Java™ Open Source Programming

With XDoclet, JUnit, WebWork, Hibernate

Joe Walnes

Ara Abrahamian

Mike Cannon-Brookes

Pat Lightbody

WILEY

Wiley Publishing, Inc.

Vice President and Executive Group Publisher: Richard Swadley
Vice President and Executive Publisher: Bob Ipsen
Vice President and Publisher: Joseph B. Wikert
Executive Editorial Director: Mary Bednarek
Editorial Manager: Kathryn A. Malm
Executive Editor: Robert Elliott
Senior Production Editor: Fred Bernardi
Development Editor: Kevin Shafer
Production Editor: Pamela Hanley
Media Development Specialist: Kit Malone
Permissions Editor: Carmen Krikorian
Text Design & Composition: Wiley Composition Services

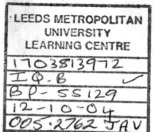
Library of Congress Cataloging-in-Publication Data:

Java Open source programming : with Xdoclet, JUnit, WebWork, Hibernate
(Java Open Source Library) / Joe Walnes ... [et al.].
    p. cm.
  ISBN 0-471-46362-0 (PAPER/WEBSITE)
  1. Java (Computer program language) 2. Open source software. I.
Walnes, Joe, 1978-
  QA76.73.J38J3785 2003
  005.2'762--dc22

                                                      2003020242

ISBN: 0-471-46362-0

Printed in the United States of America

10 9 8 7 6 5 4 3 2 1

Contents

Acknowledgments

Martin Fowler, despite being busy with his own book, proved invaluable with his improvements and guidance along the way. Ben Hogan and Erik Hatcher managed to consistently provide us with an awesome amount of feedback with little notice. Dan North requires a special mention for not only providing great reviews but for saving us in the eleventh hour by helping to rewrite a chapter. Special thanks to Gavin King for fast and accurate review of the Hibernate-related chapters in the final periods of the book.

Of course, this book would be nothing without the patience of our many reviewers: Andy Pols, Aslak Hellesoy, Damian Guy, Darren Hobbs, Hooman Mehr, Ivan Moore, Jason Carriera, Jeremy Stell-Smith, Lisa Van Gelder, Mathias Bogaert, Matt Ho, Mike Roberts, Mike Royle, Owen Rogers, Rachel Davies, Rachel McConnell, Rebecca Parsons, Scott Farquar, Steve Freeman, and Tim Mackinnon.

Rickard Oberg and Matt Baldree also played an important role in the creation of this book. Without them, we would never have gotten started.

We would also like to thank the teams behind the Open Source tools that we used, for providing those excellent tools and responding to our requests. We thank Bob and the rest of the team at Wiley for constantly supporting us.

Mike would like to thank his co-authors, the Atlassian development team (Scott, Owen, Anton, Jeff, Bobby, Dave, Edwin); his "work" mates (Mike, Gavin, Jason, Jeremy, Eugene, Rickard and more); his Sydney mates (Niki, Alina (Kins), Sarah, Camilla, Will, Hoey, Tex, Kel, Nuts, et al — you know who you are) and, last, but certainly not least, his family (Mum, Dad, Jace, Tora, Andrew, James, Holly, and little Phoebe). He'd also like to thank anyone who read the previous sentence and is still searching for his or her name — he forgot you and apologizes profusely.

Joe would like to thank all his fellow ThoughtWorkers; it's a humbling experience working with them. Special thanks to Dan North for encouraging him to reach that bit further (not just the top magazine rack) while keeping his feet on the ground. Paul Hammant always looks out for him and provides solid experiences that have driven his techniques. Paul, Dan, Laura Waite, and Tim Bacon have always been there for him when he needed them and have been excellent coaches, mentors, and friends. Charles Lowell, Chris Stevenson, Drew Noakes, Duncan Cragg, Gregor Hohpe, Jeremy Stell-Smith, Jonathan Rasmusson, Martin Fowler, Mike Roberts, and Tim Mackinnon have been a constant inspiration to work with, amongst many other names. Thanks to Trevor Mather for the support and for not being what Dan said you'd be.

Joe thanks his family (Mum, Gay Dad and Tilly) for the support. Most important, Joe thanks his loving fiance, Jaimie, for sticking by and loving him all the way through the ordeal. Right back at ya!

Ara would like to thank his co-authors; he learned a lot from them during writing the book. He would also like to thank his colleagues at Eedé and Roxcel (Behrang, Nazanin, Iman, Arbi, Nassim, Ali, Ramin, Mohammad and Dr. Mohammad, Jarek, and Mr. Lehmann) for their support; especially his creative ex-boss (Hooman) and Dr. Arsanjani (his first coach in software development techniques); and his best friends (Teodik, Armond, Farzad, Raymond, Telma, Abtin, Artin, Arin, Nasser, and Ali). Without your support and encouragement, it would have been impossible to engage in such a long and huge project. He thanks his family (Mom, Dad, Razmik, Emma, Alice, Seda, and Narbeh) for their support. Ara loves you all!

Pat would like to thank all his co-workers at Cisco and Spoke who helped him along the way. Special thanks to Mike Schwartz for his extra effort in providing invaluable feedback. He'd also like to thank Adam Fleming, Marshal Dhillon, Michael Artamonov, and Dan Libicki for their willingness to subject themselves to the ideas presented in this book in a first-hand experience. A very special thanks goes out to Professor Bill Griswold for being a great teacher and having a strong influence on this book. Finally, he would like to thank his friends and family for supporting him throughout the writing process. Mom, Dad, Chris — you're the best!

About the Authors

Joe Walnes is a consultant for ThoughtWorks (www.thoughtworks.com), a systems integration company that specializes in Agile development techniques for the enterprise. His areas of expertise lie in Extreme Programming coaching for developers, design techniques for object-oriented and component-oriented systems, and simplifying J2EE development. In his (minimal) spare time, he works on Open Source projects, many of which can be found at www.opensymphony.com and www.codehaus.org.

You can read his blog at: http://joe.truemesh.com.

Ara Abrahamian is a freelance consultant specializing in developing Enterprise Java solutions. He's been involved in various J2EE projects all around the globe, as a consultant or technical leader. His areas of expertise are code generation, attribute-oriented programming, and software automation techniques. He is also active in many Open Source projects, including XDoclet as the leader of the project. His other area of interest is adapting lightweight methodologies such as XP to large distributed teams.

You can read his blog at: http://freeroller.net/page/ara_e.

Mike Cannon-Brookes is the founder of Atlassian (www.atlassian.com), a cutting-edge J2EE applications and services company in Sydney, Australia. Atlassian makes top-class J2EE software applications including JIRA, a leading issue-tracking and project-management system. Mike specializes in building brilliantly simple, usable J2EE Web applications and also founded JavaBlogs (www.javablogs.com), a Web-based, Java-focused blog aggregator. He also founded the OpenSymphony (www.opensymphony.com) project and works on WebWork, SiteMesh, and other Open Source projects. On weekends, he likes to be distinctly Australian — drinking, gambling, and enjoying the best country on earth.

You can read his blog at: http://blogs.atlassian.com/rebelutionary.

Pat Lightbody currently lives in San Francisco and works in Palo Alto at a startup company called Spoke Software, which specializes in enterprise software using social networking to enhance sales performance. Before that, he worked as a software engineer at Cisco Systems and attended the University of California, San Diego, where he received his B.S. in Computer Science. He also works on various Open Source projects, primarily WebWork, XWork, and OSWorkflow, all of which can be found at www.opensymphony.com.

You can read his blog at: http://blogs.atlassian.com/psquad.

Introduction

In today's IT environment, Java is a leading technology in the world of enterprise development. As management demands more from technology, complexity in infrastructure seems to grow exponentially, leaving many unable to keep up with the demands of such a fast-paced world. These complexities can be seen in the over-evolving Java 2 Enterprise Edition (J2EE) specifications. This unnecessary complexity drove us to discover ways of simplifying development.

Now, don't get us wrong; we love J2EE! But why does it take so long to get stuff done? We (the authors of this book) were all early adopters of J2EE, grappling with concepts and complexities as they evolved. It was painful, but over time, we started making use of reusable Open Source tools that dramatically reduced the time taken to develop these applications. We also started questioning which technologies were actually helping us and which had become a hindrance.

This book is about using development techniques and Open Source tools to lower the cost of building enterprise applications. We aim to show you how to bring these together to build a real-world application while avoiding complexity and embracing simplicity. We will help you extend your knowledge of Java and the J2EE framework so that you can begin using the millions of dollars of free research and development just waiting to be utilized.

Not only will this book teach you how to utilize Open Source technology that you can put to work for you immediately; it will also strengthen and broaden your development philosophies in such a manner that, like us, you will soon find yourself scratching your head in wonder and asking "Why didn't I do this a long time ago?"

Why You Need This Book

This book takes on two goals that will benefit you both immediately and in the future:

- The most immediate goal is that you will become more familiar with just a few of the hundreds of amazing Open Source technologies available for use.

- Furthermore, the simple techniques and philosophies we shall introduce will be applicable today and long into the future, even when current technologies may have been replaced by better alternatives.

We shall apply these technologies and techniques by recreating Sun's Java Blueprint: the infamous PetStore application. Our implementation of the PetStore will not be an exact carbon copy, but rather an improvement all around, in terms of usability, architecture, and simplicity. We call this project *PetSoar* because the development of the projects just soars along. Outlined here are the various technologies and skills that are presented throughout this book.

Who Should Read This Book?

Just as this book has two major goals, technology and techniques, there are also two groups of readers that this book caters to (although usually these two groups actually consist of the same set of people).

The first group consists of anyone who wishes to learn about cutting-edge Open Source Java components. In this book, we will take an in-depth look into several prominent Open Source projects that aid in enterprise development, including JUnit, Ant, Hibernate, WebWork, SiteMesh, XDoclet, and Lucene. If you're not already familiar with these projects, odds are you're at least familiar with the problems they are trying to solve. We will show both the problems that each tool addresses, as well as give you a step-by-step guide to using these tools in a real-world application.

The second group consists of anyone who has grappled firsthand with project complexities spinning out of control. We've found that these complexities are actually the result of developers thinking that complex requirements require complex solutions. Instead, in this book, we will show you how to apply the principle of simplicity to achieve your goals in the shortest amount of time. We will do this by following the development of the PetSoar application using *Test Driven Development (TDD)*, a practice that exudes the idea that less is more.

Conventions

In this book, we use various methods of calling text out to you for different reasons. For example, when we want you to type something, we bold the text that we want you to type, as in "Type **ls -l** and press Enter." When we mention commands, filenames, or directories, we use what's called monofont (or a fixed-width font) to call out the text of that item. For example, "As you can see, the `ls` command lists two files: `fileone.txt` and `filetwo.lgz`, both of which are located in the `directoryone` directory."

How This Book Is Organized

This book is divided into three distinct parts, with the majority of the content in Parts II and III.

Part I: Introduction

The first part of the book will serve as a roadmap to what we plan to discuss in the rest of the book. Here we will introduce the tools we are going to cover as well as discuss the PetSoar application overview and architecture.

Part II: Building Your Open Source Toolbox

The second part of the book will introduce you to the many Open Source projects that we have come to include in our "developer's toolbox" over the years of working with J2EE. We will discuss reasons why each technology is useful, lessons learned from using the product, and finally alternative Open Source projects that may offer similar or complementary functionality.

Part III: Developing the Application

The last part of the book is dedicated entirely to using these Open Source projects to implement various features required by the PetSoar project. In these chapters, we will also formally introduce you to the development philosophies outlined here and show you how you can successfully meld them into your professional career, resulting in incredibly successful applications. This part shows how the technologies and techniques come together to deliver an application.

While the book has been designed to be read linearly, we know that, because we are writing to several different audiences, some of you may skip certain chapters or parts of this book. If you are already a power-user of a particular technology described in Part II, you can easily skip that section. Or, if learning a particular tool is all you want to do, head straight for Part II. Or if you are building an enterprise application that is not Web-based, you can skip the appropriate chapters in Part III.

Beyond the Book

This book gives you a good start on Open Source tools as well as building real applications while focusing on simplicity, but the help doesn't end here. For starters, this book has a companion Web site that's located at the following URL:

```
http://www.wiley.com/compbooks/walnes
```

Featured at the site are:

- The PetSoar application ready for download for you to try out on your own personal machine

- Any updates and addendums to the book itself

- A mailing list to discuss the tools and techniques used in this book with the authors and other readers

- Technology updates to help you keep pace with the advancements in the tools and technology since publication time

Also, consider checking out *J2EE Open Source Toolkit: Building an Enterprise Platform with Open Source Tools* by John T. Bell, James Lambros, and Stan Ng (John Wiley & Sons: Hoboken, NJ, 2003), another title in the Java Open Source Library that shows you how to build an enterprise development platform using Open Source tools, including many of the same tools discussed in this book. We'll refer occasionally to that book in this one.

One

Introduction

In Part I, we provide a brief introduction of what you can expect throughout the rest of the book. This is divided into two core sections: Open Source tools and application development techniques. In Chapter 1, we provide you with an overview of the tools detailed in this book and then discuss the philosophies you can expect to see championed. In Chapter 2, we tie those tools together with the development philosophies by discussing the general architecture taken to build the PetSoar application. By the end of these two chapters, you should have a clear idea of what to expect for the remainder of the book.

Overview of the Book

In this chapter, we briefly discuss the things to come — primarily what the tools we'll employ when building PetSoar as well as the development-process philosophies we'll be covering.

Using Open Source Technologies

Open Source Software (OSS) is an interesting phenomenon that, in the last few years, has really begun to show its incredible staying power. With the widespread usage of the Apache HTTP Server, the Linux operating system, and lately the JBoss application server, it is clear that Open Source technology can be as good as or better than commercial offerings. Open Source Software also has many advantages. The most significant being that the source is freely available, which means that you can customize, tweak, and learn from code written by your peers. This minimizes risk because you can always modify the code to meet your custom needs.

It is sometimes challenging to determine whether an individual OSS project is going to survive. A good metric is whether the project has unit tests and good test coverage. Another is the size of the community that is both developing and using the project. By valuing either, you should find it easy for defects to be addressed as they are discovered. However, the most important factor is whether you are willing to work directly with the source code. If you are willing to contribute back to the project or make modifications for your own personal needs, the public success of the project is largely irrelevant once you've adopted the code as your own. By investing yourself in knowing the project at a level deeper than just a cursory glance, you can guarantee the success of integration with your project — even if the OSS project itself is not considered a widespread "success."

Through the widespread use of simplicity and decoupling in your application design, we will show you how utilizing Open Source technology can actually reduce the points of failure in your application and increase overall system stability and robustness while your application remains maintainable and flexible.

In this book, we draw upon several Open Source products. Some will be offered under an umbrella organization, such as Apache Jakarta or OpenSymphony, while others are more independent, such as Hibernate or XDoclet. Following is a list of the Open Source products presented in this book and in the PetSoar application:

- *JUnit and Mock Objects* — A test harness and library designed to assist with rapid and robust unit testing.

- *OpenSymphony WebWork* — A Model-View Controller (MVC) framework that easily allows for pluggable view technologies and extensible configuration. We present examples of using both of these popular frameworks.

- *Hibernate* — A transparent and powerful object/relational persistence and query service.

- *OpenSymphony SiteMesh* — A Web-page layout system and Web-application integration system that transparently aids in the creation of large sites with a common look and feel.

- *OpenSymphony OSCache* — A utility component that enables developers to easily cache slow dynamic sections of Web sites, which results in pages that load hundreds of times faster.

- *XDoclet* — A code-generation tool originally popularized for Enterprise JavaBeans (EJB) deployments but now in use for a wide variety of tasks. We will show how it can be used to simplify the configuration of Hibernate.

- *Jakarta Lucene* — A high-performance, full-text search engine that is applicable in any project that demands text-based searching.

- *Jakarta Commons* — A repository of simple, reusable Java components that is applicable to everyday development.

Each product we use specializes in simplifying one (and only one) problem. Leveraging fine-grained OSS components in a larger application design can produce great time and cost savings.

Understanding Design and Development Philosophies

Besides the numerous quality Open Source projects that we will introduce and use in this book, we will also go one step further and show you first-hand, through the development of PetSoar, how to apply the philosophies presented here in your own projects. While there are many small techniques and principles that you'll find in the remaining chapters, they can all be classified in one of three categories:

- Test First
- Less is More
- Always Ask the Dumb Questions

Test First

During our careers as software engineers, the authors of this book have all come to the same conclusion. In order for complex, secure, stable software applications to succeed, proper testing must take place throughout the entire development lifecycle. Unfortunately, as the world grows and the pace of business increases, the time allocated for proper testing has shrunk to only a fraction of the time that is needed. In this book, we show you that the philosophy of writing tests *before* writing your actual code is more than just an academic proposition by Extreme Programming advocates. Whether you are an "Extreme" programmer or not, we maintain (and will demonstrate) that properly designed unit tests written at the onset of a development task can not only secure the stability of your code, but it can also *speed up* the development process with the pleasant side effect of saving your sanity.

Less Is More

Building on the principle of Test First, we also show you that, when given the choice between "less" and "more," a software developer will reap the benefits if "less" is chosen. For example, unless there is compulsory evidence that a project requires the use of an *Enterprise JavaBean* server, it is usually advantageous to avoid over-architecting and avoid such heavier implementations. *Such simplicity is the primary belief presented in this book. We show you how you* can apply simple, abstract, modular solutions toward your business requirements so that, if a heavier implementation is required, it is trivial to scale up the lighter-weight solution.

Always Ask the Dumb Questions

Before thinking about how any code is to be implemented, take a step back and ask yourself what you actually need to achieve to meet the business requirements. Let's face it. Writing software is the easy part. Writing software that meets requirements is where we often fall down.

It's important to get a broad understanding of *what* the software should do before even considering *how* it should be implemented. In many cases, it may be that J2EE or even Java is the wrong solution to your problem. Always pay careful attention to what the best solution actually is. Don't try to fit a solution to the wrong problem.

To do this, ask the dumb questions. Ask the really dumb questions. The simplest dumb question is *"why?"* Why does a button need to be placed there? Why is an extra field needed? Why does a JMS queue need to be used? The higher up you go (that is, the closer to the requirements and further from the implementation), the more likely you are to discover something that may fundamentally change the way you implement the solution. Even if you don't discover anything new, you will at least be reassured that you have understood the requirements.

Only after discovering the broad overall goal of the requirement should you start thinking about the details of implementation. Before and during implementation, you should *continually ask questions*. Ask the dumb questions and *then* ask detailed questions related to the fine-grained implementation. These questions can be answered in the form of a formalized specification document or a friendly chat by the coffee machine. Only through repeated questioning can a developer truly pick the brain of the client and implement the best solution possible. We do not, however, recommend asking these kinds of questions if you are a certifiable psychic or a mind reader.

Exploring the PetSoar Project

The PetSoar project may have begun as a way to showcase the technologies and techniques presented in this book, but it is a project that will continue to grow and flourish long after this book's publication. By reading this book, you will begin to understand the development ideologies used during the initial implementation of PetSoar. However, we highly encourage every reader to actively seek out the source code of this project and further enhance it by applying derivatives of the technologies and philosophies presented here. Pet-Soar will surely be a very active and dynamic project so that you can continue to learn and grow as a software developer — even after you've read this book.

The Web site for this project is `http://www.wiley.com/compbooks/walnes`. Here, you will find Book errata (hopefully, this section will be fairly desolate) as well as an online demo of PetSoar and downloadable source code. It is our sincere hope that, if you are not already an Open Source contributor, the PetSoar project and book could motivate you to begin to actively seek out and develop alternative products that hold your attention. Lastly, the PetSoar application presented in this book at the time of publication may or may not be the same PetSoar you'll find on the Web site. As time goes on, future iterations of this project should further increase the simplicity, scalability, robustness, and general usability of the application.

Sticking to the Basics

As you read this book, remember that the overall theme is *less is more* — achieved through *simplicity*. Simplicity can be a challenging task to undertake, especially when being bombarded with more and more complex specifications and products on a daily basis. The best advice we can offer is to take your time and understand that moving from complexity to simplicity is not an easy task and may take several project iterations before you truly feel comfortable developing applications in this manner. If you already embrace this philosophy, we recommend that you use this book as a guide to alternative ways to implement this development approach.

Summary

This chapter has provided an overview of material to be discussed throughout this book. We examined Open Source technologies that have played a key role in the development of the PetSoar application as well as the philosophies we followed when developing PetSoar. We described in general terms the PetSoar application, which will serve as the foundation for discussions throughout this book.

CHAPTER 2

Application Overview

This chapter is a broad overview from 30,000 feet of how we use the tools and techniques discussed in this book to build PetSoar, specifically how the tools and techniques fit together.

Looking at Yet Another Pet Store?

PetSoar is not unique in its field. There are many other groups implementing their own pet stores to demonstrate the power of their technologies. Strangely, there seem to be more pet-store technology demonstrations on the Internet than applications really trying to sell pets!

Sun originally built their application to demonstrate J2EE. This has been revised as J2EE has updated. Microsoft built a similar store to show how an equivalent application can be built with .Net. From this point on, a plague of stores popped up. Each was built by using different technologies. All were competing to gain the title for the best store.

The two main benchmarks that have been used in these comparisons are blatant and easy to prove:

- *Performance* — How many concurrent visitors can use the store, how fast can the application respond, and how many transactions can be performed per second.

■ *Lines of code* — Quite simply, how many lines of code, including configuration, the store was implemented in.

While our PetSoar takes the preceding points into account (that is, the application must be fast and shouldn't consist of massive amounts of code), we focus on something that seems to be less prominent in the other implementations — *maintainability.*

THE OTHER STORES

If you're curious, here's a short summary of some of the other store implementations lurking out there.

These implementations change regularly, and the implementation notes listed here are just to give you a broad overview of the store. For the most up-to-date details, visit the relevant Web sites.

◆ **PetStore:** `http://java.sun.com/blueprints/code/`

This is the original application released by the J2EE Blueprints group of Sun to act as an example usage of the (then new) J2EE technology stack. It makes heavy use of JSP, Servlets, EJB, Web services, and JMS. The unfortunate downside to demonstrating so much of J2EE is that it's big and can be quite confusing.

◆ **.Net PetShop:** `http://www.gotdotnet.com/team/compare/petshop.aspx`

Released by Microsoft to promote .Net, this implementation consists of a Web-based ASP.NET front end that uses ADO.NET to access the database. Logic is mostly stored in database-stored procedures or the code behind (the controller) of the Web pages. The .Net PetShop boasts considerably fewer lines of code than the Sun implementation. It's not Java, but it's worth a look if you're interested in .Net.

◆ **JPetStore:** `http://www.ibatis.com/jpetstore/jpetstore.html`

Released by iBatis to compete with the .Net PetShop, this implementation uses JSP and Jakarta Struts for the Web-tier (a Java object-based domain model), and the iBatis Database Layer to map the objects to database tables. A Web service is provided by Java API for XML Messaging (JAXM). All technologies powering this application are either standard J2EE technologies or Open Source products. No stored procedures or code generation is used.

◆ **XPetStore:** `http://xpetstore.sourceforge.net/`

An Open Source implementation that minimizes the lines of code by making heavy use of code generation, there are two versions of this available. One uses standard EJB technologies with Struts and JSP, while the other is a more trimmed-down version that makes use of lighter-weight technologies such as Hibernate, WebWork, and Velocity. Both use

> XDoclet and SiteMesh. We recommend having a look at this application
> because it uses many of the same technologies used in this book.
>
> ◆ **PetMarket:** `http://blueprints.macromedia.com/`
>
> The PetMarket is an alternative front end to the standard Sun PetStore
> built with Macromedia FlashMX. It's very pretty and demonstrates a nice
> alternative to using standard HTML for Web applications. The view layer is
> created using Flash, the controller using ActionScript, and the back-end
> business logic is encapsulated in standard Java objects. Have a look — it's
> impressive.

Understanding the Importance of Maintainability

Maintainability is the ability to change an application after the initial delivery. This may be to add new features, improve usability, fix bugs, improve performance, or even overhaul the architecture.

It's short-sighted to assume that, after the initial delivery, things will never change. Business processes are constantly changing, particularly in the IT world, and the software must keep up.

Typically, throughout the lifetime of an application, the cost of maintenance outweighs the cost of initial delivery. On top of that, there's the additional cost to the business of *not* being able to change functionality. Developing for maintainability has a higher return on investment in the long run.

Clean and flexible designs, code quality, and testing all contribute to maintainability. Unfortunately, as the pressure to reduce time-to-market intensifies, these values are usually the first to be sacrificed to deliver more quickly. This is far more expensive in the long run.

The development team should *not* be responsible for holding back the business because they want to change. Therefore, always develop with maintainability in mind.

Understanding the Requirements of PetSoar

Our PetSoar application is to be kept intentionally simple so we can spend more time emphasizing the techniques to develop the application rather than showcasing the end result. There are two types of users of the application: a customer and a store owner.

The requirements are as follows:

- A store owner should be able to maintain an inventory of pets that are currently in stock. The pets should be categorized.

- A customer should be able to visit the store's Web site and browse through the pets. A customer should be able either to select a category to view a pet or to perform a text-based search for a pet.

- If a customer finds a desirable pet, the customer should be able to add it to a shopping cart. When the customer is satisfied, he or she should be able to go to a checkout screen and place an order for all the pets in the store.

To keep the example application simple, this book does not go into the details of what happens once the order is placed.

Examining the Architecture and Technologies

The core platform used for development is *JDK 1.4.x* with the *Servlet 2.3* and *JSP 1.2* APIs from the *J2EE 1.3* standard. It's worth noting that PetSoar doesn't use all J2EE features such as JMS or EJBs. In all cases, we aim to use the simplest tool for the job.

Figure 2.1 shows all these frameworks, along with their places and relationships in the big puzzle of the architecture.

NOTE The technologies used throughout this book are only several of many possible recommendations. If you prefer to use other technologies, such as Jakarta Struts instead of WebWork, go ahead and do so. The beauty of Open Source Java is that it's very easy to mix and match. All applications should use the best combination to fit the stated needs, and we don't agree with a concrete prescribed technology set.

Looking at the Architecture

The core functionality of the application is made up of a collection of services. Low-level services provide system functionality, such as indexing a document or persisting on object. Higher-level services provide business logic, such as maintaining the pet inventory or processing the shopping cart on checkout.

Services are layered on top of each other to build the application. Each service follows the façade design pattern and encapsulates the complexities of logic and external APIs behind a very simple interface.

Layering services together in this way is known as a *service-oriented architecture* and, at the expense of more classes, simplifies the code greatly throughout the application by organizing it into modules that specialize in only doing one thing and doing it well. Code is clearer and contains less duplication. This increases the maintainability of the application in the long run.

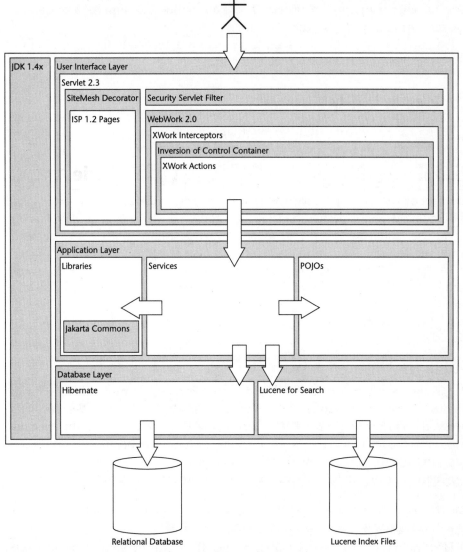

Figure 2.1 The components of the application

Applications built with technologies such as Common Object Request Broker Architecture (CORBA), Enterprise JavaBeans (EJB), and Simple Object Access Protocol (SOAP) Web services make use of this architecture. However, these technologies are often distributed, which opens a can of worms for complexity related to security, lookup, and network latency. Our implementation makes use of the architecture but does not distribute these services. Thereby, this rids us of these complexities.

Plain Old Java Objects (POJOs) are used to represent the business entities such as pets, categories, or orders. These are defined in simple JavaBean-like classes. These can be passed among the services.

How we implement and assemble services is explored in Chapter 14 of this book and the domain model in Chapter 15.

Looking at Utility Libraries

There are a few core frameworks that we use in many places in PetSoar. Some components from the *Jakarta's Common* project are among those.

We use *Commons Lang*'s reusable utility classes for implementing `hash-Code()`, `equals()`, and `toString()` methods for the domain objects. It also has a set of very handy utility classes for working with strings and getting and setting JavaBean properties via reflection code.

We use *Commons Digester* to load XML files. Many applications separate configuration into XML, and Digester simplifies this greatly.

We use *Commons Logging* to log activities of the site. Logging is a very useful technique to track what's going on in the running code. It also helps find bugs more easily.

All these components are discussed in Chapter 11.

Using Persistence and Searching

Persistence is a very critical part of any enterprise system. PetSoar is implemented to save and load its data to and from relational databases. Any relational database can be used for storing the data. This is possible because *Hibernate*, the framework used by PetSoar for handling persistence of objects, supports a wide range of relational databases.

Hibernate can persist a standard POJO — provided that we supply a complimentary `xml` file that defines its mappings to the database. *XDoclet*, a code-generation tool that uses JavaDoc comments of the source code, is used for auto-generating these Hibernate mapping `xml` files.

Hibernate is discussed in Chapter 5, and XDoclet is explained in Chapter 8.

It's worth noting that the persistence-specific code isn't littered throughout the code base and encapsulated behind dedicated services, which makes the code much cleaner. This is shown in Chapter 15.

Searching the site for pets is one of the most important features of a pet shop. Thanks to *Jakarta Lucene*, PetSoar can handle sophisticated Google-style full text searches. Lucene is covered in Chapter 8. In Chapter 18, we show how Lucene is actually integrated into the application.

Using the Web Front End

PetSoar is a Web application. The entire user interface is accessible through a Web browser. The Web-based interface and interaction is implemented by using *XWork* and *WebWork 2*. XWork is a generic and extensible MVC framework. WebWork 2 builds upon XWork to provide a rich framework for building Web applications.

The view layer of PetSoar is implemented as *JSP*. WebWork comes with some built-in JSP tags for creating HTML user interfaces. These tags are used for creating all the screens and forms in PetSoar.

The model is composed of POJO domain objects and services.

The controller consists of a set of Web-independent XWork action classes. These actions are used for responding to operations initiated by the user via the browser. So, to respond to a click on a "create order" link, an XWork action dedicated to that task is defined and triggered by WebWork.

XWork comes with a very strong validation mechanism. Basic validation such as checking that a mandatory field is indeed filled by the user is programmed with XWork's validation system.

XWork and WebWork are discussed in Chapter 6.

Another interesting part of WebWork is support for *Inversion of Control (IoC)*. IoC is a very powerful pattern for creating and looking up resources and dependencies of components. As an example, thanks to WebWork's IoC support, we don't have to pollute the action classes with low-level HTTP session access code for storing a shopping cart in a user's browser session. We let WebWork take care of it, and we instead concentrate on coding the pure business logic of the cart. IoC is explained in detail in Chapter 14.

SiteMesh is used to further simplify the view layer of the site. SiteMesh is a framework for defining the layout and navigation for the site. Based on the Decorator design pattern, SiteMesh decorates each page of the site with layout and navigation. SiteMesh is discussed in Chapter 7. Chapter 17 also demonstrates how SiteMesh is used along with Cascading Style Sheets (CSSs) and other techniques for the layout of PetSoar's Web interface.

Sign-in and access control is another part of the site. Users can sign up to the site and thereafter sign in and track their orders. Also, some features are only allowed to administrators of the site. PetSoar uses a simple *servlet filter* for protecting pages. The filter sits in front of the Web pages and prevents anonymous or unprivileged users from accessing protected pages. Security and access control are discussed in Chapter 20.

Testing

A very important aspect of developing maintainable applications is testing. Code should be tested to assure that modifications to it or developing new features don't break.

JUnit is used for unit testing the code. Unit tests test a very fine-grained piece of functionality in isolation. We also look at *Mock Objects*, which help you test classes that would otherwise be very awkward to test in isolation. JUnit and Mock Objects are covered in Chapters 3 and 4, respectively. Throughout the book, and especially in Chapters 13 and 14, we also discuss techniques for writing more effective unit tests and more testable code.

All unit tests are run as part of the automated Apache Ant-based build process. Ant is a tool for creating build scripts for automating various tasks such as compiling, testing, packaging, and deploying applications.

As well as covering the tools for unit testing, we also introduce a technique that can help you design very clean and maintainable code and give you unit tests for free. This is *Test Driven Development (TDD)* — a well-used and effective technique commonly used in projects that follow agile development methodologies such as Extreme Programming (XP). TDD is introduced in Chapter 13 and used heavily throughout the Part III of the book to build the actual application.

Summary

This chapter has provided a glimpse of the kind of technologies we typically use to build simple and maintainable Web applications. We've discovered the importance of maintainability. We've explored the requirements of the PetSoar application while looking at the basic architecture, utility libraries, and Web front end of the application.

Two

Building Your Open
Source Toolbox

In Part II of this book, we formally introduce several high-quality Open Source projects that are best-of-breed solutions for the various problems they address. While there are always alternatives to the tools discussed here, we have chosen these tools because we believe they provide the simplest and highest-quality solutions for our problems. Of course, not everyone will agree with us, so we discuss alternatives as well.

We cover a wide range of tools: indexing and searching services, MVC frameworks, persistence layers, code generation, testing, and user interface decorators. On top of these core tools, we discuss many smaller, but still very valuable, tools such as logging, caching, and configuration. Finally, we discuss tools that can assist in communication throughout a project.

CHAPTER 3

Unit Testing with JUnit

This chapter introduces unit testing, distinguishes it from other types of testing, and shows how unit testing can help you deliver more robust code with a lower bug rate in less time. *JUnit* is used to help achieve this since it's the de facto unittesting framework for Java. JUnit is used extensively throughout this book and is perhaps one of the most important and valuable technologies used in any development team, which is why it's introduced early on.

Types of Testing

There are many types of testing strategies used in software development. Unfortunately, many of these strategies are beyond the scope of this book.

In a typical software project, there are two types of tests that are most important: *programmer tests* and *customer tests*. These are otherwise known as *unit tests* and *acceptance tests*, respectively.

Unit tests and acceptance tests are equally important and, as such, should not be overlooked when developing any sort of serious enterprise or large-scale application.

Table 3.1 compares unit tests and acceptance tests.

Table 3.1   Unit Tests vs. Acceptance Tests

UNIT TESTS...	ACCEPTANCE TESTS...
Defined by developers	Defined by customers
Build confidence in developers	Build confidence in customers
Test small units in isolation	Test the entire application
Low-level	High level
Run very quickly	May take much longer
Programmatically driven	Done by hand or via a script
100% automated	Mixture of automation and manual intervention
Not end-to-end	End-to-end
Example test: The database pool should request more resources under high loads.	Example test: The monthly report should contain the correct total for all invoices sent out since the last report.

These two testing techniques complement each other. Neither on its own is sufficient. Many projects tend to use one but not the other.

- *Without unit tests,* acceptance tests become very tedious to write and run. Many more combinations need to be tested, since there is less confidence in the underlying code. This results in much more manual labor.

- *Without acceptances tests,* there is no process for determining when the software meets the requirements of the customer. This results in *vague* development cycles that drag on and on.

The remainder of this book looks at the process of unit testing and how it can become part of your daily routine as a developer. Aside from explaining the core tools to help in this, we explore techniques for writing code that is more robust as well as simpler and easier to maintain.

Using JUnit

JUnit is *the* unit testing framework for Java. It is the Java member of the xUnit family, a set of tools for unit testing across many languages. Of course, JUnit is Open Source and available from http://www.junit.org.

To get started with JUnit, simply download the jar and add it to your classpath.

Features of JUnit

JUnit provides the following features:

- It provides an API that allows you to create a repeatable unit test with a clear pass/fail result.
- It includes tools for running your tests and presenting the results.
- It allows multiple tests to be grouped together to run in a batch.
- It is very lightweight and simple to use. It takes little time to learn how it works, and it won't add bloat to your application.
- It is designed by experienced developers for experienced developers. There is no fluff around the edges, pointless wizards, or marketing hype. It does exactly what it says on the tin and no more.
- It's extensible. If you want it to do more than it says on the tin, you can easily extend it to do so.
- It's the de facto unit testing framework for Java. There is a large community of developers using it. Many free extensions are available to help you use it in specific situations. Plus, countless articles and books on the subject are available. This also means it's integrated with most major IDEs.

Writing a Unit Test

To demonstrate how to use JUnit, we use it to help implement a simple CSV parser. For brevity, we will not test every feature required of a CSV parser — just enough to demonstrate JUnit.

The basic class for doing the parsing looks like the following. We have not yet tested nor verified that this implementation works correctly. We will do so by writing unit tests in just a moment.

```
[CsvParser.java]

package csvparser;

import java.util.StringTokenizer;

public class CsvParser {

  private String[] currentLine;

  public void parse(String inputLine) {
    StringTokenizer tokenizer = new StringTokenizer(inputLine);
    currentLine = new String[tokenizer.countTokens()];
```

```
      for (int i = 0; i < currentLine.length; i++) {
        currentLine[i] = tokenizer.nextToken();
      }
    }

  public String get(int columnIndex) {
      return currentLine[columnIndex];
    }
  }
```

To create a unit test, follow these basic steps:

- Create a class that extends junit.framework.TestCase (from the junit jar).
- Create a public void method within this class whose name starts with "test." The rest of the method name is up to you. For example, testUpdateAccount().
- In this method, call out to the code that is to be tested and verify that the actual values returned match those that are expected by using the assertEquals() method.

The simplest test to start with for the CsvParser is to parse a single line and verify that the results returned match what is expected. Following the previous guidelines, a test can easily be created to check this:

```
[TestCsvParser.java]

package csvparser;

import junit.framework.TestCase;

public class TestCsvParser extends TestCase { // extends TestCase

  public void testParseSimpleLine() { // method name starts with 'test'
    CsvParser parser = new CsvParser();
    parser.parse("Bill,Gates,555-1234");

    // verify actual results equal those that are expected
    assertEquals("Bill", parser.get(0));
    assertEquals("Gates", parser.get(1));
    assertEquals("555-1234", parser.get(2));
  }

}
```

TIP It is good practice to use descriptive names for test methods that describe what the test is doing rather than the name of the method it is testing. This makes tests more readable when they are looked at later.

The first thing the test does is instantiate a new CsvParser before handing it a sample line to parse. The remainder of the test verifies the results from the parser equal the expected results.

The `assertEquals()` method is passed two arguments: The first is the result expected, and the second is the actual result. If one of the assertions fails, the test case fails.

NOTE The assertion methods provided by JUnit should not be confused with the "assert" keyword that was introduced in JDK1.4.

Running a Unit Test

With the test created, it must be executed. JUnit is bundled with a GUI for running tests. To launch it:

1. Ensure the JUnit jar is in the classpath.

2. Compile the code to be tested and the test cases.

3. Launch the class: junit.swingui.TestRunner. Pass in the fully qualified class name of the test case to execute.

Figure 3.1 shows the results of executing the test with the JUnit GUI.

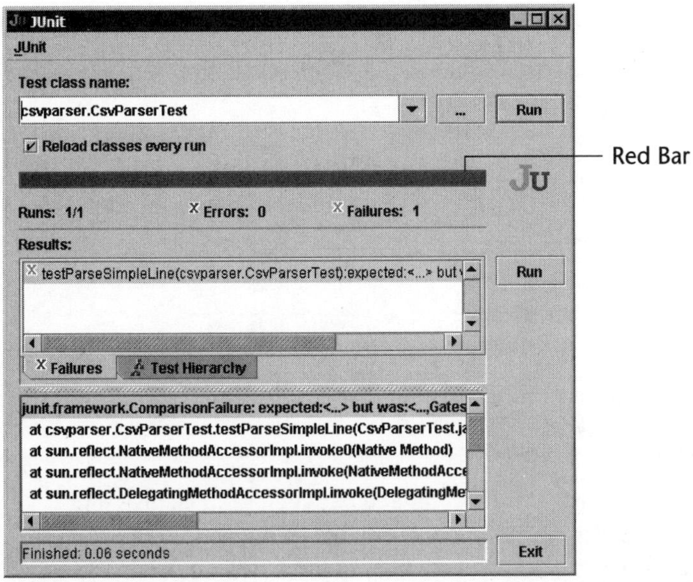

Figure 3.1   The JUnit test runner with a failing test. The *Red Bar*.

The most important feature of the test runner is the large *Red Bar* in the middle of the screen. When all the tests are passing, the bar will turn green.

The list box in the middle of the screen lists the tests that failed, shows the test method, which test class it belongs to, and the reason for the failure. The box at the bottom of the screen shows the full stack trace of the test failure.

In this case, the test failed because the first assertEquals() was passed a value of "Bill,Gates,555-1234" instead of what was expected. Looking carefully, we can see that this is happening because StringTokenizer, by default, tokenizes on whitespace characters and nothing else. However, we really want to tokenize on commas. We've found a bug!

With the failing test in place, it is now easier to fix the CsvParser class since there is a simple indication as to whether it works — the *Green Bar*. To implement it, the StringTokenizer class can be passed a second argument to the constructor, namely the strings to tokenize on:

```java
[CsvParser.java]

package csvparser;

import java.util.StringTokenizer;

public class CsvParser {

  private String[] currentLine;

  public void parse(String inputLine) {

    currentLine = new String[tokenizer.countTokens()];
    for (int i = 0; i < currentLine.length; i++) {
      currentLine[i] = tokenizer.nextToken();
    }
  }

  public String get(int columnIndex) {
    return currentLine[columnIndex];
  }
}
```

Recompiling the code and running the test again yields a *Green Bar* (see Figure 3.2). The CsvParser works.

TIP Although the classes have to be recompiled between each change and running the test, the JUnit test runner is smart enough to detect that the classes have been recompiled and will automatically reload them without having to be restarted. This shaves considerable time from running tests since the JVM startup overhead is removed for individual test runs.

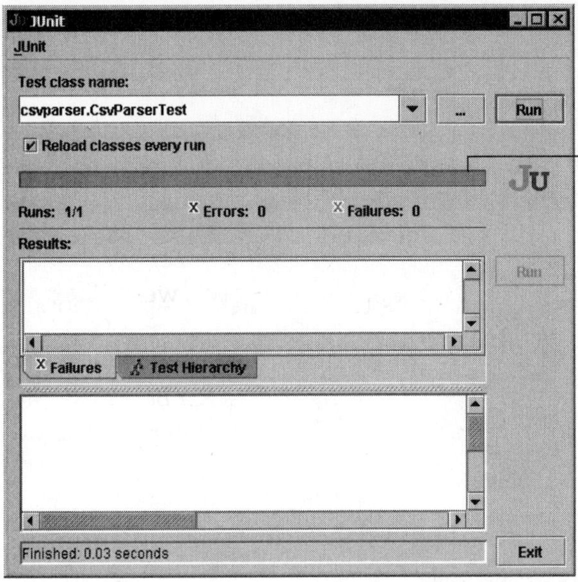

Green Bar

Figure 3.2 The JUnit test runner with a passing test. The *Green Bar*.

Running Multiple Tests

To add more unit tests, simply create more methods in the test class.

The TestCsvParser currently has only one basic test defined. This is not enough to be confident that it works correctly.

A second test can be added to ensure it can parse multiple lines:

```
[TestCsvParser.java]

package csvparser;

import junit.framework.TestCase;

public class TestCsvParser extends TestCase {

  public void testParseSimpleLine() {
    // ...
  }

  public void testParseMultipleLines() {
    CsvParser parser = new CsvParser();

    parser.parse("Fred,Flintstone,555-1111");
    assertEquals("Flintstone", parser.get(1));

    parser.parse("Barney,Rubble,555-2222");
```

```
    assertEquals("Rubble", parser.get(1));
  }

}
```

Now, running the test class again — exactly as before — runs both tests. JUnit automatically runs all methods starting with the name "test" in a class.

This test passes the first time. The implementation of CsvParser was just too good.

Now we can try testing a more awkward situation, such as what happens when one of the values in the CSV line is empty.

```
[TestCsvParser.java]

package csvparser;

import junit.framework.TestCase;

public class TestCsvParser extends TestCase {

  public void testParseSimpleLine() {
    // ...
  }

  public void testParseMultipleLines() {
    // ...
  }

  public void testEmptyValues() {
    CsvParser parser = new CsvParser();
    parser.parse("Madonna,,555-9999");
    assertEquals("Madonna", parser.get(0));
    assertEquals("", parser.get(1));
    assertEquals("555-9999", parser.get(2));
  }

}
```

Running this test results in a Red Bar! The testEmptyValues() test failed (see Figure 3.3), which reports the following error:

```
expected: <> but was : <555-9999>
```

NOTE When displaying error messages, JUnit surrounds values with < and > for clarity.

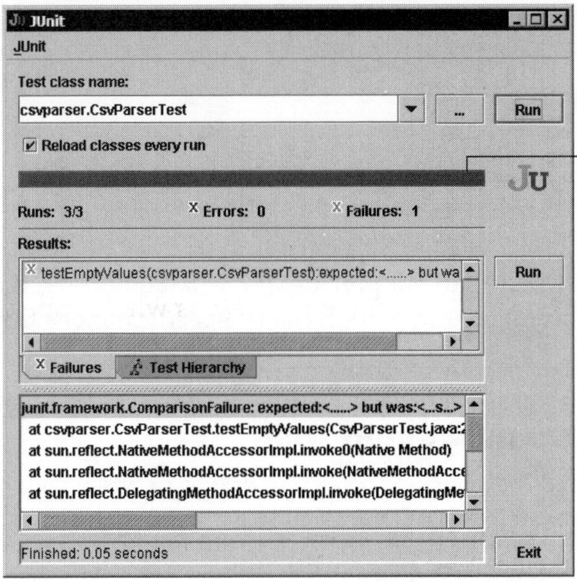

Figure 3.3 That *Red Bar* again — catching a potential bug

Looking closer, we can see the second assertion is failing. When the Csv-Parser encounters a blank token, it skips it and returns the next value along instead. This is clearly not the desired behavior.

Unfortunately, this is because java.util.StringTokenizer is being used to split the string up. This class ignores blank tokens. So, it may not be possible to use it in the CsvParser.

Not a problem. With the unit test is in place, it should be trivial to rip out the guts of the CsvParser and replace it with something that is up to the task. Hunting around the JDK API docs, we can see there's a more effective way to split strings by using `String.split()`, which is introduced in JDK1.4.

The CsvParser can be improved to make use of that instead.

```
[CsvParser.java]

package csvparser;

public class CsvParser {

    private String[] currentLine;

    public void parse(String inputLine) {
```

```
    currentLine = inputLine.split(",");
  }

  public String get(int columnIndex) {
    return currentLine[columnIndex];
  }

}
```

Now, the test class can be run, and all of our previously created unit tests can check that the new implementation conforms to the same specification as the previous one.

Everything You Need to Know about JUnit

So far, this chapter has introduced the core of JUnit. To finish the JUnit introduction, we can look at everything else you need to know about it to get by on a daily basis. Be thankful that there's not a lot to learn.

Assertion Methods

A number of methods are available to perform assertions from tests. Each method has two forms, one of which has an additional first argument for reporting an error message upon failure (see Table 3.2). This is useful if you have many assertions in a single test method, and it isn't obvious which is failing.

Table 3.2   Assertion Methods

METHOD	DESCRIPTION
`assertEquals(Object expected, Object actual);` `assertEquals(String message, Object expected, Object actual);`	Check that two values are equal by using the standard `Object.equals()` method. Overloaded versions of this method also exist for all primitive types.
`assertTrue(boolean condition);` `assertTrue(String message, boolean condition);`	Check that a value evaluates to true.
`assertFalse(boolean condition);` `assertFalse(String message, boolean condition);`	Check that a value evaluates to false.
`assertNull(Object value);` `assertNull(String message, Object value);`	Check that a value is null.

Table 3.2 *(continued)*

METHOD	DESCRIPTION
`assertNotNull(Object value);` `assertNotNull(String message, Object value);`	Check that a value is not null.

`assertSame(Object expected, Object actual);`
`assertSame(String message, Object expected,`
`        Object actual);`
	Check that two values are the same — that is, the same reference.

`assertNotSame(Object expected, Object actual);`
`assertNotSame(String message, Object expected,`
`        Object actual);`
	Check that two values are not the same reference.

`fail();` `fail(String message);`	Fail the test, no matter what. An example of when this is useful appears in the next section.

Exception Handling

It is common for code under test to call methods that can throw checked exceptions. Rather than using ugly try/catch clauses in the test case, the test method can just have the throws clause in its signature.

```java
public void testSomething() throws IOException {
  Something s = new Something();
  s.doStuff(new FileReader("..."));
  // ...
}
```

If an exception is thrown when the test is executed, JUnit will catch, fail the test, and report the failure in the test runner.

To specifically verify that an exception has been thrown, a try/catch block can be used that causes the test to fail if it gets to a certain point without encountering an exception.

```java
public void testAnExceptionIsThrown() {
  Something s = new Something();
  try {
    s.processNumber("cat");
    fail("Expected an exception");
  } catch (IllegalArgumentException goodException) {
    // good - this was expected.
  }
}
```

Test Suites

The JUnit test runner is capable of running only a single test class at a time. This is problematic because, as soon as you get beyond one test class in the system, you will need a way of running them all in one go.

Test suites come to the rescue. A *test suite* is a test class that aggregates the tests from other classes into one big test.
The steps to creating a test suite are as follows:

1. Create a normal class.

2. Create a single method in the class with the signature `public static junit.framework.Test suite()`.

3. Within that method, instantiate a new junit.framework.TestSuite instance.

4. Add the test classes to be included in the suite by using the `TestSuite .addTestSuite(Class testClass)` method.

5. Return the suite.

For example, to create a test suite that includes the TestCsvParser and TestSomething classes:

```
package csvparser;

import junit.framework.Test;
import junit.framework.TestSuite;

public class MyTestSuite {

  public static Test suite() {
    TestSuite suite = new TestSuite();
    suite.addTestSuite(TestCsvParser.class);
    suite.addTestSuite(TestSomething.class);
    return suite;
  }

}
```

Now, to run both test classes in one batch, invoke the test runner. Pass the name of the test suite as an argument instead of an individual test class.

Test Runners

So far, this chapter has used the junit.swingui.TestRunner application for running tests. This is not the only option.

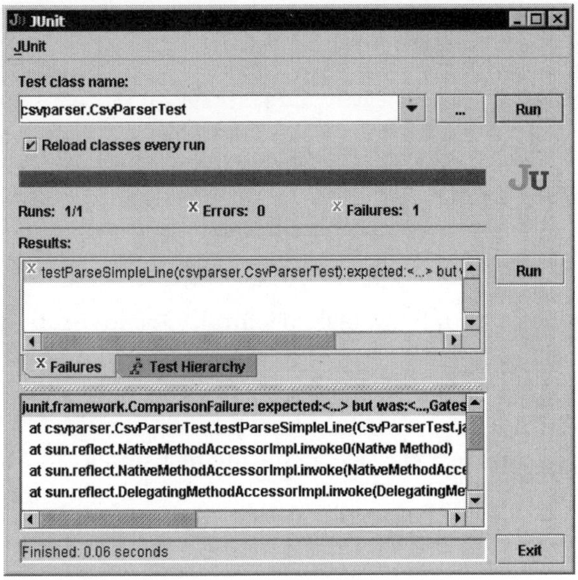

Figure 3.4   The swing test runner

Swing Runner

This is the most commonly seen test runner. As shown in Figure 3.4, this test runner provides plenty of visual feedback, such as the progress of the currently executing test and the huge Green/Red Bar. One advantage this test runner has over the others is that it can automatically reload classes without having to restart the JVM on each execution. Because of this test runner, when we refer to Green/Red Bar, we mean that a test is passing or failing.

Text Runner

Designed for the diehard console geeks, the text runner is free from fluffy GUIs. It outputs the results of the tests in a concise view on the console.

The console test runner has an advantage in that it can easily be called from other applications as well as build files and scripts. It returns a non-zero return code if there are any failures.

When code passes, the test text runner displays the following:

```
...
Time: 0.191

OK (3 tests)
```

When code fails, the test text runner displays the following:

```
...F
Time: 0.03
```

```
There was 1 failure:
1) testEmptyValues(csvparser.TestCsvParser) ComparisonFailure:
   expected:<> but was:<555-9999>
        at csvparser.TestCsvParser.testEmptyValues(TestCsvParser.java:29)

FAILURES!!!
Tests run: 3,  Failures: 1,  Errors: 0
```

Ant JUnit Task

Jakarta Ant comes bundled with a custom JUnit task to simplify the invocation of JUnit from the build file.

To use it, copy the `junit` jar file into the ANT_HOME/lib. This enables the <junit> task to be used.

The <junit> task can run individual test classes, including test suites:

```
<target name="test" depends="compile" description="Run unit tests">
  <junit>
    <classpath>
      <fileset dir="lib"/>
      <pathelement path="build"/>
    </classpath>
    <test name="csvparser.TestCsvParser"/>
    <test name="csvparser.TestSomething"/>
  </junit>
</target>
```

It can also run all test classes in a directory that match a pattern:

```
<target name="test" depends="compile" description="Run unit tests">
  <junit>
    <classpath>
      <fileset dir="lib"/>
      <pathelement path="build"/>
    </classpath>
    <batchtest>
      <fileset dir="src">
        <include name="**/*Test*.java"/>
      </fileset>
    </batchtest>
  </junit>
</target>
```

The default behavior for the <junit> task is to create no output if the tests pass or a single one-liner stating a failure if any of the tests failed.

```
[junit] TEST csvparser.TestCsvParser FAILED
```

If all you care about is whether there are any failures, this is enough. However, to diagnose why the tests have failed, you typically need more information. The

<junit> task can have nested <formatter> elements to specify how the test results are formatted.

Following are three types of formatter elements:

- *brief* — Shows a brief summary of why a test failed
- *plain* — As brief as the preceding element, but also includes details of how long each test took to run
- *xml* — Verbose output that includes as much information as possible about the test, including system properties passed to the test, any output to System.out or System.err, timings of each test, and details of failures

The brief and plain formatters are useful for viewing. Whereas, the xml formatter is suited for processing by other applications to obtain information about the test results.

By default, a formatter will output the results to a file in the current directory, one file per test class. To output the results to the console, the usefile="false" attribute can be used.

The following target outputs a brief summary of test failures to the console and a more verbose test report in XML to files named after the tests.

```
<target name="test" depends="compile" description="Run unit tests">
  <junit>
    <classpath>
      <fileset dir="lib"/>
      <pathelement path="build"/>
    </classpath>
    <test name="csvparser.TestCsvParser"/>
    <test name="csvparser.TestSomething"/>
    <formatter type="xml"/>
    <formatter type="brief" usefile="false"/>
  </junit>
</target>
```

The output to the console is as follows:

```
[junit] Testsuite: csvparser.TestCsvParser
[junit] Tests run: 3, Failures: 1, Errors: 0, Time elapsed: 0.11 sec

[junit] Testcase: testParseSimpleLine took 0.01 sec
[junit] Testcase: testParseMultipleLines took 0 sec
[junit] Testcase: testEmptyValues took 0.01 sec
[junit]     FAILED
[junit] expected:<> but was:<555-9999>
[junit] junit.framework.ComparisonFailure: expected:<>
                                      but was:<555-9999>
[junit] at
        csvparser.TestCsvParser.testEmptyValues(TestCsvParser.java:20)
```

```
[junit] Testcase: testEmptyValues
[junit] TEST csvparser.TestCsvParser FAILED
```

IDE Integrations

Many modern IDEs provide JUnit integrations to allow tests to be easily launched from the environment. Besides convenience, this also allows the debugger to be used to track down problems with little effort.

In most cases, these are simply shortcuts for compiling the tests and launching the JUnit test runner. Don't underestimate the value of this. It's incredibly useful to have a one-click compile and be able to view test results.

A few of the IDEs go one step beyond that and provide a JUnit runner integrated into the development environment. That's what integrated development environments are supposed to do, right? This prevents the need for having to switch between windows, which often slow because of garbage collection kicking in on window switches, and allows easy cross-referencing of test results with code. That is, you can click a test failure and jump to the line of code that caused it.

Figure 3.5 and Figure 3.6 show examples of IDE integrations.

TIP If your IDE does not provide JUnit integration, it's not the end of the world. Assuming you can launch Java applications from the IDE, you can launch the JUnit test runner as if it were one of your own classes. If the environment supports macros, it may be possible to wire up a shortcut key to run the current test case. Explore your environment. It's worth investing a little effort to make day-to-day development faster. And don't forget about the debugger!

Setting Up and Tearing Down the Environment

It is common for tests to have to set up the environment to a known state before running. This could include creating a set of objects populated with known values or connecting to a database. Likewise, many tests must ensure that the environment is cleaned up correctly before proceeding, such as closing resources like database connections or file streams. This environment is often referred to as a *fixture* in the JUnit and other xUnit family documentation.

This can lead to duplication in individual test methods, since each test requires a similar setup, and nasty try/finally blocks to ensure resources are closed correctly.

```
public class TestDatabase extends TestCase {

  public void testStuff() {
    Database db = new Database("localhost");
    db.open();
    try {
      // ... some test code
```

```
      } finally {
        db.close();
      }
    }

    public void testMoreStuff() {
      Database db = new Database("localhost");
      db.open();
      try {
        // ... some more test code
      } finally {
        db.close();
      }
    }

  }
```

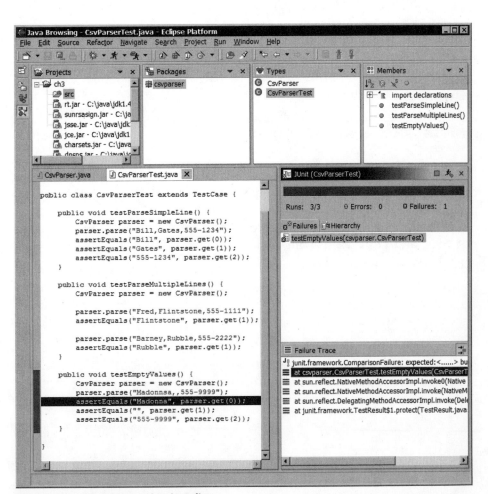

Figure 3.5   JUnit integration in Eclipse

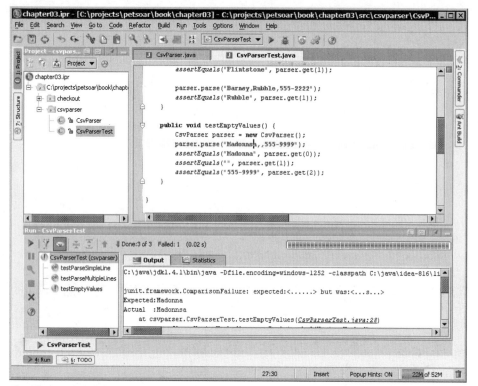

Figure 3.6   JUnit integration in IntelliJ IDEA

Fortunately, JUnit provides a mechanism for ensuring that a piece of code is run before and after each test method in a class, regardless of whether the test passed, failed, or threw an exception.

To set up and tear down tests correctly, simply override the protected `setUp()` and `tearDown()` methods, respectively. Thus, the previous code could be simplified as follows:

```
public class TestDatabase extends TestCase {

  private Database db;

  protected void setUp() {
    db = new Database("localhost");
    db.open();
  }

  protected void tearDown() {
    db.close();
  }

  public void testStuff() {
    // ... some test code
```

```
  }

  public void testMoreStuff() {
    // ... some more test code
  }

}
```

This is somewhat more readable, don't you think? The duplicated clutter from the test methods has been removed.

When JUnit executes the test method, the following methods are called in order. Between each group of setup/test/teardown blocks, a new instance of the test case is created. This means that one test cannot be dependant on the state of another test, which is always a good thing.

```
Instantiate test class.
Call setUp().
Call testStuff().
Call tearDown().

Instantiate test class.
Call setUp().
Call testStuff().
Call tearDown().
```

TIP A good practice is to ensure that your unit tests correctly set up and tear down the full environment correctly. This allows tests to be instantly run in isolation or as part of a batch in an automated manner without added manual intervention.

Extensions

To complement JUnit, many tools are available from `http://www.junit .org/`. This list is ever-changing, and it's worthwhile to check up on it from time to time to see if there's anything there that can help you.

Some of the more useful add-ons include the following:

- **XMLUnit** — A collection of assertions for comparing the structure of XML documents or specific subsets. See `http://xmlunit. sourceforge.net/`
- **jWebUnit** — A library for interacting with Web applications over HTTP from unit tests. See `http://jwebunit.sourceforge.net/`

- **JUnitPerf** — A JUnit extension that allows tests to be run repeatedly by simultaneous threads to test the performance and concurrency of code. See `http://www.clarkware.com/software/JUnitPerf.html`

- **Cactus** — A toolkit to allow unit tests that run in remote servers, such as application server or Servlet engines, to be tested. See `http://jakarta.apache.org/cactus/`

For a more detailed look at JUnit, and many of its extensions, refer to the book *JUnit in Action* by Vincent Massol with Ted Husted (Greenwich, Conn: Manning Publications Company, 2003).

Summary

In this chapter, we looked at how writing unit tests in JUnit can help you quickly find bugs and make changes to your code without the worry of breaking things — just as we did with the CsvParser. This safety net speeds up development because less time is spent worrying about what might be broken if a change is made. We also examined the core features of JUnit, including test fixtures (environments) and various assertion methods. Both of which will be very useful once you begin writing large test suites.

Chapter 4 expands on unit testing by looking at how to test object collaborations by using a technique known as mock objects.

Chapter 13 looks beyond the technology and into a technique known as Test Driven Development that can radically change the way code is developed.

Testing Object Interactions with Mocks

Chapter 3 looks at the basics of unit testing and demonstrates how a fairly straightforward class can be tested. This chapter expands on these points and looks at the problems associated with testing classes in larger applications that interact with other classes.

Using *mock objects* or *mocks* is a technique that allows you to unit test how objects interact with each other. In addition, we introduce the Mock Objects Library, which provides the necessary infrastructure for using this technique.

Testing Object Interactions

In a typical JUnit test, some data is set up that is passed to the code under test, and the return value is verified. All this does is test data — or state.

Exploring Some Pitfalls of Testing State

Although testing state is relatively straightforward, when it comes to building a real application, it has some downsides. These downsides include the following:

- Too many dependencies
- Too much exposure

- Too much state to manage
- Too hard to test

Too Many Dependencies

A unit test is meant to test just a small unit of code.

Sometimes, you can be testing a class that uses another class that uses another class that uses another class that uses another class and so on.

This can lead to a lot of required setup work and have a high execution cost. A single method may require many other objects to be instantiated, including external resources such as files or database connections.

Besides the high execution cost of this, it also makes tests harder to manage. If the behavior of one class is changed, this could bubble up and affect all the classes that depend on it. In turn, it could cause all the tests for these classes to fail. This makes it difficult to change the behavior of systems without causing a test maintenance nightmare.

Too Much Exposure

One of the many benefits of Object Oriented Programming is that objects encapsulate data and behavior by exposing an interface to work with. If using an object, you need to know *what* it does but not necessarily *how* it does it.

For example, a system can contain an OrderDispatcher class that is responsible for ensuring orders are dispatched to the warehouse. In order to test any *other* external class that may interact with this class, the OrderDispatcher would have to be opened up to allow the unit test to check if a particular order has been dispatched. This would require the class to expose the orders it contains.

This violates encapsulation. What the OrderDispatcher does with orders is its own business. By exposing the data structure of the underlying orders, you require knowledge about the internals of the class. This also makes it harder to maintain the class. It is possible that it would make more sense to store the orders in a hashtable rather than a list or even to fire them onto a JMS queue and forget about them. These details should not be exposed by the class.

Too Much State to Manage

Setting up the environment and tearing it down again is complicated. There are a lot of variables to consider in a large system, and it's often just too complicated or costly to do for each unit test.

A tell-tale sign of this is that, in order to set up a class for a unit test, you must load a properties file, instantiate a factory, connect to a database, set up some context objects, and so on. In each of these processes, there's a lot of state to consider, and it can make tests tedious to write and brittle because the structure of these items changes.

Too Hard to Test

Some APIs are difficult to test against. These can be standard JDK or J2EE APIs, third-party libraries, or your own code.

An obvious example is testing that an e-mail has been sent and contains the correct body. To do this, you have to execute the code under test, then create some more code to log in to an e-mail account, download the messages, search for the correct message, and test that it contains the correct body. Ouch!

Besides being complicated to write, there are many other factors that make this a brittle test. The test requires a mail server for delivery to be available plus a mail server for picking up mail. If these are separate servers, the test mail may fail because the mail hasn't been transferred quick enough between the two. If multiple developers run the test at the same time, the tests could get the messages muddled up.

Again, because of the many layers that are built on top of this, there are many tests in your application that depend on this fragile testing technique.

A less obvious example is when you want to test how code behaves in situations that are harder to simulate in tests, such as a JDBC driver drops a connection midway through a transaction.

Exploring the Alternative: Testing Interactions

An alternative to testing state is to test the interaction of objects. That is, verify that one object calls methods on another object in a certain way.

To test whether a particular button on a coffee machine adds milk to the coffee, the test can be written in two ways:

- *Testing State* — Does the `Coffee.getIngredients()` method contain milk?
- *Testing Interaction* — Was the `Coffee.addIngredient()` method called with milk as an argument?

From the OrderDispatcher example used previously:

- *Testing State* — Does the order exist in the list of dispatched orders?
- *Testing Interaction* — Was the order dispatched?

From the email example used previously:

- *Testing State* — Is the message in the mailbox?
- *Testing Interaction* — Was the message sent?

Table 4.1   Testing State vs. Testing Interaction

PROBLEM WITH TESTING STATE	CONSEQUENCE OF TESTING INTERACTION
Too many dependencies	Interactions can be tested without worrying about what the dependencies actually do. So long as the dependencies are interacted with correctly, the test can pass. This eliminates the need for dependencies of dependencies to be set up.
Exposing too much	The internals of objects remain internal. The state is never interrogated.
Too much state to manage	With fewer external dependencies to set up, less state must be managed from tests.
Some things are very hard to test	It's less important what the hard-to-test dependencies actually do when executing the test so long as the interactions with them can be tested.

Although the difference between the two approaches is subtle, it's enough to address many of the pitfalls related to testing state. Table 4.1 looks at how testing interaction overcomes many of the problems associated with testing state.

Testing interactions sounds great in theory, but they can be very difficult to put into practice. The next section shows how easy it can be.

Using Mock Objects

A technique to help test the interactions of objects in isolation is to use a *mock object*. The remainder of this chapter explores what mock objects are and how to use them.

A mock object is often referred to simply as a *mock*.

NOTE To get more information on mock objects, visit http://www.mockobjects.com/. This site contains articles, frequently asked questions, and relevant links related to the subject.

Example Scenario

Here's the scenario. A checkout facility is required that is responsible for processing a customer's shopping cart, invoicing the customer, and dispatching the customer's order. This entails five objects:

- *Customer* — Provides information about the customer making the purchase
- *ShoppingCart* — Provides information about what the customer is purchasing
- *Invoicer* — Sends an invoice via e-mail to the customer and a copy to the accounts department's mainframe
- *OrderDispatcher* — Sends messages to the warehouse that instructs an order to be dispatched
- *Checkout* — Encapsulates the process required to complete the transaction, sends an invoice for the contents of the shopping cart, and requests the order dispatch

Figure 4.1 shows this process.

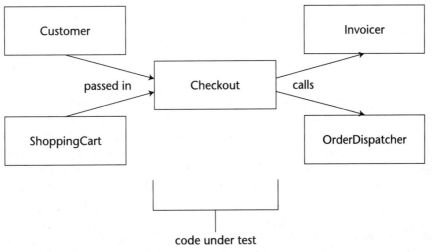

Figure 4.1 Class interactions

For this scenario, the class being tested is Checkout. The interfaces for the other classes look like this:

```
public interface Customer {
   String getName();
   String getAddress();
   String getEmail();
   long getNumber();
   // more...
}

public interface ShoppingCart {
   long[] getItemNumbers();
   float getTotalAmount();
   // more...
}

public interface Invoicer {
   void invoiceCustomer(long customerNumber,
                        String customerEmail,
                        float amount);
}

public interface OrderDispatcher {
   void dispatchItem(long itemNumber,
                     String name,
                     String address);
}
```

Each of these interfaces will have a corresponding class implementation that has not been shown here for brevity. We recommend using interfaces in this way to help separate the details of *what* a class does from *how* a class does it.

Although not strictly necessary in many circumstances, this interface/implementation separation emphasizes the fact that classes should encapsulate the internals of how they work and provide clients to the class a simplistic API to work with. Even though this API may never be used outside of your project, thinking in terms of small APIs can greatly improve the design of your code, which, of course, leads to simpler enhancements, evolution, and maintenance.

Another benefit of separating interfaces in this way is that it helps solve the problem of testing the Checkout class by using mock objects.

Understanding the Role of a Mock Object

Mock objects allow the classes surrounding the class under to test to be replaced with fake or mock versions. This allows a class to be tested in isolation from its dependencies.

Because the interfaces from the dependencies have been separated from their implementations, a new implementation of the class can be substituted — the mock.

When testing a class, a mock is set up for each dependency that class has and is then passed to the class under test. The class under test thinks it's dealing with real objects; however, these mocks are merely simulating the environment to enable isolated and thorough testing.

Each unit test customizes the behavior of the mock, depending on what functionality needs to be tested in the class under test. For each method a mock simulates, the following criteria can be set up:

- *Expectations* — How the mock expects the code under test to interact with it. If these expectations aren't met, the test will fail.

- *Return values* — Any values the mock may need to return to the code under test.

Looking back at the scenario, to test that the Checkout class talks to the OrderDispatcher correctly, a mock OrderDispatcher can be substituted in the test that verifies that its methods are called correctly, as shown in Figure 4.2.

Understanding the Mock Objects Library

To help out in using mock objects, you can use the Open Source (yay!) library available from `www.mockobjects.com`, which is aptly called the *Mock Objects Library*.

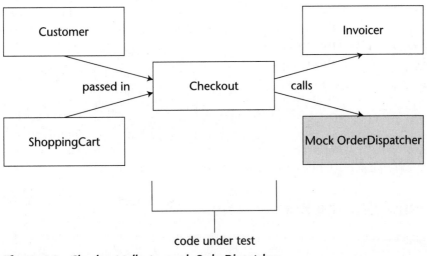

Figure 4.2 Checkout talks to mock OrderDispatcher.

The Mock Objects Library contains the following parts:

- An expectation library to help define the expectations when creating mock objects

- Alternative APIs for many of the common JDK and J2EE libraries, including network sockets, I/O, JDBC, Servlets, JMS, JNDI, and Java-Mail. These alternative APIs extend the conventional APIs to include clean interface separations from implementations, which allows code that depends on these interfaces to be passed mock implementations — as well as any other custom implementation — as needed.

- Mock implementations for the APIs mentioned previously

- A library for dynamically creating mocks at runtime from your unit tests without having to define extra classes. This uses dynamic proxies.

NOTE *Dynamic proxies* are a feature added to Java 1.3. As you may know, the Proxy Pattern is nothing more than providing implementation through indirection. Essentially, a class can implement an interface and, rather than contain any real logic or computation, it can just redirect calls to another object — hence the name *proxy*. A dynamic proxy is the same thing. The only difference being that the proxy implementation is created at runtime. This is perfect for creating fake implementations of your services inside of unit tests.

You do not need to know how to use dynamic proxies to use the mock objects framework. However, if you're interested, you can read more about it in the JavaDoc for java.lang.reflect.Proxy.

Using Dynamic Mocks

The most useful part of the Mock Objects Library is the ability to rapidly create a mock implementation of any interface using a dynamic proxy.

Following is a short tutorial to get you started with the library to help test the Checkout class from the previous scenario. The Checkout class looks like this:

```
public class Checkout {

  private OrderDispatcher orderDispatcher = new OrderDispatcherImpl();
  private Invoicer invoicer = new InvoicerImpl();

  public void process(ShoppingCart shoppingCart, Customer customer) {
    // send invoice
    invoicer.invoiceCustomer(customer.getNumber(),
                             customer.getEmail(),
                             cart.totalAmount());
```

```
      // dispatch items
      long[] itemNumbers = cart.getItemNumbers();
      for (int i = 0; i < itemNumbers.length; i++) {
        orderDispatcher.dispatchItem(itemNumbers[i],
                                     customer.getName(),
                                     customer.getAddress());

      }
    }
  }
```

Creating Mocks

Creating mocks is easy. Simply instantiate the com.mockobjects.dynamic
.Mock class, and pass the interface you intend to mock in the constructor.
    For our scenario, we can set up the mock Invoicer and OrderDispatcher like so:

```
Mock orderDispatcher = new Mock(OrderDispatcher.class);
Mock invoicer = new Mock(Invoicer.class);
```

Substituting Objects

To get the class under test (Checkout) to use the mocks, the real Invoicer and
OrderDispatcher instances need to be substituted for the mocks. There are
many ways to do this. However, the simplest practice is to add setter methods
on the Checkout class.

```
public class Checkout {

  private OrderDispatcher orderDispatcher = new OrderDispatcherImpl();
  private Invoicer invoicer = new InvoicerImpl();

  public void setOrderDispatcher(OrderDispatcher orderDispatcher) {
    this.orderDispatcher = orderDispatcher;
  }

  public void setInvoicer(Invoicer invoicer) {
    this.invoicer = invoicer;
  }

  // ...

}
```

With these setters in place, the real implementations can be easily substituted for the mock implementations.

The Mock class can generate a proxy that implements the required interface being mocked by calling the `proxy()` method. This proxy is what the class under test interacts with:

```
Checkout checkout = new Checkout();

checkout.setOrderDispatcher((OrderDispatcher) orderDispatcher.proxy());
checkout.setInvoicer((Invoicer) invoicer.proxy());
```

Defining the Expectations

Now that we've handed these two mocks off to the Checkout object, we must somehow provide a way to test Checkout's *interaction* with them. We can do this by providing *expectations* to the mocks. An expectation is a method call, including arguments, which will be called on the mock instance. Looking at the Checkout implementation, we can expect that Invoicer's `invoiceCustomer()` method is called.

An example of what this looks like is shown here:

```
invoicer.expect("invoiceCustomer", C.ANY_ARGS);
```

The `expect()` method tells the mock that it should expect that the `invoiceCustomer()` method be called.

The C.ANY_ARGS argument is called an *argument constraint*. It says that any arguments can be passed to `invoiceCustomer()`, and the expectation will be met. The C class is a utility class with static methods provided by the Mock Objects Library.

Understanding Argument Constraints

Just expecting that a method name is called is often not enough to test a class' interaction with outside resources, such as Invoicer. To be more precise with your expectations, constraints can be placed on the expectation as to which arguments are allowed to be passed in.

Constraints are represented by the com.mockobjects.constaint.Constraint interface. This interface has a single `boolean eval(Object o)` method that is used to determine if a constraint is met or not. The Mock Objects framework ships with several implementations for this interface, such as IsEqual, IsAnything, IsInstanceOf, IsNot, and many more. You can use these prebuilt constraints to narrow the precision of your expectation.

The `expect()` method allows for an array of constraints to be passed as an argument, one constraint for each argument that will be verified in the method. Since `invoiceCustomer()` has three arguments, a more precise expectation might look like this:

```
invoicer.expect("invoiceCustomer", new Constraint[] {
    new IsEqual(new Long(123)),
    new IsEqual("duke@ilovejava.com"),
    new IsEqual(new Float(100.50))
});
```

This expectation means that the invoiceCustomer() method is expected to be called, but, furthermore, it is expected that the arguments will be equal to 123, "duke@ilovejava.com," and 100.50.

A slightly more flexible expectation may look like:

```
invoicer.expect("invoiceCustomer", new Constraint[] {
    new IsAnything(),
    new IsInstanceOf(String.class),
    new IsGreaterThan(100)
});
```

Writing out these constraint arrays can be somewhat tedious. So, the C utility class can be used to cut down the amount of code required. For example, an expectation that only uses the IsEqual constraint can be shortened to:

```
invoicer.expect("invoiceCustomer",
    C.eq(new Integer(123), "duke@ilovejava.com", new Float(100.50)) );
```

The C utility class contains several methods to help make creating constraints easier for you. It provides an args() method that can be used to construct Constraint[] arrays, which lets you avoid the cryptic new Constraint[] {...} syntax.

It also provides many methods and public fields for using common constraints, such as eq(), not(), IS_NULL, IS_NOT_NULL, and so on. Furthermore, methods such as eq() and not() are designed to take both objects as well as primitives, which allows you to avoid having to write code such as new IsEqual(new Long(123)).

Verifying Expectations

Once expectations, including detailed constraints, have been specified, there must be a way to verify that the expectations were indeed met. Fortunately, this is very easy to do. Some of it happens automatically, such as a check against constraints when the mock's method is called. This means that, if your code calls invoiceCustomer() with unexpected arguments, the unit test will fail immediately.

However, there must be a way to see if invoiceCustomer() was ever called at all. This is just a matter of simply calling the mock's verify() method, which will in turn verify that all the expectations were met correctly. If the expectations aren't met, the test will fail. A complete test looks like this:

```
// create a Checkout to test
Checkout checkout = new Checkout();

// Create some mock dependencies
Mock orderDispatcher = new Mock(OrderDispatcher.class);
Mock invoicer = new Mock(Invoicer.class);

// Create some values to pass in
Customer customer = new CustomerImpl(123, "Duke",
    "duke@ilovejava.com", "101 Java Dr., San Jose, CA 95126", 100.50);
ShoppingCart cart = new ShoppingCartImpl(99.99, new long[] { 1, 2, 3 });

// Substitute the dependencies of the Checkout with the mocks
checkout.setOrderDispatcher((OrderDispatcher) orderDispatcher.proxy());
checkout.setInvoicer((Invoicer) invoicer.proxy());

// Setup expectations of how the Customer should interact with its
// dependencies

invoicer.expect("invoiceCustomer",
    C.eq(new Integer(123), "duke@ilovejava.com", new Float(100.50)) );
orderDispatcher.expect("dispatchItem", C.args(
    C.IS_ANYTHING, C.eq("Duke"),
    C.eq("101 Java Dr., San Jose, CA 95126")));
// Execute the code under test
checkout.process(customer, cart);

// Verify the expectations were met
invoicer.verify();
orderDispatcher.verify();
```

It is important to `verify()` the mocks at the *end* of the test; otherwise, there would be no calls to verify yet.

Setting Up Return Values

Sometimes, just verifying that a method is called isn't enough. In the last example, we created a CustomerImpl object to represent our customer, Duke. But, what if the customer object were too complex to create like that? We'd have to mock it, which means that the mock now has to *return* values as well, specifically for calls to getName(), getAddress(), getEmail(), and getNumber(). Consider replacing the following code:

```
Customer customer = new CustomerImpl(123, "Duke",
    "duke@ilovejava.com", "101 Java Dr., San Jose, CA 95126", 100.50);
```

Use the following code instead:

```
Mock customerMock = new Mock(Customer.class);
customerMock.matchAndReturn("getName", "Duke");
customerMock.matchAndReturn("getAddress",
                           "101 Java Dr., San Jose, CA 95126");
customerMock.matchAndReturn("getEmail", "duke@ilovejava.com");
customerMock.matchAndReturn("getNumber", new Long(123));
Customer customer = (Customer) customerMock.proxy();
```

The `matchAndReturn()` method simply returns a preset value when the named method is called.

While this change looks more complex, it actually gives us more power. We can now write the Checkout unit test without CustomerImpl even being created yet, a very powerful feature that we will explore more in Chapter 13 when we discuss Test Driven Development. The unit test now truly runs in isolation!

> **NOTE** Note that, in the last example, there were no constraints given to the expectations. For methods that have no arguments, there is clearly no need to provide any constraints. Therefore, the API has simpler versions of methods like `matchAndReturn()` **and** `expect()` **that take no constraints.**

Summary

In this chapter, we looked at the complexity of testing large programs and the difference between testing state and testing interaction. After seeing that it is sometimes better to test interaction than state, we then looked at mock objects as a way to do this. By using mock objects, we were able to test some advanced code in isolation without requiring any external resources, such as a database.

Chapter 13 introduces a concept called Test Driven Development (TDD) that will show how the fundamentals learned in this chapter, and Chapter 3 can be used as a design and development process — not just for testing. From there, we use Test Driven Development to create the rest of the PetSoar application by using the tools and technologies that will be introduced in the remainder of the book.

CHAPTER 5

Storing Objects with Hibernate

This chapter shows you how to simplify the persistence of objects by using Hibernate. In the first part of the chapter, we explain Hibernate, persist a simple object model in a database, and query on it. In the second part, we examine the options Hibernate provides for handling complex relations between objects and its support for persisting a hierarchy of classes. We introduce you to some of the most popular tools for working with Hibernate and provide a brief comparison between Hibernate and other competing persistence technologies.

Understanding the Complexities of Persistence

One of the most complicated and time-consuming tasks of developing an enterprise application is writing the code to store and load data from a database at the appropriate times.

At some point, the state of your application must be persisted — most likely to a relational database. Following are some obstacles to overcome with this:

- *Mapping an object model to a relational schema* — The types of relationships exhibited differ between the two types of models. For example, relational databases model one-to-many and many-to-many relations; whereas, object models model association, aggregation, composition, multiplicity, and inheritance.

- *Keeping your object model and database schema in sync* — Why should you have to? If you define a Person class with all its fields, you shouldn't have to duplicate your effort by defining the same structure in a table. What happens when you change the class but you forget to change the schema?

- *Persisting and retrieving an object from a database* — Writing SQL for all the fields is very tedious and error-prone. It is another thing that also has to be updated when the model changes.

- *Maintaining relationships* — When an object is retrieved that is associated with a second object, where should the code go that retrieves this second object? When should it be called?

- *Querying data* — Where do you write code to find all Person objects who are born in a particular year?

- *Performance* — Executing an SQL hit for every single operation is slow and puts a lot of overhead on the server. Techniques such as caching, lazy loading, and eager loading must be employed to improve performance.

The actual work required to achieve all this is possible but very repetitive, which adds to development time. However, like all repetitive tasks, tools can be of assistance. Hibernate is one of those.

Persisting Objects with Hibernate 2

Hibernate version 2, which will be referred to from here on as *Hibernate*, is a free and Open Source Object-Relational Mapping (ORM) framework available from `http://hibernate.sourceforge.net`.

Hibernate is not an abstract, high-level persistence framework like JDO or EJB CMP. Unlike those frameworks, it doesn't try to abstract away completely to a generic persistence framework that is applicable to mapping to relational, object-based, or mainframe databases. It specializes only in transparent persistence of objects in relational databases and, thereby, has an API that is more intuitive for working with relational databases. Also note that, unlike those standards, Hibernate is not currently an implementation of any industry standard.

Hibernate tries to accomplish what is known as Transparent Persistence in its best and most realistic form. *Transparent Persistence* means that, in order to add the persistence functionality to classes, you don't have to modify the classes to adapt to the persistence mechanism. Some frameworks, such as JDO, use byte-code modification to accomplish this. So, in those systems, the compiled classes are enhanced by some persistence-specific bytecode. Hibernate, on the other hand, does essentially the same thing but in runtime. The advantage of this approach is smoother development cycles because no extra step is added to the build process of the application to enhance the compiled classes with persistence code.

Hibernate works with many different database brands, such as Oracle, DB2, Sybase, PostgreSQL, and MySQL, to name a few. It understands different SQL dialects of these databases and tries to take advantage of all optimizations possible in the SQL dialect of each of these databases. It's worth mentioning that Hibernate is independent of any application server and works on any of them. It even works in environments other than J2EE application servers. For example, you can easily use it in a client-server Swing application or in JUnit test cases.

Hibernate comes with a framework for storing objects in relational tables. It provides an API to load those objects back in memory, either directly by using the primary keys or by using a sophisticated query language called Hibernate Query Language (HQL). It provides other services such as caching and database schema generation, too.

Let's start learning Hibernate with a very simple example. We will do normal database operations such as inserting, updating, removing, and searching on a simple object model that will be persisted into a HypersonicSQL database. We've chosen the HypersonicSQL (HSQL) database for this sample because it's a pure Java database and can be very easily embedded into any Java application with no setup required. The application itself won't do anything useful. It consists of some model classes and some code for testing them.

NOTE Although we use HypersonicSQL as the database in this chapter, Hibernate can be used with most JDBC-enabled databases, including MySQL, PostgreSQL, Oracle, and SQL Server.

Creating the Persistent Classes

The object model consists of two classes. The ContactInfo class has firstName and lastName String properties, a phone property of type PhoneNumber, and an ID field of type long, which will be mapped to the primary key of the table it's persisted to.

```
[ContactInfo.java]

package contacts;

public class ContactInfo {

    private long id;
    private String firstName;
    private String lastName;
    private PhoneNumber phone;

    public long getId() {
        return id;
    }
```

```
    public void setId(long id) {
        this.id = id;
    }

    public String getFirstName() {
        return firstName;
    }
    public void setFirstName(String firstName) {
        this.firstName = firstName;
    }

    public String getLastName() {
        return lastName;
    }
    public void setLastName(String lastName) {
        this.lastName = lastName;
    }

    public PhoneNumber getPhone() {
        return phone;
    }
    public void setPhone(PhoneNumber phone) {
        this.phone = phone;
    }
}
```

The PhoneNumber class has countryCode, areaCode, and number properties — all of type String. PhoneNumber does not have any ID properties. A PhoneNumber is dependent on a ContactInfo object and can't exist without a ContactInfo. ContactInfo has a reference to PhoneNumber.

```
[PhoneNumber.java]

package contacts;

public class PhoneNumber {

    private String countryCode;
    private String areaCode;
    private String number;

    public String getCountryCode() {
        return countryCode;
    }
    public void setCountryCode(String countryCode) {
        this.countryCode = countryCode;
    }

    public String getAreaCode() {
```

```
        return areaCode;
    }
    public void setAreaCode(String areaCode) {
        this.areaCode = areaCode;
    }

    public String getNumber() {
        return number;
    }
    public void setNumber(String number) {
        this.number = number;
    }
}
```

Notice that the classes are plain old Java objects (POJOs). The only constraints set by Hibernate are that each class must have a public default constructor that takes no arguments, and each persistent field requires a getter and setter method. Although, they don't have to be public.

Mapping the Classes to a Database

With the classes in place, they can be mapped to a database schema.

The ContactInfo class is *composed* of some simple values and a PhoneNumber class. This means that every PhoneNumber instance always belongs to a single ContactInfo instance. In Hibernate-speak, the PhoneNumber class is a *component* of ContactInfo.

This relationship means the two classes can be mapped to a single database table:

```
TABLE CONTACTS
    FNAME               VARCHAR(30)
    LNAME               VARCHAR(50)
    PHONEAREACODE       VARCHAR(3)
    PHONECOUNTRYCODE    VARCHAR(5)
    PHONENUMBER         VARCHAR(15)
    PK                  BIGINT not null
```

Hibernate needs to know how to map the classes to this schema. To do this, a mapping file must be created.

A *mapping* is defined in a simple XML file named CLASS.hbm.xml, where CLASS is the name of the class to be persisted. This file should reside in the same directory or jar file as the compiled class.

```
[ContactInfo.hbm.xml]
<?xml version="1.0"?>
<!DOCTYPE hibernate-mapping PUBLIC
    "-//Hibernate/Hibernate Mapping DTD 2.0//EN"
```

```
            "http://hibernate.sourceforge.net/hibernate-mapping-2.0.dtd">

    <hibernate-mapping>

        <class name="contacts.ContactInfo" table="CONTACT">

            <id name="id" column="PK">
                <generator class="increment"/>
            </id>

            <property name="firstName" column="FNAME" length="30"/>
            <property name="lastName"  column="LNAME" length="50"
                        not-null="true"/>

            <component name="phone">
                <property name="areaCode"      column="PHONEAREACODE"
                                               length="3"/>
                <property name="countryCode"  column="PHONECOUNTRYCODE"
                                               length="5"/>
                <property name="number"        column="PHONENUMBER"
                                               length="15"/>
            </component>

        </class>

    </hibernate-mapping>
```

<hibernate-mapping>

This is the root element of the mapping file. Inside this element, multiple <class/> elements can be defined, but only a single <class/> is normally defined. This describes the mapping for the class after the CLASS.hbm.xml file is named.

<class>

The mappings for a class — and its components — are defined in the <class> element. The *name* attribute is the fully qualified name of the class that the mapping is being defined. The *table* attribute specifies the database table to which this class maps. Hibernate currently supports mapping one class to one table.

Inside the element are definitions for each of its fields.

<property>

The mapping for each of the primitive fields is defined by the <property> element. Each primitive property of the class maps to a single field of the database table. *Name* is the name of the Java property being mapped. It's mapped to a column defined by the *column* attribute.

We can also optionally define the *length* attribute to hint the length of the SQL data type that Hibernate will use if creating a schema, such as VARCHAR(25). Hibernate can do all the persistence operation without the *length* field being present. This field is used only for generating the database schema from the mapping file. The *not-null* attribute is also optional and only effective for the schema-generation tool provided by Hibernate, which we will cover shortly.

By default, Hibernate guesses which getter or setter method of JDBC Result-Set or PreparedStatement it should use. For example, if the property is of String type `ResultSet.getString()`, it is used for loading the value from the database. On the database side, the String field can be mapped to a database-specific type, such as VARCHAR, TEXT, or any other vendor-specific type. Hibernate maintains a default mapping between Java types and database types for each brand of database. The mapping can be used for generating database schema from mapping files. Of course, it is possible to redefine a mapping. For example, we can map a specific String field to a CLOB type instead of the default VARCHAR type. This is accomplished by nesting a column element inside the <property> element.

<id>

Each persistent object should have a unique identifier. The identifier maps to the primary key of the table to which the class is mapped. The nested <id> element defines the mapping for the identifier property. Hibernate supports IDs of primitive types, such as integer or long, and composite IDs. The <id> element is used for defining primitive types as primary keys.

It is a good practice in database design to use primary keys that have no business meaning and are auto-generated. Hibernate supports different ID generation schemes, but you can add your own by implementing the net.sf.hibernate.id.IdentifierGenerator interface. We use the built-in "increment" ID generation mechanism. Hibernate supports these ID generation schemes:

- increment — Generates decimal numbers that are guaranteed to be unique within a single JVM

- identity or sequence — Uses identity or native sequence columns of the underlying database. Many databases support identity columns that are auto-generated and filled by the database when a new record is inserted.

- uuid.hex or uuid.string — Uses a UUID algorithm to generate identifiers of type string that are unique within a network (the IP address is used)

- hilo or seqhilo — Uses a hi/lo algorithm to efficiently generate identifiers of type long. The biggest benefit of this algorithm is that it reserves a chunk of IDs in one shot and assigns one to each new record from the chunk. When all IDs from the chunk are consumed, a new chunk is reserved. This technique leads to less database access for primary key generation because IDs are assigned from the chunk that is in memory.

- assigned — Lets the application itself assign an identifier to the object. It's useful for rare cases when the ID should be calculated from the properties of the domain object.

- foreign — Uses the identifier of another associated object

The choice of the ID generation mechanism is largely dependent on the application requirements. If an ID unique to a single JVM is acceptable for a particular application, it is the most efficient one. A database-dependent mechanism such as identity or sequence is mostly used in environments in which many applications developed in different languages and environments work with the database. In such an environment, the only universal mechanism that all these applications can rely on is the ID generation provided by the underlying database.

<component>

This defines what Hibernate calls a *component*, which is a dependent class that does not have a primary key of its own. Its life is dependent on the existence of another object, and it is mapped to the same table of the wrapping class.

PhoneNumber is such a component type, and the phoneNumber property is mapped to a <component> element. A PhoneNumber without a ContactInfo object is meaningless.

Because of the nature of this relationship, it makes more sense to store both the ContactInfo and PhoneNumber in a single CONTACT table with additional columns to facilitate the PhoneNumber.

The properties of the PhoneNumber component type are mapped to the columns of the CONTACT table by the same <property> element we saw before.

Configuring Hibernate

Before we can store and retrieve instances of ContactInfo to and from a relational database by using Hibernate's API, we should first configure Hibernate.

Hibernate needs a minimum of these jar files in order to operate:

- `hibernate2.jar` — All the Hibernate interfaces and implementations are in this jar file. While working with Hibernate, only classes from Hibernate itself are used by the developer, and the rest of the following jar files are used by Hibernate internally.

- Several Jakarta Commons components — `commons-beanutils .jar`, `commons-collections.jar`, `commons-digester.jar`, `commons-lang.jar` and `commons-logging.jar`. We'll become familiar with some of them in Chapter 11.

- `cglib.jar` — Hibernate uses this to enhance compiled classes in runtime by persistence-specific code.

- `odmg.jar` — Hibernate provides an optional implementation of ODMG's API.

- `xml-apis.jar` and `dom4j.jar` — This is needed for working with XML configuration files.

In our sample application, we will use the Open Source HSQL database, which is downloadable free of charge from `http://www.hsql.org/`. To use it, we must include `hsql.jar` in our application. We could, of course, use any other supported database instead.

Now we should configure Hibernate to connect to the HSQL database and also load and use the XML mapping files we created.

To configure Hibernate, we should create a file named `hibernate .cfg.xml`. Hibernate expects to find this file from the classpath of the application. Here is the `hibernate.cfg.xml` of our sample application, which connects to an embedded HSQL database and lists the `ContactInfo.hbm .xml` mapping file for the only persistable class of our application:

```
<?xml version='1.0' encoding='utf-8'?>
<!DOCTYPE hibernate-configuration PUBLIC
    "-//Hibernate/Hibernate Configuration DTD//EN"
    "http://hibernate.sourceforge.net/hibernate-configuration-2.0.dtd">

<hibernate-configuration>

    <session-factory name="/jndi/ContactsSessionFactory">

        <!-- properties -->
        <property name="hibernate.connection.driver_class">
            org.hsqldb.jdbcDriver
        </property>
        <property name="hibernate.connection.url">
            jdbc:hsqldb:dbdata
        </property>
        <property name="hibernate.connection.username">sa</property>
```

```
<property name="hibernate.connection.password"></property>
<property name="hibernate.dialect">
    net.sf.hibernate.dialect.HSQLDialect
</property>

<property name="hibernate.connection.pool_size">4</property>

<property name="hibernate.show_sql">true</property>

<!-- mapping files -->
<mapping resource="contacts/ContactInfo.hbm.xml"/>

</session-factory>

</hibernate-configuration>
```

An XML file is adhering to the `hibernate-configuration-2.0.dtd` file. The <hibernate-configuration> root element contains a single <session-factory> element. This element defines how Hibernate should obtain a Session for working with the database. It has a name that is actually the JNDI name the database DataSource is bound to. If we were to run our application inside of a J2EE application, we would define a DataSource in our favorite application server and specify the JNDI name of the DataSource in the name attribute of <session-factory>. We'll run our sample application as a normal Java program that has a `main()` method. In this case, this is just a symbolic name given to the session factory used.

Two main elements under the <session-factory> element are <property> and <mapping>.

We can define many properties for the session factory. In the case of a stand-alone application such as this sample application, we should provide the JDBC driver class name, connection string, user name, and password. The hibernate.connection.driver_class, hibernate.connection.url, hibernate.connection.username and hibernate.connection.password are specified for connecting to the embedded HSQL database instance.

Hibernate also needs to know which *dialect* to use when talking to the database because each database product is slightly different. Hibernate uses a dialect to define the specifics of how best to store data and how to make optimizations. For example, to store a String of 400 characters in MySQL, you would use a column of type TEXT; whereas, in Oracle 9, you would use VARCHAR2(400). The hibernate.dialect property refers to a class that configures these optimizations. Hibernate is bundled with dialect classes for most relational database products. However, if one is missing, you can easily create your own by adapting one of the existing ones.

Connection pooling is a very powerful technique for lowering the performance overhead of opening and closing the database connection. The pool holds a number of open connections all the time and serves them one-by-one to the caller. When the client is done with the connection, it is returned to the pool and is ready to be served to other callers. In case of a J2EE application, the application server is responsible for handling connection pooling. Connections are then retrieved via the DataSource facility. For an environment outside of a J2EE application server, we can use Hibernate's built-in connection-pooling mechanism. We use the built-in facility for this sample and configure the number of pooled connections to four by using the hibernate.connection .pool_size property.

Another useful property that we will use in this application is hibernate .show_sql, which tells Hibernate to output any SQL statement it runs on the console. This is very useful for learning which statements Hibernate eventually runs for persisting objects.

Next comes one or more <mapping> elements. All the XML mapping files of the persistent classes should be listed here; otherwise, Hibernate can't figure out which classes are persistable and by which mapping file.

Obtaining a Session

Now that we have a `hibernate.cfg.xml` file, we should load it and let Hibernate use it. This is accomplished by the following piece of code:

```
import net.sf.hibernate.HibernateException;
import net.sf.hibernate.cfg.Configuration;

...
Configuration config = new Configuration();
config.configure();
```

Hibernate comes with a flexible configuration API. Creating a Configuration object and calling `configure()` on it to load the `hibernate.cfg.xml` file. Some applications demand loading the configuration file from other locations, such as somewhere on the disk or network. Hibernate provides more advanced method for these cases.

Next, we should run Hibernate's SchemaUpdate to generate the database schema.

```
// update database schema if required
new SchemaUpdate(config).execute(true);
```

SchemaUpdate generates DDL statements and runs them to generate the database schema. Because we've enabled the hibernate.show_sql property, we see the statement being executed on the console:

```
create table CONTACTS (PK BIGINT not null, FNAME VARCHAR(30), LNAME
VARCHAR(50) not null, PHONE_COUNTRY_CODE VARCHAR(5), PHONE_AREA_CODE
VARCHAR(3), PHONE_NUMBER VARCHAR(4), primary key (PK))
```

As you can see, the table and column names and their type and length are extracted from the `ContactInfo.hbm.xml` mapping file. Note that Hibernate mapped the ID of type long to BIGINT. This is the default mapping for this type for HSQL.

We're now ready to start persisting object with Hibernate's API. We interact with Hibernate via the net.sf.hibernate.Session interface. Session is the interface that has low-level service methods such as `load()`, `save()`, and `find()`.

Each session is backed by a java.sql.Connection instance. Session uses this connection object to run SQL statements. On the other hand, Session is like a transaction or a conversation with the underlying database. We call methods such as `save()` and `load()`, but we should eventually finish our conversation and let Hibernate run all the operations that it recorded during the conversation. By using a single object to track this conversation, Hibernate can act very smartly. For example, it can skip saving unmodified objects. It can also cache loaded objects. So, if consecutive requests to load an object are received, they are served from the cache instead of running any SQL statement. This is known as the *Unit of Work* pattern.

Sessions are created by using the SessonFactory interface, which we configured in the `hibernate.cfg.xml` file. The following code creates a SessionFactory instance and obtains a Session from it:

```
import net.sf.hibernate.HibernateException;
import net.sf.hibernate.Session;
import net.sf.hibernate.SessionFactory;


...
SessionFactory result = config.buildSessionFactory();
Session session = sessionFactory.openSession();
```

SessionFactory is typically a singleton class. One instance is used for the entire application in the particular JVM. It is created once and used thereafter for creating Sessions. It's thread safe so we can obtain Sessions from it without worrying about concurrent threads. Session itself is not thread safe, and we should be careful not to share it with other threads. In fact, we should get a Session, use it, and close it when we are done with our conversation with the database.

The next sections show how to use the Session interface for performing common persistence operations.

Storing Objects in the Database

Let's first insert a ContactInfo instance into the database:

```
ContactInfo contact = new ContactInfo();
contact.setFirstName("Bart");
```

```
contact.setLastName("Simpson");

PhoneNumber phone = new PhoneNumber();
phone.setCountryCode("999");
phone.setAreaCode("666");
phone.setNumber("6969");

contact.setPhone(phone);

try {
    session.save(obj);

    session.flush();
    session.connection().commit();
}
catch(Exception e) {
    session.connection().rollback();
}

System.out.println("contact:" + contact);
```

We create a ContactInfo object and save it by using the save() method of the Session object that we've already obtained. Calling save() by itself doesn't make Hibernate run any SQL INSERT statement. We should finish our conversation by calling the flush() and commit() methods. Also notice that, if something goes wrong, Hibernate throws an Exception that we respond to by catching and rolling back the operation by calling rollback() on the underlying Connection object.

Let's see what's printed on the console as a result of running this code:

```
Hibernate: insert into CONTACTS (FNAME, LNAME, PHONE_COUNTRY_CODE,
PHONE_AREA_CODE, PHONE_NUMBER, PK) values (?, ?, ?, ?, ?, ?)

contact:contacts.ContactInfo@147358f[
id=69220892179431424,firstName=Bart,lastName=Simpson,
phone=contacts.PhoneNumber@190a0d6[
countryCode=999,areaCode=666,number=6969]]
```

Based on the ContactInfo.hbm.xml mapping file, Hibernate generates the SQL statement. Note the values of the properties of the ContactInfo object after saving it in the database. Specifically notice that the "increment" ID-generation mechanism that we chose to use generated a unique value for the ID property. A record is added to the CONTACTS table with that primary key value.

The next thing we'll do is modify this object and update the database content with it:

```
contact.setLastName("Williamson");
contact.getPhone().setNumber("7777");
```

```
try {
    session.update(obj);

    session.flush();
    session.connection().commit();
}
catch(Exception e) {
    session.connection().rollback();
}
```

The code is similar to the previous one except that, this time, we use the update() method instead of save() to update an existing object. This is the SQL statement that was run:

```
Hibernate: update CONTACTS set FNAME=?, LNAME=?, PHONE_COUNTRY_CODE=?,
PHONE_AREA_CODE=?, PHONE_NUMBER=? where PK=?
```

We can also use the saveOrUpdate() method instead of save() or update(), and Hibernate will determine automatically which to call. The saveOrUpdate() method looks at the value of the ID property to find that out. To help Hibernate make the correct decision in this regard, we should give it a hint about IDs for new objects and existing ones. This is accomplished by adding an unsaved-value attribute to the mapping file of ContactInfo:

```
<id name="id" column="PK" unsaved-value="0">
    <generator class="increment"/>
</id>
```

If it's a value other than the specified 0, Hibernate assumes it's an existing object. Calling saveOrUpdate() is not different from the previous codes:

```
try {
    session.saveOrUpdate(obj);

    session.flush();
    session.connection().commit();
} catch(Exception e) {
    session.connection().rollback();
}
```

Deleting an object from the database is equally easy. We just need to call the delete() method:

```
try {
    session.delete(obj);

    session.flush();
    session.connection().commit();
```

```
} catch (Exception e) {
    session.connection().rollback();
}
```

It runs the following SQL:

```
Hibernate: delete from CONTACTS where PK=?
```

Retrieving Objects from the Database

We can either retrieve a specific object from the database by doing a "retrieval by identifier" or by using the querying facility.

The first one is used when we know the primary key of the object we're looking for. To load an object by its identifier, we should use the `load()` method:

```
try {
    contact = (ContactInfo)session.load(ContactInfo.class,
                        new Long(69220892179431424));

    session.flush();
    session.connection().commit();
} catch (Exception e) {
    e.printStackTrace();
    session.connection().rollback();
} finally {
    System.out.println("loaded contact:" + contact);
}
```

The `load()` method accepts two parameters: the type of the object and its ID.

Depending upon whether we're running this code by using the same active Session or in a new Session, we would see different responses on the console. If we called `load()` on the Session instance that we used in the previous part, we would see nothing on the console because it's served from the cache of objects attached to the Session that the Session keeps. Persistent objects are always attached to an active Session; otherwise, they are transient until they are reattached to a Session. Methods such as `update()` only reattach an object to a Session. Later on `flush()`, the actual database operation takes place. Of course, as expected, on a freshly opened Session, a SQL select statement is run to load the object from the database because no such object with the specified ID already exists in its cache of attached objects.

Querying Persistent Objects

Now let's load all objects of the ContactInfo type and print them on console. To do so, we can use *Hibernate Query Language (HQL)*. HQL is a simple language similar to SQL designed for running object-based queries.

```
try {
    List contacts = session.find("FROM contacts.ContactInfo");

    session.flush();
    session.connection().commit();

    for (int i = 0; i < contacts.size(); i++) {
        ContactInfo contactInfo = (ContactInfo) contacts.get(i);
        System.out.println("contactInfo:" + contactInfo);
    }
} catch (Exception e) {
    e.printStackTrace();
    session.connection().rollback();
}
```

To execute an HQL statement, we use the `find()` method. What we give the `find()` method to execute is an HQL statement that is considered an "object query language." As you can see, nowhere in the query is there anything about the table or columns. Instead, object and properties are used. So, a statement like FROM contacts.ContactInfo means select all objects of the contacts.ContactInfo type. Under the covers, Hibernate translates this object query to a SQL query like this:

```
Hibernate: select contacti0_.PK as PK, contacti0_.FNAME as FNAME,
contacti0_.LNAME as LNAME, contacti0_.PHONE_COUNTRY_CODE as PHONE_CO4_,
contacti0_.PHONE_AREA_CODE as PHONE_AR5_,
contacti0_.PHONE_NUMBER as PHONE_NU6_ from CONTACTS contacti0_
```

HQL has syntax very similar to SQL except that it uses classes and properties instead of tables and columns. Instead of tables, we specify class names. Instead of columns, we specify properties. Later in this chapter, you will learn how easy it is to query on relations between tables or, more correctly, to query on associations between objects. It even supports sophisticated query functions such as `max()`, `avg()`, and `order by`.

To query all ContactInfo objects that have a firstName value of Bart, we should write the following code:

```
try {
    String firstName = "Bart;"
    List contacts = session.find(
        "select c from contacts.ContactInfo c where c.firstName=?",
```

```
        firstName, Hibernate.STRING);

    session.flush();
    session.connection().commit();

    for (int i = 0; i < contacts.size(); i++) {
        ContactInfo contactInfo = (ContactInfo) contacts.get(i);
        System.out.println("contactInfo:" + contactInfo);
    }
} catch (Exception e) {
    e.printStackTrace();
    session.connection().rollback();
}
```

Here we use the overloaded version of find() that accepts parameters and parameter types, too. The select c from contacts.ContactInfo part tells Hibernate the expected type of the found objects. The c is an alias name that we then use in the where clause in the where c.firstName=? part. Hibernate substitutes the ? sign by the parameter value that we pass in as the second argument. This parameter's type is specified by the third argument.

If more than one parameter is needed in a query, the third overload form of find() can be used, which accepts an array of parameters and the corresponding array of Hibernate parameter types.

Here are some more advanced queries:

```
from contacts.ContactInfo c order by c.firstName asc, c.lastName desc
```

This query shows the use of the order by clause. One or more properties can be specified with their order type — ascending or descending.

```
select count(c) from contacts.ContactInfo c
```

This query returns a List containing a single Integer object that holds the count of all contacts available in database. Note how something other than the persistence class is returned as the result from the query.

```
select c.firstName, c.lastName from contacts.ContactInfo c
```

This query shows partial selects. Instead of the full object being loaded, we can just load some specific properties of it. The returned result is a List of Lists. The outer list contains one item for each match and the inner list contains the items specified in the select clause — firstName and lastName.

The following returns a list of last names of all the contacts that have a non-null lastName.

```
select c.lastName from contacts.ContactInfo c where c.lastName is not
null group by c.lastName
```

The group by clause groups found items by lastName, exactly like SQL's GROUP BY clause. In fact, many of the HQL constructs are very similar to SQL. Refer to HQL's documentation for a complete list of supported constructs and their correct usage.

Persisting Relationships Between Objects

Let's enhance the sample we've written. We want to be able to create logical nested folders and put contacts inside of them. We also want to be able to mark some folder protected and only let a specific user access it.

The easiest way to model such a requirement is to create a Folder class that can have a list of the Folders below it and also a list of ContactInfos it contains. Then, for the protected folders, the easiest way of modeling it is to derive a ProtectedFolder class from Folder and store permission information in that derived class.

The Folder class is shown as follows. It's nothing but a simple Plain Old Java Object (POJO). It has a List of Folder objects and a List of ContactInfo objects. For both of these lists, we provide getter and setter methods plus add and remove methods for adding and removing items.

```java
package contacts;

import java.util.HashSet;
import java.util.Set;

public class Folder {
    private long id;
    private String folderName;
    private Set folders = new HashSet();
    private Set contacts = new HashSet();

    public long getId() {
        return id;
    }
    public void setId(long id) {
        this.id=id;
    }

    public String getFolderName() {
        return folderName;
    }
    public void setFolderName(String folderName) {
        this.folderName=folderName;
    }

    public Set getFolders() {
        return folders;
    }
```

```
    public void setFolders(Set folders) {
        this.folders = folders;
    }
    public void addFolder(Folder folder) {
        getFolders().add(folder);
    }
    public void removeFolder(Folder folder) {
        getFolders().remove(folder);
    }

    public Set getContacts() {
        return contacts;
    }
    public void setContacts(Set contacts) {
        this.contacts = contacts;
    }
    public void addContact(ContactInfo contact) {
        getContacts().add(contact);
    }
    public void removeContact(ContactInfo contact) {
        getContacts().remove(contact);
    }
}
```

We model the relationship between the parent folder and nested folders with a unidirectional one-to-many relationship. A unidirectional one-to-many relationship is a one-way relationship from the parent folder to the nested folders. The Java code also shows the same type of association. Folder has a list of nested folders. Another design would be a bidirectional one-to-many relationship. Not only would Folder contain a list of folders, but the nested folder would also have a reference to its parent folder.

In the database world, the one-to-many relation is modeled by putting a foreign key in the table. In our case, the FOLDERS table has a PARENT _FOLDER_PK column, which is a foreign key pointing to the row of the parent folder. Of course, in the database world, all such relations are traversable from both ends of the relations and, hence, bidirectional in nature. We can easily query for the parent of a folder. Finding all children of a folder is equally easy. It's a select statement with a where PARENT_FOLDER_PK=? at the end. On the Java side of it, modeling the association as bidirectional requires putting a get/setParentFolder in the Folder class. Hibernate, of course, can handle both cases.

The following database schema models the parent-child relationship between folders:

```
FOLDERS
    PK: BIGINT
    FOLDER_NAME: VARCHAR(30)
    PARENT_FOLDER_PK: BIGINT
```

The relationship between contacts and folders is many-to-many. A folder can have many contacts, and a contact can be a member of many folders. Such a relation can't be created in the database by putting a foreign key in the CONTACTS table like the relation between folders. Another table is needed where each row represents a relation between one folder and one contact. This third table is known as a *join table*. These are used for modeling many-to-many relationships in relational databases, and, as you can see, the relation between folders and contacts is a many-to-many one. The schema for this join table is like this:

```
CONTACTS_FOLDER_REL
    PARENTFOLDER_PK: BIGINT not null
    CONTACT_PK: BIGINT
```

Each row of this table holds the foreign keys of the respective folder and contact records.

To map Folder to the preceding schema, the following `Folder.hbm.xml` file is defined:

```xml
<hibernate-mapping>
    <class name="contacts.Folder" table="FOLDERS">

        <id name="id" column="PK" type="long" unsaved-value="0">
            <generator class="increment"/>
        </id>

        <property name="folderName" column="FOLDER_NAME" length="30"/>

        <set name="folders">
            <key column="PARENTFOLDER_PK"/>
            <one-to-many class="contacts.Folder"/>
        </set>

        <set name="contacts" table="CONTACTS_FOLDER_REL">
            <key column="PARENTFOLDER_PK"/>
            <many-to-many class="contacts.ContactInfo"
                        column="CONTACT_PK"/>
        </set>

    </class>
</hibernate-mapping>
```

Note the two <aet> elements. For the unidirectional one-to-many relation between folders and for the many-to-many relation between folders and contacts, a *set* can be used. Like the Java class, a set can contain any number of items; however, the set's order is not retained, and each item may only appear once. The *name* attribute is the JavaBean name of the Sets. We have defined `set` and `get` methods for each of the collections.

Hibernate supports different collection types. We can use java.util.List, java.util.Set, arrays, and even java.util.Map collection types. All these types can be mapped to database tables. Choosing the correct type of collection needs some analysis of the requirement. A Set doesn't allow duplicate items and doesn't keep track of their order. A List, on the other hand, is ordered and allows duplicated items.

The nested <key> element and its column attribute specify which column is used as the key for each item of the set on the table.

The type of the relation, whether it's one-to-many or many-to-many, is defined by putting a <one-to-many> or <many-to-many> element under the <set> element. The class name of the other end of the relation is specified by the class attribute. Java collections are not typed. They are just a collection of java.lang.Objects. To let Hibernate know about the type of the other end of the relation, we should provide the class name with the class attribute. By knowing the class name, Hibernate can create the correct class upon loading the object from the database.

We defined everything the one-to-many folders relations needs. But, for the many-to-many contacts relation, we should also specify the name of the join table and the name of the foreign-key column pointing to a row in the CONTACTS table. To do that, we specify the *table-name* attribute for the <set> and add a *column* attribute to <many-to-many>.

It's time to write some code to create a folder, add some contacts and nested folders to it, and finally save the whole graph of objects to the database:

```
Folder myFolder = new Folder();
myFolder.setFolderName("My Folder");

Folder friendsFolder = new Folder();
friendsFolder.setFolderName("Friends");

myFolder.addFolder(friendsFolder);

ContactInfo contact = new ContactInfo();
contact.setFirstName("Bart");
contact.setLastName("Simpson");

friendsFolder.addContact(contact);

try {
    session.saveOrUpdate(folder);

    session.flush();
    session.connection().commit();
}
catch(Exception e) {
    session.connection().rollback();
}
```

We create a folder and add another friendsFolder to it. Then, a contact is created and added to it, too. Finally, by using the same `saveOrUpdate()` methods that we used previously in this chapter, we save the root folder object.

Hibernate in some ways supports the concept of "persistence by reachability." So, if an object references another object and we save the first object, the second object is also saved. Unfortunately, the current configuration doesn't accomplish this goal. If we run the application, only a single insert statement is issued, and that statement inserts the root folder object to the database. We should instruct Hibernate to cascade the save operation to referenced objects, too.

On any relation type, be it a <list>, a <set>, or a <one-to-one> relation, we can add a cascade attribute and tell Hibernate what kind of cascading it should do. There are some different cascade types:

- cascade="save-update" — It tells Hibernate to save dependent objects of an object, too.

- cascade="delete" — When the parent object is deleted, all the dependent objects of that object are also deleted from the database. It is useful for modeling *aggregations* between objects. When the life of an object is bound to the life of its parent, that object is aggregated by the parent. Otherwise, it's an *association* between them, and both can live independently of each other.

- cascade="all" — This is a combination of save-update and delete.

- cascade="none" — This is the default that shows an association between objects.

Because the folders list is an aggregation, when we save a folder, all folders associated with it should also be saved. When we delete a parent folder, all nested folders should also be deleted. The contacts list is an association because a contact can be a member of many folders. So, when we delete one of the parent folders, the associated contacts shouldn't be deleted. Here is the modified mapping file:

```
<set name="folders" cascade="all">
    <key column="PARENTFOLDER_PK"/>
    <one-to-many class="contacts.Folder"/>
</set>

<set name="contacts" cascade="save-update" table="CONTACTS_FOLDER_REL">
    <key column="PARENTFOLDER_PK"/>
    <many-to-many class="contacts.ContactInfo"
                  column="CONTACT_PK"/>
</set>
```

When we run the application, these statements are logged on the console:

```
Hibernate: insert into FOLDERS (FOLDER_NAME, PK) values (?, ?)
Hibernate: insert into CONTACTS (FNAME, LNAME, PHONE_COUNTRY_CODE,
PHONE_AREA_CODE, PHONE_NUMBER, PK) values
(?, ?, ?, ?, ?, ?)
Hibernate: update FOLDERS set PARENTFOLDER_PK=? where PK=?
Hibernate: insert into CONTACTS_FOLDER_REL (PARENFOLDERS_PK, CONTACT_PK)
values (?, ?)
```

As you can see, the operation is cascaded to the dependent objects.

Loading this object graph to memory is nothing but calling the infamous load() or find() methods on a Session instance. The interesting part of the retrieval of an object graph in memory is that, when the root object is fetched, all referenced objects of that object are also fetched. The developer does not have to issue separate requests for loading the referenced object.

Of course, it's not always a good thing to load the entire referenced objects in one shot. In fact, this will be a performance killer for this application! With this approach, loading the root folder of the contact list will load all nested folders and contacts, and those folders will, in turn, load their own nested folders and contacts. This chain will lead to all the folders and contacts of the database to memory. Sometimes, this is what we desire, especially when we want to eagerly load all nodes of an object graph and cache it in memory. But, in many cases, it's not the desired behavior. That's why Hibernate provides a "lazy loading" scheme for referenced objects. So, if we mark a reference as lazy, Hibernate won't load the referenced object to memory when the parent object is loaded. Hibernate sits there and waits until the getter method of the reference is called. Only then does Hibernate try to load the referenced object.

So, to mark the two references, we add a lazy attribute to them:

```
<set name="folders" cascade="all" inverse="true"
     lazy="true">
    <key column="PARENTFOLDER_PK"/>
    <one-to-many class="contacts.Folder"/>
</set>

<set name="contacts" cascade="save-update" table="CONTACTS_FOLDER_REL"
     lazy="true">
    <key column="PARENTFOLDER_PK"/>
    <many-to-many class="contacts.ContactInfo"
                  column="CONTACT_PK"/>
</set>
```

It's also worth mentioning how HQL queries can be applied to object references. Suppose we want to find the count of contacts of a folder named Friends. To do so, we write the following HQL query:

```
select count( elements(folder.contacts) ) from contacts.Folder folder
where folder.folderName=?
```

We can access contacts of a folder with the folder.contacts expression. The special `elements()` function is used for selecting the underlying elements of a collection rather than the collection itself. Finally, the `count()` returns the count of the selected elements. This sophisticated query converts into a single, well-defined, and speedy SQL statement by Hibernate.

As another example, let's select all folders that have a contact with a specific firstName, such as Bart:

```
select folder from contacts.Folder folder join folder.contacts contact
where contact.firstName=?
```

Here again, we use the dotted notation to access referenced objects and their properties. Here we retrieve all folders that have a contact with a specific firstName. We use the join keyword just as in SQL.

Hibernate supports many sophisticated constructs in HQL. Refer to Hibernate's documentation for more details.

Persisting Hierarchies of Objects

No object-relational mapping discussion is complete without touching the tough issue of mapping hierarchies of objects to database tables. Unlike object-oriented languages, most relational databases do not have any notion of inheritance and class hierarchies. There are a different ways to map a hierarchy to database tables. Here is a brief list of the most popular techniques:

- *Table per concrete class* — Each concrete class is mapped to its own table. If some properties are common to many classes, they are defined in the table of each concrete class, too.

- *Table per class hierarchy* — A single table holds all the properties of all the classes in the hierarchy. The type of a row is held by using a "type discriminator" column.

- *Table per subclass* — Each concrete class is stored in its own table. Common properties are stored in a separate table, and the table of each concrete type has a relation to the table holding common columns.

These types of mappings are possible in Hibernate. The first type does not need any specific supporting code in Hibernate. In this mapping strategy, each class maps to a table directly. The table-per-class-hierarchy mapping type requires some built-in support in Hibernate. Otherwise, the developer would need to write some low-level messy code to handle it. Fortunately, Hibernate supports this mapping by what is known in Hibernate's terminology as "joined subclass."

To demonstrate this, we will add a subclass of Folder, called OwnedFolder, which contains an additional field that specifies the owner of the folder.

The *table-per-class-hierarchy* mapping strategy is attractive in this case because Folder and OwnedFolder have many common properties with less that differs.

With a single table for both Folder and OwnedFolder, a *discriminator* column must also be added to the table to allow Hibernate to distinguish which class should be loaded for a given row of the FOLDERS table.

When defining the class in the Hibernate mappings file, a discriminator value is associated with both the base class and the subclass. The FOLDERS table looks like this after this addition:

```
FOLDERS
    PK: BIGINT not null
    FOLDER_NAME: VARCHAR(30)
    PARENT_FOLDER_PK: BIGINT
    TYPE: VARCHAR(10)
    OWNER: VARCHAR(30)
```

The OwnedFolder class is implemented like this:

```
package contacts;

public class OwnedFolder extends Folder {
    private String owner;

    public String getOwner() {
        return owner;
    }
    public void setOwner(String owner) {
        this.owner = owner;
    }
}
```

We should change the `Folder.hbm.xml` mapping file and define the owner property there. Add the TYPE column to the FOLDERS table as the discriminator column:

```
<hibernate-mapping>
    <class name="contacts.Folder" table="FOLDERS"
```

```
                      discriminator-value="Normal">

        . . .


        <discriminator column="TYPE" type="string" />

        <subclass name="contacts.OwnedFolder"
                  discriminator-value="Owned">
          <property name="owner" type="java.lang.String"
                    column="OWNER" length="30"/>
        </subclass>

    </class>
</hibernate-mapping>
```

The nested <subclass> element introduces the OwnedFolder subclass to
Hibernate. Subclasses of a base class are defined in the mapping file of the base
class as nested <subclass> elements. Note how owner is defined inside the
<subclass> element.

The discriminator column is defined by the <discriminator> element. It simply
defines the name and type of the column.

Finally, notice how the discriminator-value attribute is defined for both
Folder and OwnedFolder. The discriminator-value attribute of the <class>
element for the Folder class tells Hibernate that if the discriminator column
has a value of Normal, it's a row representing a Folder in the database. The
<subclass> also defines the discriminator-value attribute — this time with a
value of Owned.

Other than the mapping file, we don't need to change anything to load
members of a class hierarchy to memory or to save and query them. It follows
the same techniques that we defined in the previous parts of this chapter. Only
the querying part needs some explanation.

Hibernate queries are aware of class hierarchies. So an HQL statement such
as from contacts.Folder loads all Folder objects, including those that are
instances of OwnedFolder. This enables you to take advantage of inheritance
and polymorphism in your persistent objects. However, using a statement like
from contacts.OwnedFolder query loads OwnedFolder objects. Hibernate can
even handle querying over classes higher in the hierarchy. For example, from
java.lang.Object selects all objects available in the database! Under the covers,
Hibernate translates this abstract query to one or more queries that load all
instances derived from the specified type. This is a very powerful feature of
Hibernate's HQL and a feature unavailable in SQL itself.

Understanding the Hibernate Toolset

Hibernate has a rich toolset for various tasks. A combination of Hibernate with these tools makes Hibernate a very easy to use object-relational mapping framework. We don't give a detailed description or usage of these tools here. Refer to the documentation of each of these tools for more details.

Hibernate comes with a set of built-in Ant tasks, such as SchemaExport and SchemaUpdate. We've already seen SchemaUpdate in this chapter. There's an Ant task equivalent of it also provided. We can use the SchemaExport Ant task to generate DDL files containing CREATE TABLE statements. Both of these tasks are smart enough to be able to connect to existing databases and generate any ALTER TABLE statements necessary to upgrade a schema.

Apart from these built-in Ant tasks, Hibernate has very strong backing from other third-party tools such as XDoclet.

XDoclet can be used for auto-generating Hibernate mapping files from source code. Using this technique, we can greatly simplify the way we define the object-relational mapping information. In Chapter 9, we will specifically discuss this in more detail.

MiddleGen is another very useful tool that, in fact, sits on top of XDoclet and generates the source code of persistent classes from the database table. So, if we have an existing database schema, MiddleGen can generate the Java source code for an object model based around this schema. MiddleGen is Open Source and free and can be downloaded from `http://middlegen.codehaus .org/`.

Comparing Hibernate with Competing Technologies

In this section, we will compare Hibernate with some of the most popular competing technologies. It is intended as a brief comparison and is nowhere near complete or extensive.

Hibernate vs. EJB

EJB provides a semi-transparent persistence mechanism with the Container Managed Persistence (CMP) specification. The biggest differences between Hibernate and CMP beans are:

- CMP is *intrusive*; whereas, Hibernate is *non-intrusive*. With Hibernate, any POJO can be persisted without having to alter the design or implement interfaces specific to the persistence tool.

- CMP beans are designed as coarser-grained components; whereas, Hibernate leans toward fine-grained POJOs. When developing with CMP, you tend to define big, coarse-grained CMP components. Modeling small classes such as PhoneNumber is considered a bad practice in EJB.

- EJBQL, the object query language of EJB, is very limited. It doesn't support inheritance and polymorphism as Hibernate does. It also doesn't support many features of HQL, such as its rich set of functions and outer join and inner join facility.

- Testability of code is lost with EJB. You can't test an EJB outside of its container. On the other hand, you can easily run JUnit tests for Hibernated classes by just running the normal JUnit test runner. In the case of EJB, most people give up testing CMP beans because they have to deploy the bean on the container every time they want to test something and use a server side JUnit test runner such as Cactus.

- Hibernate can be run in non-J2EE environments. We can use Hibernate in a classic two-tier architecture. We can pass persistent objects around on the wire very easily. But serializing and transferring EJB beans is not possible.

- The `ejb-jar.xml` file where the EJB beans are defined is amazingly complicated in comparison with Hibernate's human-readable mapping files. Add to this complexity the mapping files of each EJB server vendor. It's considerably harder to manage even by using a tool such as XDoclet or any IDE. One of the most complicated parts of EJB is, of course, the container managed relations (CMR).

- In most containers (not all though!), performance is poorer than Hibernate. This is because a CMP bean has layers other than just persistence, such as security, transaction, and remote access calls. Normally, these services are not needed for persistent objects. In a typical service-oriented J2EE architecture, these services are provided by separate façade objects.

- Hibernate runs on any application server without the need for any change to the code or the mapping files. To make CMP beans deploy and run on a different application server, considerable effort is required. Needless to say, different application servers support different sets of persistence features, and the application is not guaranteed at all to work on an application server that does not support a persistence feature used by the application.

- Hibernate is not a standard; whereas, EJB is.

Hibernate vs. JDO

JDO is a relatively new transparent persistence standard, which is currently supported by many former object database vendors and some object-relational mapping vendors. JDO is very similar to Hibernate. Like Hibernate, but unlike EJB, it works with POJOs.

The biggest difference between Hibernate and JDO is that JDO defines a very abstract API for any persistence system. Theoretically, JDO can be used to persist objects in nonrelational databases, such as object database, mainframe databases, or even flat files. Hibernate, on the other hand, is only for relational databases. This difference leads to different persistence APIs.

Another big difference is that JDO accomplishes transparent persistence via bytecode enhancement. So, to make a POJO JDO persistable, a JDO enhancer application should be run on the compiled classes. This tool adds JDO persistence plumbing code to the bytecode of the POJOs. Hibernate, on the other hand, performs the same operation in runtime; hence, easier and faster development cycles occurs because there's no need to run a tool each time a persistable class is modified. Hibernate's runtime approach has very little performance overhead.

There are many smaller differences between these two technologies. JDOQL, JDO's query language, is considerably more limited than HQL. Also, JDO leaves the definition of object-relational mappings to the vendors. This leads to the same problem EJB has: Porting from one vendor to another takes a lot of effort.

Hibernate vs. DAO Frameworks

Finally, the easiest way of handling the tough persistence problem is to code in JDBC directly. The biggest problem with this approach is that hand-coded statements aren't as flexible as the vast set of options provided by smart object relational mapping frameworks such as Hiberante. While with a simple change of an attribute in the mapping file we can map and fine-tune the mapping of a POJO, accomplishing the same thing with raw JDBC and SQL requires a considerable amount of coding — possibly by changing many SQL statements in many different parts of the code.

Summary

In this chapter, you first learned about the complexities of persistence. You then learned how to configure Hibernate and how to obtain a Session object for working with the persistence framework. You learned how to use Hibernate to define the mapping for a simple object model. Then you performed various common persistence operations on this sample object model, such as saving, loading, and querying on it. You then learned how to persist relationships between objects and how to map a hierarchy of classes to relational tables. Finally, we discussed some useful tools for easier Hibernate development and showed a brief comparison between Hibernate and some of its competing technologies.

CHAPTER 6

Model View Controller
with WebWork

This chapter examines how we can build clean, simple, and maintainable Web-based user interfaces. We introduce the Model View Controller (MVC) pattern and show how it can be applied to the user interface of a Web application. We will do this by using the Open Source framework called WebWork.

By using WebWork, we build a small user interface to introduce its important features before looking in detail at how rich validation rules can be added to the application. WebWork is built on an underlying project called XWork; thus, we also discuss what XWork is and how it relates to Web-based applications. We discuss the Command Design Pattern — as made famous by the Gang of Four — and show how XWork provides a framework based around this pattern as well as several other powerful patterns that will make your application development much smoother.

WebWork 2 is used throughout this book.

Understanding Model View Controller (MVC)

Model View Controller (MVC) was a technique devised in the late 1970s by the SmallTalk community. It simplifies the development of user interfaces by cleanly separating code into three layers: the model, the view, and the controller.

When dynamic Web applications started to become mainstream in the mid-1990s, most of the concepts that applied to traditional user interface (UI) development temporarily went out the window as developers struggled to come to grips with the new medium. Very quickly, Web-application development became laborious and awkward. Over time, as comfort levels increased, the original MVC concepts were revised to suit the Web application model.

There are many variations of MVC to suit different scenarios. Arguably, the most practical for Web applications is *Model 2*.

Examining the Model Layer

The model layer represents the business domain. The model serves two primary purposes:

- To expose data encapsulated by the application, such as listing products in the inventory
- To allow business logic to be performed on the model, such as purchasing a product

Depending on the programming paradigm used, typical implementations of the model could be any of the following:

- Java objects
- Enterprise JavaBeans (EJB)
- Database-stored procedures
- Web services
- CORBA services

For clarity, we'll use Java objects to build our model because these are the simplest and most flexible.

Following are two important design features to bear in mind when developing the model:

- All interactions or data required by the system should be exposed via the model.
- The model should not be aware of the user interface at all. Unless directly applicable to the model, things like fonts, colors, layout, and HTML should never be dealt with in the model. By keeping the model nonvisual, we can reuse it from any type of user interface — whether it be graphical, a Web page, a command line, or a Web service. This also promotes a clean separation of roles. Business-logic developers need not concern themselves with presentation and vice-versa.

Examining the View Layer

The view layer is responsible for taking data from the nonvisual model and mapping to a visual presentation for the end user.

For Web-based J2EE applications, JSP is the most common view layer, and we will be using it in this book.

Design considerations for the view include the following:

- The view should only read data from the model and display it to the user. It should not handle user-input validation or make modifications to the model.

- The view should never contain business logic but rather only presentation logic. For example, the model determines whether an account is overdrawn, and the view determines how it should display accounts if they are overdrawn.

Examining the Controller Layer

The controller layer responds to user input, manipulates the model, and determines which view to display next. The controller acts as the *glue* between the model and the view.

In Model 2, a controller layer is split into *actions*. An action represents a task the user wants to perform, such as submitting an application or clicking a link for additional information. In Web applications, there is typically a direct correlation between a browser making an HTTP request and an action being invoked. The controller itself is a Servlet that manages the flow between actions and views.

Tasks that can be performed by an action include the following:

- Validating incoming user input, such as options selected or values entered in a form

- Mapping user inputs to business-logic methods exposed by the model, such as setting the amount of money to be transferred from a form field

- Determining the correct view to display to the user next

- Providing the appropriate parts of the model to the view

Tying It All Together

When a request is made from a browser, the following interactions occur between the model, view, and controller (see Figure 6.1):

1. A Web browser makes an HTTP request that is then dispatched to an action.

2. Optionally, the action manipulates the model based on the user input.

3. The action forwards the request to the view with a reference to the model.

4. The view pulls data from model via the action.

5. The resulting data is returned to the browser.

Looking at Reasons to Use MVC

While MVC can initially seem daunting, it can drastically simplify large or complicated Web-based applications. Following are some reasons that you may want to use MVC:

- Business logic can be developed in isolation from the user interface, which allows problems to be neatly encapsulated and developers with different specialties to work on the same system without stepping on each others' toes.

- With business logic encapsulated in the model, the model alone can express the intentions of the system, which makes the system easier to understand and maintain.

- Multiple interfaces can be built on top of the same model without having to duplicate business rules. These could be different Web interfaces — perhaps for advanced or administration users — desktop clients, PDAs, phones, command-line interfaces, or Web services.

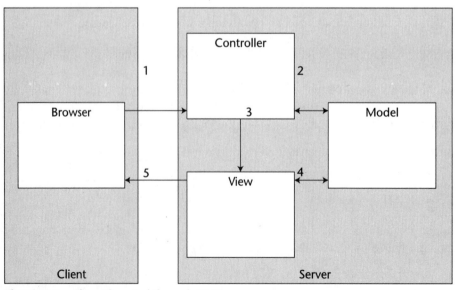

Figure 6.1   Flow of control through MVC

- User interfaces are typically difficult to test. With the separation of layers, the model and controller have no presentational logic, which makes them much easier to test. Views are relatively less error-prone than these two other layers.

- Because the views contain only presentational logic — that is, little or no code embedded — they can easily be maintained. A Web designer with little or no programming knowledge can easily maintain the pages.

- UI developers can determine how best to develop user interfaces without worrying about the details of business rules.

- The flow between Web pages can be easily altered.

- Because the model, view, and controller layers are decoupled, each becomes easier to refactor, break down into components, and reuse.

- UI elements can be moved between pages easily.

- The Action classes make unit testing much easier.

Understanding MVC, WebWork, and XWork

As you can imagine, by using MVC in your application, you will most likely end up with many views, models, and actions. There must be a way to easily manage all these various parts to your application in a standard way. This is where XWork and WebWork step in, two complementary modules for you to use to rapidly develop clean, modular code that conforms to the MVC design pattern.

Exploring XWork

XWork is a generic command framework that can be used for executing arbitrary units of work. This follows the *command pattern* very closely, which is really nothing more than a single interface, *com.opensymphony.xwork.Action* that all units of work must implement.

When each action is executed, a return code is given to the XWork framework. This code is a simple String such as "success" or "error" that indicates to the framework what the result of the action is. A *result* can be anything. In the Web context, it is usually a JSP or HTML file.

Besides results and actions, XWork provides many other advanced features such as an expression language, a validation framework, and support for interceptors. All of these advanced features will be discussed later in this chapter.

XWORK'S MODULARITY

Because XWork acts as a small, command-pattern framework to be used by other applications, it has been designed from the ground up to support modularity. For example, its default configuration can be easily overridden and embedded into existing configuration systems. The nice thing about using XWork Actions is that they aren't tied to the Web and can be reused very easily. The following projects all support XWork actions, which means your code can integrate with these projects without modification:

◆ *WebWork* — The most obvious integration is WebWork. WebWork, version 1, was originally the command-pattern framework as well as the Web features bundled into a single project. After seeing the power of separating the two, XWork and WebWork 2.0 were born.

◆ *JPublish* — JPublish is an Open Source Web publishing and application framework that cleanly separates developer roles. Versions 3.0 and beyond include support for XWork actions in addition to the JPublish API from previous versions.

◆ *OSWorkflow* — Besides being a perfect fit for the request/response paradigm, the command pattern also works very well for units of work in relation to business workflow. OpenSymphony's OSWorkflow module supports XWork actions for executing whenever a business process takes place, such as reviewing a document or updating an account.

Exploring WebWork

While XWork provides the core framework for actions and results, WebWork is a component on top of XWork that adds Web-specific features. Specifically, WebWork provides three core features: *dispatchers, Web-specific results*, and a library of *tags* to be used in the view layer.

A dispatcher is responsible for handing off incoming Web requests to the appropriate actions. In Web applications, the most common way to invoke an action is either via a Servlet or a Filter. WebWork comes with both. For example, the ServletDispatcher, when mapped to the URL pattern `*.action`, will allow you to execute the foo action when `http://myserver/foo.action` is requested.

Once a dispatcher causes an action to be invoked, some sort of result must be returned. XWork contains a rich framework for result types that WebWork utilizes to provide several Web-specific results, such as support for Request-Dispatchers and HTTP Redirects. Both are core parts of the Servlet specification.

Lastly, when each result is returned, usually a JSP or other view technology is executed. Rather than have Web pages exposed to clunky XWork APIs, WebWork provides a large suite of built-in JSP tag libraries to assist with Web development. Besides JSP support, there is tag support for other view technologies such as Velocity, XML, and JasperReports.

WHAT ABOUT STRUTS?

An alternative framework to WebWork is Jakarta Struts. Struts is a very popular framework used widely in the Java world. Struts and WebWork both build upon the same concepts of Model 2 MVC.

The advantages of Struts include the following:

♦ *Mature product* — This is one of the first MVC frameworks to make use of Servlets and JSP.

♦ *Huge community* — There are many developers out there with Struts skills to provide support or even work for you.

♦ *Documentation* — Many articles and books have been written on the subject.

♦ *Tool support* — There are many tools available, such as IDE plugins, or extension libraries designed to work with Struts.

The advantages of WebWork include the following:

♦ *Simpler to learn* — You'll see how easy it is to get started in the next section.

♦ *Easy to extend for custom needs* — The source code is minimal and has been designed with customization in mind. If WebWork doesn't behave how you want it to, you can easily modify or extend it.

♦ *Clean API* — The interfaces used in WebWork are all very clean and simple.

♦ *Decoupled from the Web tier* — It is easy to reuse actions in Swing applications, Applets, Web Services, EJBs, custom workflow engines, or unit tests.

♦ *Easy to test* — Because of the simplicity of WebWork and how decoupled it is from the Web tier, it suits the processes of Test Driven Development.

Both frameworks are powerful and can simplify your development greatly. This book primarily focuses on WebWork; thus, going into the details of Struts is beyond the scope of this book. For more information, see *Mastering Jakarta Struts*, by James Goodwill (Indianapolis: Wiley Publishing, 2002).

Struts is available from http://jakarta.apache.org/struts/.

Taking an In-depth Look at Actions

For now, we will not touch on dispatchers, results, or any of the advanced features of XWork. Rather, we will dive right into a simple example of an XWork action and explain what is happening. Then, we will discuss how to configure XWork to use this action and show the bare basics involved for executing this action in your Java application.

A Simple XWork Example

Following is the typical HelloWorld example that we all have grown to love. But rather than saying hello to the world, we're going to personalize this message. To do this, the HelloWorld action will have one input: name. Likewise, it will have one output: greeting. When this action executes, the greeting will be constructed to be personalized for the name of our choosing.

> **TIP** In XWork, inputs and ouputs are treated as *JavaBean properties*. As such, Actions are really nothing more than a JavaBean or Plain Old Java Object (POJO) that implements the Action interface.

All actions in XWork must implement the Action interface:

```
package com.opensymphony.xwork;
```

```
public interface Action {
  public static final String SUCCESS = "success";

  public String execute();
}
```

Here is the simple HelloWorld action implementing this interface:

```
package helloworld;
import com.opensymphony.xwork.Action;

public class HelloWorld implements Action {
    String name;
    String greeting;

    public void setName(String name) {
        this.name = name;
    }

    public String getGreeting() {
        return greeting;
    }

    public String execute() {
        greeting = "Hello, " + name;
        return SUCCESS;
    }
}
```

The only special thing to note is the return value of the `execute()` method. As you can see, it is returning the String constant SUCCESS. This result value, as well as others not shown here, is built into the Action interface for the sake of simplicity. The most common return values are SUCCESS, INPUT, ERROR, NONE, and LOGIN. As such, these are all built into the Action interface as constants. If you need a different return code, you can just as easily return any String value you please. Return codes are totally arbitrary.

Configuring XWork

Now that we've built an action, the next step is to configure XWork so that we can use it. Because XWork is designed to be used in many different environments, such as the Web, workflows, or in your own application architecture, the configuration is not specific to Web applications. As such, result mappings for SUCCESS, like in our example, must be explicitly mapped to a result type.

For now, we won't discuss results, interceptors, or other features in XWork. These will be discussed later in this chapter. As we go over each topic, we will revisit the configuration to show the new features. Following is the most bare-bones configuration possible, in a file called xwork.xml:

```
<!DOCTYPE xwork PUBLIC "-//OpenSymphony Group//XWork 1.0//EN"
                "http://www.opensymphony.com/xwork/xwork-1.0.dtd">
<xwork>
    <package name="default">
        <action name="hello"
                class="helloworld.HelloWorld">
        </action>
    </package>
</xwork>
```

As you can see, the HelloWorld class has been mapped to an action named hello. Furthermore, this action is included in the package default. *Packages* are just simple ways to categorize actions. This is useful when your application is very large, and you have hundreds of actions. Packages can extend other packages by inheriting their various attributes such as results and interceptors.

Lastly, packages can be bound to an — optional — namespace. By default, all packages are in the empty namespace — that is, the empty string "". Namespaces are useful to avoid naming conflicts with your actions — just like packages do in Java. Because we have only one action so far, we'll use the default namespace.

Structuring Your Actions (Action Composition)

Before we actually run this action, let's take a moment to look at a slightly more complicated action that provides an even more personalized greeting. To create the new greeting, the action requires three values: a last name, a city, and whether the person being greeted is a male or female.

There are two ways we can approach this problem. The first and most obvious way is to add new properties to the action, which ends up with three properties total. This technique is considered "thin" because the object graph is very flat. After all, there is only one object involved here:

```java
public class ThinHello implements Action {
    String name;
    String city;
    boolean gender;
    String greeting;

    public void setName(String Name) {
        this.name = name;
    }

    public void setCity(String city) {
        this.city = city;
    }

    public void setGender(boolean gender) {
        this.gender = gender;
    }

    public String getGreeting() {
        return greeting;
    }

    public String execute() {
        greeting = "Hello " + (gender ? "Mr. " : "Ms. ") + name
            + ", say hello to my friends in " + city;
        return SUCCESS;
    }
}
```

While this does indeed fill the job, it feels a bit odd and would probably make most Object-Oriented Programming (OOP) gurus sick to their stomachs. Because actions are really just simple Java objects, there is nothing holding us back from decomposing ThinHello into a deeper, more object-oriented structure:

```java
public class Person {
    String name;
    String city;
    boolean gender;

    // getters and setters for each property
}

public class DeepHello implements Action {
    Person person;
    String greeting;

    public void setPerson(Person person) {
        this.person = person;
```

```
    }

    public Person getPerson() {
        return person;
    }

    public String getGreeting() {
        return greeting;
    }

    public String execute() {
        greeting = "Hello " + (person.getGender() ? "Mr. " : "Mrs. ")
                + person.getName()
                + ", say hello to my friends in " + person.getCity();
        return SUCCESS;
    }
}
```

As you can see, this new design is much better in terms of object reuse and general OOP practices. Even better, when we get to discussing XWork's Expression Language support, you'll find that referencing these object graphs is as trivial as a call to person.name. Thus, this promotes good design in all your action and model code.

We generally call this type of action a *model-driven* action because it is actually reusing pieces of our model. The first action we saw can be referred to as a *field-driven* action because the data is stored by fields within the action itself.

Calling an Action from XWork

Back to the simpler HelloWorld example, let's write some code that finally causes this action to be executed. In XWork, all actions are invoked via an ActionProxy, a piece of code that manages the command execution lifecycle from start to finish. The following code will get a handle to an ActionProxy for the "hello" action, execute it, and then print the return code as well as the greeting.

```
package helloworld;
import com.opensymphony.xwork.ActionProxyFactory;
import com.opensymphony.xwork.ActionProxy;

public class Main {
    public static void main(String[] args) throws Exception {
        ActionProxyFactory factory = ActionProxyFactory.getFactory();
        ActionProxy proxy =
                factory.createActionProxy("", "hello", null);
        System.out.println(proxy.execute());
        HelloWorld hello = (HelloWorld) proxy.getAction();
        System.out.println(hello.getGreeting());
    }
}
```

To get a handle to an ActionProxy, we must use the ActionProxyFactory. By using the `createActionProxy()` method, we pass in the namespace — "" in this case — and the action name, hello. The third argument, which is currently null, is for extra context values and will be discussed momentarily. The output of this code is as follows:

```
success
Hello, null
```

This makes sense since our action is returning SUCCESS, and the name used to construct the greeting was never set. But, clearly, we need to set the name property somehow if we want this program to do anything remotely useful.

Using Parameters and the ActionContext

Now that we have the basic action executing, the next step is to somehow get that name property set to a value of our choosing. In the previous example, we said that the third argument of `createActionProxy()` was used for extra context values.

In XWork, whenever an action is executing, there is a context in which it runs called the ActionContext. XWork is based upon the single-thread model; thus, its ActionContext is implemented as a java.lang.ThreadLocal, which is introduced in Java 1.2. A ThreadLocal provides a simple mechanism for storing and retrieving objects from a central storage space while ensuring that each storage space is only accessible from a single thread. This allows an object to maintain states for multiple threads at the same time.

This means that code both internal to XWork and WebWork, as well as any of your own code, may access context information about the action invocation via a simple call to the ActionContext:

```
import com.opensymphony.xwork.ActionContext;
...
ActionContext ac = ActionContext.getContext();
Map params = ac.getParameters();
```

Because ActionContext is a ThreadLocal, the static call to `getContext()` will return a different context for each thread, which means multiple actions may be executing on different threads at the same time.

An ActionContext is really nothing more than a simple map containing all the relevant information needed to execute an action as well as extra information that might be important. One such piece of extra context information is a map of parameters that can be treated as inputs to the action invocation.

Following is an example of how we can create these parameter mappings to make the greeting more personable:

```
package helloworld;
import com.opensymphony.xwork.ActionProxyFactory;
import com.opensymphony.xwork.ActionProxy;
import com.opensymphony.xwork.ActionContext;

import java.util.HashMap;
import java.util.Map;

public class Main {
    public static void main(String[] args) throws Exception {
        Map params = new HashMap();
        params.put("name", "Patrick");

        Map extraContext = new HashMap();
        extraContext.put(ActionContext.PARAMETERS, params);

        ActionProxyFactory factory = ActionProxyFactory.getFactory();
        ActionProxy proxy =
                factory.createActionProxy("", "hello", extraContext);
        System.out.println(proxy.execute());
        HelloWorld hello = (HelloWorld) proxy.getAction();
        System.out.println(hello.getGreeting());
    }
}
```

As you can see, the name property was given a value of Patrick. The parameters map was then placed in another map called extraContext, which is then placed in the ActionContext when a call to `createActionProxy()` is made. The output is now:

```
success
Hello, Patrick
```

Great, this is much better. But what about the Web? So far, we haven't seen anything that really knocks our socks off. The real magic is when we apply this generic command framework to the Web environment and get WebWork involved. To do so, the most obvious thing would be having some sort of Web page displayed when an action is finished executing, such as one that displays the greeting message.

Applying Newton's Third Law of Physics

As Newton's Third Law of Physics says, "for every action there is an equal opposite reaction." We don't want the exact opposite action to take place. That is, negating the action's side effects would render the process rather useless. For every action, we'd like there to be some sort of reaction or, more precisely, a *result* that illustrates what just took place. For example, if an action is called UpdateAccountBalance, we might want the result of the action to display the new account balance. In the case of HelloWorld, we'd like the result of the action execution to be a Web page displaying the greeting.

Understanding XWork Results and Action Chaining

As already discussed, actions must return a String when they are finished executing. XWork then uses this String to find a result type for that action in `xwork.xml`. A result type is a class that implements *com.opensymphony .xwork.Result*. By default, the only result class included with XWork is ActionChainResult. This is useful if you wish to have another action executed immediately after your first action has executed. By chaining many actions together, complex logic can be formed from simple building blocks.

All results take parameters in `xwork.xml` that are used to specify the behavior of the result. An example of *action chaining* in `xwork.xml` is as follows:

```
<xwork>
    <package name="default">
        <result-types>
            <result-type name="chain"
                class="com.opensymphony.xwork.ActionChainResult"/>
        </result-types>

        <action name="foo" class="mypackage.FooAction">
            <result name="success" type="chain">
                <param name="actionName">bar</param>
            </result>
        </action>

        <action name="bar" class="mypackage.BarAction">
        </action>
</xwork>
```

In this situation, after foo is finished executing, if the return value of its `execute()` method is SUCCESS, the bar action will execute immediately afterward. Chaining actions together can be very powerful, but the chain eventually has to end — whether a single action is being executed or a long chain of many actions. Next, we will discuss results used specifically for the Web environment.

Examining WebWork Results and the Servlet Environment

WebWork provides several implementations of the Result interface to make Web-based interaction with your actions very simple. The following results are included with WebWork:

- *ServletDispatcherResult* — The Servlet specification provides for javax.servlet.http.HttpServletRequest to support RequestDispatchers. A RequestDispatcher allows an existing HTTP request to be used to request alternative content on the Web-application server. Using this feature, this result allows you to display JSP or HTML pages while the URL of the original request is still in the browser location. This result effectively forwards the request to the location specified.

- *ServletRedirectResult* — This is similar to the dispatcher result. Except, rather than forwarding the request to the location specified, the response is told to redirect the browser to that location. The consequence of doing this means that a second HTTP request takes place; thus, the action that was just executed is no longer available because actions are built on the single-thread model. The advantage of this is that the user's browser is not actually pointing to the new location, which means that clicking reload will not cause the action to be executed again.

- *VelocityResult* — WebWork supports many view technologies. If your view is a Velocity template, it's possible to use the dispatcher or redirect results to display the page. However, doing so involves more computation by the Servlet container than is necessary. Using the VelocityResult will read the Velocity template immediately and render its output directly to the HttpServletResponse's output.

NOTE Velocity is a popular template engine used heavily by many WebWork users as well as users of other alternative MVC frameworks such as Struts. WebWork requires that Velocity be enabled and working because it is used internally by the framework. However, it does not require that you use it for your application's views. You can find out more about Velocity at
http://jakarta.apache.org/velocity.

Other results are also included with WebWork, but these three are the most frequently used ones. Result types are specified on a per-package level and are inherited by subpackages. Following is an example xwork.xml file that shows two different actions using the dispatcher and redirect results.

```
<xwork>
    <package name="default">
        <result-types>
            <result-type name="dispatcher"
class="com.opensymphony.webwork.dispatcher.ServletDispatcherResult"/>
            <result-type name="redirect"
class="com.opensymphony.webwork.dispatcher.ServletRedirectResult"/>
        </result-types>

        <action name="hello1"
```

```
            class="helloworld.HelloWorld">
            <result name="success" type="dispatcher">
                helloworld.jsp
            </result>
        </action>

        <action name="hello2"
            class="helloworld.HelloWorld">
            <result name="success" type="redirect">
                helloworld.jsp
            </result>
        </action>
    </package>
</xwork>
```

TIP XWork's configuration allows you to specify the default result type for each package. This is useful so that the most common result you are using, such as dispatcher, does not need to be specified for every action result. Also, each result supports a default parameter that can make specifying results even simpler. We're using the default abbreviated notation here. To use the full notation, we have to specify the dispatcher result's "location" parameter, which means this result could read: `<result name="success"><param name="location">helloworld.jsp</param></result>`.

Because most results in a Web application have a single location parameter, the abbreviated notation is generally preferred.

TIP Notice in the preceding `xwork.xml` example that HelloWorld is used for two actions. This technique is called *action aliasing* and is very useful when you want to use the same business logic with different results.

Configuring WebWork

WebWork must first be properly configured to use any of the WebWork features we are about to discuss. Doing this is as simple as ensuring that both `xwork-1.0.jar` and `webwork-2.0.jar` are in `WEB-INF/lib` and then adding the following to `web.xml`:

```
<web-app>
    <display-name>A WebWork Example</display-name>

    <servlet>
        <servlet-name>webwork</servlet-name>
        <servlet-class>
            com.opensymphony.webwork.dispatcher.ServletDispatcher
```

```
        </servlet-class>
    </servlet>

    <servlet>
        <servlet-name>velocity</servlet-name>
        <servlet-class>
          com.opensymphony.webwork.views.velocity.WebWorkVelocityServlet
        </servlet-class>
        <load-on-startup>1</load-on-startup>
    </servlet>

    <servlet-mapping>
        <servlet-name>velocity</servlet-name>
        <url-pattern>*.vm</url-pattern>
    </servlet-mapping>

    <servlet-mapping>
        <servlet-name>webwork</servlet-name>
        <url-pattern>*.action</url-pattern>
    </servlet-mapping>

    <taglib>
        <taglib-uri>webwork</taglib-uri>
        <taglib-location>/WEB-INF/lib/webwork.jar</taglib-location>
    </taglib>

</web-app>
```

There are three things of importance here:

1. WebWork's primary dispatcher is a Servlet. In this configuration, it has been mapped to `*.action`, but this mapping is entirely up to you. Some prefer `*.jspa` or `*.do`.

2. WebWork requires that Velocity be initialized correctly before it can be used. Doing this is as simple as ensuring that the WebWorkVelocity-Servlet has a load-on-startup parameter set. If you aren't planning to use Velocity at all, you can skip this.

3. Lastly, in order to use the JSP taglibs, you must specify them in `web.xml` as shown.

Understanding the Role of the Dispatcher

Now that we know how to make the results of actions appear on the Web, the next step is to somehow cause an action to be invoked from a Web browser. The most obvious choice is to write a Servlet that executes the ActionProxy code we previously looked at. The parameters of the HTTP request would be added to the parameters map; thus, this makes inputs to actions from the Web

very easy. WebWork ships with such a Servlet, com.opensymphony.webwork
.dispatcher.ServletDispatcher.

ServletDispatcher must be mapped to a URL pattern such as `*.action`.
When a request for hello.action is made, for example, the dispatcher recog-
nizes that the hello action must be executed. Furthermore, all important
information that is unique to Servlets, such as the HttpServletRequest,
HttpServletResponse, and HttpSesssion, is placed into the ActionContext so
that it may be retrieved by either your code or by results that need that info
such as the ServletDispatcherResult.

This Web-specific information can be retrieved from the ActionContext by
using its `get()` method with the key being values stored in the WebWork-
Statics interface. Alternatively, WebWork provides a ServletActionContext that
has several static methods to do this for you.

```
import com.opensymphony.xwork.ActionContext;
import com.opensymphony.webwork.WebWorkStatics;
import com.opensymphony.webwork.ServletActionContext;

ActionContext.getContext().get(WebWorkStatics.HTTP_REQUEST);
// OR...
ServletActionContext.getRequest();
```

What all this means is that a request to `http://myserver/hello`
`.action?name=Patrick` would cause our HelloWorld action to be executed
with the property name set to a value of Patrick. If a parameter is part of the
request, but there is no associated property in the action, the parameter is
ignored. Likewise, if there is no parameter in the request for a property in the
action, the property is never set and stays as its original value. This is usually
null unless you specifically initialized it to something else.

Namespaces

As previously mentioned, namespaces are very important when there are
hundreds of actions to keep track of. In the world of the Web, namespaces are
commonly managed by using *paths*. ServletDispatcher will look at the entire
request path and use that to construct both the action name as well as the
namespace.

A request to /foo/bar.action means that the action named bar in the /foo
namespace will be searched for. If that action doesn't exist, XWork will fall
back to the default namespace and try to find an action named bar there. If
neither can be found, an error will be reported by the ServletDispatcher:

```
There is no Action mapped for namespace /foo and action name bar
```

Exploring Example Views in JSP and Velocity

Now that we know how to invoke actions from the Web as well as have their results render a JSP, HTML file, Velocity template, or just about anything else that can be viewed in a Servlet container, the next step is to actually write some simple pages that will be the views in our MVC application. Let's build a simple page that displays the greeting by using JSP.

HelloWorld in JSP

Following is the JSP source for `helloworld.jsp`, as referenced in the `xwork.xml` configuration shown previously.

```
<%@taglib uri="webwork" prefix="webwork"%>
<html>
    <head>
        <title>HelloWorld output</title>
    </head>
    <body>
        The HelloWorld action greets you:
        <webwork:property value="greeting"/>
    </body>
</html>
```

The only two parts of particular interest are the *taglib reference*, which is required by all JSPs that want to use the WebWork JSP tags. The other part is, of course, the webwork:property tag. This is how we can retrieve properties of the action and display them in the Web page.

Some people find the performance of JSPs to be too slow. Others feel that view layers shouldn't be as powerful as JSP allows. Regardless of their reasons, there are many people that choose to use Velocity templates instead. The template for the same view in Velocity would be:

```
<html>
    <head>
        <title>HelloWorld output</title>
    </head>
    <body>
        The HelloWorld action greets you:
        $greeting
    </body>
</html>
```

Now let's try out this action and see if it works as expected. Pointing your Web browser to `http://myserver/hello1.action?name=Patrick`, you can see that the HTML generated is:

```html
<html>
    <head>
        <title>HelloWorld output</title>
    </head>
    <body>
        The HelloWorld action greets you:
        Hello, Patrick
    </body>
</html>
```

JSP Tags

We've already seen the property tag in action. Now, let's look in depth at the various JSP tags that WebWork comes with and see how they can be used to make your views more dynamic. For a full tag reference, see the WebWork Web site at `http://www.opensymphony.com/webwork`.

The Property Tag

As we already saw, the property tag can be used to print the value of a property. This tag is, by far, the most commonly used tag when writing JSPs for WebWork. Luckily, it is incredibly simple. Just fill the *value* attribute of the tag with the *expression* you wish to display.

The Push Tag

WebWork is considered a hierarchical MVC framework because it supports a stack-based system for values that your view layer might require. These values are stored in the ValueStack, which will be discussed shortly. The push tag can be used to push items on to the stack for more advanced data display in your JSPs:

```
<%-- this... --%>
<webwork:push value="person">
    <webwork:property value="name"/>
</webwork:push>

<%-- ... is the same as this ... --%>
<webwork:property value="person.name"/>
```

The Set Tag

Sometimes it is important to be able to place references to objects or properties, such as the greeting, in another location. In JSPs, it is common to place objects in the page, request, session, or application scope. Using the set tag, it is possible to do this:

```
<webwork:set value="greeting" name="greeting" scope="session"/>
<%= session.getAttribute("greeting") %>
```

Now the greeting has been saved to the user's session and can be printed — as we've done here — or used in other pages.

The If/ElseIf/Else Tags

Control flow in the view layer can be very important. WebWork provides three JSP tags that can be used to specify view behavior under certain circumstances only. Let's recall the DeepHello action we previously looked at and now create a view that displays the text in blue if the person is male and pink if the person is female:

```
<%@taglib uri="webwork" prefix="webwork"%>
<html>
    <head>
        <title>DeepHello color output</title>
    </head>
    <body>
        The DeepHello action greets you:
        <webwork:if test="person.gender == true">
            <font color="blue">
                <webwork:property value="greeting"/>
            </font>
        </webwork:if>
        <webwork:else>
            <font color="pink">
                <webwork:property value="greeting"/>
            </font>
        </webwork:else>
    </body>
</html>
```

The Iterator Tag

The iterator tag is the second most frequently used tag in WebWork. At the most simple level, it iterates over any "iteratable" object. Java has no concept of an "iteratable" object. It is not an *iterator*, but it is rather any object with a list of elements that can be traversed in a defined order.

Currently, WebWork can iterate over:

- Any collection, such as a List, Set, or Map
- Any class implementing java.util.Iterator or java.util.Enumeration
- Any array

The iterator tag does not distinguish among the different types of iteratable objects. For whichever it is given, the tag will loop over each element in turn, putting each in "context" during the body of the tag. Following is an example:

```
<webwork:iterator value="people">
    <li><webwork:property value="name"/>,
        <webwork:property value="city"/></li>
</webwork:iterator>
```

Suppose that an action had a java.util.List property called people. If the view for that action is supposed to display the name and city of each person in that list, the previous code fragment would do the job.

The Action Tag

Sometimes, using the ServletDispatcher to execute actions doesn't suit our needs. Suppose we want to point the browser directly to a JSP but still display the greeting generated by HelloWorld. This can be done by using a JSP tag that executes an action using the ActionProxy— just like ServletDispatcher does. Parameters are pulled from the HTTP request or can also be programmatically passed in:

```
<webwork:action id="hi" name="hello">
    <webwork:param name="name" value="'Patrick'"/>
</webwork:action>
<webwork:property value="#hi.greeting"/>
```

Here, the action tag is told the name of the action it is going to execute — in this case, hello — as well as the ID to store that action object in the Action-Context — in this case, as hi. We give the action a parameter — just as we've done in the past. But, this time, we use the webwork:param tag. Finally, when the action tag closes, the action is executed, and values from that action can now be retrieved. We can use the property tag to pull values from the ActionContext by using the # operator. More information on this will come later.

Looking at Component-Based Web Development

Until now, the only way we've been providing input to our various "hello" actions is either via the XWork API or an HTTP GET request. Of course, for real Web applications, we require a nice UI for users to enter input. WebWork provides a very rich set of components to assist with this.

Before we dive into code examples, let's think about what a typical form element must do. It must:

- Allow users to enter data
- Constrain the data to certain possible values, such as a drop-down selection
- Display error messages if the entered data is considered invalid
- Display labels to describe the data being entered
- Make sure that the data entered is associated with the right property

In WebWork, there is a large set of tags for each type of HTML form element, such as textfield, select box, radio, check box, and so on. Each of these tags takes care of the stated requirements automatically for you, which allows you to develop your JSPs in a very simple, componentized manner. So, rather than coding hundreds of input textfields throughout your UI, you can now just drop in textfield modules wherever you need.

TIP **For error messages to be displayed when data is considered invalid, XWork's validation framework must be employed. Later in this chapter, we will discuss validation and how it applies to the UI tags.**

Let's look at a simple input page for the DeepHello action:

```
<%@taglib uri="webwork" prefix="webwork"%>
<html>
    <head>
        <title>DeepHello Input</title>
    </head>
    <body>
        The DeepHello action requires some info from you:
        <webwork:form action="deephello.action">
            <webwork:textfield label="Name" name="person.name"/>
            <webwork:textfield label="City" name="person.city"/>
            <webwork:textfield label="Gender" name="person.gender"/>
            <webwork:submit value="'Say Hello'" />
        </webwork:form>
    </body>
</html>
```

As you can see, this JSP is very simple and contains very little HTML. Instead, it is comprised of callouts to tags that will, in turn, generate HTML form elements for you. The generated HTML of such a page is as follows:

```
<%@taglib uri="webwork" prefix="webwork"%>
<html>
    <head>
        <title>DeepHello Input</title>
    </head>
    <body>
        The DeepHello action requires some info from you:
        <table>
            <form action="deephello.action">

                <tr>
                    <td align="right" valign="top">
                        <label class="label">Name:</label>
                    </td>
                    <td>
                        <input type="text" name="person.name" value=""/>
```

```
                        </td>
                    </tr>
                    <tr>
                        <td align="right" valign="top">
                            <label class="label">City:</label>
                        </td>
                        <td>
                            <input type="text" name="person.city" value=""/>
                        </td>
                    </tr>
                    <tr>
                        <td align="right" valign="top">
                            <label class="label">Gender:</label>
                        </td>
                        <td>
                            <input type="text" name="person.gender"
                                            value=""/>
                        </td>
                    </tr>
                    <tr>
                        <td colspan="2">
                            <div align="right">
                                <input type="submit" value="Say Hello"/>
                            </div>
                        </td>
                    </tr>

                </form>
            </table>
        </body>
    </html>
```

The JSP tags have now been expanded to HTML form elements with their attributes specially populated with the pertinent information for the property we are asking for input on. When the form is submitted, the values entered will be passed off to the corresponding setter methods of the action.

Some of the form elements included with WebWork are:

- Text field
- Select box
- Text area
- Submit button
- Hidden value
- Password field
- Form element

There are a few more advanced tags as well, such as the doubleselect tag. You can learn more about these tags by consulting the WebWork documentation at http://www.opensymphony.com/webwork. Throughout this book and in the PetSoar application, these tags will be heavily used so you can also see them in action.

Themes

The default tags, while functional, are very bare bones. Often, we want to spice up the UI a bit by using Cascading Style Sheets, colors, different fonts, and so on. We need a way to *theme* the UI components specially tailored for our needs. All the tags support an attribute or theme that allows you to specify the location of the templates used to generate the various form elements. Each Velocity UI component is defined in a corresponding Velocity template file.

For example, if you want to create a new theme called "aqua," create a directory called templates in the root of your Web application. In that directory, create a subdirectory called aqua. There, you can place Velocity templates that match the JSP tag names. So, if you wish to create a new look for the textfield tag, write a textfield.vm template.

We recommend you consult the default templates as a starting point before writing your own templates. They do a great job of reusing as much as possible, such as error reporting, labels, and positioning.

Once you've written your own complete theme, you can use that theme by specifying the theme attribute in each JSP tag:

```
<%@taglib uri="webwork" prefix="webwork"%>
<html>
    <head>
        <title>DeepHello Input</title>
    </head>
    <body>
        The DeepHello action requires some info from you:
        <webwork:form action="deephello.action">
            <webwork:textfield theme="aqua" label="Name"
name="person.name"/>
            <webwork:textfield theme="aqua" label="City"
name="person.city"/>
            <webwork:textfield theme="aqua" label="Gender"
                        name="person.gender"/>
            <webwork:submit theme="aqua" value="'Say Hello'" />
        </webwork:form>
    </body>
</html>
```

Of course, having to write theme="aqua" for each UI component could soon become quite a chore! As such, WebWork allows you to specify the default theme for the JSP tags by creating a file called `webwork.properties` in `WEB-INF/classes` and placing the following line in it:

```
webwork.ui.theme=/templates/aqua/
```

Now you can control the look and feel of your entire Web application with a single configuration change.

Writing Your Own Component

Sometimes the default components work perfectly fine 99% of the time, but, in rare situations, you need something unique. Writing an entire theme for 1% of the time is rather painful. So, WebWork instead allows you to create custom components to solve these unique situations.

Suppose that normally you want your textfields to be very basic — just as the default ones are. But, in a couple pages in your application, you require a special textfield with a popup JavaScript-based calendar to allow users to select a date. You can solve this by creating the template, calendar.vm, and placing it in `/templates/xhtml`, in which xhtml is the default template library. Then, using the webwork:component tag, you can utilize this new template:

```
<webwork:component template="calendar.vm" label="Birthdate"
name="birthday"/>
```

If your component requires special parameters that can't be defined in the webwork:component tag's attributes, such as label or name, you can use the webwork:param tag to pass in extra parameters:

```
<webwork:component template="calendar.vm" label="Birthdate"
name="birthday">
    <webwork:param name="showWeekends" value="true"/>
</webwork:component>
```

By using themes and custom templates, you can begin to build a very rich and modular library of UI elements that can be easily reused.

One Small Problem

One thing we'd like to point out is that our original example was slightly flawed. To refresh your memory, it was:

```
<%@taglib uri="webwork" prefix="webwork"%>
<html>
    <head>
        <title>DeepHello Input</title>
    </head>
    <body>
```

```
        The DeepHello action requires some info from you:
        <webwork:form action="deephello.action">
            <webwork:textfield label="Name" name="person.name"/>
            <webwork:textfield label="City" name="person.city"/>
            <webwork:textfield label="Gender" name="person.gender"/>
            <webwork:submit value="'Say Hello'" />
        </webwork:form>
    </body>
</html>
```

The problem is that the input for the male/female selection is currently a textfield. That means the user must actually type "true" or "false." A better way to ask for the information would be in the form of a drop-down labeled "Gender," which allows the user to select either Male (true) or Female (false). We can do this by replacing the textfield with the following:

```
<webwork:select label="Gender" name="person.gender"
        list="#{'true' : 'Male', 'false' : 'Female'}"/>
```

Let's break this down. The label is still Gender, and the name is still person.gender, which maps to the Person object's boolean property, gender. The only new part is this list attribute. What exactly does all that stuff do? What you are seeing is the first real taste of one of the most powerful features XWork and WebWork offer: an expression language (EL). We will now discuss the EL and explain why it is so powerful.

Expressing Yourself

As we just saw, there are times when we need to express some information, such as the possible list of choices, that probably isn't suitable to be represented in the domain model (person) or the action (DeepHello). Because a selection of Male or Female could just as easily be Man or Woman, Boy or Girl, or Guy or Gal, this clearly indicates this choice should be made at the view level, which is typically a JSP or Velocity template.

Velocity has its own template language that we won't discuss, but JSP has no standard language for it — except for Java itself. The WebWork tags act as an interface not only to the data that the action class exposes, but also to the expression language that XWork natively supports.

In the previous examples, the value attribute of all the tags was considered a *parsed expression*. That is, the content in the value attribute would be parsed and then evaluated as an expression. XWork's EL is built upon the *Object Graph Navigation Language* (OGNL) available at http://www.ognl.org. It is an expression language for getting and setting properties of Java objects. It also has robust support for data-type conversion, collection manipulation, method calling, and most other features that the full-blown Java language can do.

The OGNL Web site comes with a very nice set of documents; thus, we won't cover too many of the basics here. However, we will discuss the additional features that XWork provides on top of OGNL's base language.

> **NOTE** Recently, JSTL became the standard expression language for the JSP specification. While WebWork does support JSTL at a basic level, OGNL is the EL of choice for the JSP tag libraries because of the incredible power that OGNL has over JSTL. OGNL is more than just an expression language. It provides a framework that can be extended by many projects. Not only does XWork use OGNL, but other projects have extended it as well, such as Jakarta's Tapestry project (http://tapestry.jakarta.org). With that said, JSTL and OGNL have a very similar syntax, which makes moving between the two trivial.

Using Basic Expressions

We will now cover a few basic expressions in OGNL just to get your feet wet. For more OGNL basics, check out the excellent documentation on the Web site.

Properties

As with most Java-based expression languages, OGNL is built upon the JavaBean standard. This means that properties are represented in an object by getter and setters methods. If the property is read-only, only a getXxx() method exists. Likewise, if it is write-only, only a setXxx() method exists. And, of course, read-write would include both. As the JavaBean standard indicates, the type returned by the getter must be the *same* type of the argument in the setter method.

```
public class Person {
    String name;
    String city;
    boolean gender;

    // getters and setters for each property
}
```

Looking at the Person class again, we can see that an expression of name would call the getName() method; thus, this results in the name property of the person we wish to evaluate upon. The same would work for the other properties as well.

Now suppose Person has two new properties: father and mother of type Person. If we were to find the mother's maiden name, the expression would now be mother.name. What this means is that if you wish to select a subproperty, you can use *dot notation* — just as we do in Java with objects.

Method Calls

Now that we've discussed properties, method calls are not much different. The only catch is that the entire method name must be given, and parentheses must be used to distinguish a method call from a property name. That means that `method.name` and `mother.getName()` will, in fact, evaluate to the same value.

If you wish to call a method that takes arguments, that works exactly as you might expect, `mother.hasChildWith(father)` would evaluate to true. Using literals is also legal: `father.olderThan(50)`. Using Strings in your expressions is as easy as quoting them. However, some situations make it impossible to use double quotation marks, such as when giving the expression as a JSP tag attribute. So, using single quotation marks also works. All of the following expressions are legal and do the same thing:

```
mother.setName("Sharii")
mother.name = "Sharii"
mother.setName('Sharii')
mother.name = 'Sharii'
```

Static Fields and Method Calls

Sometimes, calling static methods and accessing static fields is important. One such scenario might be that you have some String constants in your action class, and you want to display that value on a Web page. There are many other situations where static access is important as well.

Normally, OGNL allows for static access by using the syntax @package .ClassName@FIELD or @package.ClassName@method(args). However, this can get pretty messy in your JSPs. So, XWork provides an easier way. Rather than using the entire package and class name to specify a class, we can use the shorthand "vs."

This means that if we wish to display the HELLO public static field of our HelloWorld example action, the JSP might contain:

```
<webwork:property value="@vs@HELLO"/>
```

NOTE The reference to "vs" actually stands for ValueStack. We will discuss what the ValueStack is later in this chapter.

Using Advanced Expressions

Now that we've gone over the simpler stuff, let's look at more advanced things you might want to do. While OGNL is very similar to the Java syntax, some things are not included with Java and are borrowed from other languages, such as C. We will now discuss some of the features of the EL that aren't immediately obvious to users familiar with other expression languages such as JSTL.

Dealing with Collections

The most common usage of the EL in WebWork is dealing with collections, such as creating new Lists or Maps as well as selecting elements in them. Creating Lists and Maps in OGNL is very simple. A List can be created by using the syntax {e1, e2, ...} and a Map by using #{ k1 : v1, k2 : v2, ...}. As we saw previously, a drop-down selection box for the gender of a person can be generated with:

```
<webwork:select label="Gender" name="person.gender"
          list="#{'true' : 'Male', 'false' : 'Female'}"/>
```

The expression for the list attribute is essentially resulting in a Map being created that maps the String "true" to the String "Male" and the String "false" to the String "Female." The individual elements in List construction — as well as the key/value pairs in Map construction — can also be regular OGNL expressions. This means that the following, while probably an unfair question to ask, is perfectly valid syntax:

```
<webwork:select label="Favorite Parent" name="person.favoriteParent"
          list="{person.father.name, person.mother.name}"/>
```

Often, it is important to see if an element is in a collection. This, as well as its opposite, can be done with the in and not in operations. Examples of this are 'foo' in {'foo', 'bar'} and 'baz' not in {'foo', 'bar'}.

Lastly, you sometimes might want to select only a subset of a collection. Doing this is called *projection*. Projection involves taking a larger collection and selecting zero or more elements in the collection to result in a smaller collection. The general syntax is collection.{X selection}. Here, collection is the actual list or map you plan to project upon. X indicates the type of projection you are planning to do:

- ? — Select all the elements matching the selection logic.
- ^ — Select only the first element matching the selection logic.
- $ — Select only the last element matching the selection logic.

Finally, the selection part is called the selection logic and is the actual filter that determines which elements should be included in the projection and which should not. You can use the #this operator to perform logic queries on the individual elements in the collection. For example, the following expression will select all male relatives from a person's "relative" property, which is a List: person.relatives.{? #this.gender == true}.

Constructors

Suppose you need a query that requires an object to be created. Just like in Java, you can use the new operator in OGNL to create new objects. Following is an example of an expression that checks, rather indirectly, if a person's father's name is James from San Jose:

```
person.father.equals(new Person("James", "San Jose", true))
```

Context Variables and the Root Variable

The last thing to discuss, as it is pertinent to our next topic, is OGNL's notion of context variables and the *root variable*. The way OGNL works is that there is always a context, which is essentially a Map that contains a mapping of variable names to variable objects.

You can refer to an object in the context with the # operator. This means, if the context contains two variables, foo and bar, you can refer to them as #foo and #bar, respectively. However, having to prefix each and every expression would get tedious. So, the concept of a root, or default, variable was introduced. What this means is that, if foo and bar are both in the context map and foo is also the root variable, #foo.baz and baz are actually the same expression.

It turns out that the ActionContext in XWork, which is a map, is, in fact, the same OGNL context. This means that anything in the ActionContext can be referenced by using this operator. As we showed before, the action JSP tag can be used as:

```
<webwork:action id="hi" name="hello">
    <webwork:param name="name" value="'Patrick'"/>
</webwork:action>
<webwork:property value="#hi.greeting"/>
```

Because the ID was "hi," the action object itself was then mapped to the "hi" variable name in the OGNL context (ActionContext), and thus the expression #hi.greeting now makes perfect sense.

Understanding the ValueStack

As we just discussed, OGNL normally supports a single root object and any number of named context variables. However, WebWork is slightly different in that, rather than a single root object, there is a single root stack called the *value stack*.

This means that, rather than only one object in the root context, any number of objects can all be considered to be in the root context. The best way to see this is to look at a few examples. Suppose that the stack contains two items: foo and bar. Also, the context contains a third item, baz. The context can then be visualized as shown in Figure 6.2.

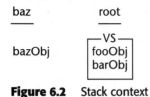

Figure 6.2   Stack context

A query such as #baz.bazName would access the bazName property of the bazObj — as we've already seen. The tricky part is when we issue a query such as fooName or barName. In the case of fooName, when fooName is a property of fooObj but not barObj, the stack would be traversed from the top down until a match was found. In this case, a match would be found at the top of the stack.

In the second case, barName, fooObj would first be looked at, but, because it has no barName property, the next object on the stack, barObj, would be evaluated. Lastly, if a property, such as bazName or noName, is accessed on the root object and all elements in the stack have been exhausted, null will be returned.

Accessing Stack Elements

Under some circumstances, it is important to be able to skip some elements on the stack when traversal begins for a property or method name. For example, suppose the stack contained two Person objects. If your query was just name, the name of the person on the top of the stack would be returned. To get the name of the person lower in the stack, the query would be [1].name.

Accessing items other than the top of the stack is as simple as using array notation, where the index is the location of an item in the stack, with zero being the top of the stack.

Examples Using the JSP Tags

The application of the value stack may be hard to see until you've seen it in action. We can do this by showing a few JSP examples that take advantage of the behavior of the unique features that the value stack offers.

```
<webwork:iterator value="relatives">
    <webwork:property value="[1].name"/> -> <webwork:property
value="name"/>
</webwork:iterator>
```

Here, we are iterating over the List of relatives on the Person object. For each iteration over the relatives List, the current relative will be *pushed* onto the stack. That means that, inside of the iterator block, a query of name would return the relative's name — not the name of the person who has these relatives. To query that name, we have to use [1].name instead. The output of that JSP snippet might look like:

```
Pat -> Shari
Pat -> James
Pat -> Chris
```

Another JSP tag that illustrates the features of the value stack is the push tag. This tag allows you to push items onto the stack, which makes queries simpler. The following two JSP blocks produce the same output, but, as you can see, one is much easier to read.

```
<webwork:property value="person.mother.name"/>
<webwork:property value="person.mother.age"/>
<webwork:property value="person.mother.hairColor"/>
<webwork:property value="person.mother.favoriteColor"/>

<webwork:push value="person.mother">
    <webwork:property value="name"/>
    <webwork:property value="age"/>
    <webwork:property value="hairColor"/>
    <webwork:property value="favoriteColor"/>
</webwork:push>
```

Exploring Type Conversion

One thing that has always been a bit of a pain with Java-based Web development is its support — or lack of it — for typing. In languages such as Perl and PHP, where types aren't strongly enforced as in Java, dealing with the typeless nature of the Web is very easy.

The HTTP spec does not allow types to be defined for GET or POST parameters. This means that Java code must do the type conversion for you. For Servlets, all parameters come in as either String or String[], which means that it is usually up to your code to convert these to the actual type.

Fortunately, XWork provides a very strong type-conversion system to allow you to reuse type-conversion logic throughout your application. While it might be perfectly legal to make all your actions' properties String and then convert them in the execute() method, this is cumbersome and makes you focus on things other than business logic.

A better way is to make your actions and classes use the types you'd want them to use and then provide XWork with some information on how it should handle converting from type X to type Y or vice-versa. Let's look at some examples to see this in action.

Digging into a Date Example

One of the more common things we'd like to read as well as display in a Web system is a date. Suppose we want our application to be hardcoded on the format MM/dd/yyyy. We want to specify conversion both to and from String. To do so, all we'd need to do is implement the TypeConverter interface or extend DefaultTypeConverter, which does much of the work for you.

NOTE As we all know, the MM/dd/yyyy format is a U.S. thing, and other countries use different formats to express a date. While XWork does have broad support for i18n, we won't be discussing it in this chapter because it is a huge subject. If you'd like to find out more about XWork and WebWork's supports for i18n, check the OpenSymphony Web site for documentation.

```
package myfirstconverter;

import ognl.DefaultTypeConverter;

import java.util.Map;
import java.util.Date;
import java.text.SimpleDateFormat;
import java.text.ParseException;

public class DateConverter extends DefaultTypeConverter {
    public Object convertValue(Map context, Object obj, Class type) {
        SimpleDateFormat sdf = new SimpleDateFormat("MM/dd/yyyy");

        if (type == String.class) {
            Date date = (Date) obj;
            return sdf.format(date);
        } else if (type == Date.class) {
            String date = (String) obj;
            try {
                return sdf.parse(date);
            } catch (ParseException e) {
                return null;
            }
        }

        return null;
    }
}
```

As you can see here, the DateConverter class is actually very simple. If we are being requested to convert to a *String*, we use the `format()` method of SimpleDateFormat. If we are being requested to a *Date*, we use the `parse()` method. By using a type converter such as this, we can allow our action classes and models to keep their original types and still handle the loose typing problem that the Web environment creates.

Specifying Default Conversion Rules

Now that we know how to create type converters, the next task is to make sure XWork actually uses them. There are two ways to do this. The first way is to define a *default rule* such that this type converter is used, anytime a particular type, such as java.util.Date, is encountered.

Default rules can be specified in the `xwork-conversion.properties` file, located in `WEB-INF/classes`. The format of this file is:

```
full.name.of.Type=full.name.of.TypeConverter
```

If we want our DateConverter to be applied to all dates in our application, we just add the following entry:

```
java.util.Date= myfirstconverter.DateConverter
```

NOTE XWork ships with a large set of default converters that are built to handle most of the common types you encounter, such as Date, String, List, Map, all the primitives, arrays, and others. These default types are stored in xwork-conversion.properties that are bundled in the XWork jar file.

Specifying New Conversion Rules

Sometimes, we don't want to use the default conversion rules but rather a more granular manner. XWork allows you to specify type converters on a per-class, per-property basis as well. This means that you might want to use the DateConverter by default, but, for some classes, you want to use a DateAndTimeConverter instead.

To do this, you must create a file of `ClassName-conversion.properties` in the same package as the class you want to define the rule upon, where ClassName is the name of your class. In this file, you then map properties of the class to type converter classes.

For example, if we want to allow a way to input a Person as String such as Patrick, San Francisco, true, we could create a type converter to break this string up and create a Person object. To make sure that this type converter is used only for the DeepHello action class, we create a file called `DeepHello-conversion.properties` with the following content:

```
person= myfirstconverter.PersonConverter
```

Separating Concerns with Interceptors

Aspect-Oriented Programming (AOP) is considered the next step in the evolution of software development. While AOP is only just becoming mainstream, there are concepts it uses that have actually been around for quite a while. AOP has interceptors that can be wrapped around method calls, field reads and writes, and many other things.

XWork borrows from the ideas in AOP as well as those presented long ago by design pattern experts. It provides for the ability to configure interceptors around calls to the execute() method of your action. These interceptors can do things before and after the execute() method is called, including short-circuiting calls to execute() entirely.

Looking at Configuration and Interceptor Stacks

Interceptors within XWork are configured in stacks, which can be applied to any action or package of actions. A stack of interceptors is applied in the order they are defined. Let's first look at how to define interceptors. We'll then look at how to apply interceptors to actions and packages.

```
<interceptors>
    <interceptor name="timer"
class="com.opensymphony.xwork.interceptor.TimerInterceptor"/>
    <interceptor name="logger"
class="com.opensymphony.xwork.interceptor.LoggingInterceptor"/>
    <interceptor name="params"
class="com.opensymphony.xwork.interceptor.ParametersInterceptor"/>
    <interceptor name="component"
class="com.opensymphony.xwork.interceptor.component.ComponentInterceptor
"/>
    <interceptor name="validator"
class="com.opensymphony.xwork.validator.ValidationInterceptor"/>

    <interceptor-stack name="defaultStack">
        <interceptor-ref name="timer"/>
        <interceptor-ref name="logger"/>
        <interceptor-ref name="params"/>
        <interceptor-ref name="component"/>
    </interceptor-stack>

    <interceptor-stack name="validatingStack">
        <interceptor-ref name="defaultStack"/>
        <interceptor-ref name="validator"/>
    </interceptor-stack>
</interceptors>
```

Here, you can see we define five interceptors and two stacks. The second stack is actually an extension of the first stack, but it adds an extra interceptor after the original four — validator. This is good when you want to apply only some interceptors to certain actions and other interceptors to other actions.

Now let's look at how we can apply these interceptors to our familiar Hello-World action:

```
<action name="hello1"
        class="helloworld.HelloWorld">
    <interceptor-ref name="defaultStack"/>
    <result name="success" type="dispatcher">
        <param name="location">helloworld.jsp</param>
    </result>
</action>
```

Sometimes, we don't want to specify the interceptor-ref for every action, but rather for an entire package, and all actions in that package will use that default interceptor-ref:

```
<package name="default">
    ...
    <default-interceptor-ref name="defaultStack"/>

    <action name="hello1"
            class="helloworld.HelloWorld">
        <result name="success" type="dispatcher">
            <param name="location">helloworld.jsp</param>
        </result>
    </action>
</package>
```

Using default-interceptor-ref is good because you can use the defaultStack without having to explicitly reference it. Then, in situations where you don't want to use defaultStack, but rather validatingStack, you can override the default.

Using LoggingInterceptor

Interceptors can do many different things, but they conceptually all work the same way. To understand the flow of execution, the simplest interceptor to look at is the LoggingInterceptor. Suppose we had the following action that was configured to use the LoggingInterceptor:

```
public class PingPong implements Action {
    public String execute() {
        System.out.println("Ping... Pong!");
        return STRING;
    }
}
```

> **INVERSION OF CONTROL**
>
> As usual, there's more than one way to do things. We mentioned that interceptors can be used to handle transactions. Built upon XWork's interceptor support, XWork also contains an Inversion of Control (IoC) framework that can be used to handle things such as transaction management as well. But rather than making a TransactionInterceptor, XWork's IoC framework allows you to write a transaction *service* that has `init()` and `dispose()` methods called before and after the `execute()` call that is courtesy of the interceptor. Chapter 14 discusses IoC in much more detail.

When this action gets called, the output to the console would be:

```
Starting execution stack for action pingpong
Ping... Pong!
Finishing execution stack for action pingpong
```

As you can see, the LoggingInterceptor merely prints statements before and after the call to `execute()`.

Building Your Own Interceptor

Using the simple power of interceptors, you can now begin to write interceptors to handle security or transactions or anything else you can dream up. For example, a security interceptor might be configured to allow only the `execute()` call to pass through if a user had already been authenticated. A transaction interceptor might start a transaction before the call to `execute()` and then, after the call, either commit or rollback. The possibilities are truly limitless.

Validation — A Powerful Interceptor

One area of Web-application development we haven't looked at is validation. You should always validate any data received from end users, and a Web application is no different. Let's look briefly at how validation could be done by hand and then at the XWork validation framework, which makes validation easier by decoupling the validation rules for an action from the action itself.

Exploring an Example without XWork Validation Framework

Let's look at how we might add our own validation to the HelloWorld example. At the moment, there is no validation at all. So, what should we validate? Well, in this case, it's very simple.

There is only one field (name) and we should validate that the user entered a correct value for it. This means the name String must be not null and must have at least one character in it.

Let's look at some code to see how we would do this:

```java
import com.opensymphony.xwork.ActionSupport;

public class HelloWorld extends ActionSupport {
    String name;
    String greeting;

    public void setName(String name) {
        this.name = name;
    }

    public String getName() {
        return name;
    }

    public String getGreeting() {
        return greeting;
    }

    public String execute() {
        if (name == null || "".equals("name")) {
            addFieldError("name", "You must specify a valid name.");
            return ERROR;
        }

        greeting = "Hello, " + name;
        return SUCCESS;
    }
}
```

We're extending ActionSupport, which is a useful abstract base action class that adds internationalization support and error-message handling. Our validation happens in the first four lines of the `execute()` method, as follows:

- The conditional clause does the actual check that the name field, which is automatically set by WebWork by using the `setName()` method, is not null and not "". That is, it has a length greater than 0.

- If the field validation fails, we add an error message to the name field. ActionSupport handles two types of error messages: field-level and action-level errors. The UI components will automatically look for this error when displaying the field and display it if it exists.

- Lastly, we return to an ERROR view, rather than the SUCCESS view, since this action didn't successfully execute. The ERROR view can be the same page as our originally submitted JSP — presumably with error messages printed.

Writing validation code like this gives us very fine-grained control. However, it tends to result in a significant duplication in validation code among different actions and bloats our action unnecessarily. Let's look now at the validation framework provided by XWork that solves these problems.

Exploring an Example with XWork Validation Framework

XWork comes with a very neat validation framework built in. Instead of validating your inputs in code, validation is handled by a series of pluggable Validator classes and XML configuration files that map the validators to actions and fields. The framework decouples validation from the action itself and allows for much greater reusability of individual validations.

So, how is this framework used? Let's rewrite the previous example to use it. First, our action becomes much simpler:

```
import com.opensymphony.xwork.ActionSupport;

public class HelloWorld extends ActionSupport {
    String name;
    String greeting;

    public void setName(String name) {
        this.name = name;
    }

    public String getName() {
        return name;
    }

    public String getGreeting() {
        return greeting;
    }

    public String execute() {
        if (hasErrors()) {
            return ERROR;
        }

        greeting = "Hello, " + name;
        return SUCCESS;
    }
}
```

Note that our `execute()` method just checks if there are any errors at all. If there are, it returns the ERROR view. So, where are the errors added, and how do we define our validation? Let's look at the `HelloWorld-validation` `.xml` file, which is placed in the same package as the HelloWorld action itself:

```
<validators>
    <field name="name">
        <field-validator type= "requiredstring" >
            <message>Please enter a valid name.</message>
        </field-validator>
    </field>
</validators>
```

The requiredstring validator does exactly the same thing as our earlier code, which validates that a String is not null and has a length greater than 0. The difference is that, this time, we're taking that validation and applying it to a particular field (name) with a particular error message. We could then reuse this validation elsewhere or apply other validations to the same field. Now we know how to validate an action so let's look at how we set up the validation framework itself.

Using Built-In and Custom Validators

Validation is applied by a single interceptor class, ValidationInterceptor, which must be in your interceptor stack for validation to occur. Apart from that, all we need to do is define the set of validators our validations can use.

Validators are defined in a `validators.xml` file, which are stored in the `WEB-INF/classes` directory of your Web application. Let's look at a sample of that file, which shows the eight built-in validators:

```
<validators>
    <validator name="required" class="com.opensymphony.xwork
.validator.validators.RequiredFieldValidator"/>
    <validator name="requiredstring" class="com.opensymphony.xwork
.validator.validators.RequiredStringValidator"/>
    <validator name="int" class="com.opensymphony.xwork.validator
.validators.IntRangeFieldValidator"/>
    <validator name="date" class="com.opensymphony.xwork
.validator.validators.DateRangeFieldValidator"/>
    <validator name="expression" class="com.opensymphony.xwork
.validator.validators.ExpressionValidator"/>
    <validator name="fieldexpression" class="com.opensymphony.xwork
.validator.validators.FieldExpressionValidator"/>
    <validator name="email" class="com.opensymphony.xwork
.validator.validators.EmailValidator"/>
    <validator name="url" class="com.opensymphony.xwork.
validator.validators.URLValidator"/>
</validators>
```

The built-in validators validate fields, Strings, number and date ranges, e-mail addresses, URLs, and arbitrary expressions. However, they are by no means a complete set. They are the basic validations you will reuse many times, but it's likely your application will require you to write custom validator classes. This is, of course, very simple to do!

Validators must implement the com.opensymphony.xwork.validator.Validator interface and come in two types: action and field validators. These implement the com.opensymphony.xwork.validator.FieldValidator interface. Action validators provide validation of the action overall; whereas, field validators are used to validate individual fields.

To write a custom validator, the easiest way is to extend one of the provided base classes — ValidatorSupport and FieldValidatorSupport — for action validators and field validators, respectively.

Let's build a sample custom validator class for our HelloWorld action. As well as validating that the name is a nonzero length String, let's assume we wanted to verify that the name submitted was the name of someone in our system. We might do this like so:

```
public class SystemUserValidator extends FieldValidatorSupport {
    public void validate(Action action) throws ValidationException {
        String fieldName = getFieldName();
        String username = (String)this.getFieldValue(fieldName, action);

        if (UserManager.getUser(username) == null) {
            addFieldError(fieldName, action);
        }
    }
}
```

Our validator gets the field value out of the action — in our case, the submitted name — and then tries to use some UserManager class to look up the user in the system. Our UserManager returns null if the user is not valid. So, all we have to do is add the error message to the action in that case.

To use this validator against the action, we don't need to modify the action at all. We need to add the following line to `validators.xml`:

```
<validator name="properuser"
class="com.ouraplication.validators.SystemUserValidator"/>
```

And then update the `HelloWorld-validation.xml` file as follows:

```
<validators>
    <field name= "name" >
        <field-validator type= "requiredstring" >
            <message>Please enter a valid name.</message>
        </field-validator>
        <field-validator type= "properuser" >
            <message>The name entered is not a valid user.</message>
        </field-validator>
    </field>
</validators>
```

Our name field will now be validated by both classes, and our action now validates both that the name is a valid String and that it matches a user within our system. We can also reuse our SystemUserValidator class in other actions by simply adding it to their -validation.xml file.

Using the Expression Validator

One particularly powerful validator that comes with XWork is the Expression-Validator. It simply validates that a given OGNL expression — evaluated against your action — returns true.

As we have just seen, writing custom validators in Java classes is relatively easy, but, most of the time, it is unnecessary. Frequently, the ExpressionValidator can be substituted to create custom validations by using just XML.

Assume we are validating a new user signup action. Most user signups require a user to enter the desired password twice to confirm they did not make a mistake the first time they typed it. Now, we could validate that these two passwords are the same by writing a PasswordConfirmationValidator class to compare them. However, we can do this same task by using the existing expression validator, as follows:

```
<field name="confirm">
    <field-validator type="fieldexpression">
        <param name="expression"> password.equals(confirm)</param>
        <message>The two passwords entered don't match.</message>
    </field-validator>
</field>
```

This sample shows the expression validator in use. The expression to be evaluated is specified in the "expression" parameter of the validator. In this case, the expression validated is password.equals(confirm). Where do these values, password and confirm, come from? Our expression validator will get the field values out of our action by using getPassword() and getConfirm() and then check that they are equal.

The expression validator allows us to write very powerful validations without writing any Java code, and, because it uses OGNL, the same expression language as the rest of XWork, creating new validations is very simple.

Summary

In this chapter, we took an in-depth look at XWork and WebWork. We discussed the basics of MVC as well as the notion of actions in terms of XWork. We then looked at how WebWork provides view support on top of XWork and how the OGNL expression language can be used for very powerful queries of your Java object models.

Next, we looked at the advanced features, such as the ValueStack, type conversion, interceptors, and validation. There is much more to XWork and WebWork, but this chapter should provide more than enough information to get you started and writing your own MVC-based application by using these technologies.

Simplifying Layout with SiteMesh

It is likely you've come across problems mixing layout-specific HTML (such as corporate branding) with the content of the application (such as JSP forms or search results). If not handled properly, code can become very messy and hard to maintain.

To solve these problems, this chapter takes a step back from HTML and looks at how you could approach these issues in an object-oriented world. We look at some specific design patterns that are commonly used in non-Web GUI application development (such as Swing). We introduce SiteMesh, an Open Source tool that can help you implement these patterns using HTML and JSP, and show some examples of it working. Lastly, we offer you some general tips and tricks to help get the most out of SiteMesh.

Identifying Problems with Layout

As developers, we constantly strive to create clean, elegant, and simple code (we hope!). Clean code can make a system easier to write, read, and maintain. When working with Java code, we can use OO design techniques to simplify the problem; however, these solutions do not map so well to HTML and JSP.

Let's use a login screen as an example:

```html
<html>
  <head>
    <title>Please login</title>
  </head>
  <body>
    <form action="login.action" method="post">
      <input type="hidden" name="section" value="store">

      Login Name:<br>
      <input type="text" name="loginname"><br>

      Password:<br>
      <input type="password" name="password"><br>

      <input type="submit" value="Login">
    </form>
  </body>
</html>
```

This code is simple. Every tag has an obvious meaning. The screen has all the content to meet the requirements of the login screen. Figure 7.1 shows what it looks like. It seems to be lacking something.

Of course, the combined forces of the boss and the graphic designer need it to look more graphically pleasing, as in Figure 7.2.

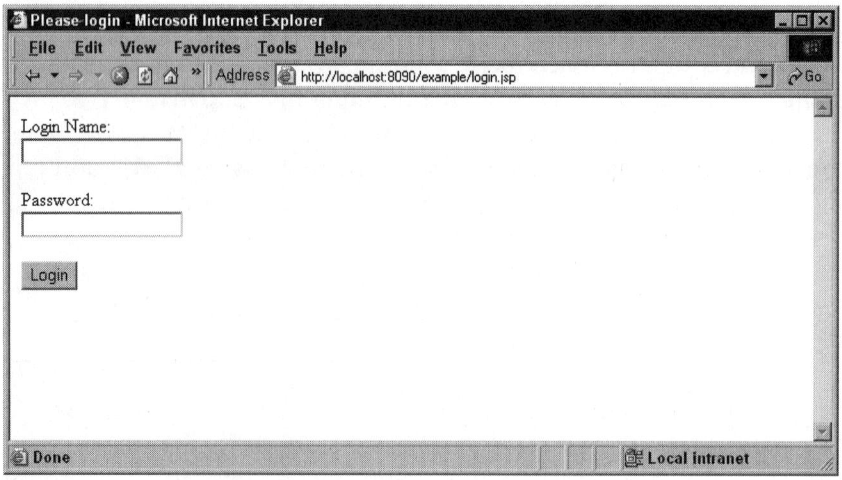

Figure 7.1   A functional login window

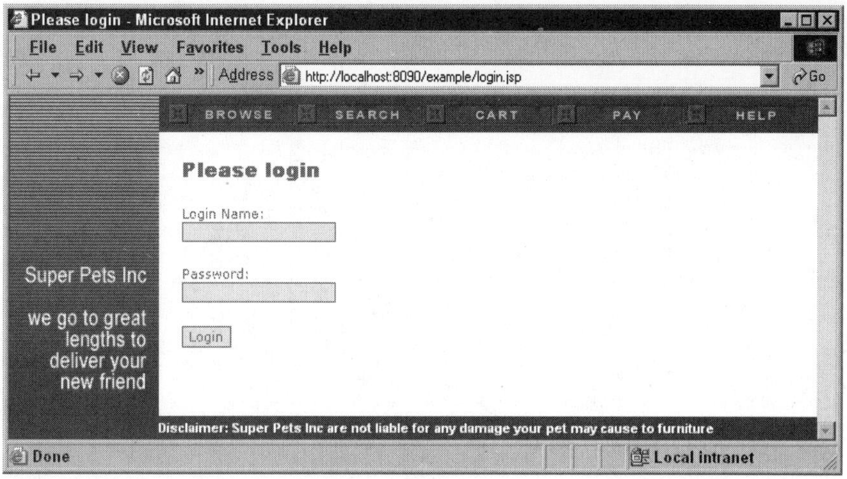

Figure 7.2   A prettier functional login window

With some HTML wizardry, the screen can easily be modified to meet this requirement; however, the original 20 lines of HTML jump up to 300. As more and more ideas are added to the layout, the HTML grows and grows, dwarfing the actual elements that make the content of the page in the first place: the login form and fields.

As these elements disappear into the page, it becomes less obvious how the form works, making it harder to maintain and increasing the chance of bugs. For example, from the original form, it is very obvious that there's a hidden input field called "section." If this was mixed up with lots of layout-specific HTML, there's a high chance the element could be missed when examining the code.

Now when a new page is added to the application it is likely that much of the layout of the login screen must be applied to this, too. The HTML could be copied and pasted from the login screen, but that would lead to duplication (something we are always keen to avoid in development) and is particularly tricky because it is heavily interweaved with the login form, which is not part of our second page. As more and more pages are added to the application, so is more and more HTML, causing a code explosion and maintenance nightmare.

If we were looking at multiple pages of Java code and spotted duplication, we could easily solve this by refactoring the duplication into common. Likewise, a server-side include (SSI) allows us to do this with JSP. If we were to look at the layout and content-specific elements across the various pages, we would likely see a lot of duplication that can be separated into include files methods (see Figure 7.3).

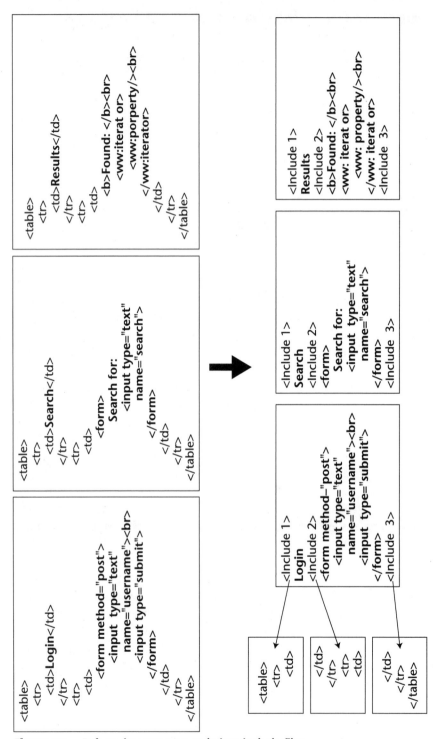

Figure 7.3   Refactoring common code into include files

But adding server-side includes leads to more complexity. Consider this piece of code:

```
...
<table>
  <tr><td style="color:navy; font-size:20px">
     <img src="widget.gif" width="10" height="20">
Search form
  </td></tr>
  <tr><td style="font-face: arial">
    <img src="gradient-begin.gif"><br>
    <form action="search.action">
      <input type="text" name="query">
      <input type="submit" value="Search">
    </form>
    <br><img src="gradient-end.gif">
  </td></tr>
</table>
...
```

The layout-specific elements can easily be extracted into include files, shortening the page to:

```
...
<jsp:include page="form-header.jsp"/>
Search form
<jsp:include page="form-middle.jsp"/>
<form action="search.action">
  <input type="text" name="query">
  <input type="submit" value="Search">
</form>
<jsp:include page="form-footer.jsp"/>
...
```

This simplifies the content by separating the layout, but that simplification comes at the expense of the maintainability of the layout. For example, `form-middle.jsp` contains

```
</td></tr>
<tr><td style="font-face: arial">
  <img src="gradient-begin.gif"><br>
```

That's a very confusing piece of code. It's not even well-formed HTML. Maintaining lots of these snippets of code gets complicated very quickly. It's very hard to design layout in this way, as it's not obvious how each of the snippets are assembled in the page. The snippet of code is incomplete.

It is also beneficial to make use of specialized Web-development tools that can aid in designing complicated pages, such as WYSIWYG editor packages; however, these tools are effective only when developing entire pages — they provide little help for malformed include snippets.

JSP SERVER-SIDE INCLUDES

JSP supports two different forms of server-side includes: those that insert the included file at JSP compilation time and those that insert the included file at runtime.

Compile-time includes look like the following:

```
<%@ include file="mypage.jsp" %>
```

These includes

- ◆ **Can only include JSP pages.**

- ◆ **Do not allow a different file to be included at runtime. In the preceding code, mypage.jsp is constant — it cannot be changed.**

- ◆ **Allow variables to be shared between files, which can offer convenience but can also lead to confusion if variable declarations are hidden.**

- ◆ **Can cause problems with JSP pages built using these types of includes because pages are often incomplete, resulting in badly formed HTML in multiple files.**

- ◆ **Do not add any overhead at runtime.**

Runtime includes look like the following:

```
<jsp:include page="mypage.jsp"/>
```

or

```
<% pageContext.include("mypage.jsp"); %>
```

These type of includes

- ◆ **Are not restricted to JSP includes; you could use static files or the results from other Servlets.**

- ◆ **Allow the include file to be dynamically chosen at runtime.**

- ◆ **Run within their own scope; that is, variables are not shared between them. However, values can be explicitly passed between the pages using the <jsp:param> tag. These values have to be strings and are handled by the included file as if they were parameters posted to the page.**

- ◆ **Require extra processing by the Servlet container at runtime.**

In short, runtime includes offer greater flexibility, whereas compile-time includes perform better. Choose the one that best suits your needs.

Using the Object-Oriented Solution

If we were dealing with layout problems in a traditional GUI application (that is, not a Web-based application), we could consider looking at any design patterns that may solve this. So let's do that by treating the various components that make up a page as objects so we can make use of the same patterns.

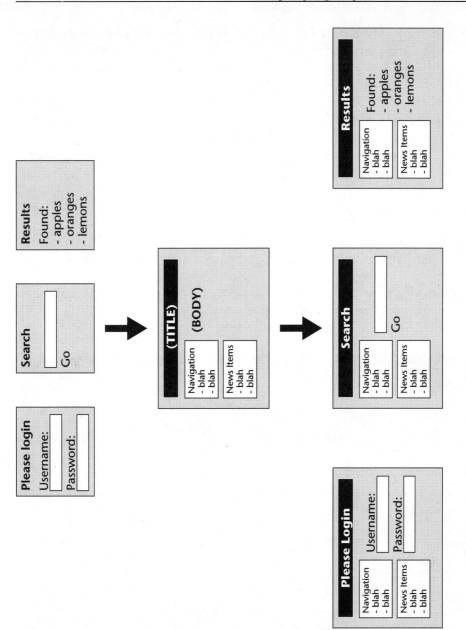

Figure 7.4 Plain content pages combined with a decorator to produce the best of both worlds

Decorator Design Pattern

The decorator design pattern can be used in a GUI to apply a visual style known as a *decorator* to any other component. Decorators can be created with standard JSP pages using a simple tag library. A decorator contains the layout of the page and placeholders for inserting the content in the relevant places. The decorator itself looks like a standard HTML page, allowing it to be easily maintained even with visual Web-design tools.

Other components need not be aware of the decorators that are to be applied to them and vice-versa. This decoupling makes it easy to match components and decorators together in different combinations.

In the context of our Web application we can use the contents as components and the layout as a decorator, as shown in Figure 7.4.

Composite Design Pattern

The composite design pattern allows for components to be nested inside other components, which in turn allows components to be assembled in a treelike structure to form more complicated layouts.

Take the example of a portal. There are many components that are assembled together in a treelike structure to make the page (see Figure 7.5).

Figure 7.5 A typical Web page

These components can be broken down and assembled in a treelike structure such as the one shown in Figure 7.6. The page contains regions for navigation, information, header, and the body. The body in turn contains smaller regions for the welcome and main headline.

Combining the Patterns

Combining the decorator and composite design patterns, we can assemble a Web page using pages, includes, and decorators, as shown in Figure 7.7.

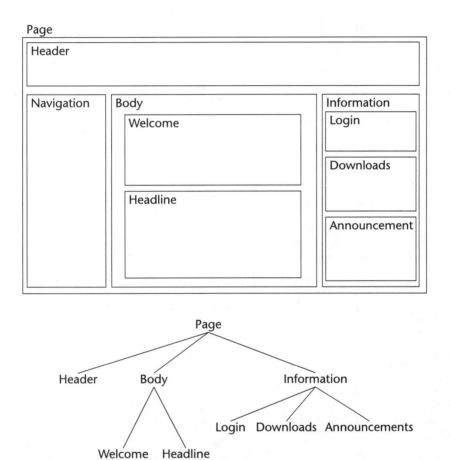

Figure 7.6   Web page components broken down into tree structure

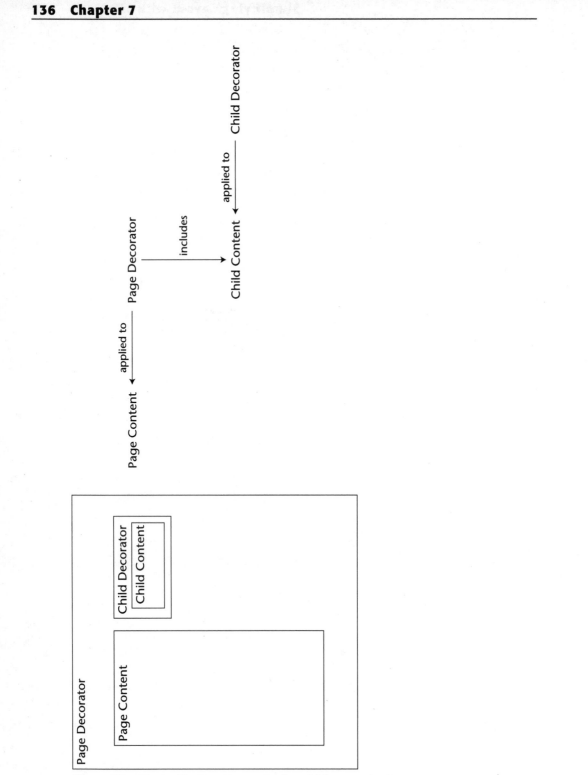

Figure 7.7   Page with decorator containing child component

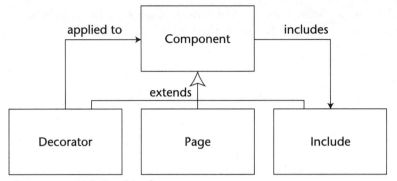

Figure 7.8   Relationships between components

The core of the page is the *page content*. This has the *page decorator* applied to it. The *page decorator* itself includes further content — the *child content*. Like the other content, the *child content* has a *child decorator* applied to it.

If we treat pages, includes, and decorators as object-oriented (OO) classes, we can create a superclass called *component* that simplifies the relationships. In this case, pages, includes, and decorators are all components that can be applied to one another as follows:

- Components can contain includes.
- Decorators can be applied to components.

This can be summarized as a UML class diagram (see Figure 7.8). *Decorators, Pages,* and *Includes* all extend the abstract type *Component*. Any type of *Component* can include an *Include*. A *Decorator* can be applied to any type of *Component*.

Looking at the relationships in this way helps to simplify how a page can be built up in a compentized manner.

Implementing the Solution with SiteMesh

If the components of the page were simple objects, the implementation of complicated page layouts in a way that separates content from layout would be easy. However, mapping this to HTML is slightly trickier because an HTML document isn't a structure you can apply OO patterns to — it's a chunk of text. That's where SiteMesh comes in.

SiteMesh is system that can be added to a Web application that facilitates the use of these patterns in the HTML world. SiteMesh can be downloaded from the following URL:

```
http://www.opensymphony.com/sitemesh/
```

NOTE Installation instructions are bundled with the download. The remainder of this chapter assumes SiteMesh has been installed.

SiteMesh Fundamentals

SiteMesh is based on the Servlet 2.3 API and consists of an engine that can parse outgoing pages or page fragments, determine if any decorator needs be applied, and merge the appropriate decorator.

SiteMesh has been designed to be nonobtrusive to the content of the application and thus does not impose any requirements as to how the HTML is generated. Content can come from a static .html file, JSP, Servlet, MVC framework, an XSL transform, or even a legacy CGI script, making it easy to retrofit SiteMesh to existing Web applications.

NOTE By default, SiteMesh processes only HTML content — media such as images, PDFs, and downloads are ignored.

NOTE Although JSP is used to define decorators in the examples given here, other view technologies can be substituted, such as Velocity.

The process of the applying a decorator to a page is as follows (see Figure 7.9):

- When an HTTP request is made to the Servlet container, SiteMesh intercepts the request, using a Servlet Filter, and captures the resulting HTML.
- This HTML is then parsed and any relevant content is extracted into a Page object.
- A DecoratorMapper is queried to determine which Decorator need be applied.
- The Servlet container forwards the request to the JSP containing the decorator.
- The decorator generates the layout HTML with the content pulled from the Page object.

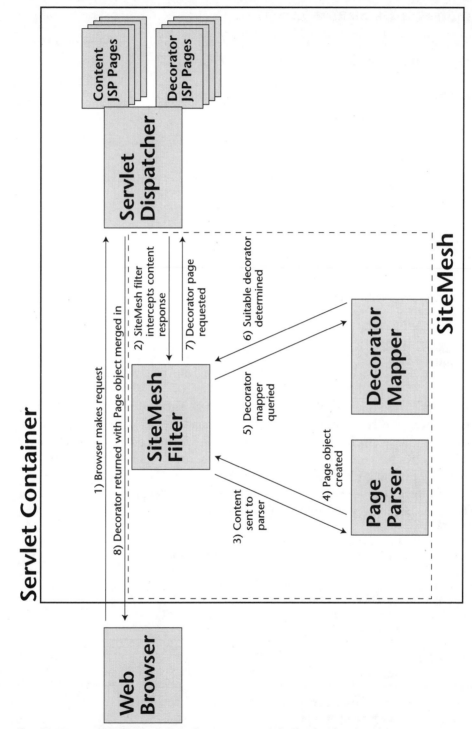

Figure 7.9   Interaction between the components in the Servlet container

Creating a Decorator

Let's revisit the original code sample and apply a new layout with SiteMesh. The plain login form looks like this (refer to Figure 7.1):

```
<html>
  <head>
    <title>Please login</title>
  </head>
  <body>
    <form action="login.action" method="post">
      <input type="hidden" name="section" value="store">

      Login Name:<br>
      <input type="text" name="loginname"><br>

      Password:<br>
      <input type="password" name="password"><br>

      <input type="submit" value="Login">
    </form>
  </body>
</html>
```

A decorator looks like a standard Web page but focuses on layout (see Figure 7.10). This is where all the smart graphics, tables, flashy DHTML doodaahs, and CSS styles reside. The actual content is omitted; instead, JSP tags are inserted as placeholders where the title, header, and body of the original content will be substituted when the decorator is applied. Because the page takes the structure of a standard HTML document, it is easier to maintain and is friendly to visual Web-development tools.

The following code shows a very simple SiteMesh decorator. For brevity, the HTML has been cut down to the bare minimum.

```
[decorators/simple.jsp]
<%@ taglib uri="sitemesh-decorator" prefix="decorator" %>
<html>
  <head>
    <title><decorator:title/></title>
    <link rel="stylesheet" href="style.css">
    <decorator:head/>
  </head>
  <body>
    <table width="100%">
      <tr>
        <td class="title" colspan="2">
          <decorator:title/>
        </td>
```

```
        </tr>
        <tr>
          <td class="body">
             <decorator:body/>
          </td>
        </tr>
      </table>
    </body>
  </html>
```

In order for SiteMesh to determine which decorator (if any) to apply to a page, a mapping needs to be set up in the `decorators.xml` file, which resides in the `WEB-INF` directory.

Each decorator requires a name to uniquely identify it and the location of the page that contains the layout. A *pattern match* is required to define which URLs the decorator will be applied to. Pattern matches can use wildcards and regular expressions. We shall set up a decorator that matches all page URLs in the Web application using the * wildcard.

```
[WEB-INF/decorators.xml]
<decorators>

  <decorator name="simple" page="decorators/simple.jsp">
    <pattern>*</pattern>
  </decorator>

</decorators>
```

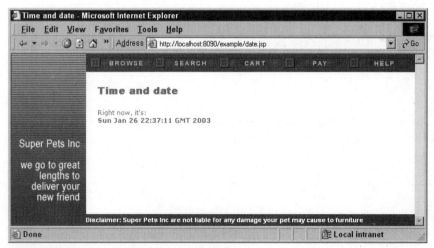

Figure 7.10   Decorated time and date page

If we visit the login form again, it now looks somewhat different (refer to Figure 7.2).

We can now create additional content pages and SiteMesh will decorate these, too, without any modification — no extra work is required because the wildcard pattern will match all requests (see Figure 7.10).

```
[date.jsp]
<%@ page import="java.util.Date" %>
<html>
  <head>
    <title>Time and date</title>
  </head>
  <body>
    Right now, it's:<br>
    <b><%= new Date().toString() %></b>
  </body>
</html>
```

Composing Pages

We've seen how SiteMesh can apply decorators to pages; now let's assemble a page from more pages and decorators.

Let's suppose we want to extend our decorator to allow it to act as a container for another component. Let's use the login page as the child component. This page has no decoration, though, so it needs its own decorator.

We already have three out of four of these components — the child decorator does not exist yet. This can be just like the first decorator; however, this decorator is just for a small window of a page.

NOTE The child decorator can be used to apply layouts to smaller components such as forms or portal windows.

```
[decorators/window.jsp]
<%@ taglib uri="sitemesh-decorator" prefix="decorator" %>
<table class="window">
  <tr>
    <th><img src="snazzy.gif"><decorator:title/></th>
  </tr>
  <tr>
    <td>
      <decorator:body/>
    </td>
  </tr>
</table>
```

In order for SiteMesh to know where this decorator is located, an entry is made to `decorators.xml`. However, because this decorator is not to be applied to a page, we leave the pattern matching out. When building the parent decorator, we can explicitly state which child decorator is to be used.

```
[WEB-INF/decorators.xml]
<decorators>

  <decorator name="simple" page="decorators/simple.jsp">
    <pattern>*</pattern>
  </decorator>

  <decorator name="window" page="decorators/window.jsp"/>

</decorators>
```

Finally, the parent decorator is modified to contain the reference to the child component. The `<page:applyDecorator>` tag includes another component and applies the new decorator to it.

```
[decorators/simple.jsp]
<%@ taglib uri="sitemesh-decorator" prefix="decorator" %>
<%@ taglib uri="sitemesh-page" prefix="page" %>
<html>
  <head>
    <title><decorator:title/></title>
    <link rel="stylesheet" href="style.css">
    <decorator:head/>
  </head>
  <body>
    <table width="100%">
      <tr>
        <td class="title" colspan="2">
          <decorator:title/>
        </td>
      </tr>
      <tr>
        <td class="body" valign="top">
          <decorator:body/>
        </td>
        <td valign="top">

          <page:applyDecorator name="window" page="login.jsp"/>

        </td>
      </tr>
    </table>
  </body>
</html>
```

NOTE Although the included `login.jsp` is a full HTML document, only the actual body of it is displayed in the page. This means that text outside of the `<body>` tag will not be displayed in the final page, as shown in Figure 7.11.

Another approach we can take to inserting a composite component is to apply a decorator to an inline fragment of page by providing a body to the `<page:applyDecorator>` tag. The body of the content is obtained from the body of the tag, and the title is passed in as an attribute (see Figure 7.12).

```
[decorators/simple.jsp]
...
<td valign="top">

  <page:applyDecorator name="window" page="login.jsp"/>

  <page:applyDecorator name="window" title="Disclaimer">
    This site is not legally binding in any way. <br>
    All rights reserved. Elvis has left the building.
  </page:applyDecorator>

</td>
...
```

Figure 7.11   Screenshot of final page

Figure 7.12   Final page with inline decorator

Exploring SiteMesh

The fundamentals of SiteMesh are generally enough to be productive with immediately; however, it is useful to know a bit more detail about two areas of the system: how to get to content from decorators and how the correct decorator is selected for the page.

Getting to the Content

Let's examine in more detail how the content and layout pages are merged. SiteMesh has a `PageParser` object that takes the data outputted by the content page and parses it into a `Page` object. This `Page` object is later made available to the decorator page.

> **NOTE** The parser in SiteMesh has been built with one thing in mind: performance. The actual overhead and time added to a request is minimal, making it feasible to use SiteMesh in sites that receive heavy traffic. The performance bottlenecks in a Web application are typically caused by network latency such as the incoming HTTP request, database queries, or RPC calls.

Any data held in the Page object can be inserted into the decorator, either via the decorator JSP tag library or by programmatically accessing the object, which is stored as an attribute in the HTTP request.

As well as the head, title, and body, a page has a number of keyed properties associated with it that allow data to be passed from the content to the decorator using HTML tags.

An example of a property the decorator can access is an HTML <meta> tag. This is a standard HTML tag that can appear in the <head> of a document, which is used to attach meta-data to the document. Every <meta> tag that appears in the content is available to the decorator.

To demonstrate this, we will create a decorator that displays the title and author of each page as part of the layout. Suppose a content page has the following header:

```
<html>
  <head>
    <title>Press Release</title>
    <meta name="author" content="Jaimie Calderwood">
  </head>
  . . .
```

A decorator can access both the title and author properties using the JSP tags:

```
<%@ tablib uri="sitemesh-decorator" prefix="decorator" %>
. . .
<b>Title:</b>  <decorator:title/> <br>
<b>Author:</b> <decorator:getProperty property="meta.author"/> <br>
. . .
```

Alternatively, the properties can be accessed using the Page object. To make this available to the JSP page as a scriptlet, the <decorator:useHtmlPage> tag is used. This is useful if more complicated logic is required (such as conditionals or string manipulations). The following snippet is functionally identical to the previous snippet:

```
<%@ tablib uri="sitemesh-decorator" prefix="decorator" %>
. . .
<decorator:useHtmlPage id="content"/>
<b>Title:</b>  <%= content.getTitle() %> <br>
<b>Author:</b> <%= content.getProperty("meta.author") %> <br>
. . .
```

The output from this decorator, once the content has been merged in, will thus look like the following:

```
<b>Title:</b>  Press Release <br>
<b>Author:</b> Jaimie Calderwood <br>
```

Table 7.1 lists the common operations for retrieving the data contained in the content from the decorator. It lists the Java methods and JSP tag equivalents — you can use either.

The following properties can be retrieved from the content:

- Content of the <meta> tags.

- Attributes of the <body> tag.

- The content of the SiteMesh-specific <parameter> and <content> tags.

This is better illustrated by looking at an example piece of HTML:

```
<html>
  <head>
    <title>The title</title>
    <meta name="author" content="Somebody">
    <meta name="category" content="News">
  </head>
  <body onload="alert('hi')">

    <parameter name="icon" value="urgent.gif">

    <p>Hello world</p>

    <content tag="summary">
      Short summary
    </content>
  </body>
</html>
```

Table 7.1   Accessing Data from the Page Object

JAVA METHOD	JSP TAG	DESCRIPTION OF CONTENT
String getTitle()	<decorator:title [default="..."]/>	Retrieve the value of the <title> tag. If content does not have a title, default will be substituted.
void writeHead(OutputStream out)	<decorator:head/>	Write the contents of the <head> tag, excluding the title.
void writeBody(OutputStream out)	<decorator:body/>	Write the contents of the <body> tag.
String getProperty(String key)	<decorator: getProperty property="..." [default="..."]/>	Retrieve the value of a specific property in the page. If the property does not exist, default will be substituted.
Map getProperties()		Retrieve all key/value properties of the page.

With this content, the following properties will be available in the `Page` object:

```
meta.author    = Somebody
meta.category  = News
body.onload    = alert('hi')
page.icon      = urgent.gif
page.summary   = Short summary
```

Passing properties around this way allows pages to pass data to the layout. An example of this is a page specifying the category of the site it is in by using a <meta> tag so that the decorator can adjust the color scheme accordingly.

Mapping Decorators

Recall that after a page has been parsed, a `DecoratorMapper` (hereafter referred to as a *mapper*) is queried to determine which decorator to apply to the content. SiteMesh has the ability to plug in additional mappers to allow custom rules to define how a decorator is selected.

Mappers can be chained together, allowing a mapper to select a decorator or, if it cannot, to delegate to another mapper. This relationship is known as the *Chain of Command* design pattern.

SiteMesh is bundled with a collection of useful mappers in the com `.opensymphony.module.sitemesh.mappers` package. These mappers are described in Table 7.2.

Table 7.2 DecoratorMappers Bundled with SiteMesh

CLASSNAME	DESCRIPTION
ConfigDecoratorMapper	Reads the `decorators.xml` file to select a decorator based on a URL pattern.
FrameSetDecoratorMapper	Ensures that HTML pages containing a `<frameset>` tag are not decorated.
PageDecoratorMapper	Allows a content page to choose its own decorator by specifying a `<meta name="decorator" content="...">` tag.
PrintableDecoratorMapper	If a URL is requested with `printable=true` as a parameter, this mapper forces the use of the decorator named `"printable"`. This is typically used to serve up printer-friendly versions of pages.

Table 7.2 *(continued)*

CLASSNAME	DESCRIPTION
AgentDecoratorMapper	Allows alternative decorators to be used depending on the type of browser accessing the site. For example, a specialized decorator could be served if the visitor is using Internet Explorer.
OSDecoratorMapper	Allows alternative decorators to be used depending on the operating system that the browser accessing the site is running on.
LanguageDecoratorMapper	Allows alternative decorators to be used depending on the language settings of the browser accessing the site.
RobotDecoratorMapper	Allows a specialized decorator to be served if the site visitor is a search engine robot. Generally, it is friendlier on the robot if minimal layout HTML is returned, thereby maximizing the effectiveness of the content.

By default, SiteMesh has the following `DecoratorMappers` setup (chained in the same order):

- `PageDecoratorMapper`
- `FrameSetDecoratorMapper`
- `PrintableDecoratorMapper`
- `ConfigDecoratorMapper`

To add new decorators to the chain, the SiteMesh configuration file must be modified. The default SiteMesh configuration is stored inside `sitemesh.jar` in a file named `sitemesh-default.xml`. If this file is copied to the `WEB-INF` directory and renamed to `sitemesh.xml`, SiteMesh will read its configuration from there instead.

Implementing custom mappers is beyond the scope of this book. More information on custom mappers can be found at the SiteMesh Web site: `http://www.opensymphony.com/sitemesh`.

Using Tips and Tricks

SiteMesh is a very flexible tool, and as such some best practices have developed over time as to how to get the most value out of it. The following sections briefly look at some of those practices to use SiteMesh optimally within your application.

Group Decorators Together

It often makes sense to group decorators and their included files into a single directory tree (such as /decorators) within your Web application. This helps to mentally differentiate between presentation and content.

Don't Be Afraid to Include

SiteMesh doesn't replace server-side includes; it makes them componentized. Includes are still useful when using SiteMesh! For example, often you will have multiple decorators for your application, all of which include a common footer — perhaps containing legal and copyright information. It makes sense, then, to put this common information into a single JSP file and include it from each of your decorators.

The important thing is to ensure all files containing HTML (whether from a content page, a decorator, or include) contain valid HTML (that is, well-balanced tags).

Following is an example of a good include:

```
<div class="someStyle">
  <b>Disclaimer: All facts on this site are fictional.</b>
</div>
```

And the following is an example of a bad include (the HTML is not well formed):

```
    </td>
  </tr>
  <tr>
    <td>
      <div class="someStyle">
        <b>Disclaimer: All facts on this site are fictional.</b>
      </div>
    </td>
```

CSS Is Your Friend

These days, all graphical browsers support Cascading Style Sheets (CSS). Your application can benefit from having a common style sheet (or perhaps a set of style sheets if your application is large) to provide a common stylistic look and feel to each of the elements on the page, such as form controls and text sizes.

Because the content and presentation are combined into a single resulting HTML page, using CSS with SiteMesh helps tie the two layers together nicely. The same style sheet will be decorating both (as they produce one page) so fonts and colors flow seamlessly between the layers.

We will discuss CSS, as well as other tools to help with look and feel, in more detail in Chapter 17.

Minimize HTML

As a general rule, try to keep your HTML code as simple as possible — in both tiers. Beyond the KISS (Keep It Simple, Stupid!) principle, writing simple HTML helps in the content layer by making it easier to decorate with a decorator.

Separate Your Concerns

It is uncommon to meet people with both excellent development skills and excellent Web-design skills. Development and design are very different tasks; hence your company hired different people to do them.

SiteMesh separates the concerns of layout from the concerns of content, enabling different people to specialize in different layers without stepping on each other's toes.

SiteMesh also makes it easier for different tools to be used for the two layers. For example, it may be preferable to use a Java-aware IDE to edit the JSPs containing the content, whilst a more graphical WYSIWYG tool can be used for layout.

Summary

In this chapter, we've outlined the problems with mixing layout and content code in pages — namely, that it causes duplication and makes it very hard to maintain. We looked at how server-side includes can help but only to an extent.

We then took a step back and analyzed how we could solve the problem in an object-oriented world. We identified how the decorator design pattern can be used to separate layout from content and how the composite design pattern can be used to break pages into discrete components that can be arranged in a nested structure.

We used SiteMesh to actually map these OO solutions to an HTML-based application, which allows us to create decorators in HTML that are easy to maintain. This results in a clean separation between layout and content that is easier to maintain.

We then looked in more detail at how SiteMesh parses content pages and how decorators are mapped to page. Finally, we looked at some techniques to help get the most out of SiteMesh.

Breaking the pages down into smaller components allows for components to focus on specific problems, similar to how we tackle complicated problems with OO. These finer-grained components can then be assembled together to produce the final pages of a Web application. While there are still many problems to deal with in a Web application, this simplifies one of them, allowing more time to be spent on the tougher problems.

CHAPTER 8

Adding Search Capabilities with Lucene

This chapter shows you how you can add sophisticated free text-based search operations to your application — similar to that you'd find in search engines found on the Web.

The first part of the chapter outlines some of the complexities of searching and introduces Lucene. Then you learn how to index data and perform simple queries by adding search support to the ContactInfo example we developed in Chapter 5. Finally, you will learn how to perform more sophisticated queries.

Understanding the Complexities of Searching

Any enterprise application should provide searching capabilities; otherwise, users would drown in information stored in these systems. Searching provides a convenient way of getting the desired data out of these systems. However, implementing searching can often get quite tricky.

The most common tool to aid in searching is SQL. SQL is good for simple structured searches (such as find all employees born in the sixties who work in the accounting department, ordered by last name). However, SQL often reaches its limits quickly, particularly when related to *fuzzy* text searching, large criteria sets, and ranking. SQL is also tied strongly to data stored in relational databases — which may not always be the case.

The common problems associated with searching are:

- *How do you search for the data with maximum speed and minimum overhead?* — We should respond to queries instantly. Users don't want to wait days for the result of a query. In fact, they don't even want to wait seconds — they want the results now. This means we should store the data in a format that is searchable with maximum speed and retrieves only the minimum amount of data required.

- *How do you handle queries in a user-friendly way?* — When you're searching, you expect to be able to perform case-sensitive and case-insensitive searches. You also expect to be able to search for an exact phrase or only part of a phrase. And, when you are searching the content of a document, you want the system to handle grammatical differences of nouns and verbs and return what you meant to search. It should suppress meaningless common words such as "that" and "an" and so on (known as *stop* words). Similar words should also be detected. How do you get a search for "priority" to yield results containing 'priorit*ies*'? It is also desirable to build searches from binary operators (and, or, not).

- *How do you rank results?* — If a search query returns hundreds of results, these need to be ordered with the most relevant matches first.

- *How do you search through heterogeneous document types?* — The data to be searched may be a combination of plain text, HTML, PDF documents, XML, or properties of plain old Java objects. These may be stored in memory, files, a relational database, or an LDAP server. How can a single search retrieve data from all of these sources?

Fortunately, Lucene is here to help us to overcome these obstacles.

Introducing Lucene

Lucene is a free, Open Source, high performance, and full-featured text search engine written entirely in Java and available from `http://jakarta.apache.org/lucene/`.

Lucene addresses all of the previously mentioned problems, providing a simple, yet powerful, API that can be customized for many specific needs. On top of that, Lucene boasts impressive performance even with very large amounts of data.

Understanding the Elements of Lucene

Performing a full text search in Lucene involves two steps:

- *Setting up indexes* — The data should be indexed so that Lucene can later perform efficient queries over them.

- *Creating queries and running them* — To perform a full text search, the query should be created and parsed. Then it should be run over the indexes. The found hits are returned and used by the application.

Lucene's API makes it easy to do this. Here is a bird's eye view of Lucene's API:

- *Document* — Represents an item to be searched. This can be built up from any data. A Document contains a set of named *Fields*.
- *Analyzer* — Breaks the data of a Document down into tokens that can be efficiently indexed.
- *IndexWriter* — Used for creating indexes. An Index contains the analyzed tokens from Documents, designed in a manner that is fast to query.
- *IndexReader* — Used to access the index and to perform low-level operations on it.
- *IndexSearcher* — Used for performing queries on the IndexReader.

So let's enhance the sample application we've developed in Chapter 5 and add indexing and searching to it. We will provide full text searching on the first names and last names of the contacts.

NOTE Often, there is confusion as to what Lucene is. Just as we said, it does only two things: creates indexes and searches those indexes. It does not automatically index any type of content. That means if you want Word documents, PDFs, or HTML files to be indexed, it is up to you to parse those various data formats and then pass the raw data strings to Lucene. There are numerous libraries available that can make this easier — see the Lucene Web site.

Indexing a Document

The first thing we must do is build an index of the ContactInfo instances. To build the index, an instance of Lucene's IndexWriter class is required. This class is the gateway to Lucene's indexing capabilities and allows searchable data to be written to an index.

We will create a utility class called ContactInfoSearcher for dealing with different aspects of indexing and searching for the ContactInfo objects. The following lines of code create an IndexWriter instance, which will be used by other methods of ContactInfoSearcher to perform indexing:

```
public class ContactInfoSearcher {

    String indexDir = "index"; // directory storing index files
```

```
        private IndexWriter openIndexWriter() throws IOException {
            Analyzer analyzer = new StandardAnalyzer();

            return new IndexWriter(indexDir, analyzer, true);
        }
    }
```

The `openIndexWriter` method is a simple utility method that creates an IndexWriter. Index files are created in the folder that indexDir points to, which is a directory named `index` under the current working directory. If the directory doesn't already exist, Lucene creates it for you.

The second parameter of the constructor is an instance of a subclass of analyzer. The analyzer is used for tokenizing text. Lucene comes with various built-in analyzers. Here we use StandardAnalyzer, which removes stop words ("and," "an," and so on) from the token text and normalizes it to lowercase. This is suitable for most English-language text searches.

The last argument tells IndexWriter whether to create a new index from scratch or to add documents to an existing one. Specifying *true* forces a new index to be created.

After creating the index, we build up Documents containing the fields of the ContactInfo to be indexed.

```
    public class ContactInfoSearcher {

        // ...

        private Document buildDocument(ContactInfo contact) {
            Document document= new Document();

            document.add(Field.Keyword("id",
                                     String.valueOf(contact.getId())));

            document.add(Field.Text("firstName", contact.getFirstName()));
            document.add(Field.Text("lastName", contact.getLastName()));

            return document;
        }
```

A Document consists of one or more Fields. A Field contains a key and a value, making a Document similar to a hashtable. The keys and values must be Strings. We added three fields to the preceding code, the first being the ID for the object and the second being standard Java properties.

There are four types of Fields used in Documents. Notice how the ID is of type *keyword*, whereas the firstName and lastName are of type *text*. Depending on the content of the field, you would use a different type. These are the options:

- *Field.Text* — Text fields are tokenized, indexed, and stored in the index. So they can be searched quickly because they are indexed and the content is physically stored in the index files. You shouldn't use Text fields for big data, because they can make the index files larger and larger and, hence, less efficient. We used Text fields for firstName and lastName. Because these two properties are physically stored in the index files and are indexed, we can search on them.

- *Field.UnIndexed* — UnIndexed fields are neither tokenized nor indexed, but their value is physically stored in the index. This field is typically used for storing fields that you need to display with search results, but no search is performed on them. Like Text fields, you should be careful about the size of these fields.

- *Field.Keyword* — Keyword fields are not tokenized, but are indexed and stored in the index. This is useful in cases where the original value of the field should be stored untouched (such as URLs, dates, special names, and so on). We marked id as a Keyword field. The id field actually contains the primary key of the ContactInfo object we're indexing. By storing this id, we can map the search results back to the original ContactInfo instances.

- *Field.UnStored* — UnStored fields are tokenized and indexed, but are not stored in the index. They are useful for indexing large amounts of text that does not need to be retrieved in its original form (such as the bodies of Web pages or long texts).

The final step to building an index is to add the Document to it.

```
public class ContactInfoSearcher {

    // ...
    private Document index(ContactInfo contact)
                                        throws IOException {
        IndexWriter indexWriter = openIndexWriter();
        try {
            Document document = buildDocument(contact);

            writer.addDocument(document);

            writer.optimize();
        } finally {
            writer.close();
        }
    }
}
```

To index the document, simply call the addDocument() method.

After adding a Document, the `optimize()` method is called, which optimizes the index on disk to allow for faster retrieval.

Finally, the writer should be closed when modifications are complete.

The `optimize()` method does not have to be called every time a Document is added. When adding multiple Documents in a large batch, it is more efficient to call `optimize()` at the end of the batch, like this:

```
public class ContactInfoSearcher {
    // ...
    public Document indexBatch(ContactInfo[] contact)
                                            throws IOException {
        IndexWriter indexWriter = openIndexWriter();
        try {
            // index batch
            for (int i = 0; i < contacts.length; i++) {
                Document document = buildDocument(contacts[i]);
                writer.addDocument(document);
            }

            writer.optimize();
        } finally {
            writer.close();
        }
    }
}
```

We now have a class capable of indexing ContactInfo instances. To use it, all we need to do is create a few contacts and pass them in:

```
ContactInfo joe = new ContactInfo();
joe.setFirstName("Joe");
joe.setLastName("Walnes");
joe.setId(1);


ContactInfo ara = new ContactInfo();
ara.setFirstName("Ara");
ara.setLastName("Abrahamian");
ara.setId(2);

ContactInfoSearcher searcher = new ContactInfoSearcher();
searcher.index(joe);
searcher.index(ara);
```

That's it. A contact is stored in Lucene's index files and is now ready for querying.

It's worth explaining the structure of the indexes Lucene creates. The directory where we decided to store the index files contains many different files. They are grouped together with some prefixes and different extensions.

These groups of files are called *segments*. It's the job of the `optimize()` method of IndexWriter to consolidate different segments and create a more efficient segment.

You might wonder how concurrent access to the index files is handled by Lucene. Lucene locks the index while updating it, so no more than one thread can modify the index at a time. If simultaneous modifications are possible in an application (such as modifying the index in a live Web application), you should make sure you modify only the index from one thread. There are many different ways to handle this. You can use JMS queues, a job scheduler, or any other mechanism.

Searching Documents

Now that we have an index, we should run queries on it. The basic steps are to open an IndexSearcher and pass in a Query object, which returns Hits as a result.

```
public class ContactInfoSearcher {

    String indexDir = "index"; // directory storing index files

    public Hits search(String fieldname, String criteria)
                                throws ParseException, IOException {
        // open IndexSearcher
        IndexSearcher searcher = new IndexSearcher(indexDir);

        try {
            Query query = buildQuery(fieldname, criteria);
            hits = searcher.search(query);
        } finally {
            searcher.close();
        }
    }
```

The Query object is created by the `buildQuery()` method that follows:

```
public class ContactInfoSearcher {

    // ...

    private Query buildQuery(String fieldname, String criteria)
                                throws ParseException {
        Analyzer analyzer = new StandardAnalyzer();
        QueryParser parser = new QueryParser(fieldName, analyzer);
        return parser.parse(criteria);
    }
```

To build the Query, an analyzer is required. This should be the same type of analyzer as used when building the index in the first place. A QueryParser is then responsible for taking a String of search terms and converting that into a Query.

To build a Query, two inputs are required — the *fieldName* and the *criteria*. The fieldName specifies which field to search through and the criteria is the actual term to look for. If the criteria are not formed correctly, a ParseException is thrown.

The returned Hits object contains the results of the query. The results are ordered based on rank (that is, the closest-matching search first). Table 8.1 lists the most frequently used methods of Hit.

That's the code for the searching complete. This is how the class can be used:

```
ContactInfoSearcher searcher = new ContactInfoSearcher();
// perform search
Hits hits = searcher.search("firstName", "joe or fred");

if (hits.length() == 0) {

    // no results found
    System.out.println("No results found");

} else {

    // iterate over results
    for(int i = 0; i < hits.length(); i++) {
        Document document = hits.doc(i);
        System.out.println("--- Result " + i);
        System.out.println("First Name: " + document.get("firstName"));
        System.out.println("Last Name : " + document.get("lastName"));
        System.out.println("ID        : " + document.get("id"));
        System.out.println("Score     : " + hits.score(i));
    }

}
```

Note that the query is "joe or fred." This will match the contact with a first-Name of "Joe."

Table 8.1   Frequently Used Methods of Hit

METHOD	DESCRIPTION OF RETURN VALUE
int length()	The number of results returned by the search.
Document doc(int n)	Fetch the *nth* Document in the results.
float score(int n)	Fetch the score of the *nth* hit (between 0 and 1).

Reindexing and Removing an Indexed Document

You've learned how to index and search a document. Now, what if we want to remove a document or update it? Obviously, whenever we remove or update a ContactInfo in the database, the index files should be updated, too.

To remove a Document from the index, we have to read the Index and find the location of the Document.

To read the index, the IndexReader class is used. In order for the Document to be located in the index, you must supply a Term. This is an exact match of field name and value — a unit of search. The IndexReader provides a convenience method to delete all Documents with a given Term in the document.

We can use the ID of the contact to get an exact match:

```
public class ContactInfoSearcher {
    String indexDir = "index"; // directory storing index files
    public void unIndex (ContactInfo contact) throws IOException {
        IndexReader reader = IndexReader.open(indexDir);
        try {
            Term term = new Term("id", String.valueOf(contact.getId()));

            reader.delete(term);
        } finally {
            reader.close();
        }
    }
}
```

To reindex a Document, all we have to do is unindex it and then index it again.

```
public class ContactInfoSearcher {

    // ...
    public void reIndex(ContactInfo contact) throws IOException {
        unIndex(contact);
        index(contact);
    }
}
```

Note that Lucene does not provide a facility for modifying an indexed document directly, so we have to delete the indexed one and add a new document. That's because updating a document can invalidate the indexes and the segments, so we have to remove and append instead.

Using Advanced Searching

How flexible is Lucene in tokenizing text? So far, we've only tested Standard-Analyzer by searching for "joe or fred." The QueryParser allows for very flexible criteria to be specified. Remember that the criteria are case insensitive and that the actual match can appear anywhere in the text. Table 8.2 demonstrates some of the advanced queries that can be performed.

Table 8.2   Advanced Queries

EXAMPLE	DESCRIPTION
ba*y	Wildcards can be used anywhere within a word, except at the very beginning.
(bert or ernie) and muppet not kermit	Common operators such as AND, OR, NOT are supported. Parentheses for grouping terms are also supported. The other two operators are plus signs (+) and minus signs (-). The plus sign requires an expression to exist in the field. The minus sign is the opposite.
"bert and ernie"	Surrounding words with quotes states that an exact phrase is to be used.
bart~	Fuzzy searches look for words spelled similarly, such as "bert" or "fart."
[apple to cabbage]	Range searches look for any name that falls alphabetically within this range.
"bucket spade"~5	Proximity searches ensure that the two words specified must be within a certain number of words of each other to be included.
lastName:walnes	Search another field of the document.

As you can see, these queries are fairly similar to the way you search in popular search engines found on the Web.

Customizing the Tokenization Process

The way Lucene tokenizes the text is completely dependent on the analyzer chosen. You can tell Lucene how to analyze text by composing a new analyzer out of various TokenFilter classes or by introducing your own Analyzer class. So, for example, if searching for "puppy" should return records with the words "puppy" or "puppies" in it, the StandardAnalyzer is not enough. The StandardAnalyzer only tokenizes the text by splitting the text to tokens; then it converts the tokens to lowercase and removes stop words. But it doesn't do anything for removing morphological endings from words in English. So searching for "puppy" with StandardAnalyzer would not return a result if the indexed text contains "puppies."

We need to set up a new analyzer that does that, too, so we create a new Analyzer class composed of different TokenFilter classes to achieve our goal. Here is our CustomAnalyzer class:

```
public class CustomAnalyzer extends Analyzer {
    /**
     * Processes the input by first converting it to
     * lower case, then by eliminating stop words, and
     * finally by performing Porter stemming on it.
     *
     * @param reader the Reader that provides access to the input text
     * @return an instance of TokenStream
     */
    public TokenStream tokenStream(Reader reader) {
        TokenStream result = null;
        result = new LowerCaseFilter(result);
        result = new StopFilter(result,
                                StopAnalyzer.ENGLISH_STOP_WORDS));
        result = new PorterStemFilter(result);

        return result;
    }
}
```

CustomAnalyzer extends the Analyzer abstract base class and tokenizes the text in a custom way by overriding the `tokenStream()` method. Three different TokenFilter classes are then used:

- *LowerCaseFilter* converts the text to lowercase.

- Then *StopFilter* is applied on the result returned from LowerCaseFilter to remove common English stop words such as *and*, *the*, *my*, and so on.

- Then *PorterStemFilter* is applied on that result to run the Porter algorithm on it, which removes the morphological endings from the tokens.

Lucene comes with a very rich set of built-in Analyzer and TokenFilter classes. Some of these Analyzer classes are GermanAnalyzer, SimpleAnalyzer, StandardAnalyzer, StopAnalyzer, and WhitespaceAnalyzer. Every language has a different set of stop words, and, in this case, the GermanAnalyzer class takes into account common German stop words instead of English stop words. Many different TokenFilter classes are also provided. For a complete list of these TokenFilter and Analyzer classes, refer to Lucene's documentation.

To use this new analyzer, replace all occurrences of StandardAnalyzer with CustomAnalyzer in ContactInfoSearcher, and you'll have a cleverer searching algorithm.

TIP If you change the anaylzer, you should rebuild the entire index so the documents can be tokenized effectively.

LUCENE VS. SQL SELECT OR OBJECT QUERY LANGUAGES

Weren't SQL SELECT statements designed for finding data out of a pile of data? Well, yes, but they have many limitations for performing full text searches. Even SQL LIKE keyword is not flexible enough for these kinds of searches. LIKE is not designed to handle full text searches. It doesn't know about common words such as "that" and "an." It can't treat different grammatical forms of words at all. It can even be slow because of joining tables, calling SQL functions, or loading too much data. Object query languages, such as Hibernate's query language, are another option, but in the end they also execute SQL statements, so they bear the same limitations.

Furthermore, not all SQL queries work on all databases, so portability can become a problem. For example, the LIKE operator is not supported by all vendors. Likewise, the syntax for outer joins might vary from database to database. Rather than trying to support the various incarnations of SQL, using Lucene for searching might be a better approach.

Summary

In this chapter, we've outlined the complexities of searching. We learned about Lucene and its differences with SQL SELECT queries. We learned that working with Lucene consists of two main phases: indexing documents and searching them. We learned how to index, re-index, and remove indexes, and how they are stored on hard disk. We learned about different kinds of Fields and suitable uses of each of them. Then we searched the indexes we've created with simple and complex queries. Finally, we learned how to create a custom Analyzer class and how to use TokenFilters.

CHAPTER 9

Generating Configuration Files with XDoclet

This chapter looks at how mundane artifacts such as configuration files can be autogenerated using XDoclet to add attributes to your source code. This takes a lot of the hard work out of repetitive tasks and ensures that these artifacts are kept in sync with your ever-changing code base.

Introducing XDoclet

XDoclet is a free Open Source tool for code generation and attribute oriented programming (not to be confused with *aspect* oriented programming). It's available from `http://xdoclet.sf.net/`.

XDoclet has two facets:

- Generates any kind of source code or any other kind of file — usually code or configuration files that do not necessarily need to be written by hand. You can use it to generate source code from other source code or from other external resources such as a database. For example, you can generate remote interfaces for EJB components as well as `ejb-jar.xml` deployment descriptor files for EJB applications.

- Drives the code-generation process through the use of its *Attributed Oriented Programming* facilities. This means that to have XDoclet generate all the artifacts of an EJB component, such as remote and local interfaces as well as the deployment descriptor, you must place attributes on the desired classes and methods that are relevant to the artifacts you want to generate. Those attributes act as metadata for describing the necessary information that relates to those classes and methods. XDoclet can then use this metadata to accurately generate deployment descriptors, other code, configuration files, or just about anything else that can be automatically generated but that you've previously done by hand.

XDoclet was originally called EJBDoclet because it was created to tackle the tough issue of generating EJB artifacts. Later, it was generalized to handle any code-generation task, but it's still very popular among EJB developers. This chapter does not discuss the EJB generation features of XDoclet, but rather focuses on basic concepts of XDoclet and how it can be used for generating Hibernate's configuration files.

Understanding Attribute Oriented Programming with XDoclet

In Chapter 5, we learn that Hibernate uses XML configuration files to store the object-relational mapping information. For the ContactInfo class we develop in Chapter 5, we first create by hand a mapping file like this:

```xml
<?xml version="1.0"?>
<!DOCTYPE hibernate-mapping PUBLIC
    "-//Hibernate/Hibernate Mapping DTD//EN"
    "http://hibernate.sourceforge.net/hibernate-mapping.dtd">

<hibernate-mapping>
    <class name="contacts.ContactInfo" table="CONTACTS">
        <id name="id" column="PK" >
            <generator class="vm.long">
            </generator>
        </id>

        <property name="firstName" column="FNAME" length="30"/>
        <property name="lastName" column="LNAME" length="50"/>

        <component name="phone">
            <property name="areaCode"
                    column="PHONE_AREA_CODE" length="3"/>
            <property name="countryCode"
                    column="PHONE_COUNTRY_CODE" length="5"/>
            <property name="number" column="PHONE_NUMBER" length="4"/>
        </component>
    </class>
</hibernate-mapping>
```

It's obvious that this file is human readable and easily understandable, but, in the long run, it becomes harder to keep this file updated with all the changes and refactorings during development. That's where XDoclet comes to the rescue. Instead of keeping this file up to date by hand, we use XDoclet and a set of @hibernate tags right in the source code of the ContactInfo class. We use the @hibernate.class tag to define the mapping for this class like this:

```
/**
 * @hibernate.class table="CONTACTS"
 */
public class ContactInfo {
```

This tag serves two purposes. Primarily, it's used to drive the code-generation process. The presence of the @hibernate.class tag tells XDoclet to generate the corresponding `ContactInfo.hbm.xml` file for this class. The tag is also used for putting extra metadata on the class. The table parameter tells XDoclet about the table that this class maps to. Many class-level tags (such as @hibernate.class in the case of a Hibernate persistable class, or @ejb.bean in the case of an EJB bean) act as markers that drive the code-generation process. They tell XDoclet that it should generate some artifact. Without these "driver" tags, all other XDoclet tags relating to hibernate (@hibernate.*) would be ignored in this file.

For a property like firstName, we put the @hibernate.property tag on the `getFirstName()` method:

```
/**
 * @hibernate.property column="FNAME" length="30"
 */
public String getFirstName() {
```

As you can guess, each of these attributes maps to one of the XML elements that we hand-code in Chapter 5. Here, @hibernate.property is used by XDoclet to generate a `<property/>` element in the mapping file.

Finally, @hibernate.id and @hibernate.component define the property as an ID and component, respectively, like this:

```
/**
 * @hibernate.id column="PK" generator-class="vm.long"
 */
public long getId() {
...
/**
 * @hibernate.component
 */
public PhoneNumber getPhone() {
```

Note that with this technique we don't have to supply the class attribute of the `<component/>` element, for example. XDoclet extracts the fully qualified class name from the return type of the `getPhone()` method.

TIP As you can see, you can use attributes instead of marker interfaces. One of the famous marker interfaces of Java is java.io.Serializable. A class implementing this marker interface is considered serializable by Java's IO framework. A compile time code-generation tool such as XDoclet instead relies on @tags to mark classes. The next version of JDK, version 1.5, will have built-in runtime attributes support. Like XDoclet, you will be able to mark code with attributes and add metadata to them, and those attributes will be easily accessible in runtime via a simple API. This does not mean that XDoclet will become obsolete when Java 1.5 comes out because the code and configuration generation is still incredibly important.

Understanding the Syntax of Attributes

XDoclet attributes are normal Javadoc tags. They should be contained, /** and */, and they start with an @ sign in front of them. A common error is to use /* instead of /**, which is invalid Javadoc format; as such, XDoclet doesn't recognize them. The following code won't generate anything, because the comment block doesn't start with /**.

```
/*
 * @hibernate.class table="CONTACTS"
 */
public class ContactInfo {
```

Almost all attributes adhere to @<namespace>.<tag> convention. Namespaces serve only as a grouping facility and prevent any name collision between attributes defined by different parties. It's also possible to use the @<namespace>:<tag> syntax, though this form is deprecated.

Attribute parameters come right after the @tag definition. These formats are valid:

```
/**
 * @namespace.tag param1="value1" param2="value2"
 */
```

You can break parameters into lines too, but don't forget the * sign at the start of each line:

```
/**
 * @namespace.tag param1="value1"
```

```
 *                   param2="value2"
 */
```

If an attribute supports only one parameter (unlike @hibernate.class that supports many parameters, such as table and proxy), you can skip writing the parameter name and write the value of the parameter right after the @tag definition:

```
/**
 * @namespace.tag "value1"
 */
```

And even this syntax is valid, provided that the value doesn't have any blank characters in it:

```
/**
 * @namespace.tag value1
 */
```

If a parameter value has a quote in it, you should escape it:

```
/**
 * @namespace.tag param="the value is \"bla\""
 */
```

Just like methods, constructors, and fields, XDoclet tags are inherited by subclasses. If you put a @hibernate.class tag on a base class, all subclasses will also inherit that tag, as well as its parameters. This provides a good way to define common metadata in a base class, instead of duplicating attribute values in all subclasses. For example, if you have an abstract BaseEntityObject EJB that all the entity beans of the system extend from, you can simply put a @ejb.bean attribute on the header of BaseEntityObject, and all subclasses automatically inherit it. They don't have to define the tag again to be recognized by XDoclet as EJB classes. Thus, the "driver" attribute is no longer needed directly but is instead picked up from superclasses.

Attribute parameters tags are also inherited, but can be overridden. So a Person class is defined like this:

```
/**
 * @hibernate.class table="PERSONS" mutable="false"
 */
public class Person {
```

You may have an Employee class derived from it that should be stored in an EMPLOYEES table instead of the PERSONS table defined in the Person class. You can override the table parameter like this:

```
/**
 * @hibernate.class table="EMPLOYEES"
 */
public class Personnel extends Person {
```

Note that the rest of the parameters are automatically inherited. The mutable parameter of Person is inherited by Personnel, even though the table parameter was overridden and its value was changed. You can use this approach to remove @tag duplication from the code and put common parameters on super-classes.

It's worth mentioning that some third-party tools and plugins exist that provide visual editing of XDoclet tags. Some of them are IDE plugins that provide smart autocompletion and validation for any XDoclet module. You can find an always up-to-date list of these tools on the XDoclet Web site.

Running XDoclet

XDoclet is typically executed from an Ant build script. For our sample application, we create a simple Ant `build.xml` file like this:

```xml
<project name="contacts" default="all">

    <property name="src.java"      location="src/java"/>

    <property name="build.dir"     location="build"/>
    <property name="build.java"    location="build/java"/>

    <path id="classpath.build">
        <fileset dir="lib/runtime"/>
        <fileset dir="lib/build"/>
    </path>
    <path id="classpath.runtime">
        <fileset dir="lib/runtime"/>
    </path>

    <target name="java" description="Compile Java">
        <mkdir dir="${build.java}"/>
        <javac srcdir="${src.java}"
               destdir="${build.java}"
               classpathref="classpath.build"
               debug="true"/>
        <copy todir="${build.java}">
            <fileset dir="${src.java}">
                <exclude name="**/*.java"/>
            </fileset>
        </copy>
    </target>
```

```
<target name="config" depends="java"
        description="Generate hbm files">
    <taskdef name="hibernatedoclet" classpathref="classpath.build"
        classname="xdoclet.modules.hibernate.HibernateDocletTask"/>
    <hibernatedoclet destDir="${build.java}">
        <fileset dir="${src.java}">
            <include name="**/*.java"/>
        </fileset>
        <hibernate version="2.0"/>
    </hibernatedoclet>
    <copy todir="${build.java}">
        <fileset dir="${src.java}" includes="**/*.xml"/>
    </copy>
</target>

<target name="all" depends="clean,config"/>

<target name="clean" description="Clean up built files">
    <delete dir="${build.dir}"/>
</target>

</project>
```

NOTE This book does not go into the details of Ant. For further reading, see *Java Development with Ant*, by Erik Hatcher, (Greenwich, Conn.: Manning Publications Company, 2002).

The two main targets of this build script are java and config targets. The first one compiles all java files, and the second one runs XDoclet to generate the Hibernate mapping files. When we run Ant, it runs the default target, which is the *all* target, but because this target depends on clean and config targets first, those targets are run. The *config* target itself depends on the *java* target, so that before creating the XML mapping files, all sources are compiled.

XDoclet is configured as shown here:

```
<taskdef name="hibernatedoclet" classpathref="classpath.build"
        classname="xdoclet.modules.hibernate.HibernateDocletTask"/>
<hibernatedoclet destDir="${build.java}">
    <fileset dir="${src.java}">
        <include name="**/*.java"/>
    </fileset>
    <hibernate version="2.0"/>
</hibernatedoclet>
```

The taskdef tag introduces the hibernatedoclet task to Ant. Ant comes with several built-in tasks such as javac, copy, and mkdir. XDoclet is a separate standalone product with its own Ant tasks, so we need to introduce it to Ant.

Notice the use of the xdoclet.modules.hibernate.HibernateDocletTask class in the taskdef. XDoclet has various tasks for different jobs. HibernateDoclet-Task adds the functionality of generating Hibernate artifacts to XDoclet. Various other tasks also exist (for example, EjbDoclet for generating many different EJB artifacts).

The classpathref attribute defines the classpath of the task. The classpath is where Ant looks to find the specified task class with all its dependencies. For running hibernatedoclet, we need these jar files:

```
contacts\lib\build\xdoclet-xjavadoc.jar

contacts\lib\build\xdoclet.jar

contacts\lib\build\xdoclet-hibernate-module.jar
```

The core of XDoclet is defined in the xdoclet.jar, but it also needs another core piece of it, XJavadoc, which is bundled in the xdoclet-xjavadoc.jar. XJavadoc is responsible for parsing java files and extracting the @tags from them. XDoclet uses what XJavadoc produces. As we mentioned, XDoclet has support for generating many different things. For each of these distinct jobs, an XDoclet module exists. For this application, we must use XDoclet's Hibernate module, so we add xdoclet-hibernate-module.jar to our classpath, too.

With all these dependencies resolved, we can run XDoclet's hibernatedoclet task by putting a <hibernatedoclet/> element in. The fileset-nested element of hibernatedoclet tells it where the source files are and which of them should be analyzed by XDoclet, which is all of the java files underneath the src/java directory. Finally, <hibernate version="2.0"/> runs the hibernate subtask of the hibernatedoclet task. Each of the XDoclet tasks may have many subtasks. hibernatedoclet has only a single <hibernate/> subtask, but the ejbdoclet task, for example, has many subtasks such as <remoteinterface/> and <deploymentdescriptor/>. Both tasks and subtasks define some configuration properties. The version property of the <hibernate/> subtask tells it to generate Hibernate version 2.0 mapping files.

Now we are ready to run Ant. By running it from the console, we get an output like this:

```
C:\contacts>ant
Buildfile: build.xml

clean:

java:
    [mkdir] Created dir: C:\contacts\build\java
    [javac] Compiling 7 source files to C:\contacts\build\java

config:
```

```
[hibernatedoclet] [INFO] start - -Running <hibernate/>
[hibernatedoclet] Generating mapping file for contacts.ContactInfo.
[hibernatedoclet]    contacts.ContactInfo

all:

BUILD SUCCESSFUL
```

All targets are executed one after each other based on the dependency of targets. The config target is also run, which runs the hibernatedoclet task and its `<hibernate/>` subtask that generates the mapping files for all of our persistent classes marked with @hibernate tags.

It's worth noting that running XDoclet from Ant is not the only way of running it, but it's the preferred way of doing it. An automated build process with Ant provides Continuous Integration for the application.

Martin Fowler popularized the term *Continuous Integration*, "an automated basis on which the application is built and tested automatically and periodically to catch any bugs or broken tests earlier."

Adding XDoclet to the build process adds another step to the Continuous Integration phase. By running XDoclet as a part of the build, we produce up-to-date artifacts from the XDoclet metadata. If an attribute is misconfigured or outdated because of a source-code change, the next run of the build will catch it.

Using Advanced Hibernate OR Mapping with XDoclet

In the previous parts of this chapter, we learned how to use basic @hibernate tags such as @hibernate.class and @hibernate.property. We also learned how to run XDoclet from within Ant. Now we will learn how to use XDoclet to define the object-relational mapping for Hibernate relations and joined subclasses.

In Chapter 5, we create two classes in addition to ContactInfo: Folder and OwnedFolder. Folder is a persistable object that has a unidirectional one-to-many aggregation to nested Folder objects. It also has a many-to-many association with contained ContactInfo objects. OwnedFolder derives from it, and this hierarchy is mapped to a database with a table-per-class-hierarchy strategy. The Folder class itself is annotated like this:

```
/**
 * @hibernate.class table="FOLDERS" discriminator-value="Normal"
 * @hibernate.discriminator    column="TYPE"
 */
public class Folder {
```

Most @hibernate tags map directly to elements with corresponding names in the mapping file. From the previous attributes, this piece of XML is generated by XDoclet:

```
<hibernate-mapping>
    <class
        name="contacts.Folder"
        table="FOLDERS"
        dynamic-update="false"
        discriminator-value="Normal"
    >

        <discriminator
            column="TYPE"
            type="string"
        />
```

It's roughly the same mapping file that we create in Chapter 5 by hand. In this case, the formatting is a bit different and XDoclet adds some default values for some attributes.

OwnedFolder is annotated with the following tags:

```
/**
 * @hibernate.subclass    discriminator-value="Owned"
 */
public class OwnedFolder extends Folder {
```

Here again, the @hibernate.subclass tag maps directly to the `<subclass>` element of the mapping file and the discriminator-value parameter defines the value of its discriminator-value attribute.

All primitive properties of these two classes and their ID fields are also defined by using the @hibernate.property and @hibernate.id attribute like ContactInfo.

The mapping metadata for folders property is put on the `getFolders()` method:

```
/**
 * @hibernate.set cascade="all" lazy="true"
 * @hibernate.collection-one-to-many    class="contacts.Folder"
 * @hibernate.collection-key            column="PARENTFOLDER_PK"
 */
public Set getFolders() {
    return folders;
}
```

These attributes and their parameters all map directly to the same elements that we hand-code in Chapter 5. Here is what XDoclet generates from these tags:

```
<set
    name="folders"
    lazy="true"
    inverse="false"
    cascade="all"
>
    <key
        column="PARENTFOLDER_PK"
    />

    <one-to-many
        class="contacts.Folder"
    />
</set>
```

The mapping metadata for the contacts many-to-many association is defined as follows:

```
/**
 * @hibernate.set table="CONTACTS_FOLDER_REL"
 *     cascade="save-update" lazy="true"
 * @hibernate.collection-many-to-many class="contacts.ContactInfo"
 *     column="CONTACT_PK" not-null="false"
 * @hibernate.collection-key column="PARENFOLDERS_PK"
 */
public List getContacts() {
    return contacts;
}
```

Again, thanks to the human readable form of the Hibernate mapping files, these tags translate roughly to the same readable XML elements.

Using XDoclet for Generating More Sophisticated Artifacts

Not all XML files are easily readable like Hibernate mapping files. In case of an `ejb-jar.xml`, one @ejb tag might map to many different XML elements. As an example, suppose we have an Account EJB CMP bean. By putting an @ejb.bean tag, we add some EJB metadata to it:

```
/**
 * @ejb.bean
 *     name="Account"
 *     jndi-name="ejb/bank/Account"
 */
public abstract class AccountBean implements EntityBean {
```

Now the interesting thing is how the single @ejb.bean tag of AccountBean generates a multitude of elements in the `ejb-jar.xml` file:

```
<entity >
    <ejb-name>Account</ejb-name>

    <home>test.interfaces.AccountHome</home>
    <remote>test.interfaces.Account</remote>
    <local-home>test.interfaces.AccountLocalHome</local-home>
    <local>test.interfaces.AccountLocal</local>

    <ejb-class>test.ejb.AccountCMP</ejb-class>
    <persistence-type>Container</persistence-type>
    <prim-key-class>test.interfaces.AccountPK</prim-key-class>
    <reentrant>False</reentrant>
    <cmp-version>2.x</cmp-version>
    <abstract-schema-name>Account</abstract-schema-name>
```

As you can see XDoclet generates a lot of other elements by applying some defaults or by extracting the appropriate information from the source code of the bean itself.

Now, suppose we have a CustomerBean that should have an EJB reference to Account. CustomerBean and the ejb-ref are defined like this:

```
/**
 * @ejb.bean
 *     name="Customer"
 *     jndi-name="bank/Customer"
 * @ejb.ejb-ref
 *     ejb-name="Account"
 *     ref-name="ejb/bank/Account"
 */
public abstract class CustomerBean implements EntityBean {
```

The @ejb.ejb-ref very smartly discovers the other end of the ejb reference and generates the following XML as the result:

```
<ejb-ref >
    <ejb-ref-name>ejb/bank/Account</ejb-ref-name>
    <ejb-ref-type>Entity</ejb-ref-type>
    <home>test.interfaces.AccountHome</home>
    <remote>test.interfaces.Account</remote>
    <ejb-link>Account</ejb-link>
 </ejb-ref>
```

Notice how XDoclet has discovered the other end of the ejb-ref from the ejb-name parameter of @ejb.ejb-ref. XDoclet here has searched for all source codes that have an @ejb.bean declaration with a name parameter of "Account." It then extracted the rest of the metadata such as the home and remote interface name of the referenced EJB from the metadata defined in the referenced Account class. If we were to provide this information by specifying some home, remote, or ejb-link parameters of @ejb.ejb-ref, we would have to duplicate the metadata (which is basically in the metadata of the referenced class itself).

XDoclet can be not only used for generating XML files but Java or JSP source codes, too. In the case of EJB, XDoclet is also used for generating the remote and home interface source files from the bean implementation class and the corresponding @ejb.bean and other attributes. Consider the following Stateful Session Bean implementation class:

```
package test.ejb;

/**
 * @ejb.bean name="Stateful" type="Stateful"
 */
public abstract class StatefulBean implements javax.ejb.SessionBean {
    private String x;

    /**
     * @ejb.interface-method
     */
    public String foobar() {
        return "Foobar";
    }

    /**
     * @ejb.create-method
     */
    public void ejbCreateWithParam(String x) {
        this.x = x;
    }

    /**
     * @ejb.create-method
     */
    public void ejbCreate(String x) {
        this.x = x;
    }
}
```

Each enterprise java bean has a home and remote interface. Without XDoclet, we would have to write those classes by hand, but with XDoclet we can use the <homeinterface/> and <remoteinterface/> subtasks of the <ejbdoclet/> XDoclet

task to generate them for us. This is the generated home interface for Stateful-
Bean:

```
/*
 * Generated by XDoclet - Do not edit!
 */
package test.interfaces;

/**
 * Home interface for Stateful.
 * @xdoclet-generated at 3-06-03
 * @author XDoclet
 * @version 1.2b3-dev
 */
public interface StatefulHome
    extends javax.ejb.EJBHome
{
    public static final String COMP_NAME="java:comp/env/ejb/Stateful";
    public static final String JNDI_NAME="Stateful";

    public test.interfaces.Stateful createWithParam(java.lang.String x)
        throws javax.ejb.CreateException,java.rmi.RemoteException;

    public test.interfaces.Stateful create(java.lang.String x)
        throws javax.ejb.CreateException,java.rmi.RemoteException;
}
```

A StatefulHome interface is generated. Notice how the two EJB `create()`
methods are generated based on their XDoclet annotated counterparts defined
in the StatefulBean class.

Here is the remote interface generated for StatefulBean:

```
/*
 * Generated by XDoclet - Do not edit!
 */
package test.interfaces;

/**
 * Remote interface for Stateful.
 * @xdoclet-generated at 3-06-03
 * @author XDoclet
 * @version 1.2b3-dev
 */
public interface Stateful
    extends javax.ejb.EJBObject
{

    public java.lang.String foobar(  )
        throws java.rmi.RemoteException;
}
```

Again, notice that XDoclet generated the definition of the `foobar()` remote method in this interface, based on the presence of an @ejb.remote-interface attribute on the `foobar()` method of StatefulBean class.

Understanding XDoclet Tasks and Subtasks

XDoclet comes with a rich set of built-in tasks and subtasks. Needless to say, many more of them are available from other independent sources and commercial vendors providing XDoclet support for their products.

Earlier in this chapter, we briefly discussed two of the most popular XDoclet tasks for generating Hibenate and EJB-related artifacts. Here we will provide a matrix of some built-in and popular XDoclet tasks and their subtasks, with a brief explanation for each.

EJBDoclet

Defined in class xdoclet.modules.ejb.EjbDocletTask, this task is a big wrapper for all EJB-related subtasks of XDoclet. All standard attributes are in @ejb namespace. It has the following standard subtasks:

SUBTASK	GENERATES ...
dao	Abstract Data Access Object interfaces
deploymentdescriptor	`ejb-jar.xml`
entitybmp	BMP subclass derived from the abstract bean implementation class, useful for smooth migration from EJB 1.1 to EJB 2.0
entitycmp	CMP subclass derived from the abstract bean implementation class, useful for smooth migration from EJB 1.1 to EJB 2.0
entitypk	Primary key classes
homeinterface	Home interfaces
localhomeinterface	EJB 2.x local home interfaces
localinterface	EJB 2.x local interfaces
remoteinterface	Remote interfaces
session	Session bean classes derived from the abstract bean implementation classes, useful for injecting code to a bean without touching the bean implementation itself
utilobject	Utility objects for home interface lookups from JNDI server
valueobject	Value object classes

There are also many vendor-specific EJB subtasks for various application servers such BEA Weblogic, JBoss, Orion, Sybase, SunOne, Resin, Jonas, Oracle OC4J, Borlans Enterprise Server, Pramati, Macromedia JRun, and who knows what other application servers out there.

WebDoclet

Defined in class xdoclet.modules.web.WebDocletTask, this task is a big wrapper for all Web-tier-related subtasks of XDoclet. It has the following standard subtasks:

SUBTASK	GENERATES ...
jsptaglib	`taglib.tld` files for JSP tag libraries, from @jsp tags
strutsconfig	Jakarta Struts `struts-config.xml` configuration file, from @struts tags
strutsform	Struts Form classes for EJBs, from @struts.form tag
strutsvalidationxml	Jakarta Struts `validation.xml` configuration file, from @struts:validator
webxml	`web.xml`, from @web tags

Like EJBDoclet, WebDoclet has many application-server-specific subtasks.

JMXDoclet

Defined in class xdoclet.modules.jmx.JMXDocletTask, this task is a big wrapper for all JMX-related subtasks of XDoclet. JMX stands for Java Management eXtensions and is a standard for building manageable components. All standard attributes are in @jmx namespace. It has the following standard subtasks:

SUBTASK	GENERATES ...
mlet	`mbeans.mlet` files for JMX beans
mbeaninterface	MBean interfaces for MBeans

JDODoclet

Defined in class xdoclet.modules.jdo.JdoDocletTask, this task is a big wrapper for all JDO-related subtasks of XDoclet. JDO stands for Java Data Objects and is a persistence standard. All standard attributes are in @jdo namespace. It has the following standard subtasks:

SUBTASK	GENERATES . . .
jdometadata	`.jdo` files for persistent classes

Many other subtasks are also provided for vendor-specific extensions of many JDO vendors.

HibernateDoclet

Defined in class xdoclet.modules.hibernate.HibernateDocletTask, this task only has a single `<hibernate>` subtask that is responsible for generating `hbm.xml` mapping files for persistent classes. All attributes are in @hibernate namespace.

Using XDoclet Effectively

Like any technology, using XDoclet also has some pros and cons. Overusing it may cause more damage than good, and misusing it can make the program harder to develop rather than easier to develop. Here we will provide some guidelines for proper use of XDoclet.

First of all, we divide the @attributes into two kinds: *development-oriented* and *deployment-oriented*. There's no concrete rule for deciding whether an @attribute or some of its parameters are among the first set or the second. If you feel that an @attribute belongs to the code and the @attribute adds some meta-data that nicely annotates the source code itself, it's a development-oriented @attribute.

@hibernate.property is an example of a development-oriented attribute. It nicely adds some mapping metadata to properties of persistent classes. The definition of the property and the mapping metadata logically belong to the source code. @ejb.transaction attribute is another development-oriented attribute. The developer in charge of that piece of code has counted on the method belonging to a specific transaction boundary. If we extract this transaction metadata from source code and let any third party modify it, we're changing all the assumptions that the developer of the original code has applied toward the transactional setting of a method.

Some @attributes or some parameters of some @attributes are deployment oriented. They define some of the metadata needed only during deployment of the software. Such metadata is mostly dependent on where and how the application is deployed. The JNDI name of an EJB and database schema name of a Hibernate persistent class are such deployment-focused metadata. The same EJBs are typically deployed with different jndi-names on the servers of a cluster. The database schema name of a Hibernate class is also dependent on the deployer's choice of which database to use for storing the data.

We should avoid putting deployment-oriented metadata in source code; otherwise, we have to change the @attributes of the code each time we want to deploy to a new environment. The question is how can we generate an `ejb-jar.xml` or Hibernate mapping file from development-time attributes and yet include those rare deployment-time metadata in the same generated file?

XDoclet provides two mechanisms for extracting these metadata from source code and putting them in a place other than the source code. We can either use Ant properties in attribute values or use merge files.

As an example for using Ant properties for defining deployment-time metadata, consider the database schema name of a Hibernate class. We can define it by using the schema parameter of @hibernate.class attribute like this:

```
/**
 * @hibernate.class table="FOLDERS" discriminator-value="Normal"
 *                  schema="contactsdb"
 * @hibernate.discriminator   column="TYPE" length="10"
 */
public class Folder {
```

But we're in trouble if a client wants to deploy the application on a database schema other than contactsdb. We can extract the value to an Ant property defined in the `build.xml` file and reference it in this tag like this:

```
/**
 * @hibernate.class table="FOLDERS" discriminator-value="Normal"
 *                  schema="${schemaname}"
 * @hibernate.discriminator   column="TYPE" length="10"
 */
public class Folder {
```

When building the application, XDoclet will substitute the ${schemaname} with the value of an Ant property with the same name. The property is defined like this in the `build.xml` file:

```
<property name="schemaname" value="contactsdb"/>
```

In some other cases, we can use XDoclet merge points or merge files. Merge files are like plug points in the template file used for generating stuff. Each XDoclet subtask defines a set of merge points. The list of these merge files is available in the documentation of each subtask.

Each EJB component can have a set of environment variables defined for it. The values of these variables are defined on the JNDI tree of the application server. They are clearly deployment-oriented things. So instead of putting a bunch of @ejb:env-entry tags in the source code of a bean, we can put them in a separate merge file, which is later merged into the generated `ejb-jar.xml` file during build. By looking at the documentation of `<deployment descriptor>` subtask of `<ejbdoclet>`, we find that if we create a file named `ejb-env-entries-EJBNAME.xml` we can instruct XDoclet to merge this file into the generated `ejb-jar.xml` file. Here is the definition of an EJB environment variable for the StatefulBean class:

```
[/test/ejb-env-entries-Stateful.xml]
<env-entry>
    <env-entry-name>backup-server-name</env-entry-name>
    <env-entry-type>java.lang.String</env-entry-type>
    <env-entry-value>hercules</env-entry-value>
</env-entry>
```

Using these two simple techniques, we can move deployment-time metadata out of the source code.

Summary

In this chapter, we first got familiar with the Attribute Oriented Programming concept and how this concept can by used by XDoclet to perform code generation and add metadata to source code.

We then converted the ContactInfo class from the sample application of Chapter 5 to use @hibernate attributes instead of hand-coding the mapping file. During this conversion, we learned how to use XDoclet attributes. We also learned the correct syntax of XDoclet attributes and their inheritance behavior. We then learned how to run XDoclet from within Ant to generate the Hibernate mapping files.

Then we moved on to converting more advanced Hibernate mapping, such as relations and joined subclasses to @hibernate tags.

We also learned how to use XDoclet to generate more sophisticated EJB artifacts such as EJB deployment descriptors and home and remote interfaces. We learned how XDoclet generates a lot of things from a very small number of @ejb tags and how it can cleverly extract metadata just by looking at the source code.

Then we had an overview of most popular XDoclet tasks and subtasks.

The chapter was wrapped up with some guidelines for using XDoclet more effectively. We distinguished between development-time and deployment-time metadata and learned how to use Ant properties and merge files to separate and merge deployment-time metadata into generated artifacts.

CHAPTER 10

Communication and Tools

This chapter examines some tools and techniques that will be useful in your development projects. We use PetSoar as an example project and explain some of the lessons we have learned along the way.

Communication is one of the key attributes of any successful project. Without good interteam communication, a project is sure to run into trouble during its lifetime. It is often overlooked that communication goes a lot further than just talking to others on your team! We also look at some of the different types of communication involved in a modern development project and look specifically at how to manage communication to achieve your development goals.

Tools are another key aspect of a good development project. A good developer should never use inadequate tools! We provide a quick catalog of the tools used in our project. We explain where each tool is most useful, as well as how to integrate tools to increase their overall value.

Exploring PetSoar Development

The PetSoar project was developed by four developers on four continents, each in totally different time zones. We have extracted a few self-contained "lessons" from our work, which are described in this section.

Two things are worth noting:

- Our development has been distributed, so these "lessons" may or may not apply in your environment.

- All the authors are employed to write software commercially and are very active in the Open Source world. This means that our development reflects a broad range of experience and a merging of "models."

No process is ideal for everyone. Many teams choose no process at all, and some choose to create their own; some adapt another one, while others follow an existing one religiously by the book.

We do not discuss any of the processes we used in detail. That subject forms a whole library of books itself. Whichever process you decide to use, this chapter lists some important tips that suit most processes.

Companies are willing to invest huge amounts of money in software development projects. However, often under the pressures of a project timeline, investing in "development speed" is neglected.

How do you invest in development speed? Learn to use your tools, especially your IDE, intimately. Considering that you use the IDE for most of your development day, you should train yourself to be an IDE ninja. There's no excuse not to be.

You should be continually looking for ways to improve development speed. In the area of source-exploration time, consider the following:

- Learn the shortcut keys and techniques to navigate around your source code effectively. You should be able to search or follow links to items or usages of items as quickly as you can think about it.

- If you find yourself doing something repeatedly in your IDE, set up a shortcut key. If it's an operation not supported by the IDE, consider writing a macro or plugin to make it easier.

- Look around for seamless integrations between your IDE and source code control system. Having to constantly switch between the two as you want to edit code is frustrating.

To reduce the time required to build your application, consider the following:

- If your build system is needlessly repeating work at each run, try making your build more incremental. For example, ensure that it recompiles or regenerates only code that has been modified.

- If the Java compiler is taking too long, try using Jikes. This is an Open Source alternative to javac that is many times faster. It is available from `http://ibm.com/developerworks/oss/jikes/`.

- Use finer-grained build targets and choose the correct one depending on your current task. For example, you do not have to regenerate the JavaDoc documentation on every build run.

- Use different build steps for development and deployment. Although you may have to package everything into a neat JAR, WAR, or EAR file when you release the application, it is a time-consuming step while in development. If you are merely editing a JSP, you shouldn't have to invoke the build system at all. A browser refresh should suffice if the Web application is run directly from your source directory.

In the area of testing time, consider the following:

- If your integrated development environment (IDE) has built-in JUnit support, make use of it. As subtle as it sounds, ensuring that there's a key-mapping available that can compile and run your unit tests can give you those extra few seconds — important when you're running tests many times per minute.

- If a few tests are much slower than the rest, try optimizing them. Failing that, break the slow ones into a separate test suite that isn't run as regularly. You should, however, ensure that *all* tests are run before checking in any code.

- If all your tests are running slowly, determine if anything can be done to optimize them. For example, if a database connection is being re-established for every unit test, it may make more sense to share a single connection across all tests.

In the area of application startup time, consider the following:

- If the application runs in an application server, try starting the server directly from the IDE to minimize the amount of time you spend switching between applications. Most application servers are written in pure Java, so it's usually just a case of placing all the necessary JARs in the classpath and invoking the correct startup class. This makes it very easy to use the debugger because the IDE is managing the JVM.

- If the application server itself has a slow start-up time, investigate whether it has a hot-deploy capability, allowing you to start it once but to redeploy the application rapidly. You may have to modify the JVM arguments that start the server if you want to use the debugger from your IDE, as it will have to connect to the JVM remotely. Consult the documentation for your IDE and server to determine how to do this.

- If your application takes too long to start because it's so big, see if you can break it into smaller applications that can be started in isolation.

In teams that practice TDD (explained in Chapter 13), it is common to build and run your tests many times a minute.

Managing Imperfect Communication

One of the greatest contributors to successful development projects is good communication.

In this section, we look at the following:

- The different mediums in which developers can communicate
- The source code as a valuable communications tool
- The training benefits of good communications

Communicating in Every Way

Almost everything we do as developers communicates something to someone, whether it's writing a piece of source code, sending an e-mail, or writing a Web page. Table 10.1 shows a classified list of some of the communication methods you may encounter as a developer.

As an example, in the development of PetSoar and in the authoring of this book, we used every method of communication in Table 10.1 — except "over the cubicle discussions"! (These are a bit difficult when the authors are in Australia, the U.S., England, and Iran.)

One thing to bear in mind when you're communicating with other developers on your team is the permanence of the communication. Your "message" should be adjusted to take this into account. For example, a phone conversation has no permanent record, whereas a Web page is designed to be permanent. Often, these nonpermanent communication mediums generate good ideas. Developers should always be aware of the need to record this information in a permanent form (for example, quickly writing the minutes of a conference call on a Web site). This record can save time down the road, because there is less need to hold duplicate meetings and calls.

The general rules of clarity, conciseness, and consistency apply, regardless of the medium you're using. Remember, the effect of the communication is always more important than the form of communication.

Table 10.1   Communication Methods

	ONE TO ONE	ONE TO MANY
Synchronous	"Over the cubicle" discussions, phone, instant messaging, pair programming.	Meetings, conference calls, online chat.
Asynchronous	E-Mail	Mailing lists, forums, Web sites, documentation, source code.

Using Source Communication

At one time or another, every developer has been faced with a large, new code base to understand. Or perhaps you've scratched your head staring at a piece of code you wrote last week, trying to remember what it did or why you made certain decisions. This is exactly where good source communication comes in.

Source communication is a black art. There are no hard and fast rules. People often think their source speaks for itself and will be readable to the next developer. This is rarely the case! Of course, the opposite is also true — commenting too heavily (yes, we've seen classes with comments for *every* line of code) runs the risk of smothering the useful communication of the source in layers of meaningless garbage that offer little value. Overcommenting leads to code that is harder to change because you have twice as much to maintain.

Here are a few simple rules to help improve your team's source communication:

- *Always strive to write simple, understandable code* — Writing readable code is far more important than adding comments (which often get left until the end — or left out altogether). Your code should document itself. Also, if your code is confusing and doesn't communicate well, that is one of the sure signs that it needs refactoring!

- *Add comments only where necessary* — Comments describing *what* a class is designed to do or *why* a particular design decision was made are useful, but explaining *how* it works is a duplication of the code.

- *Always remember that JavaDoc gets generated as HTML* — Thus, you should use the hyperlinks liberally! @see should be regularly used to link classes and methods together. These techniques provide a great navigation tool to those reading or learning from your source documentation.

- *Use your unit tests as API examples* — One of the great benefits of having a comprehensive unit test suite is that you instantly get usage examples for each class. Make sure you use these! It's also a self-referential sanity check. If your unit tests do not provide good usage examples, the tests themselves probably aren't comprehensive. Your tests should describe what your code is meant to do, as well as how to use the API. The test names should also reflect this. If you do this religiously, you can find tools such as TestDox that autogenerate documentation from test names that can have surprisingly useful output. For more information, see `http://agiledox.sourceforge.net/`.

- *Use an IDE that allows you to navigate the source as if it were a hypertext environment* — Being able to navigate back and forth through a code base is brilliantly useful when you are presented with a new project. (See the section, "Exploring Our Toolbox" later in this chapter for our recommendations).

THE "HIT BY A TRUCK" TEST

Look at a your team closely. What would happen if someone were hit by a truck tomorrow? What vital skills and information would be lost? Would the team be able to continue development? Would this person be replaceable? Consider this for each member of the team.

It's not meant to be as morbid as it sounds. Frequently asking yourself this question can show you where the high-risk zones in your project are. If you identify a member of your team whom the project could not function without, it's a tell-tale sign of where communication needs to be focused.

In practice, few developers are hit by trucks. However, ensuring that vital development knowledge is distributed has many advantages:

- ◆ The team collectively becomes more responsible for the information.

- ◆ Critical decisions can be made, questioned, and enhanced by multiple brains.

- ◆ Developers feel better about not attending yet another meeting, taking a needed vacation, or even working on a new project. Taking burdens like these off developers' shoulders can have a dramatic positive effect on collective morale and can often rekindle enthusiasm as they think about new problems.

Using Communication as a Learning Tool

Development teams aren't made up of identical drones, each with the same skills and knowledge. Different developers have different sets of refined skills. Many teams are split into junior and senior developers, while other teams don't make that distinction. Either way, everyone is good at different things and knows different information (whether technical, domain, or application specific). There is rarely one person on your team who knows everything about the application. Therefore, some members of your team will be unaware of various pieces of information. People leave. People join. Where does the knowledge go?

The challenge is to use communication as a learning tool to distribute knowledge around your development team. Communication methods can help teach new developers.

One of the aims of your development team should be to increase collective knowledge by communicating with each other and recording useful information for people who may join in the future (or those with bad memories).

Exploring Our Toolbox

There are many good development tools out there, each with its own purpose.

Here we present a list of the tools that we used on the PetSoar project and a brief overview of each tool. We also look at how learning to tie your tools together can provide a great benefit to your project overall.

Remember, the best tools are by no means the most expensive tools.

Source Configuration Management — CVS

Without question, all projects should use a source-control system. If you're not using one, we suggest that you put this book down now and install one instantly. There is no excuse for lost code.

A source-control system provides a complete audit trail of all changes on the code base. This can be used for determining what was changed in a class on a particular date or to retrieve an older version of the system.

However, the more subtle advantage of a source-control system is that it gives confidence to the developers — confidence to introduce new code to the system, to make a refactoring, to fix a bug in a radical way, or to delete dead code.

As an analogy, try walking the length of a three-meter plank of wood on the ground. It's pretty easy, isn't it? Now try walking along that same plank of wood suspended from a tower block, with no safety net. The wood hasn't changed shape, but you'll go much slower. The source-control system allows you to be daring enough to walk the plank with confidence.

For source control, we used the Open Source tool CVS. It is one of the utmost used Source Configuration Management (SCM) systems in the world. It has the benefit that both IDEs we used have good CVS support, and there are clients for all platforms. Incidentally, if you're using any version of Windows, TortoiseCVS is a fantastic way to use CVS from within Explorer. For more information, see the following:

- *CVS* — http://www.cvshome.org/
- *TortoiseCVS* — http://www.tortoisecvs.org/

Knowledge Management — Wiki

If you haven't used a Wiki before, you should try it. A *Wiki* is a group-editable Web site that is excellent for rapidly collecting and recording knowledge within a development team and providing hyperlinked paths through the information. We use MoinMoin Wiki, which is one of the more established Wiki systems out there. It is Open Source and written in Python, although there is Wiki software written in all major programming languages. On PetSoar, we used Wiki to keep schedules, manage documentation, record chat logs and meeting minutes, and much more. For more information, see the following:

- *The original Wiki* — `http://www.wiki.org/`
- *MoinMoin* — `http://moin.sourceforge.net/`
- *TWiki* — `http://twiki.org/`

Mailing List — Majordomo

Mailing lists are extremely useful for communicating to a group of people asynchronously. We used the Open Source Majordomo package, although there are a number of useful systems out there. For more information, see `http://www.greatcircle.com/majordomo/`.

Real-time Discussion — IRC and Instant Messaging

There are many ways to conduct online discussions in real time. For our group meetings, we used Internet Relay Chat (IRC), simply because IRC clients exist for all platforms that the developers were using. With PetSoar, these meetings were held online because of the distributed nature of the team. In your development team, this would be the equivalent of a weekly meeting, so a conference room would serve the same purpose. The ideal is to have a standup meeting in the coffee area if you have one.

For one-to-one communication, an instant messaging (IM) application (such as Jabber, AIM, or Yahoo!) can be used. IM is very useful when developing in tandem with someone who is not in proximity with you (physically speaking). These clients can also be used for group discussions if there is a standard client across your development team. Jabber is fully Open Source; however, all the tools listed previously are freely available for use. For more information, see the following:

- *Jabber* — `http://www.jabber.org/`
- *AIM* — `http://www.aim.com/`
- *Yahoo* — `http://messenger.yahoo.com/`

IDEs — IDEA and Eclipse

IDEs are a highly contested topic, and I'm sure everyone already has his or her favorite. The two IDEs used by our team are IDEA (commercial software from IntelliJ) and Eclipse (Open Source from IBM). Both have excellent source navigation and productivity features, including CVS clients. Both allowed us to increase our development speed by developing inside the IDE (including running all tests and debugging the application deployed in the application server). It is important to feel comfortable with your IDE. If you don't know your shortcut keys, learn them. If you don't like how it's configured, customize it. You spend most of your development time in your IDE, so make it good time. For more information, see the following:

- *Eclipse* — `http://www.eclipse.org/`
- *IDEA* — `http://www.intellij.com/`

Issue Tracking and Task Management — JIRA

Keeping track of the issues that arise during a software project, both during development and in production, is a very important task. For our issue tracking, we used JIRA (commercial software from Atlassian) because it was the tool that best fit our needs. There are Open Source alternatives that you may want to try — the most popular of which is Bugzilla, developed by the Mozilla project.

- *JIRA* — `http://www.atlassian.com/`
- *Bugzilla* — `http://www.mozilla.org/bugzilla/`

Using Continuous Integration

Continuous Integration is the concept popularized by Martin Fowler of Extreme Programming (XP) fame. His original article about the concept can be found at the following address:

`http://www.martinfowler.com/articles/continuousIntegration.html`

We've already learned about the importance of a fully automated build and test process that allows a team to build and test their software many times a day. An automated build based on Ant is a reliable mechanism for ensuring consistent build procedures for each of the team members. But there's still something that running Ant individually can't provide: building and testing the integrated work of the team.

While developing one component of a software product, the developer responsible for that part can build and test the changes individually. However, often in a team environment, changes made by one developer to some part of the system break another part developed by another developer. Sometimes a change can introduce bugs in other parts of the system. The difficulty in integrating the work of a developer to the system is more severe if the integration is not taking place very often. All developers have bad memories of bugs introduced by integrating some piece of work very late into the system. We need to run all test cases upon integrating any new work into the system; otherwise, there's no way to make sure that a change doesn't break the system. Further, we need to do it as many times as possible to reduce the scope of searching for bugs, thus making fixing them easier and faster. This process is called *continuous integration*. That is: integrate often and let an automated build and test happen when integration happens.

There are two Open Source products that assist with automating continuous integration: CruiseControl and AntHill, which you can find at the following locations:

- *CruiseControl* — `http://cruisecontrol.sourceforge.net/`
- *Anthill* — `http://www.urbancode.com/projects/anthill/`

Both of these products essentially do the same thing: they monitor your version-control repository for changes and then run predefined build tasks (usually Ant targets) and send out notifications of successes or failures. These types of builds are called *event-driven builds*. Event-driven builds can be very powerful because they quickly notify the development team when things are going wrong. Essentially, they ensure that the entire team has a sense of responsibility for the project's current status, not just the individual code they "own." In a sense, this promotes the idea that there is no code ownership, but rather everyone shares ownership with everyone else (a strong theme in XP-style development).

We recommend that even if you are using your IDE for most of your tasks (such as launching unit tests), placing these tasks in your Ant build as well allows event-driven builds to also take part in the development cycle. Without a way to run unit tests from Ant, there is no way Anthill or CruiseControl can notify your team when code in the repository is failing its tests.

If you choose not to use an event-driven build system, you might still want to have all check-ins to the code repository trigger a notification e-mail to be sent to all the developers. While this doesn't automatically ensure that the build continuously stays in tip-top shape, it still helps you see when someone has updated code and gives you the opportunity to see if change has affected anything in the overall project.

Tying the Tools Together

Having good development tools is one thing, but you must also look at the value that can be generated by tying your tools together. With PetSoar, we did this in a number of ways:

- All of our meeting logs from IRC and IM chats were archived on our Wiki online for future reference. Meeting minutes and action lists were also created manually from these logs and stored on the Wiki or within JIRA. This allows us to easily reference and search all discussions that have occurred regarding the project, as well as see which tasks are assigned to whom.

- We connected our CVS server to our mailing list via a script called syncmail (`http://syncmail.sourceforge.net`). This sort of integration is fantastic for interteam communication. Anytime any of us made a change to the source base, it was e-mailed with a log of the change to all developers. This allows everyone to stay up to date with the changes taking place using only his or her e-mail client. An alternative to syncmail is CVSSpam (`http://www.badgers-in-foil.co.uk /projects/cvsspam/`).

- The mailing list was used to develop discussions over time, the result of which was turned into a document on the Wiki. This is a good example of using communication media for their best purposes and recording the useful information that results from synchronous communication.

All of the tools that your development team uses are useful by themselves, but remember to look for the points of interconnectivity between them to increase the communication value and their value to your project!

Summary

In this chapter, we've looked briefly at the importance of communication. Building PetSoar would have been impossible without good communication among the team members. We've seen that there are many forms of communication (including morning meetings, chatting to the developer sitting next to you, documentation, source code, and online chats).

We've also looked at the actual tools we've used to get our work done and how they relate to each other. Becoming intimate with your IDE is extremely important, as it will help you develop faster. Using a source code control package is vital because it allows you to make changes in confidence with a safety net in case anything goes wrong. Ensuring that your IDE and source control system are seamlessly integrated will allow you to get on with writing code without obstructions from the source control system. Your source control system also automates some communication by notifying other team members of changes. This in turn sparks up conversations.

Think carefully about how your tools can interact with each other, making your days more productive and improving communication at the same time.

CHAPTER 11

Time-Saving Tools

This chapter looks at some useful small utility components that can make development simpler.

To start with, we will look at *OSCache*, a component that can cache portions of JSP pages, enabling better scalability and improved performance. We'll then take a look at some utilities that can simplify everyday Java code. *Commons Lang* is a collection of utility classes that supplement the java.lang package and *Commons Collections* contains extensions and additions to the JDK Collections APIs. We shall also look at *Commons Logging*, an adapter that provides a common interface to many logging frameworks, such as Log4j and the java.util.logging added in Java 1.4. Finally, we'll look at how *Commons Digester* can aid in parsing (digesting!) XML files into JavaBeans given a simple set of patterns and rules.

For each component, we explain what its aims are and give some examples of its usage. For the complete documentation, see the Web site for each component. These components can be downloaded from `http://jakarta`
`.apache.org/commons/` and `http://www.opensymphony.com/`.

Understanding Utility Components

A utility component is small, simple, and reusable and performs a single function. Individually, each utility component isn't large enough to warrant its own chapter, but together they can contribute significantly to a project.

While all components are supposed to be small, simple, and reusable, by nature, utility components are quite hard to define. The border between a utility component and a larger-grained component is subjective.

Rather than exploring a specific definition, let's look at a few rules that generally indicate a *good* utility component:

- *Lightweight* — Utility components are usually much smaller and simpler than full-blown components. For example, Hibernate is a heavyweight component with a 760K JAR file including many configuration options, whereas Commons Logging is a very lightweight component with only a 26K JAR file including one main configuration parameter.

- *Focused* — A utility component should be designed to provide one simple, focused function. As an example, Commons Digester does one thing and one thing only — digesting XML files into Java Beans.

- *Flexible* — Utility components should be extremely flexible and configurable for different situations. For example, Commons Logging is adaptable to use many different underlying logging systems.

- *Friendly* — Everyone likes friendly people who play well with others. The same applies to utility components. They should integrate well with other components and continue the existing design thinking. For example, Commons Collections builds on the design of the JDK Collections API with many new collections, but integrates well into existing applications because it reuses many of the JDK Collections interfaces.

- *Nonintrusive* — A utility component shouldn't change the way you have to code and design your application. It should fit into your design rather than make you design for it.

Understanding OSCache

Performance and scalability of an application can be greatly dependent upon the caching strategies used within it. The Web is a request-response based medium, which often means that subsequent requests requery the same piece of data over and over.

OSCache is a utility component that solves this problem by caching postprocessed JSP fragments in the Web-tier. A simple example may help more clearly explain why OSCache is so useful.

Introducing SampleNews.com

Let's imagine a typical online news site called SampleNews.com, which consists of a front page with a list of headlines updated once an hour.

Without caching, each time a person visits the site to read the front page, a new request is created, which fires off some sort of server-side code, which talks to the database to get a list of headlines, which a JSP then iterates over and renders into HTML for the user.

Now imagine that ten people visit this site every second. That's ten server-side processes, ten JSPs executing, and ten database queries. The database queries are most important, because they are generally the most resource-intensive part of a request.

If the headlines for this site are only updated once an hour, almost every one of these requests is a waste of resources, because each is querying and iterating the exact same data again and again!

OSCache solves this problem simply by caching the generated HTML fragment the first time a request is run. For subsequent requests, the cached portion is served to the end user, thereby reducing the number of database hits.

Using the Loop Test

The loop test is a simple example that shows the benefits OSCache can provide. It is a simple loop that iterates ten million times, printing the counter after every millionth iteration.

The code for looptest.jsp is as follows:

```
<%@ taglib uri="oscache" prefix="cache" %>

<%
long before = System.currentTimeMillis();

for (int i = 0; i < 100000000; i++) {
    if (i % 10000000 == 0)
        out.print(i + "<br>");
}

long uncachedTime = System.currentTimeMillis() - before;
%>

Uncached time taken = <%= uncachedTime %>ms.<p>

<%      before = System.currentTimeMillis(); %>

<cache:cache>
<%
for (int i = 0; i < 100000000; i++) {
        if (i % 10000000 == 0)
            out.print(i + "<br>");
}
%>
```

```
</cache:cache>

<%      long cachedTime  = System.currentTimeMillis() - before; %>

Cached time taken = <%= cachedTime %>ms.<p>

Caching is <%= uncachedTime / Math.max(cachedTime, 1) %>% faster.
```

This JSP

- Imports the OSCache tag library (line 1)
- Loops ten million times without any caching and calculates the time taken (lines 3 – 14)
- Loops ten-million times with a simple cache and calculates the time taken (lines 16 – 29)
- Calculates how much faster the cached loop was than the uncached one

Here is a sample of what the results look like the first time the JSP is run:

```
0
10000000
20000000
30000000
40000000
50000000
60000000
70000000
80000000
90000000
Uncached time taken = 4907ms.

0
10000000
20000000
30000000
40000000
50000000
60000000
70000000
80000000
90000000
Cached time taken = 4958ms.

Caching is 0% faster.
```

The loops each took the same amount of time! Let's try executing it again and see what happens:

```
0
10000000
20000000
30000000
40000000
50000000
60000000
70000000
80000000
90000000
Uncached time taken = 5037ms.

0
10000000
20000000
30000000
40000000
50000000
60000000
70000000
80000000
90000000
Cached time taken = 1ms.

Caching is 5037% faster.
```

The second execution was much faster than the first. The first time loop-test.jsp executes, the content between the `<cache:cache>` tags is executed and cached (here stored in memory). The second time the JSP is executed, the tag will look for the cache content, find it in memory, and return it — without ever actually executing the loop.

This is the essence of where OSCache provides a speed improvement. As long as a cached fragment exists, the JSP code between the cache tags is never actually executed, thus saving time.

Also note the simplicity of what we did here. We didn't alter our JSP in any way to account for a caching strategy; we simply imported the OSCache tag library and used it. A 5000 percent speed improvement with two lines of code? Not bad at all! (Note: 5000 percent performance improvements are not guaranteed — this is a very simplistic example!)

Exploring the OSCache Tag Library

We've just met the `<cache>` tag, which is one-third of the OSCache tag library! The tag library is very simple, consisting of the following three tags:

- `<cache>` — The main OSCache tag, it indicates a cacheable fragment of the JSP page. This tag governs the scope, key, and duration of the cache content.

- `<usecache>` — If this tag is present within the body of a `<cache>` tag, it will force the use of cached content if possible.

- `<flush>` — This tag flushes specific caches or all caches.

Now let's look at some of the OSCache key concepts; then we'll build a more complex example that uses all three tags.

Understanding OSCache Concepts

Each cache entry has three main attributes — key, scope, and duration — all of which were automatically chosen for us in the previous example. We'll also look at how cache entries are flushed or refreshed.

Cache Key

The *cache key* is a simple String, a unique primary key of the cached fragment. It is specified in the key attribute of the `<cache>` tag. If no key is specified, the request URI with a full query String is used instead.

This means that if you set a specific key for your cache fragment, you can share cached content among multiple JSP pages. Alternatively, if you have only one cached fragment on a single page and you don't want to share that cached fragment, you don't need to specify the key at all.

Scope

Each cache entry has a particular *scope*. The cache scopes reflect the scopes available in JSP — application and session. Scope is specified by a simple String in the scope attribute of the `<cache>` tag.

> **NOTE** Request scope would be useless for a cache — think about it!

Application scope is the default, meaning that the cached content will be the same for the whole application.

Alternatively, by using a session scope for your cache, you now have a cache for each user session. This is useful in scenarios where the content of the page is not frequently updated but is different for each user of your application.

As an example of where a session-scoped cache is useful, imagine an e-mail application. Each user has unique e-mail content, but new e-mail is retrieved only once an hour. For the rest of that hour, the inbox listing page could be cached with a session scope.

Duration

Each cache entry has a set *duration*, the length of time until the cache is refreshed. By default, the duration is set to one hour. Obviously, if you have content that needs refreshing more often, you should specify a small duration and vice versa.

The cache duration can be set in two ways:

- The *time* attribute of the <cache> tag indicates duration in seconds. For example, <cache:cache time="30"> will cache the entry for 30 seconds.

- Using the *duration* attribute of the <cache> tag, we can specify a duration using either the Java SimpleDateFormat syntax or the industry standard ISO-8601 date format. For example, <cache:cache duration="30h"> will cache for 30 hours using the SimpleDateFormat syntax or <cache:cache duration="XXXXX"> using the ISO-8601 date format.

Looking at a Caching Time Example

Let's look at a slightly more complicated example utilizing some of the new features we have just learned about:

```
<%@ page import="java.util.Date"%>
<%@ taglib uri="oscache" prefix="cache" %>

The time is <%= new Date() %> uncached.

<p>

<cache:cache key="timer" duration="10s">
The time is <%= new Date() %> cached in the Application Scope.
</cache:cache>

<p>

<cache:cache key="timer" duration="10s" scope="session">
The time is <%= new Date() %> cached in the Session Scope (session ID:
<%= session.getId() %>).
</cache:cache>
```

So, what can we learn from this example?
First, loading up the page in a browser will give us something like this:

```
The time is Mon Jan 13 19:22:27 EST 2003 uncached.
The time is Mon Jan 13 19:22:27 EST 2003 cached in the Application Scope.
```

```
The time is Mon Jan 13 19:22:27 EST 2003 cached in the Session Scope
(session ID: JLGKBHDOCOPN).
```

All three times here are the same because the content is being cached for the first time. Waiting a few seconds (less than 10) and reloading gives you a page like the following:

```
The time is Mon Jan 13 19:22:31 EST 2003 uncached.
The time is Mon Jan 13 19:22:27 EST 2003 cached in the Application Scope.
The time is Mon Jan 13 19:22:27 EST 2003 cached in the Session Scope
(session ID: JLGKBHDOCOPN).
```

Looking closely at the seconds of each time stamp, we can see that the two cached entries (with the key "timer") have not changed, even though time has moved forward four seconds. Also note that as we have not changed session, the session and application scoped-cache entries are identical.

Now let's load up the page from another machine to simulate another session; you'll see a page like this:

```
The time is Mon Jan 13 19:22:36 EST 2003 uncached.
The time is Mon Jan 13 19:22:27 EST 2003 cached in the Application Scope.
The time is Mon Jan 13 19:22:36 EST 2003 cached in the Session Scope
(session ID: JLGKBHDOCOPN).
```

Here, the session-scoped time has changed because this computer is another session, but we see the same application cache entry!

Finally, wait another few seconds, and reload from the second computer. You will see the following:

```
The time is Mon Jan 13 19:22:42 EST 2003 uncached.
The time is Mon Jan 13 19:22:42 EST 2003 cached in the Application Scope.
The time is Mon Jan 13 19:22:36 EST 2003 cached in the Session Scope
(session ID: JLGKBHDOCOPN).
```

We can see from this last result that the ten-second duration has elapsed and that the application-scoped cache entry has been refreshed. Also, note that the session-scoped entry has not changed, as it was refreshed less than ten seconds ago.

Looking at Advanced OSCache Features

OSCache has a few more features that are beyond the scope of this book, but let's briefly look at some of the other features that you might want to investigate in more detail.

Caching Binary content

The OSCache tag library is only one "interface" into controlling OSCache. Another is the CacheFilter. This is a Servlet 2.3 filter that caches entire responses, not fragments of pages.

The benefit of the CacheFilter is that it can cache responses that contain binary content, which is most useful for caching dynamically generated images, PDF documents, and ZIP files.

Java API

OSCache has a full Java API to manipulate the various caches. This enables you to write a class to flush particular caches from within your application or to add cached content to a particular key.

For example, thinking back to our SampleNews.com example, using the Java APIs you could automatically flush the headline cache from your back-end code whenever a new story is posted.

Error Tolerance

One of OSCache's best side effects is that it gives your application great error tolerance. If an exception or error occurs while processing a JSP page, you can instruct OSCache to serve cached content instead of the error.

Disk Persistence

All the examples we have seen use memory persistence, meaning the cache entries are only stored in memory. Restarting the server or application would clear all the caches. OSCache can, however, be configured to use disk caching as well, where cache entries are written to disk — thereby surviving a server restart.

This small section provides an idea of the great performance improvements that OSCache can provide for almost any J2EE application. For downloads and documentation, look at the OSCache Web site (`http://www.opensymphony.com/oscache`).

Understanding Commons Lang

Commons Lang (`http://jakarta.apache.org/commons/lang.html`) provides a series of helper classes for the java.lang package API, including String manipulation methods, basic numerical methods, object reflection, creation and serialization, and system properties.

It also provides some builder objects to make it simpler to overload common java.lang.Object methods such as `toString`, `hashCode`, and `equals`.

There are more helper classes in Commons Lang than we can cover here. We will look at the most useful methods and classes, but to find out more, browse the well-written API docs (`http://jakarta.apache.org/commons/lang/api/index.html`).

Exploring Most Useful Classes

Here are some of the more useful classes in the Commons Lang component, with the exception of the builder classes, which are covered in the next section. Included in org.apache.commons.lang are the following:

- *StringUtils* — This class contains many very useful methods for manipulating String objects including case manipulation, text formatting and padding, along with some simple search-and-replace methods.

- *SystemUtils* — A collection of simple methods to determine the version of the current JVM.

Included in org.apache.commons.lang.exception are the following:

- *NestableException* — A simple exception class that handles nested exceptions. This works the same way as the JDK 1.4 class for those using previous JDKs.

- *ExceptionUtils* — A collection of utility methods for manipulating Throwable objects and Exceptions.

Using Builder Classes

The builder classes in Commons Lang are used to provide a simple way to safely override common methods from java.lang.Object — namely, `toString()`, `equals()`, and `hashcode()`.

All the builder classes come with two varieties — those that use reflection and those that must be explicitly constructed. As we'll see in the following examples, reflection variety is simpler to write but will execute marginally slower and can have security permission problems.

As an example, let's build a simple Customer bean using the build classes:

```
import org.apache.commons.lang.builder.ToStringBuilder;
import org.apache.commons.lang.builder.EqualsBuilder;
import org.apache.commons.lang.builder.HashCodeBuilder;

public class Customer {
    String name;
    boolean male;
```

```
    int age;

    public Customer(String name, boolean male, int age) {
        this.name = name;
        this.male = male;
        this.age = age;
    }

    public String toString() {
        return new ToStringBuilder(this).
            append("name", name).
            append("male", male).
            append("age", age).
            toString();
    }

    public boolean equals(Object o) {
        if (!(o instanceof Customer)) {
            return false;
        }
        Customer rhs = (Customer) o;
        return new EqualsBuilder()
                    .append(name, rhs.name)
                    .append(male, rhs.male)
                    .append(age, rhs.age)
                    .isEquals();
    }

    public int hashCode() {
        // you pick a hard-coded, randomly chosen, non-zero, odd number
        // ideally different for each class
        return new HashCodeBuilder(17, 37).
            append(name).
            append(male).
            append(age).
            toHashCode();
    }
}
```

We can see from this class that the ToStringBuilder, EqualsBuilder and HashCodeBuilder have simplified the writing of those methods. To add new fields, simply add the relevant `.append()` clause for each field you want to include, and the builder class does the rest of the work for you.

The builder classes handle many of the tricky tasks in writing these methods, such as

- Providing human-readable field names
- Handling null values
- Handling all types, including collections and arrays

Using the ToStringStyle class, we can govern the output of the `toString()` method, configuring things such as whether or not fields are displayed and printing on single or multiple lines. See the API documentation for more details on this.

The default output of the previous Customer class is:

```
Customer@15ff48b[name=Fred Flintstone,male=true,age=30]
```

Using another style (ToStringStyle.MutliLineStyle), the output looks like this:

```
customer.toString() = Customer@15ff48b[
  name=Fred Flintstone
  male=true
  age=30
]
```

We can see now that the builder classes are extremely useful, but they still require a little modification each time a field is added or removed.

Let's take a look at how we can use the reflection methods of the builder classes to make the previous class simpler:

```
import org.apache.commons.lang.builder.ToStringBuilder;
import org.apache.commons.lang.builder.EqualsBuilder;
import org.apache.commons.lang.builder.HashCodeBuilder;

public class ReflectionCustomer {
    String name;
    boolean male;
    int age;

    public ReflectionCustomer(String name, boolean male, int age) {
        this.name = name;
        this.male = male;
        this.age = age;
    }

    public String toString() {
        return ToStringBuilder.reflectionToString(this);
    }

    public boolean equals(Object o) {
        return EqualsBuilder.reflectionEquals(this, o);
    }

    public int hashCode() {
        return HashCodeBuilder.reflectionHashCode(this);
    }
}
```

While the reflection methods are very useful and we tend to use them in our own applications, they are no magic bullet. As when using all powerful things, you must be aware of the downsides as well as the positives before using them.

Positives of reflection builder classes include the following:

- They make your code instantly easier to maintain as you have less code duplication. New fields automatically become used in the built methods.

- Errors become less likely in your code because reflection can't forget to check certain fields.

Negatives of reflection builder classes include the following:

- They are slower because of the reflection being used. Depending on what JDK you are using (JDK 1.4 is much faster at reflection) and the performance needs of your application, this may or may not be an issue. (Note that it is generally good practice to start with the slower, simpler option and then optimize later if it is deemed a performance issue.)

- To access private fields, the reflection methods must use Field.setAccessible to temporarily change the visibility of fields. This will fail under a security manager unless the appropriate permissions are set.

As we have seen, the Commons Lang component is very useful for augmenting almost every class we write, especially the builder classes.

Understanding Commons Collections

The second of the Jakarta Commons utility components we'll discuss in this chapter is Commons Collections. The Java Collections API was introduced in JDK 1.2 and has been very useful for standardizing the collections and data structures used in Java programs. Most of the Java2 APIs have become significantly easier to use because of the Collections API.

Commons Collections is useful for a few reasons:

- It provides special implements of existing interfaces in the standard collections API, such as List, Map, and Collection, such as Bag and Buffer.

- It supports adapters and converters from the older collections in Java1, such as Enumeration and static arrays, to the newer collections in Java2.

- It has utility methods for manipulating collections, such as union, intersection, and closure.

As with Commons Lang, we'll discuss some of the most useful classes in the Commons Collections component. You will want to explore the API documentation yourself to learn more about the details and other features offered by this component.

Included in the package org.apache.commons.collections are the following:

- *Bag* — An interface (with implementations in DefaultMapBag, HashBag, and TreeBag) of a bag data structure. A *bag* is a collection of objects that retains a count of the number of times each unique object occurs in the collection. For example, this is useful in a shopping-cart scenario where your collection might contain two apples, one orange, and three mangos.

- *BeanMap* — An implementation of Map for JavaBeans that uses introspection to get and put properties of the bean.

- *Buffer* — A *buffer* is a collection that allows objects to be removed in some well-defined order. The removal order can be based on insertion order (for example, a FIFO queue or a LIFO stack), on access order (for example, an LRU cache), on some arbitrary comparator (such as a priority queue), or on any other well-defined ordering.

- *CollectionUtils* — A group of useful Collection-related utility methods, including methods to select and filter elements, compare different collections, and modify elements within collections.

- *SequencedHashMap* — A map of objects whose mapping entries are sequenced based on the order in which they were added (that is, the key set iterator iterates in the order the items were added). We have found this extremely useful for small maps where entry order matters (such as for creating select boxes on a Web page).

Included in the package org.apache.commons.collections.comparator are the following:

- *ComparatorChain* — A ComparatorChain is a Comparator that wraps one or more Comparators in sequence. The ComparatorChain calls each Comparator in sequence until it gets a nonzero result, or the end of the chain of comparators is reached (and zero is returned). This Comparator's sorting algorithm is very similar to multicolumn sorting in SQL, and this class allows Java classes to emulate that kind of behavior when sorting a List.

- *ReverseComparator* — Using the decorator pattern, the ReverseComparator reverses the order of any other comparator.

Understanding Commons Logging

Unlike Lang and Collections, Commons Logging is not a group of useful classes with a common purpose. Rather, it is a very thin adapter to different logging libraries.

Traditionally, logging within a Java program is done by primitive means such as `System.out.println()`. Using a logging API is good practice because you can generally enable or disable logging through a configuration file without changing any code within your application.

Currently, the supported logging APIs are as follows:

- *Log4j* — the Open Source logging component from Jakarta (`http://jakarta.apache.org/log4j`), used by a large proportion of Java applications.

- *Logging API* — The new Sun logging API introduced in JDK 1.4 (javax.logging).

- *LogKit* — Another Jakarta logging API that originated from the Avalon project.

- *SimpleLog* — A simple logger that logs messages to the console.

- *NoOpLog* — Another simpler logger that ignores all messages.

The obvious question is why would we want to use Commons Logging rather than one of the logging APIs directly? Surely it would be simpler to just choose an API and stick to it.

Looking at Advantages of Commons Logging

Let's look at the advantages of Commons Logging:

- It has no compile-time or runtime dependencies on any particular logging package. As we'll see, Commons Logging largely configures itself based on what is available on the classpath.

- You have the added flexibility to change logging implementations without changing any of your code.

- The Commons Logging API is very simple and clean, which allows you to avoid the complexity of some of the larger logging packages until you need to use it (if you ever do).

The only real disadvantage is that you have one extra dependent JAR and another API to learn (albeit very similar to both JDK Logging API and log4j). Commons Logging is used in many Open Source projects because the authors know that they cannot predict what logging framework might be used by consumers of their project. Rather than lock down to a particular framework, they use Commons Logging and leave the final choice up to the consumer.

Looking at a Simple Example

Here is a simple example of a class that uses Commons Logging to log a few basic messages:

```
import org.apache.commons.logging.Log;
import org.apache.commons.logging.LogFactory;

public class SimpleLoggingExample {
    private static Log log =
                LogFactory.getLog(SimpleLoggingExample.class);

    public static void main(String[] args){
        log.debug("This is a debug message");
        log.warn("This is a warning message");
        log.error("This is an error message");
    }
}
```

Depending on your environment, Commons Logging will use a different logging implementation by default. If Log4J is available in the classpath, this will be used. Failing that, if the platform is Java 1.4 or higher, the standard Java logging framework will be used. If neither of those is available, the SimpleLog implementation bundled with Commons Logging will be used. This simply outputs messages of type WARN, ERROR, and FATAL to the console.

Commons Logging can be configured by a variety of mechanisms, including a System property, a property file in the classpath, and the classpath itself. For full details of the configuration options and mechanisms, see the online documentation at http://jakarta.apache.org/commons/logging/api/index.html.

For now, let's just configure it the simplest way by using a System property and the SimpleLog:

```
java -cp commons-logging.jar -Dorg.apache.commons.logging.Log=
    org.apache.commons.logging.impl.SimpleLog    SimpleLoggingExample
```

This will print the following:

```
[WARN] SimpleLoggingExample - -This is a warning message
[ERROR] SimpleLoggingExample - -This is an error message
```

As you can see, Commons Logging is an extremely flexible utility component that provides a simple way to adapt to different underlying logging mechanisms. For more information, you can visit the Commons Logging Web site at http://jakarta.apache.org/commons/logging.html.

ALTERNATIVE XML DATA-BINDING TOOLS

There are many frameworks and components that convert XML into Java classes and vice versa, including Castor and JAXB. Each has its own advantages and disadvantages, but here are the reasons we use Commons Digester:

◆ It doesn't force a close correlation between the Java class and the XML file, because of the way it combines XML patterns and rules. This is a big advantage as a utility component because it means you can use Digester with existing XML files and Java classes without modification.

◆ Once you have learned the syntax of XML patterns and how the basic rules are used, it is very simple and fast to develop with.

Also, it is worth noting that Digester only marshals XML ⇨ Java, whereas other components may be bidirectional.

Understanding Commons Digester

Commons Digester is a popular utility component that processes XML into Java objects. If you have done any XML processing, you know that there are traditionally two ways to do it — DOM and SAX. Neither of these methods is simple, and each requires a considerable amount of XML processing code to perform the operations that you want.

The idea behind the Digester package is to configure a series of rules that are triggered by matching certain patterns. *Rules* are actions that modify Java objects in some way (for example, creating objects, executing methods, or setting bean properties). Digester itself ships with a rich set of predefined rules but includes the ability to create your own rules if needed.

Traditionally, when reading an XML file into some sort of an object hierarchy, your code is 80 percent XML manipulation and 20 percent object manipulation. Digester is a huge improvement over this traditional processing model. It allows you to focus on exactly how the XML relates to your class architecture, rather than the minutiae of parsing XML.

Looking at a Digester Example

This example builds an object model describing the legends of Java programming. First, let's look at the XML file we're going to process:

```
<legends>
    <legend>
        <name>Bill Joy</name>
        <achievement>The father of Java.</achievement>
    </legend>
    <legend>
        <name>Joshua Bloch</name>
```

```
        <achievement>Sun Architect and author of "Effective Java
Programming Language Guide"</achievement>
        </legend>
</legends>
```

It's a fairly simple XML format but works for the purposes of this example. Now let's see the object model:

```java
public class Legend {
    String name;
    String achievement;

    public String getName() {
        return name;
    }

    public void setName(String name) {
        this.name = name;
    }

    public String getAchievement() {
        return achievement;
    }

    public void setAchievement(String achievement) {
        this.achievement = achievement;
    }

    public String toString() {
        return "Legend(Name: " + name
            + " Achievement: " + achievement + ")";
    }
}
```

Again, this is a very simple bean. Now we must create a class that actually uses the Digester to turn our XML into our model.

The first thing we do is create a Digester object:

```java
Digester digester = new Digester();
```

Then we add to it a series of rules determining what to do when a particular XML pattern is encountered.

```java
digester.addObjectCreate("legends", ArrayList.class);
digester.addObjectCreate("legends/legend", Legend.class);
digester.addBeanPropertySetter("legends/legend/name", "name");
digester.addCallMethod("legends/legend/achievement", "setAchievement", 1);
digester.addCallParam("legends/legend/achievement", 0);
digester.addSetNext("legends/legend", "add");
```

Each pattern-rule pair is added by one of the preceding `digester.addX()` methods.

An *XML pattern* is an expression that matches specific XML elements with processing rules. Let's look at the XML file again, with the associated expressions listed for each element:

```
<legends>                           [legends]
    <legend>                        [legends/legend]
        <name />                    [legends/legend/name]
        <achievement />             [legends/legend/achievement]
    </legend>
    <legend>                        [legends/legend]
        <name />                    [legends/legend/name]
        <achievement />             [legends/legend/achievement]
    </legend>
</legends>
```

Note that the XML patterns are very similar to XPath expressions and to the WebWork expression language (using slashes instead of dots).

Following is an explanation of what each of these rules does:

- `addObjectCreate()` — This method creates an object of the specified class. Digester will create an instance of ArrayList and put it onto the parse stack when it matches the `legends` expression.

  The parse stack is made available during the context of the XML parsing for manipulation by the rules being processed.

  Similarly, the Digester will create an instance of the Legends model bean and add it to the parse stack, above the ArrayList already created.

- `addBeanPropertySetter()` — This method sets a bean property of the current object on top of the stack. We set the bean property `name` (through the `setName()` method) of the current object on the top of the stack (which will be the current Legend instance when this pattern is matched).

- `addCallMethod()` and `addCallParam()` — These methods work together to call a method on the current object. These call the `setAchievement()` method of the current Legend object to the content of the `<achievement>` XML element. This is just a bean property. This could be achieved more simply using `addBeanPropertySetter()`, but we used it here to demonstrate how the Digester can be used to call any method with parameters.

- `addSetNext()` — This is one of a group of methods that manipulates the stack. This method pops the top object off the stack (in this case, a Legend object) and passes it to the named method on the object below it (in our case, the `add()` method of the original ArrayList.)

With the rules set up, the only remaining step is instructing Digester to process the XML file and produce the object model.

```
File input = new File("legends.xml");
List legends = (List) digester.parse(input);
```

Note that the `parse()` method returns the object on the bottom of the parse stack, which in our case is the ArrayList created initially. This List contains Legend objects.

And that's it!

Most Digester usages are similar in form to the preceding example, but there are a lot of other built-in rules that you can use depending on your needs.

Understanding Digester Rules

As mentioned previously, Commons Digester ships with a rich set of standard rules built in. You can also add your own rules if you have more very complex processing requirements, but normally the standard rules will suffice.

Here is a very brief summary of the standard rules. For more details, see the Digester API docs online at `http://jakarta.apache.org/commons/digester/api`.

Object-creation rules include the following:

- *ObjectCreateRule* — Creates an object of the specified class and pushes it onto the stack.

- *FactoryCreateRule* — Creates an object using a specified factory class and pushes it onto the stack.

Property-setting rules include the following:

- *SetPropertyRule* — Sets an individual property on the object at the top of the stack, based on attributes with specified names (used for constructs like `<legend name="Mike" />`).

- *SetPropertiesRule* — Works like the SetPropertyRule except that it sets multiple properties (for constructs like `<legend name="Mike" city="Sydney" />`).

- *BeanPropertySetterRule* — Used to set a bean property based on character data enclosed by the specified XML element (for example, `<name>Mike</name >`).

Method-calling rules include the following:

- *CallMethodRule* — Calls a method on the object on top of the stack. Parameters to the method are given by subsequent applications of the CallParamRule.

- *CallParamRule* — Sets a method parameter from an element's XML attribute or enclosed character data.

Stack-manipulation rules include the following:

- *SetNextRule* — Pops the top object off the stack and passes it to a named method on the second to top object. It is often used to insert a bean into a container object.

- *SetTopRule* — Pops the second-to-top object from the stack and passes it to a named method on the top object. Note that this is the opposite of the preceding rule!

- *SetRootRule* — Pops the top object off the stack and passes it to the bottom object of the stack, the root object.

You have now seen how Commons Digester makes processing XML into a Java class hierarchy much easier. For more details on the rules and the API documentation of Digester itself, see the Web site at `http://jakarta.apache.org/commons/digester.html`.

Summary

We have looked at a handful of reusable useful components that can make everyday development easier.

OSCache, as simple as it is, can vastly improve the performance of JSP pages (and other content) with very little effort.

Commons Lang and Commons Collections offer an enhanced set of features to the core JDK. We've looked at some of the features, such as the builder classes, which aid in the generation of tedious repetitive methods such as `toString()` and `equals()`. Commons Logging offers a very simple abstraction over the logging dilemma.

Finally, we saw how Commons Digester makes it much easier to transform XML files into an object model.

There are many Open Source components out there that can aid you in this way, so hunt around. It's rare to find components that do *exactly* what you need, so a good strategy for component selection is to look for tools that are very fine-grained (that is, do only one thing, but do it well) and easily extensible (be sure to get the source code).

Three

Developing the Application

In Part III of this book, we will begin to create the PetSoar process using the tools outlined in Part II. We will follow the application development process beginning with how the automated build system is created. From there we will introduce Test-Driven Development (TDD). Using TDD, we will then dive right in to creating domain objects with Hibernate, accessing these objects through a web interface with WebWork, and searching via Lucene. We'll also look at simple ways to secure the application, as well as how to deal with common requirements in most applications, such as a session-level service like a shopping cart. Finally, we'll take a long look at componentization in both code and user interface and how we can effectively manage these components to create a simple, re-usable toolbox to further speed up application development.

CHAPTER 12

Setting Up the Development Environment

To support the development of source code, a flexible development environment must be created. Development environments are often given little or no thought and end up changing drastically many times through the life of a project. While it should be expected that build environments will evolve over time, a solid start can go a long way toward ensuring that your build process can keep up with product development. Often, the development environment can contribute the most day-to-day efficiencies, or lack thereof.

This chapter examines the build environment we'll use for the PetSoar project and shows how it enables us to rapidly code, test, and deploy project releases. While we will cover topics usually associated with build environments, such as compilers and automated build systems, we will also discuss detailed techniques and tips that can be used to speed up development outside of the typical "code, build, test" paradigm. Much like the code in the system, the build environment must also be kept flexible so that it can be adjusted to suit the project as it evolves. The most important concept that we will stress is that the developer's environment should serve the developer, not the other way around. Only then can productivity be maximized.

TIP While this chapter gives you a good look at how to set up a development environment using Open Source tools, the focus of this book is building an application using Open Source tools, not building the environment itself. A companion book in the Java Open Source Library, *J2EE Open Source Toolkit: Building an Enterprise Platform with Open Source Tools* by John Bell, Jim Lambros, and Stan Ng (Wiley Publishing, Hoboken, NJ: 2003), guides you through the plethora of Open Source tools available to assist you in choosing your tools and then using them to build your development environment.

Working from Within the IDE

For many projects, especially smaller ones, developers often require nothing more than a simple IDE to manage all their development needs. Compiling sources is often all a developer requires in order to effectively work. Thankfully, just about any modern IDE can handle compiling sources. Some IDEs, such as IntelliJ IDEA, offer multiple ways to compile sources: make project, rebuild project, and compile individual source. Other IDEs, such as IBM's Eclipse, compile sources as they change automatically. Among all the high-quality IDEs available for you to choose from, there should be one that suits your needs and feels comfortable to you. The IDE is undoubtedly the place where you, as a developer, will spend most of your time, so it is nice that it can handle the build process as well. But sometimes you may require something that the IDE can't do.

TIP We know that IDEs are a very personal choice and that no two people work exactly the same way. Even more, we're aware that some people don't even use full-blown Java IDEs but instead opt for more general-purpose tools such as Vim or Notepad. While we don't have anything against these programs (we're all Vim users, if you're curious), we highly recommend that you look at more advanced IDEs that are specifically built for Java development. Through features such as rich debuggers, unit test support, application server integration, and support for complex refactoring, the productivity gained by modern IDEs is indeed measurable. Following is a list of free and commercial IDEs you may wish to check out:

- **Eclipse:** http://www.eclipse.org/
- **NetBeans:** http://www.netbeans.org/
- **IntelliJ IDEA:** http://www.intellij.com/
- **JBuilder:** http://www.borland.com/jbuilder/
- **Pramati Studio:** http://www.pramati.com/

The Problem: IDEs Don't Automate

While IDEs attempt to provide as much functionality to you as possible, they can't truly provide every feature you might require for your application development. One example of such a need that is very common and yet not supported by most IDEs is to build a Web Application Resource (WAR) that can be deployed by Servlet containers such as Apache Tomcat. While this can be done manually using the `jar` tool that comes with Sun's Java2 SDK, doing this takes time and requires that the developer remember to package all the classes, JSPs, images, libraries, and configuration files correctly. Naturally, most developers are likely to tire of this quickly.

Other examples of tasks that are not always supported by IDEs and can become tedious quickly are:

- Running unit tests
- Generating JavaDocs
- Deploying code to application servers
- Generating code reports

None of these tasks is particularly hard to do. However, these tasks will be required to be run countless times through the life cycle of a project. Following are some reasons why IDEs are not good candidates for handling all build tasks:

- Though they can compile and package code very easily, there's little room for automating steps such as bundling and deployment. Without an automated build process, you end up preparing a list of actions that need to be performed manually, one after another, by the developers to test the application, create a deliverable bundle of the application, or deploy the software to test or production environments.

- Many different IDEs are in use today, but there's no easy way to transfer one person's IDE settings to another user. IDE settings are mostly local to one computer. Sometimes it's even hard to transfer settings from an old version of an IDE to a new one! Without common settings, releases and builds may become inconsistent.

- IDEs are not very scalable for big projects. If the project has a single deliverable, an IDE may suffice. But when the project consists of many subcomponents, or when the project should support different deployment environments, it gets very difficult to manage building, bundling, testing, and deployment.

Given the preceding lists and the desire to avoid repetitive tasks, there needs to be a way to automate some of our build by using tools other than the IDE.

The Solution: Automated Build Tools

While the IDE works very well for some tasks, it fails miserably at other tasks, so you should look at alternatives. The most universally known build tool is Make. In the world of Java, Make has been replaced by Apache Ant. Both tools are designed to ease the pain of executing repetitive tasks such as those identified in the previous section. Ant was built from the ground up to support just about every need a developer might have for his or her build process. So, rather than use the limited IDE, let's look at using Ant for our build needs instead.

Why do you need an automated build? A software development team is much like a factory. As in a production line, many steps are required to produce a software product. The following list contains some of the typical steps (in no particular order):

- Source code is written, according to some coding conventions.

- Source code is compiled and properly packaged.

- Other artifacts are produced: design diagrams, deployment descriptors, or configuration files to name several examples.

- Documentation is generated for the consumers of the application, as well as for the benefit of the team itself.

- The software is tested to ensure that no change to the source code can break the working application and that the results are audited to be correct.

- The software might finally be deployed to a test or production environment. This might involve sophisticated packaging tasks.

In real-world applications, several other steps are also involved. It is important that a system is in place that allows these tasks to be automated correctly and reliably.

Traditionally, software developers have performed these steps manually. Because of this, whenever a developer would make some changes to the source code, he or she would manually build the changes and test them, manually deploy the altered code to the test environment, prepare a distribution, and perform various other chores. Doing this involves a repetitive, monotonous process. Aside from humans not liking repetitive monotonous tasks, humans are particularly error prone when engaging in such tasks.

Using an automated build process, such as Ant, will alleviate most, if not all, of these problems. Instead of having to perform these steps repetitively, we can employ a script to handle these steps for us. We still have to write the actual script of course, but this upfront cost is much less than the overall cost of doing the repetitive tasks.

Using Ant for All Your Building Needs

Ant has native support for compiling sources, managing files, generating reports, building .war files, and just about anything else you can imagine. Thus, Ant appears to be the perfect candidate for what we're looking for. After identifying our build requirements, we can create a build.xml file that implements all these needs and is run by Ant. Great, so it sounds like we're all set to begin development, right? Not just yet.

The Problem: Ant Isn't the Silver Bullet

While it might appear that Ant is the silver bullet for building your application, several weeks of use might make some things painfully clear. Rather than let you discover these potential pitfalls yourself, we'll save you the time and just tell you: Ant, or any other automated build tool, is a *heavyweight* process. For example, launching Ant requires that a new JVM be invoked before the Ant process can even run. Even the fastest machines still require a half second or so time to invoke the JVM. This means that even the most trivial task takes some time to launch via Ant.

Half a second or a second or even ten seconds may not seem like a big deal. And it isn't — when you look at it in the context of a single occurrence. But when taking into account that a developer compiles hundreds of times a day, the time can quickly add up. In the end, Ant does not perform as fast as you can work and can possibly slow you down.

The Solution: Use What Makes Sense

So, Ant does all we want, but does it slowly. Our IDE does only some of what we want, but does it quickly. What are we to use? The obvious answer is, of course, that we use *both*! Surprisingly, many developers stick to only a single method of building their applications and end up either dealing with the slowness (using Ant) or repeating tasks by hand (using an IDE). There is no reason why you cannot use both Ant and your IDE to do some things quickly and some things in an automated manner. Essentially, find the best way to do something, and do what makes sense to be as productive as possible.

Using the Hybrid Approach

As we've already established, there is no such thing as a silver bullet when it comes to software development environments, but that doesn't mean we can't come very close. Using the basic concept of maximizing productivity, we can see that combining the positive attributes of Ant and your IDE can ensure that you are executing tasks in the quickest possible manner. We call this the *hybrid approach* because it involves taking the best attributes from several techniques and combining them to form a hybrid development environment.

Table 12.1 lists some of the build requirements for the PetSoar application and details how we reached them, using either our IDE or Ant or both. We choose the method to execute these tasks based solely on the method that can allow the task to be invoked and finish in the shortest possible time. The goal here is to invest in development speed above all else.

NOTE Later we will discuss how tasks such as running unit tests or deploying the application can be done in your IDE. Some IDEs have native support for these operations, but even if your IDE doesn't, almost any Java IDE can perform these tasks with a bit of work.

Companies are often willing to invest huge amounts of money in the tools and technologies that make their development process faster, producing higher quality code in shorter time. However, under the pressures of a project time-line, *investing in development speed* is often neglected.

How do you invest in development speed? Learn to use your tools, especially your IDE, intimately. If you use the IDE for eight hours every day, everyone on your team should be an IDE guru; there really is no excuse not to be.

Your team should also be continuously looking for ways to improve development speed. Is it faster to run your tests inside the IDE? Can you run the entire application server inside the IDE? Can you easily navigate the source and learn about new pieces of code in your IDE? Can you optimize your Ant scripts to run faster?

Table 12.1   Build Requirements

TASK	EXECUTION
Compile sources	Primarily done in the IDE, but also done in Ant as required by other tasks
Run unit tests	Primarily done in the IDE, but also done in Ant as required by other tasks
Run application locally	IDE
Generate JavaDocs and test reports	Ant
Build `.war` file	Ant
Deploy application	Ant

Small up-front investments in development speed will pay off handsomely in the long term. Imagine this example: Assume your developers run your Ant build script an average of 100 times a day during a three-month project. We'll assume, generously, that a "developer day" includes five hours of solid development work. Therefore, there are 60 developer days in the three-month project.

Now if you can optimize the script to cut just 15 seconds from your build process, you'll save almost 25 minutes a day — or gain more than five developer days *per developer* during the project! Think about it carefully — cutting 15 seconds from your build process has just given you five extra days in a 60-day project.

Is it worth spending an hour to optimize that script?

NOTE One of the authors of this book lives by a three-second rule: the time from which he writes a line of code to the time he sees his test result should take no more than three seconds. This is because he has a small brain and can only handle making tiny changes at a time and doesn't have the patience to wait for a long build cycle, as he tends to forget his flow of thought after about four seconds of daydreaming. What were we talking about?

Laying Out Your Project

Now that we have reinforced the notion that a development environment should serve the developer and not vice versa, we need to decide on a way to organize our sources and supporting files for the PetSoar application. When it comes to the issue of organizing your project, there are generally two ways to structure your files:

- Files are organized by type.
- Files are organized to simplify deployment.

No matter which option you choose, the important thing to remember is that there should be some sort of structure to your project, as chaos will lead you nowhere fast.

Structuring by Type

Structuring your project based around the various sources, libraries, resource files, and so on is a simple hierarchical approach to managing your project.

The basic idea is to build a tree, starting at the root directory of your project, which represents all the kinds of files your project contains. Generally, there are three high-level types of files in a project: sources, libraries, and documentation. Using this as a starting point, your project directory structure would look like the following:

```
+ project
  |---- docs
  |---- lib
  \---- src
```

Once these high-level file types have been identified, we can then drill down a little deeper. For example, there might be two kinds of documentation: requirements and mockups. There are also usually at least two types of libraries: runtime and buildtime. Lastly, there are many types of sources to manage. We'll start with three types: Java sources, test sources, and JSPs:

```
+ project
  |---- docs
  | |---- requirements
  | \---- mockups
  |---- lib
  | |---- buildtime
  | \---- runtime
  \---- src
    |---- java
    |---- test
    \---- jsp
```

Continuing this process, you will eventually find a hierarchical structure to store your files. This is very nice because it leaves no room for confusion as to where new files should be placed in your project. Finally, we need to decide how *temporary* files are stored (that is, files that aren't really part of your project but are created during the build process, such as compiled files). Following the previous example, we end up with a structure such as:

```
+ project
  |---- build
  | |---- java
  | \---- test
  |---- docs
  | |---- requirements
  | \---- mockups
  |---- lib
```

```
|  |---- buildtime
|  \---- runtime
\---- src
   |---- java
   |---- test
   \---- jsp
```

This structure is logical and provides a simple and effective approach for storing and managing project files. However, it isn't without faults. By sticking to a rigid structure like this, it becomes more difficult to construct other structures that may be required by application servers that deploy your code. In the next section, we will discuss an alternative approach to storing your files that eases this pain.

Structuring by Deployment

In the previous example project, structure, libraries, JSPs, and compiled classes existed in different branches of the directory tree. Recall that the Servlet specification defines a `.war` file to be in the following structure:

```
+ jsps
  \---- WEB-INF
    |---- web.xml
    |---- classes
    \---- lib
```

As you can see, this is different from the structure previously discussed. So would there be a benefit in structuring your project in a way that is closer to this? After all, Ant can be directed to gather your various files and create this structure, so why bother storing your project files this way?

We come back to the issue of investing in developer speed. Suppose a developer needs to deploy his application to a Web-application server to debug it. He or she has two options:

1. Run Ant, which constructs a `.war` file, copy the file to a deployment location, start the application server in debug mode, and finally connect the IDE to the application server using remote debugging.

2. Launch the application server in debug mode from within the IDE, and point the server to the project's preconstructed application.

While the second option may only be 10 or 15 seconds faster than the first option, that 10 or 15 seconds will quickly add up, just as we pointed out in the "The Hybrid Approach" section earlier in this chapter, possibly saving days over the life of the project. Using the previous structuring technique as a base, a structure employing this technique might look like the following:

```
+ project
  |---- build
  | \---- test
  |---- docs
  | |---- requirements
  | \---- mockups
  |---- lib (previously lib/buildtime)
  \---- src
    |---- java
    |---- test
    \---- webapp
     \---- WEB-INF
       |---- classes (previously build/java)
       \---- lib (previously lib/runtime)
```

Arguably, this structure is not as refined or clean as the previous ones we have looked at. Of course, the advantage is that an application server need only be pointed to `src/webapp` to deploy the entire application right away.

Picking a Structure

Choosing a particular project structure can be a difficult task, as there is no science to it. In the end, the best choice is the one that limits your time building and allows more time to be spent developing. Should you dismiss structuring your project by file types if you know you will be deploying your application a lot? Should you dismiss modeling your project after its deployment if you desire a strict hierarchy for file types? The answer to both is "no." Rather, it is important to do a complete analysis before committing to a project file structure — this decision will most likely remain in effect for a very long time.

For example, depending on the application server you are using, there are ways to deploy your project without storing your files in the .war specification. While Tomcat does not allow this type of behavior, Jetty does. Not only should these types of scenarios help you decide your file structure, but they might also help you decide *how* you will use your build environment as well, such as which Servlet container should be used for development (Jetty over Tomcat, for instance).

And What about PetSoar?

As it turns out, we all generally like a strict hierarchy in our projects, and as such we opted to follow the "structure by type" example for PetSoar.

However, we committed to this decision only after we were sure that an application server existed that could accommodate quick development using this structure. Caucho Resin is very good at this and is free for development, so we felt confident that all of our bases were covered.

As PetSoar development progressed, we kept asking ourselves, "Is this the fastest way to do this?" If we answered "no," we would reevaluate the file structure and return to development. Following is the final directory layout we used:

```
+ project
  |---- build
  | |---- java
  | \---- test
  |---- docs
  |---- lib
  | |---- buildtime
  | \---- runtime
  \---- src
    |---- java
    |---- test (unit and acceptance tests)
    \---- webapp (jsp files)
       \---- WEB-INF
       |---- classes (configuration files)
       \---- web.xml
```

This approach takes a little from both methods and has turned out to be a very good way for the four of us to rapidly write and test code.

In this section, we have stressed the importance of being able to quickly deploy your application. Later in this chapter, we will go into the details as to how we deployed PetSoar in our IDE using Resin. However, before we do this, we'd like to further stress the desire to be able to complete build tasks in the smallest amount of time possible. In the next section, we will apply this principle for running unit and acceptance tests — something that can take as little as a few milliseconds or as long as several hours.

Managing Unit Tests

Testing your application should be a large part of your development cycle and should be equally represented in your build environment. Chapter 13 shows you how to develop your code using Test Driven Development — meaning that unit tests are written first and then the actual code follows. However, unit tests aren't the only kinds of tests that will be required to effectively guarantee the quality of your application.

In addition to unit tests, it is common to have automated *acceptance tests* as well as scripts that ensure the proper behavior of your application at the UI layer. Because there are many kinds of tests that you may need, there needs to be a way to distinguish these tests from each other. As we've already shown, the PetSoar test code is all located in src/test. In this directory, you will find both acceptance and unit tests.

Understanding Test Types

The two different types of tests being used in PetSoar are:

- *Unit Tests* — These test only individual units of code, typically at the class level. Unit tests usually take only a few seconds to run and traditionally don't require external services to be running, such as databases or LDAP servers. Because unit tests run so quickly, they are often run countless times throughout a developer session.

- *Acceptance tests* — These tests ensure that the functionality of a system, typically involving many classes and services working in conjunction, is behaving as expected. These tests usually take much longer to run and may require that external services such as databases are running. Because these tests take longer to run and require more setup, they are typically not run as often as unit tests.

Because we want to invest in development speed, we need to identify what our goals are for testing and then ensure that the test environment allows us to reach these goals as quickly as possible. Here are our goals:

- To be able to run all tests with one command
- To be able to run only unit tests or acceptance tests
- To be able to run only the majority of fast unit tests, thereby allowing developers to run *most* of the tests in a very short time

Now that we've identified the three main goals we wish to achieve in our testing environment, we can begin to write some test suites that help us reach these three goals.

The testing framework being used in PetSoar is JUnit, which is discussed in detail in Chapter 3.

JUnit supports test suites, which are nothing more than a collection of tests that all run together. Using this feature of JUnit, we've created four test suites for PetSoar:

- *UnitTestSuite* — Contains all unit tests *except* the slow-running tests
- *SlowUnitTestSuite* — Contains only unit tests that take a relatively long time to run (by slow, we mean longer than a second)

- *AcceptanceTestSuite* — Contains only the acceptance tests
- *CompleteTestSuite* — Aggregates the preceding three suites

At this point, any test that is written must be added to the correct test suite so that it can actually be represented in the testing process of the build. Now that the test suites have been created, let's integrate these suites into `build.xml`:

```
<target name="test" depends="java, config" description="Run unit tests">
    <mkdir dir="${test.results}"/>
    <junit haltonfailure="true" fork="true">
      <sysproperty key="basedir" value="${test.results}"/>
      <formatter type="xml"/>
      <formatter type="plain"/>
      <formatter type="brief" usefile="false"/>
      <classpath>
          <path refid="classpath.build"/>
          <pathelement path="${build.java}"/>
          <pathelement path="${build.test}"/>
      </classpath>
      <test name="org.petsoar.CompleteTestSuite"
            todir="${test.results}"/>
    </junit>
</target>
```

This Ant target runs a single test (or test suite, as the case is here): `CompleteTestSuite`. Because `CompleteTestSuite` contains the other three suites, this ensures that all tests, both unit and acceptance, are run when the user enters the `ant test` command. This satisfies our first of three objectives: the desire to run all tests using a single command.

The other two objectives can be met by individually running the other test suites. We choose not to provide any sort of Ant task that runs these test suites because we require running *all* the tests from within Ant only. However, we still have a great desire to run other test suites inside our IDE — especially the fast unit tests. Luckily, most modern IDEs, such as IDEA and Eclipse, natively support JUnit. The final result is that the most common tasks, running a single test case or a small set of fast test cases, can be accomplished quickly without ever leaving the IDE — once again maximizing developer productivity.

Examining Test Suites, JUnit, and Batch Testing

For those of you familiar with JUnit, you may be wondering why we don't use the `batchtest` feature provided by the Ant-JUnit integration. The `batchtest` feature is a very easy way to identify all the tests in your code base (usually using a pattern such as `Test*.java`) and run them individually. We use test suites for three reasons:

- Test suites provide a good way to distinguish varying degrees of tests (acceptance, fast, and slow).

- The `batchtest` feature of JUnit runs each test using its own class-loading environment, making each test usually have at least a half-second startup time. Using a test suite avoids this delay and thereby makes your tests run considerably faster.

- Because test suites are a standard JUnit feature, they can be run outside of Ant, whereas the `<batchtest>` feature is unique to Ant only. If we didn't use test suites, we would not be able to run all of a single type of test (unit or acceptance) within our IDE.

There are some downsides to using this technique. For example, we must now be very careful to ensure that new unit tests are added to the test suite; otherwise, they will never get run. One way around this limitation is to make the test suite look in our test sources for test classes and then run them.

Also, because all the tests are being run in a single suite, they share the same class-loading environment. While this enhances developer speed, it does mean that individual tests must be careful to properly initialize and dispose of static settings that could otherwise corrupt tests run later in the suite.

Using Version Control

Now that we've decided on a layout for all our sources and project files, as well as decided on a standard way to construct our test environment, it's important to ensure that all our files are secured via source control. Without question, all projects should use a source control system.

The obvious advantage of a source control system is that it provides a complete audit trail of all changes on the code base. This can be used for determining what was changed in a class on a particular date or to retrieve an older version of the system.

However, the more subtle advantage of a source control system is that it gives confidence to the developers: confidence to introduce new code in the system, make a refactoring, fix a bug in a radical way, or delete dead code. Try walking along a three-meter plank of wood on the ground. It's pretty easy, isn't it? Now try walking along that same plank of wood suspended from a tower block. The wood hasn't changed shape, but you'll go much slower. The source control system allows you to walk the wood with confidence.

NOTE Don't actually try walking along a plank of wood, especially if it's suspended from a tower block; you could get hurt or, at a minimum, look very silly.

For source control, we used the Open Source tool CVS.

Deploying PetSoar

Most IDEs can support compiling sources and running tests just like Ant does. One of the more complex but valuable features we'd like our IDE to provide is the ability to quickly deploy the entire application to an application server for end-to-end testing. Because PetSoar deploys on any Servlet 2.3 compatible container, we've chosen to use Caucho Resin as the container of choice for development. While Resin is not a totally free product, it is free for development use and suits our needs very well.

Because only a handful of IDEs support native integration with Servlet containers, we'll show you a more general approach using Resin to launch PetSoar and give access to quick and easy debugging. We chose Resin as the Servlet container only because we think it provides the easiest way to configure and deploy a Web application that is not yet in deployable form, as discussed previously. Without this ability, it would not be in our benefit to have chosen the project structure for PetSoar that we did.

Resin, like all other Java Servlet containers, is nothing more than many Java classes bundled together. When you run your favorite application server, you are really just invoking the server's main Java class. For example, Resin's main class is `com.caucho.server.http.HttpServer`. Knowing this, we can configure our IDE to launch Resin specifically tailored to the PetSoar project in its developmental form (see Figure 12.1).

TIP There are many servers available to you for deployment, some Open Source, some commercial. Depending on your circumstances, different servers may suit you. Refer to the documentation to see how feasible it is to launch the server from within your IDE. Making development speed your number-one priority, either choose a project layout that works with your application server or an application server that works with your project layout. Whatever you do, don't get stuck having to run slow builds several times a day!

Most IDEs allow you to launch a Java class, such as Resin's main class, in either normal mode or debug mode. By choosing to launch Resin in debug mode, you can place break points in your code or third-party code such as WebWork if you have the sources readily available. Debugging is by far the easiest way to track down bugs in your application, especially in the areas of integration with other components.

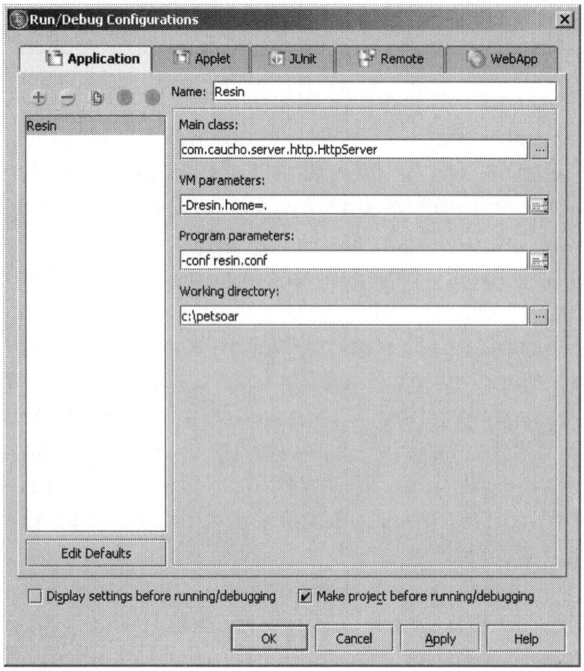

Figure 12.1 Configuration for launching Resin from IDEA

By launching Resin directly from the IDE, you can step through code much quicker than if you use remote debug methods. It also means that you can quickly bring the application server up and down as you need to, all from within your IDE. We recognize that not all applications can be deployed in such a simple manner (the use of EJBs usually makes this much more complicated), but the idea we are showing you is that your efficiency can often be increased if the build environment can accommodate ways for you to work without leaving your IDE.

Clearly it is much quicker to click the "Launch" button from within your IDE than to run the .war Ant target, launch Resin standalone, and finally connect your IDE to Resin using remote debugging. While the time saved may only be 15 seconds, or a minute or two, time quickly adds up and can cost you dearly.

TIP As of JDK 1.4, many debuggers now support the HotSwap capability. HotSwap is a technology that allows developers to "inject" modified code into a running process via the debugger. This means you can make changes to your code and they can be automatically run without restarting the JVM, or even redeploying your application.

Summary

This chapter provided a high-level discussion of the build process used in the PetSoar application, as well as several alternatives that can be employed. The most important thing to remember is that the build environment should be suited to maximize developer productivity. If you find yourself being slowed down by your build structure, it's time to reevaluate your build and release cycle. Chances are that the same results can be reached using a much faster build cycle.

Above all else, you should be intimate with your IDE and your build process. Through the use of continuous integration and fast build cycles, you should find that the development speed at which your team can operate will be much faster than it has been in the past. And if you find yourself repeating the same task more than a few times, that usually means it's time to automate that task rather than to keep repeating yourself. The upfront cost will certainly pay off in a very short amount of time.

CHAPTER 13

Understanding Test Driven Development

Test Driven Development (TDD) is a modern technique for software design that is both simple and incredibly powerful. TDD is a practice heavily adopted by the Extreme Programming (XP) community. The addition of TDD to your software-design toolbox can prove remarkably beneficial for all your software development — regardless of whether you wish to use other features of XP. TDD is a very simple idea: *Before you write your code, write your unit test*. At first glance, it can be difficult to see the benefits of testing like this — don't worry; everyone feels that way. Also, while it sounds like a deceptively simple concept, it can take a while to get used to testing first. However, once you get the hang of it, it can be remarkably addictive, and the quality of your code rapidly improves.

This chapter provides you with a small taste of what TDD is all about. We will introduce you to the reasons why TDD is important and powerful. We will then show you an example scenario of where TDD proves extremely valuable, increasing productivity and decreasing the chance of bugs. Finally, we will show you some useful design patterns that can make TDD even easier to master.

NOTE For a full tutorial on TDD, see *Test-Driven Development by Example* by Kent Beck (Boston: Addison Wesley Professional, 2003).

Why Test First?

The most common reaction to TDD is the question, "Why would you test before you even have an application to test?" This is an understandable question, given that most traditional development techniques preach that testing should only occur once the coding cycle has been completed.

Remember that the goal of this book is to promote simplicity above all else when it comes to application development. Much of achieving this simplicity can be accomplished by using TDD. While testing first may initially seem counter-intuitive, it provides several important benefits over writing tests after you've written your code.

First, let's remember why we test our code: to have confidence that it does what it is supposed to do.

Testing last is boring, and developers tend to not stick to the habit of writing tests if they can get away with it. After writing some code that you've manually tested by hand (not through unit testing), you know it works — so why bother writing a test? Also, as we will show later, making code "testable" usually involves some small level of refactoring to accommodate automated unit tests. If your code has already been written, the incentive to alter it only for the purpose of accommodating unit tests that you know will pass is very small. Time would probably be better spent moving on to the next feature.

The reality is that code changes. It may change because of a bug, new feature, optimization, or refactoring. But as soon as it changes, it needs to be retested. An automated unit test ensures that the class still lives up to its original requirements after modification. If new functionality is being added to your code, new tests must also be written. As long as you follow this regimen, you can be confident that your code is always completely and properly tested. Whether unit tests are written first or last, they must be written to properly ensure that the quality of your project is as high as possible.

Testing First vs. Testing Last

The most obvious advantage of writing your unit tests first is that you no longer need to do any sort of manual testing during the process of writing your code. All you need to do is run your test suite after making any code modifications; if the tests pass, you can stop writing your code. Ask yourself this question: How often do you write some code and then jump through hoops halfway through the code completion just to make sure your changes are actually working the way you had hoped?

Manual testing, on the other hand, requires a considerable amount of work, whether it be writing a very basic command-line program or setting up a rudimentary user interface. With a complete automated test suite, you have only to click a single button ("Run tests" in your IDE), and very quickly you know whether your latest changes were correct or require more work. As your software programs increase in scope and size, the effectiveness of the tests must increase; otherwise, you will drown in bug fixing and not be able to provide new features or enhancements. Also, the chance increases that eventually the entire project will grind to a halt.

Writing tests last is a very difficult undertaking. As already mentioned, it's hard to get excited about writing unit tests for code that has already been verified to work. Furthermore, how can you really know when to *stop* writing tests if you write them after you have written the code? Suppose you write a single test and it passes. Great! But should you write another? Possibly. Then another? Maybe. How long do you continue until you are satisfied? This question cannot be answered, because the behavior of the code was defined when you were writing the code, not the tests. By switching the order, the tests dictate the behavior; therefore, it is much clearer when you should stop testing and move on to another task.

Testing first also prevents feature creep by developers because developers are only writing code to pass tests, not to add features. The tests themselves map to features, but they are much more closely tied to actual customer requirements. When developers begin to write code without trying to make tests pass, they can often fall into the trap of trying to predict future customer requirements — an often fatal mistake for any project.

Tests as Documentation

Not only do the tests provide confidence in your code; they also serve as fantastic sources of documentation for your developers.

Assuming that you have more than one developer working on the project, no one will intimately know every class and method. By having your code fully unit-tested at all times, you have a true library of usage examples for each class and method. Second, doing TDD means that your test should cover all possible behaviors for a method, which means that your documentation covers the method in precise detail without any added useless fluff. If your tests are wrong, the compiler or JUnit will complain, so the tests are *always* up to date with the latest code contracts. This is exactly what developers look for in code documentation — that it covers every class, is precise, and is always updated.

If you've ever worked on a large project with pages and pages of written documentation, you'll know that the likelihood of its being up-to-date with the actual code itself is very slim. The momentum of a project almost always means that the documentation updates lag behind the code evolution — if the documentation is ever updated at all. Having a comprehensive test suite built first is a perfect way to avoid this scenario. Your test suite, and hence your documentation, is written *before* the code.

Software Design Through Test Driven Development

Besides the obvious advantages of having continually tested code, TDD greatly enhances the quality of your software design. By testing first, the modularity of your code quickly comes into shape because you are writing a test for a small piece of code that has no obvious connections to other code (whether existing or yet to be written).

Writing your test first is also an exercise in defining the "black box" characteristics of your code. To properly write a unit test, you must:

- Define the inputs as well as the expected outputs. This means your test becomes a specification by example — not a complete specification, but extremely valuable nonetheless, as it communicates understanding of the intention of the code.

- Test for any side effects the code may have as well as the situations, inputs, or external resources that may cause the code to throw an exception or have any other unusual behavior.

- Define the external resources required by the code you are testing before you actually write the code.

Determining the inputs, outputs, and external resources, as well as defining the behavior of the code, effectively sets up the interfaces, requirements, and *contract* of your code without writing a single line. In this way, TDD is *interface focused* — that is, it examines what a class looks like and what it does, not how it does it. When it finally comes time to write the code (after you've written the initial test), much of the framework for your class or method has already been defined. All that is left is to fill the empty spots until the tests pass.

> **NOTE** A *contract* is defined as an agreement between the users of an interface and the author of the implementing code. The contract, in effect, is how a particular piece of code would be used. Unit tests are very good at exposing that contract through example.

Later in this chapter, we will define the TDD cycle in more specific terms, followed by a real-world example showcasing the benefits of this process.

Narrowing the Requirements

Just having a list of requirements for a project is not enough. Not only do most requirements documents not list all the requirements that clients expect; they usually do not go into the level of detail required to develop and design an application in the most efficient possible manner. Having the most detailed requirements possible for the code we are currently writing is especially important when using TDD because to develop from the top down, as described in the "Work from the Top Down" section later in this chapter, you need to fully understand what you are being asked to create.

We call this search *narrowing the requirements* — continually asking questions and ensuring that the scope of the code you are about to write is perfectly matched to the absolute smallest requirement identified by the client, project manager, or analyst. Because you will be writing the tests first, this task isn't as hard as if the test were being written last. That's because a test is essentially a programmatic way to represent those narrowed requirements. This is good because it means that it is possible, once the requirements have been drilled down to their lowest level, to make an almost one-to-one mapping of requirement to unit test.

Surely you've faced a situation where the requirements given to you did not explicitly outline every detail to be implemented. Since programmers are mathematical and logical thinkers by our very nature, it is often frustrating when we are asked to infer a certain level of requirement details in a project. Instead of employing our creative sides in these situations, it is often better to continue to ask for more details rather than to make assumptions for the client. This approach has two major benefits:

- The client is not surprised when the system is finally used. That is because the features have been verified and supplied by the client or a liaison representing the client.
- Every requirement has been effectively stamped with approval; every unit test written by the team of developers acts as a programmatic stop-gate for unwanted bugs. This means that if undesired behavior does creep into the code base, it will immediately be detected because at least one unit test will fail.

Understanding Testing Techniques

Later in the chapter, we'll showcase an example scenario using TDD, but first we will present some very useful techniques when utilizing TDD in a real-world project. You may find these techniques slightly different from your usual practices.

The following sections define some techniques that are helpful when using unit tests during your development process. These techniques are even more important if you take the extra step and use TDD.

> **NOTE** These are just some techniques that we have learned over time through the experience of overall project design and development as well as the practice of TDD. These techniques and tips are meant to serve as guides, not as hard rules. As you continue to travel down the road of TDD, you will build your own style and may or may not adopt some or all of the techniques outlined here.

Place Unit Tests in the Same Package As Your Code

A good reason for placing your unit tests in the same package as your code is so that the unit tests have access to protected and default methods and fields in the class. In general, most of your unit tests will deal only with public-access methods, but once in a while you may want to test smaller subcomponents of your class that traditionally would not be exposed as public. By placing the unit test in the same package, you can leave the subcomponent methods as protected or default access and still unit-test them.

Never Skip Failing Tests

No matter how much of a rush you are in, never let a failing test make it into the code repository. If you *strictly* follow a TDD process, this issue will not come up. However, if you don't adhere strictly to TDD, you should make absolutely sure that all tests pass before committing any code to the repository. In general, it is a good idea to run your entire test suite just before checking your code into your code repository and also before you go home at night! Don't be afraid to leave a failing test that hasn't been checked in on your machine over night — it is often a good way to start the day.

Isolate the Untestable Using Mock Objects

Code that must access networks, databases, hardware, or GUIs is often very hard to test. Save these tests for acceptance tests, and instead isolate this code from your other code. As mentioned previously, you can do this by using a number of smaller, modular classes instead of a single monolithic class. It is also important to allow your code to have these untestable components easily replaced. Your unit test can replace the object with a mock instance, thereby bypassing the untestable component.

If the object that you want to mock is not under your control and does not implement an interface, we recommend that you write a class that delegates to the untestable class and use that to create a mock instance.

When to Use Interfaces and Classes

One issue that is hard to resolve, primarily because there is no exact science to it, is when to use interfaces and when to just write classes (or abstract classes) directly. Even in the PetSoar application, there is not one specific way of doing things. For example, Pet is a concrete class with no interface, while PetStore is an interface with a separate implementation.

Often, personal judgment and experience will help one arrive at a decision of whether to use an interface or not. In PetSoar we used interfaces in any case where there would be medium-to-complex code implemented. Otherwise, if the object was very trivial like the Pet object (which is nothing but a Plain Old Java Object, or POJO), we made a simple class because there was no concern of any complexity fouling up our tests. Remember that just because an external class *can* be tested, it might still be easier to write tests using mock objects in place of a complex-but-still-testable object.

TIP A good rule of thumb is to start with a class and settle with that until you need an interface for any reason (note that requiring a mock object to test properly is a valid reason). Once you establish that an interface is needed, simply refactor to extract the interface.

Stick with Simplicity

Simplicity is one of the core messages throughout this book. Make your tests simple but effective, and remember that simplicity does not mean useless, stupid, or easy. In fact, keeping your design and associated tests as simple as possible can be very hard, but the effort is well worth it. While sometimes it may seem almost *too* simple, within time you'll see the simplicity begin to pay off in a big way. By maintaining an architecture with simplicity at its heart, you'll find that unit tests will be easier to write and that future modifications to your application will come with ease.

Be careful, though, not to confuse simplicity with weakness, nor should you assume that simplicity is an easy task. In fact, keeping your architecture simple is one of the biggest challenges a software developer can face.

We stress this point because the use of TDD effectively ensures that your software design stays as simple as possible. This is because TDD requires that small, simple steps be taken before each new piece of development may take place. When you follow this practice, your code automatically develops in a modular and simple manner.

Work from the Top Down

Sometimes you may find yourself creating mock objects for code that doesn't even exist yet. For example, in developing PetSoar, one could have written a mock PetStore *before* the real PetStore class was ever created. This type of top-down approach ensures that each component is tested before the smaller, more detailed components are even created. By taking this approach, you may find yourself deriving interfaces organically based on real requirements of other components. This is okay to do and in fact is a great way to ensure that your top-down design approach stays focused on the task at hand without getting sidetracked with external dependencies.

For example, traditional modular software architecture would suggest that writing a single, large class that queries and updates a database would be better implemented using many smaller, modular classes. However, when using TDD, working from the top down is often the simplest way to write an initial test. So, while you could approach TDD by writing a very complex test for the very complex code that is yet to be written, it is much more straightforward to write a smaller test that makes assumptions that other classes, also yet to be written, are going to be put in place to support the top-level test. This would effectively be the difference between the large class using JDBC directly versus a more modular-class hierarchy implementing design patterns such as data-access objects and a persistence manager. This is not to say that TDD can be used as a substitute for good design. In fact, TDD is a catalyst for better design! Not only does TDD help developers to think through the "breakage" conditions for their code; it forces them to think through the usage of your code from an external point of view first.

Knowing how to do this kind of top-down design through the use of TDD is not a trivial task. One of the best ways to do this is to continually ensure that the code you are writing is addressing only the core requirements at hand — nothing more.

> **TIP** Mock Maker (http://www.mockmaker.org) can be used to assist with this process. By working from the top down, you will find yourself making many interfaces and associated mocks before the actual interface is ever created. One option is to use dynamic mocks, as detailed in Chapter 4. Another option is to use Mock Maker to generate mock implementations of interfaces you specify. The choice is up to you — both are very powerful ways to mock your interfaces.

Use Lots of Small Objects

Extending from the top-down development approach comes the approach of using lots of smaller (and simpler) objects that all have simple tests, which tends to keep the complexity of the project under control. Don't be afraid to have many small and simple classes and associated interfaces in your code repository. Ensure that each object has a specific role and does not do too much. While sometimes it may seem redundant to those unfamiliar with your development process, this extreme level of simplicity is what makes the TDD cycle so beautifully straightforward and powerful.

Ensure That Your Test Suite Runs Quickly

To effectively follow the TDD cycle, your entire test suite should be able to run in a very short amount of time. If your test suite takes more than a couple of seconds to run, developers will run the suite less and less and thereby circumvent the entire process. By contrast, if the tests run in under a second, there is no reason why a developer couldn't run the test suite after every single change made to the code. Just as you would refactor your production code if it were too slow, you must refactor your test suite regularly to keep it efficient and up to date. Using speedy mock objects is the best way to avoid long processing time when running your test suite.

Avoid Statics and Singletons

Singletons and static methods tend to make your code nondeterministic, meaning that testing of such code can be more complicated or impossible. Because the goal of TDD is to ensure that your code is as simple as possible at the *atomic level*, it is best to avoid statics when possible.

For example, one way to avoid statics is to set up a framework that keeps track of object resources, like the Singleton Pattern does, but instead have this framework externally to apply the resource through setter methods. In the next chapter, we will explore Inversion of Control, which is one way to achieve this.

If you must use static methods or singletons, be very careful with your test fixture and ensure that the `setUp()` and `tearDown()` methods of your unit test properly initialize and dispose of the static context.

Testing the TDD Cycle

The TDD cycle, when strictly adhered to, will ensure that at any given moment the code in your project will be largely tested.

We say largely tested, not something like 100-percent tested, because no testing methodology can promise 100-percent coverage — we'll admit that up front. However, TDD does present surprisingly high levels of completeness.

The TDD cycle is represented in Figure 13.1 and is as follows:

1. Write the initial test based upon your best estimates of the inputs and outputs of the code you need to write. This test should not even compile initially because the classes and methods it tests don't exist yet.

2. Create the interfaces, classes, and methods required so that the test now compiles and fails. Some IDEs can help with this by automatically figuring out these methods and creating them for you. Methods that have return values should return a "basic" value that requires no thought (null for Objects and 0 or false for primitives).

3. Implement the code that is to be tested and continue writing until the test passes.

4. Refactor the resulting code to improve the design and remove duplication.

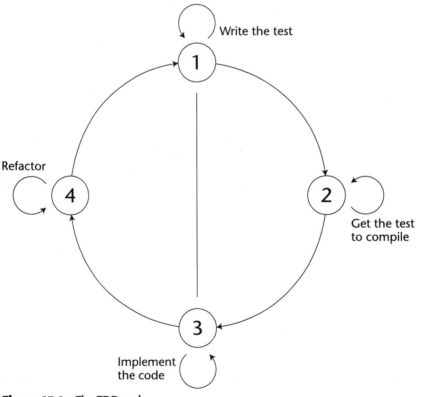

Figure 13.1   The TDD cycle

Example Scenario Using TDD

To better see the benefits of testing first, we will create a new feature and then add new requirements to that feature using TDD.

To illustrate the TDD, we shall implement a simple class for stripping XML tags from a string.

Step 1

Following the TDD cycle, we write the tests first. The way to get started is to write the simplest possible test. This is Step 1 of the testing cycle.

```
public void testStripTags() {
  // the first thing we do is instantiate
  // the class we want to test...
  TagStripper stripper = new TagStripper();

  // ... then we test the behavior
  assertEquals("hello, ",
               stripper.strip("hello, <world>"));
  assertEquals("this  hello",
               stripper.strip("this <is> hello"));

  assertEquals("not bold",
               stripper.strip("<b>not bold</b>"));
}
```

This simple test has defined the signature for a new method called `strip()` and how the method is expected to behave.

Step 2

Step 2 of the testing cycle is to write the stub classes, interfaces, and methods so that the new tests will compile, run, and fail.

```
public class TagStripper
  public String strip(String content) {
    return null;
  }
}
```

Now the test compiles and can be run. If all is going according to plan, a Red Bar (indicating test failure) should be produced by your test runner.

```
testStripTags: expected:<hello, > but was:<null>
```

NOTE We use the terms *Red Bar* and *Green Bar* heavily throughout the rest of the book to indicate test failures and passes, respectively.

The test failed because the expectations did not match the return value (null).

This Red Bar acts as a sanity check. If a Red Bar were not received, it would alert you to the fact that all is not as expected. Maybe the wrong test case is being run (a common mistake), the tests are not actually testing anything useful, or perhaps the functionality is there already and you forgot about it. Sometimes we even throw in deliberate "bugs" as a sanity check that our test code is working as we expect.

Step 3

We are now free to actually start writing the implementation code of the tagstripper, running the test each time we think we are close to passing. This is Step 3 of the testing cycle.

The simplest way to strip out the tags to get the test to pass is to use a regular expression.

```
public String strip(String content) {
    return content.replaceAll("<.+>", "");
}
```

To complete Step 3, a passing test is required. Running the test yields a Red Bar.

```
testStripTags: expected:<not bold> but was:<>
```

This is caused by the regular expression being greedy and matching the pattern from the opening angle bracket in the first tag to the closing angle bracket in the last tag. Without a test, this could have slipped by.

By adding a question mark after the plus, we can force the pattern to not be greedy.

```
public String strip(String content) {
    return content.replaceAll("<.+?>", "");
}
```

Now the test is run again, and you should get a Green Bar indicating that the test passes.

Look at how simple the code is. The entire method simply uses a five-character regular expression. This kind of simplicity is common in TDD.

That's Step 3 completed.

NOTE The previous code uses the regular-expression enhancements added to Java in JDK1.4. If you require regular-expression support on earlier versions of the JDK, you can make use of the Jakarta RegExp project (which provides a simple-to-use regular expression engine) or Jakarta ORO (which adds a full suite of text-processing tools). Following are the URLs for both projects:

```
http://jakarta.apache.org/regexp/
```

```
http://jakarta.apache.org/oro/
```

Step 4

Step 4 is to refactor the code to its simplest form. In this case, there's very little that can be done to simplify further, so this stage can be skipped.

Example Scenario Revisited

You may have a nagging feeling that the code in the previous example is *too* simple. What happens if the input is null? How should the method behave? It could return null, an empty string, or throw an exception. Following are the steps for a slightly more complex example scenario.

Step 1

At the moment, the test does not define the behavior. This can be added to the test case that takes us back around to Step 1.

```
public testNullInput() {
  TagStripper stripper = new TagStripper();
  assertNull(stripper.strip(null));
}
```

This test states that if null is passed to the `strip()` method, null should be returned.

Step 2

Step 2 is to get the test to compile. It already does, as no new methods have been introduced. Running the test produces a Red Bar.

```
testNullInput: java.lang.NullPointerException
```

Step 3

On to Step 3 — aiming for the Green Bar. A simple null check in the method could fix this:

```
public String strip(String content) {
  if (content == null) {
    return null;
  } else {
    return content.replaceAll("<.+?>", "");
  }
}
```

Running the test again produces a Green Bar.

Step 4

Step 4 is to refactor the result; but again, there's not a lot that can be done to simplify it, so this stage can be skipped.

NOTE In all but the most trivial applications, this last step is one of the most important and must not be overlooked.

Remember that just because your tests pass does not mean your code is as simple as it could be. In Step 4 we look back at the code and test we have written and try to refactor them both to improve the simplicity of the code. As we have written a comprehensive test, while we refactor we can continually run our test to assure ourselves that our refactoring doesn't break anything.

Enhancing the Functionality

In order to continue the TDD cycle, whenever a new requirement, bug, or re-factoring is requested to be implemented, a test must first be written in such a manner that it first fails and then passes once the feature has been implemented.

Step 1

Let's start by adding a new requirement to the strip() method, such that it should not remove tags that start with uppercase letters. Following the cycle illustrated in Figure 13.1, the first step is to write new tests for this requirement:

```
public void testDontStripCapitalizedTags() {
  TagStripper stripper = new TagStripper();

  // do strip
  assertEquals("world",
               stripper.strip("<hello>world</hello>"));

  assertEquals("world",
               stripper.strip("<hELLo>world</hELLo>"));

  // dont strip
  assertEquals("<HELLO>world</HELLO>",
               stripper.strip("<HELLO>world</HELLO>"));

  assertEquals("<Hello>world</Hello>",
               stripper.strip("<Hello>world</Hello>"));
}
```

Step 2

Step 2 is to get the test to compile. It already does. The test runs, and it fails with a Red Bar.

```
testDontStripCapitalizedTags: expected:<<HELLO>world</HELLO>>
                              but was:<world>
```

Step 3

Step 3 is to get the test to pass. The regular expression can be modified to ensure the tag starts with a lowercase letter. Of course, a tag may also start with a forward slash, so this must be taken into account.

```
public String strip(String content) {
  if (content == null) {
    return null;
  } else {
    return content.replaceAll("</?[a-z].+?>", "");
  }
}
```

Running the test produces another Red Bar.

```
testStripTags: expected:<not bold> but was:<>
```

Oddly, the new test actually passes, but a previous test is now failing. Because the tests are automated and all the tests are run all the time, code can be changed confidently, knowing that anything that may break previous work will be caught.

This shows why it is vitally important to run all the tests regularly, not just the test that you are currently working with. Running the complete test suite after each incremental change allows you to very quickly determine the effects of the new code. Looking at it from another angle, there is nothing more frustrating than running the complete test suite after a whole day of development to find failures because you can't be sure exactly which change you made has caused the tests to fail.

The failing test occurs because the regular expression doesn't correctly match tags containing a single letter (such as </b> for example). A subtle change to the regular expression can fix this:

```
public String strip(String content) {
  if (content == null) {
    return null;
  } else {
    return content.replaceAll("</?[a-z].*?>", "");
  }
}
```

Now the test can be run to reveal a Green Bar, and Step 3 is complete.

Step 4

Again, no work is required for Step 4, as the code is very simple already and contains no duplication.

As you can see, only a slight modification was made to the original code and now all three tests pass. You have now followed three complete cycles of TDD.

Summary

TDD is one of those incredibly simple concepts to grasp, yet very hard to master. This chapter has demonstrated a real-world scenario and development cycle that showcases TDD in such a way that you can begin to apply these techniques in your projects as soon as tomorrow morning. However, it is important to remember that no one can change the development style overnight, and it will most likely take several project lifecycles before you can truly use TDD from start to finish. The rest of Part III shows you how to use the TDD cycle to build the PetSoar application.

CHAPTER 14

Managing Lifecycles and Dependencies of Components

In Chapter 13, we looked at Test Driven Development (TDD) as a means of identifying what our components actually need to do, rather than what we *think* they will need to do. This tends to lead to a smaller, more focused code base and a clearer understanding of the interactions between components. The refactoring aspects of TDD mean the code is also going to be as clean as it can be.

This chapter provides a broader definition of a component and describes a number of ways to manage dependencies between components. We look at containers and the ways in which they can help components and the idea of coupling. We introduce a pattern called Inversion of Control and explain how it can lead to cleaner, more testable, more loosely coupled code.

Understanding Components and Services

In its simplest terms, a *component* is just an object or group of objects that does something useful. The component will be available through some sort of registry, which can be as simple as a static factory method or as complex as the Java Naming and Directory Interface (JNDI) component registry in J2EE.

Typically, a component provides some sort of *service*, so the terms "service" and "component" are used largely interchangeably throughout the remainder of the book.

In this context, an application boils down to interactions between components, so it is vital that we understand exactly how components find one another and interact with one another and how they are created and destroyed (and other parts of their life cycle).

The Java language provides a nice abstraction for talking to components, in terms of interfaces and concrete classes. We can describe a component by an interface (that is, the methods it supports) and then provide a concrete implementation in a separate class that implements the interface.

Handling Dependencies

There are probably as many ways of handling component dependencies as there are programmers writing components (or at least programmers writing component frameworks). This section presents a number of these and highlights some of their strengths and weaknesses.

Using Direct Instantiation

This is the simplest case, in which we do not even use an interface to abstract our implementation. The component directly constructs an instance of its dependent, referencing the implementation of the component class:

```java
public interface Hat {
    . . .
}

public class Beanie implements Hat {
    . . .
}

public class Head {

    private Hat hat;

    public Head() {
        hat = new Beanie(); // concrete implementation
    }

    . . .

}
```

This is an example of *tight coupling*. Every time we instantiate a Head, it comes with a Beanie. This makes it much harder to test the behavior of a Head, and in particular we cannot substitute a mock Hat to see how the Head interacts with it.

TDD tends to produce quite loosely coupled systems, which is generally a good thing. The code is more maintainable because you can make a change without having to follow spaghetti links through the code base. It is also more testable because you can limit the scope within which you are testing (for example, by mocking a database connection so you don't make expensive database calls).

Using a Factory

To introduce a level of indirection, we can use a static method in a factory class. In this case, we see that the Head class doesn't directly instantiate the implementation. So, building on our existing Hat and Beanie:

```
public class HatFactory {
    public static Hat getHat() {
        return new Beanie(); // concrete implementation
    }
}

public class Head {
    private Hat hat;

    public Head() {
        hat = HatFactory.getHat(); // indirection through factory
    }

    ...
}
```

This looks a little better, because the Head no longer references the Beanie directly, but we can still get only one type of Hat.

(It is worth noting that now that we have a factory, we could make the Hat instance a Singleton just by making the `getHat()` method return a single, static instance.)

We can add methods to the factory to provide any number of Hats, but how do we tell the Head which method to call on the HatFactory?

Using a Registry

One solution is to store a *type* of Hat and have our static method instantiate the instance by reflection rather than by calling the concrete class's constructor (this is called *late binding*). This allows us to substitute a different Hat class whenever we like, which means that we could sneak in a MockHat in the setup for a test (and remember to remove it afterward).

```
public class HatRegistry {

    private static Class hatClass;

    public static Hat getHat() {
        try {
            return hatClass.newInstance(); // by reflection
        } catch (Exception e) {
            ...
        }
    }

    public static void registerHat(Class newClass) {
        hatClass = newClass;
    }

}

public class Head {

    private Hat hat;

    public Head() {
        hat = HatRegistry.getHat(); // indirection through registry
    }

}
```

At last, we have completely decoupled the type of Hat from the Head. We can now create Heads wearing all sorts of Hats just by changing the type in the registry.

NOTE The registry pattern is described in *Patterns of Enterprise Application Architecture* by Martin Fowler (Boston: Addison Wesley Professional, 2002).

Using a Container

If we follow the idea of a registry to its natural conclusion, we end up with the concept of a *container*. A container provides services to the components it contains, usually by means of some sort of *context*. The component asks the container for any services or facilities it requires. The following code illustrates a simple container context. Don't worry about the container implementation — the interesting features here are the interfaces that the container implementer (or vendor) provides and the way that our Head now gets its Hat.

```
// defined by container provider
public interface Context {
```

```
    Object getComponent(String name);
}

// defined by container provider
interface Component {
    void setContext(Context context);
}

// our own application class
public class Head implements Component {

    private Hat hat;

    public Head() {
        // nothing to do in constructor now
    }

    // called by container after constructing our Head instance
    public void setContext(Context context) {
        hat = (Hat)context.getComponent("hat");
    }

    ...
}
```

Now we can get whatever components we like from the container. The container's responsibility is to manage any resources we need, which typically requires some external configuration. This makes it much easier to write components, because we can now focus solely on the component's behavior and not worry about how we obtain any other components with which it interacts. What's more, the container can manage complex issues for us such as contention for limited resources (database connections or threads) by implementing clever pooling algorithms.

Understanding the Component Lifecycle

Some components will have a life cycle associated with them. This defines a series of states the component will exist in and typically allows only certain activities in certain states. For example, a database connection instance could be *available* or *busy* at any point and may throw an exception if we try to run a query while it is in its busy state.

An additional benefit of having the component in a container is that we can rely on the container to manage the life cycle of the component. This again simplifies the code we have to write. For example, the container could guarantee to call a reset method on our hypothetical database connection immediately before handing it to us, so that we know it will be in a consistent state.

(Many J2EE containers have exactly this sort of behavior when handling pooled resources such as database connections.)

Understanding Inversion of Control

So far, we have assumed that the component (Head) is responsible for getting its own dependent (Hat). As we introduce more components, and more dependencies between components, there could be a huge increase in the amount of code we have to write in each component just to get components talking to one another.

To recap, our journey so far in getting a Hat on our Head has led from a concrete implementation (via a factory and a registry) to a container, but throughout the journey the Head has been the master of its own destiny. Another option, which addresses the issue of managing complex dependencies, is to have the container pre-populate the component with everything it needs. This is known as *Inversion of Control* (*IoC*).

For each component we register, we tell the container (either programmatically or via an external configuration) about any dependencies the component has. Then when we ask for a particular component, the container will assemble all of its dependencies (recursively, so that any sub-dependencies are also assembled) and deliver us a fully configured component.

There is more to this than initially meets the eye, so let's explore the implications of IoC.

Examining the Benefits

Using a container that supports IoC gives us the following benefits:

- Components are easier to test. In effect, our test case becomes a container. In the setup for the test, we instantiate the component in the way the container would and configure any dependencies. Then we test the component's behavior and make various assertions about what should have happened.

- Components are easier to implement. As mentioned, there is no need to hardwire the configuration of all those dependencies in the component implementation.

- As a direct result of this, we can focus more on developing our business application and worry less about the plumbing between the components.

- It is more aligned with the spirit of TDD. We get loosely coupled components by design, which makes testing, development, and ongoing maintenance of our application easier.

Exploring the Disadvantages

However, it is not all sweetness and light:

■ The dependencies have to be declared *somewhere*. Whether this is programmatically or externally, or a combination of the two, we need to communicate to the container exactly how to manage the component.

■ Because of this, it is not immediately obvious just by looking at the component exactly what its dependencies or life-cycle constraints are. We must remember to look elsewhere at its deployment configuration.

■ Our component is now coupled to the container, either by having to be deployed with a configuration or being marked by container-specific code such as marker interfaces. This is true of virtually all containers, however, and not particular to just IoC. XWork, the IoC container we use for PetSoar, uses a combination of marker interfaces and XML configuration to define both the dependencies and the life-cycle model for the components we deploy to it. This is described in more detail later in this chapter.

INVERSION OF CONTROL IN EJB CONTAINERS

IoC is used in EJB containers. As mentioned, a container is essentially something that handles resource management for you. EJB containers call `ejbCreate()`, `ejbRemove()`, `ejbActivate()`, and `ejbPassivate()` in your business-logic code (the bean itself) at the correct times based on the life cycle of your bean. The SessionContext or EntityContext is pushed to the bean as well using the methods `setSessionContext()` or `setEntityContext()`, also called by the container. As for services, EJB containers provide essentially three services and/or resource-management features:

◆ Security — EJB provides a standard mechanism to dictate which roles have access to a particular resource.

◆ Persistence — EJB Container Managed Persistence provides a way for objects to be persisted, usually to a relational database.

◆ Transactions — Can be demarcated in six different ways in the EJB deployment descriptors, some of which automatically handle transaction behavior for you (Container Managed Transactions).

The downfall to this list is that it is static. There is no way to tell an EJB container that some of your business objects need access to the UserProfile resource. In the purest form, containers that perform passive resource management do nothing by default. It is up to the developer to provide extensions upon the framework that provide for the three preceding EJB features, as well as new features identified, such as the UserProfile, ShoppingCart, or HibernateSession resource management.

In practice, this latter constraint (coupling to the container) is not usually a handicap. We will typically choose the container as an up-front architectural decision. (Or at least we will choose the *type* of container. For example, we might decide to deploy to a J2EE Servlet container, so we will write Servlet classes that extend the javax.servlet.http.HttpServlet class, or EJBs that implement javax.ejb.EJBObject. This does not limit us to any particular vendor's container, just to a general container model.)

Understanding Separation of Concerns

In all but the simplest of systems, the fact that we are extracting the configuration details from the component is actually a good thing. We are following a well-established strategy known as *Separation of Concerns*, which says that different issues (such as implementation, deployment, and configuration) should be handled separately. Again, this is in the spirit of loose coupling. The same component could be deployed differently in different containers, or even multiple times within the same container, without any code changes to the component itself.

Using Containers to Define Scope

Of course, we are not limited to deploying components to just a single container. There is an elegant model whereby we can nest containers to allow us to limit components to a particular scope. The way it works is like this.

Each container apart from the outermost one holds a reference to a parent container. When a container identifies a dependency, it looks to see whether the dependency corresponds to a registered component. If not, it passes the request to the parent container and so on up the line until either the request is fulfilled or we run out of containers.

In the J2EE world, this is directly analogous to the Request, Session, and Application scopes of an HTTP request. We assemble three containers in a chain: the innermost container represents the Request scope, the middle one the Session, and the outer one the Application scope. Thus, if a component is in the Request scope, it will be available immediately to any component requesting it. Failing that, the container will defer to its parent representing the Session scope, and finally we fall back to the Application scope container.

In this way, we can model the behavior of an HTTP request by a simple relationship between containers.

Using XWork's Container Implementation

There are a number of Open Source IoC containers available for use. Several containers exist for the Apache Avalon project, as well as one for XWork, the underlying engine in WebWork. Because we are using WebWork, it makes sense to use XWork as our IoC container. However, the concepts and techniques offered by Avalon and XWork are very similar and, as such, are applicable to either container.

The XWork IoC implementation works in the following way:

1. Reads an XML configuration file that specifies the resource's *class, scope,* and *enabler interface.* The enabler interface must be implemented by any resource that *depends on* the resource being registered. For example, our Head would implement a HatAware interface to alert the container to the fact it requires a Hat resource.

2. Applies all resources to the object based on the enabler interfaces it implements, recursively resolving dependencies. If a resource is not yet available, it is initialized as explained in Step 3.

3. Calls the `init()` method of the action object at the start of the resource scope and the `dispose()` method at the end (if they exist and the action implements the Initializable or Disposable interface, respectively).

Configuring the Container

Let's look at an example configuration of the XWork container to get a better idea of how resources are associated with a scope and an enabler interface:

```xml
<components>

  <component>
    <scope>application</scope>
    <class>HibernatePersistenceManager</class>
    <enabler>PersistenceAware</enabler>
  </component>

  <component>
    <scope>application</scope>
    <class>DefaultPetStore</class>
    <enabler>PetStoreAware</enabler>
  </component>

  <component>
    <scope>request</scope>
```

```
    <class>HibernateTransaction</class>
    <enabler>TransactionAware</enabler>
</component>

<component>
  <scope>session</scope>
  <class>SimpleShoppingCart</class>
  <enabler>ShoppingCartAware</enabler>
</component>

<component>
  <scope>session</scope>
  <class>DefaultUserProfile</class>
  <enabler>UserProfileAware</enabler>
</component>

</components>
```

As new resources are developed in the application, you will want to create new enablers as well as define the scope for that resource. The configuration file is called components.xml and must be located in the classpath of your application (usually WEB-INF/classes). This makes it extremely easy to introduce new resource types in the PetSoar container, whereas other static containers such as EJB don't support this kind of modularity.

Understanding How the Container Works

We won't get into too much detail about how the XWork implementation works, but needless to say it is very simple and comes out to fewer than 400 lines of code — not bad considering the power that it offers! What we will discuss here is how the various container scopes tie into the Servlet-specific environment.

The core container actually does not limit itself to the three scopes we have discussed so far. In fact, the scope names could be anything you desire. The key is that there must be an instance of a com.opensymphony.xwork.interceptors .component.ComponentManager associated with each scope that you require access to. A ComponentManager is a simple class that allows the registration of resources as well as the application of those resources onto objects.

ComponentManagers may be chained together, usually ordered by scope hierarchy. This is accomplished easily because each ComponentManager has an optional "fallback" ComponentManager associated with it. In WebWork, the hierarchy for access to a ComponentManager is first *Request*, then *Session*, then *Application*. The ComponentInterceptor bundled with XWork passes a WebWork action to the ComponentManager associated with the current ActionContext, which was in turn set by WebWork's ServletDispatcher to be the Component-Manager associated with the HttpServletRequest. That ComponentManager then passes the action to its fallback ComponentManager that is associated with the visitor's session. The next fallback is then the application-level Component-Manager, which in turn has no fallback associated.

These various ComponentManagers are associated with each scope through the use of existing Servlet 2.3 Specification features. WebWork ships with two listeners and a filter that are registered in PetSoar's web.xml. The App-licationLifecycleListener implements javax.servlet.ServletContextListener and, as the specification indicates, is invoked only once for the entire application life cycle. The other listener, SessionLifecycleListener, is used for the session scope and implements javax.servlet.http.HttpSessionListener. This listener is initialized and destroyed whenever a new session in the Web application is created or invalidated. Finally, we have a filter, RequestLifecycleFilter, which is mapped to all requests and invoked for every single request.

```
[web.xml]

<web-app>

    ...

    <listener>
        <listener-class>ApplicationLifecycleListener</listener-class>
    </listener>

    <listener>
        <listener-class>SessionLifecycleListener</listener-class>
    </listener>

    <filter>
        <filter-name>container</filter-name>
        <filter-class>RequestLifecycleFilter</filter-class>
    </filter>

    <filter-mapping>
        <filter-name>container</filter-name>
        <url-pattern>/*</url-pattern>
    </filter-mapping>

</web-app>
```

In each of these three classes, a ComponentManager is created and associated with the scope. This provides for a unique ComponentManager for every unique scope possible in the application, and as such allows for proper resource management on every request to the application server.

JAKARTA AVALON

The Jakarta Avalon project is a server-framework project at Apache consisting of a number of subprojects.

At the core is Avalon Framework, a collection of common life-cycle interfaces. Complementing these are some guideline patterns:

- ◆ Separation of concerns.
- ◆ All components have an interface/implementation separation.
- ◆ Avoidance of static methods and singletons.
- ◆ Takes a container/component view of the world using IoC.

The lifecycle interfaces include initialization, disposal, starting, stopping, configuration, and dependency management to name a few. The interfaces and patterns are designed to be used both by component developers and container implementers.

There are a number of containers available that support the lifecycle interfaces developed in Avalon. One such container is Avalon Phoenix, which assists in binding components together from an assembly, configuration, advanced life-cycle management, remote component management through JMX, thread pooling, hot deployment, and environments in which components can be isolated from other components.

```
http://avalon.apache.org/
```

Testing XWork Components

As we described earlier, one of the benefits of IoC is the ease with which we can test components. Our test case simply acts like the XWork container, so we don't need to make any changes to our components in order to test them. (Another way to look at this is that having developed our component test first, it needs no additional changes to make it compatible with XWork. We just update the XML configuration details and deploy our new component.)

Let's write a test for our Head component:

[HatAware.java]

```
// name "XxxAware" required by XWork
interface HatAware {
    void setHat(Hat hat);
}
```

[TestHead.java]

```java
// support class for test case
private class HatMock implements Hat {
    private boolean hatRaised = false;

    // method from Hat interface
    public void raise() {
        hatRaised = true;
    }

    // so we can test
    public void isRaised() {
        return hatRaised;
    }
}


public class TestHead extends junit.framework.TestCase {
    public void testHeadRaisesHat() {
        // This is what XWork would do...
        Head head = new Head();
        HatMock hat = new HatMock(); // ...except this bit
        head.setHat(hat);

        // Now test behavior
        head.raiseHat();

        // And assert results
        assertEquals("Hat should be raised", true, hat.isRaised());
    }
}
```

[Head.java]

```java
class Head implements HatAware {
    private Hat hat;

    public Head() {
    }

    // from HatAware interface
    public void setHat(Hat hat) {
        this.hat = hat;
    }

    // the code we write to make the test pass
    public void raiseHat() {
        hat.raise(); // woohoo! passing test!
    }
}
```

Now all we have to do to deploy our tested Head component into XWork is a simple piece of XML configuration:

```
<component>
  <scope>application</scope>
  <class>Beanie</class>
  <enabler>HatAware</enabler>
</component>
```

We don't need to do anything else for the Head class. WebWork will recognize that it requires a Hat (and thereby construct a Beanie and set it in the Head instance) just by virtue of the fact that Head implements the HatAware interface.

Summary

In this chapter, we have seen that components are a very simple yet powerful way to model a system. Components take the concept of an object model and extend it to incorporate sophisticated runtime configuration of interactions between components. This *late binding* allows us to incorporate implementations of components that did not exist when the application was first written.

We have learned that Inversion of Control (IoC) separates the concern of implementing a component from the details of deploying or obtaining it at runtime. It is quite a subtle reworking of the idea of collaboration between components and has a number of advantages in terms of enhancing software testability and reusability.

PetSoar uses an IoC container called XWork, which is part of WebWork, to manage components and their interactions.

CHAPTER 15

Defining the Domain Model

This chapter delves into one of the most crucial layers of the application — the business logic.

It builds a domain model to encapsulate the data the PetSoar application encompasses and the business rules surrounding that data.

As well as illustrating how to make use of a persistence layer, Hibernate, this chapter shows the process of evolving a flexible domain model through test-first and refactoring techniques.

Considering the Advantages of a Domain Model

Most enterprise applications persist data in a relational database. The role of the domain model is to provide a set of classes that look similar (but not identical) to the underlying database schema.

These classes encapsulate code such as JDBC specifics and SQL queries. The most important advantage of this encapsulation is that business logic is much easier to write because it deals with plain objects but never the specifics of how to query the database. Code is more readable and easier to change.

These domain objects are easier to develop against because they are strongly typed, allowing an IDE to provide features such as code-completion, refactoring, and the ability to find usages of a particular class or field throughout your code. You do not get these benefits if you are using SQL queries directly.

Another benefit of a domain model is that it does not have to map directly to a database schema. This allows awkward tables and relations to be hidden from the application code and allows the schema to change without causing a large impact on the code that depends on it.

The downside to domain models is that they require more up-front work, because domain classes must be created, and additional code is required to transfer the state of the classes to and from the database. However, using a persistence layer such as Hibernate can vastly simplify this, because it handles the bulk of the work. Also, a tool such as Hibernate can automatically build a database schema for you, reducing the work even more.

Another perceived downside of using a domain model is performance. An optimized table join or stored procedure that can modify or query all required data in one database hit will typically outperform a domain model. However, this is at the cost of maintainability. In modern environments, faster hardware is cheap, whereas development costs are expensive. The flexibility of maintainable code (with the option to optimize bottlenecks where needed) is a lot more beneficial than the opposite.

Tackling the Layers

An application is split into layers. Each layer interacts with the layer below it and offers a level of abstraction. These layers can start as high up as a business process, going down past the user interface, database schema, operating system, and even down as far as the hardware on the motherboard. Thankfully, each is abstracted well enough so that we need not deal with the hardware specifics when implementing the business rules for an invoicing system.

As application developers, we can safely ignore many layers. However, layers we are interested in include the following:

- *Database schema* — The structure of the database
- *Infrastructure* — Nondomain specific code such as logging, security, and persistence
- *Domain model* — The domain-specific objects and business rules
- *User interface* — The face of the application that the user interacts with

Even those four layers can require a lot of work from the developer. A tough question is how to break down the work required to complete the layers and in which order to tackle them.

Comparing a Layer-Driven vs. Feature-Driven Approach

One way to organize the work required for implementing the four layers is to work on a single layer at a time, completing the entire layer before moving onto the next one. This is a *layer-driven* approach (see Figure 15.1). In many companies adhering to this strategy, a single person or a dedicated team is assigned to implementing a specific layer. This person or team effectively has some level of code ownership on the code produced for the assigned layer.

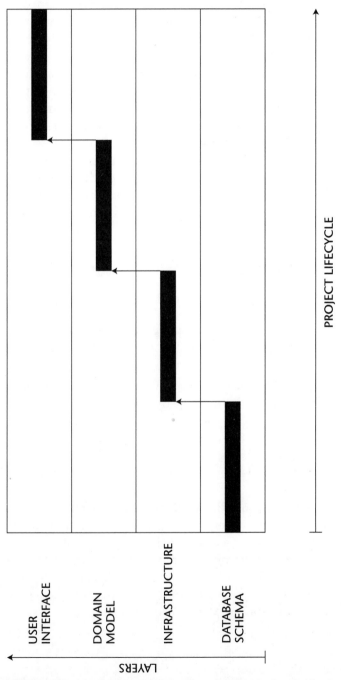

Figure 15.1   Layer-driven approach to implementing the layers

An alternate approach is to complete a very small part of one layer, a small part of another layer, until a small part of the application is complete across all layers. Then repeat the process for each new part of the application. This is a *feature-driven* approach. The goal is to implement the functionality of a single independent *story* or *feature*. So, a single person or a small team is assigned to implement a single feature of the system, and they go through layers and implement whatever is needed in each layer to accomplish the goal, which is a functional feature of the system.

The downside to using a layer-driven approach is that it gives you only one chance to get the implementation right. It is not until the final layer is implemented that an end result is seen, and at this point it is too late to go back and change other layers. This puts a large emphasis on getting the layers correct the first time and can often lead to overengineering.

On the other hand, feature-driven approaches allow small parts of applications to be completed quickly. Focusing on a smaller part of the application keeps things much simpler and reduces the risk of error. The result can be seen very early on and any bugs or improvements can be tackled on the next pass of the layer.

Choosing Bottom Up, Top Down, or Middle Out

As well as having the choice of how much work to do on each layer at a time, you can choose in which order to tackle them.

A common approach is to work your way up the layers one by one, starting from the lowest layer (the database schema) to the highest layer (the user interface). This is known as *bottom up*.

The opposite of this approach is *top down*. This is where the user interface is defined first and the layers below are defined one by one until the lowermost layer is encountered.

Another approach is to start from the domain model. Driven by the user interface requirements, we create a domain model (middle) and then map it to the persistence layer (down) and user interface (up). This is known as *middle out*.

When using TDD, a top-down or middle-out iterative approach fits nicely. For each new feature required in the system, a test can be written that allows the developer to discover which classes are required for the user interface. In implementing these, the classes for the domain model and infrastructure as well as the database schema are discovered. This approach results in code suitable to fulfill a specific user requirement but no more. For each new requirement, this is repeated, refactoring existing code where applicable.

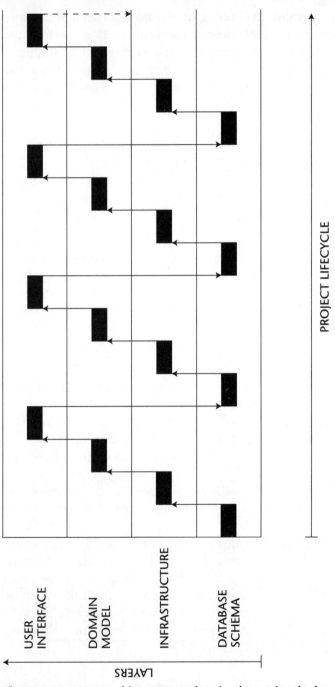

Figure 15.2   Feature-driven approach to implementing the layers

All these techniques are valid, depending on the task at hand. Sometimes the application ends up being implemented using all of these techniques. When using a feature-driven approach, it is easy to switch which technique is being used. The important thing is to select the correct technique for the feature you are going to implement. To make the correct decision, we follow two basic rules:

- *Go for the most achievable result* — It's important to make positive progress when the work starts; otherwise, the team gets lost in details and tries desperately to overcome the faced problems. There's the possibility of making mistakes or compromises just to overcome a problem. After achieving some tangible results, we're *in the coding flow* and it sounds like we can implement (and we want to implement) the whole feature piece by piece.

- *Go for some seeable results first* — We might waste a lot of time trying to implement some infrastructure code and yet, at the end of the day, have a sense of no progress at all. It's important to see some results first. Seeing the output of the program gives a more realistic sense of progress. An added benefit is that we can show the results to the client while still developing it and communicate the user story in a more hands-on and effective manner.

So we might choose to use any of the three techniques to implement a story, but when making the decision, we keep these two rules in mind.

We might choose to start from the model and the business logic if we think that it's where we can make the most progress and see some tangible results. In this case, tangible results are the output of the test cases, since there's no user interface created yet.

We might choose to start from the user interface, perhaps by just prototyping something or to show the user interface to the client or to get a better understanding of the story.

We might even use the bottom-up approach in some cases. In some cases, we might even use a little bit of bottom-up first and then middle-out for the rest. For example, we might have a legacy database schema, so we use a tool like MiddleGen to generate the persistable domain model from the database schema first and then continue implementing the rest of the story by working on the domain model. MiddleGen can generate the domain model classes annotated by XDoclet tags from the database tables.

Identifying the Current Goal

Our goal in this chapter is to develop the domain model code to facilitate the maintenance of pets in the pet store.

It must be possible for pet-store owners to add pets to the online catalog, which can be viewed by visitors to the site. Because there may be a large number of pets in the store, it should also be possible for the owner to organize them into a hierarchical category structure, which visitors to the store can use for browsing the pet selection.

We choose to use a middle-out approach. In Chapter 16, the domain model developed in this chapter will be used for implementing the user interface of the application.

During our journey in this chapter, we learn how to apply TDD techniques to create the classes representing pets and pet categories and how they are added and retrieved from the pet store. The developed domain model will be persisted in a relational database using the Hibernate object-relational framework.

So we will first try to implement the domain model and persistence logic for adding a pet to the store. Then we will retrieve pets from the store. The same is applicable to categories of pet, too. Then we will associate pets and categories to each other. The end result is the domain model of the store that is also persisted in a relational database.

Adding a Pet to the Store

For each pet in the store, we should persist fields such as name, description, and gender so they can be presented to the customer. Each pet should also be assigned a category to make it easier for a customer to browse the store if it contains many items, as shown in Figure 15.3.

To get started, we will create a class called Pet that contains information about a specific pet and a PetStore class that will act as an entry point to the contents of the store.

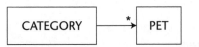

Figure 15.3 Relationships of categories and pets

We don't want PetStore to provide persistence-specific infrastructure code, as it can pollute the class and couple it to a persistence scheme. So we extract the persistence logic and put it in a separate object. This technique is generally known as the Data Access Objects (DAO) pattern. Instead of intermingling the persistence logic with the domain objects, we perform all the persistence-related operations in a separate class to handle database activity. This implementation can be hidden behind an interface allowing persistence mechanisms to be easily switched at a later date. Domain objects don't have to know about the exact persistence mechanism used, and we can easily plug a mock object implementation. We define a PersistenceManager interface for this purpose. So Pet is the description of a pet in our pet store, which is itself modeled as the PetStore class, and PetStore delegates its persistence concerns to a separate PersistenceManager interface that will have a Hibernate implementation called HibernatePersistenceManager.

We start with a test. We want to create a Pet and add it to the PetStore:

```
[TestPetStore.java]

package org.petsoar.pets;

import junit.framework.TestCase;

public class TestPetStore extends TestCase {
  public void testAddPet() {
    // create a pet
    Pet pet = new Pet();

    // add pet to store
    PetStore petStore = new PetStore();
    petStore.addPet(pet);
  }
}
```

But this test is not sufficient. It hasn't actually tested that the pet has been stored. There are two ways we can ensure the pet has been persisted.

- Allow the PetStore to hit the database and assert that we can then load the Pet back from the database.

- Don't test the persistence itself; rather, test that the PetStore made the correct method call to the PersistenceManager.

  For our current needs, we'll use the second option because:

- Our unit test should test as little as possible. This test does not test the PersistenceManager implementation itself, just that the PetStore interacts with it in the correct way.

- As the application gets bigger, more and more layers and tests are added. By testing in isolation, the entire test suite will run much faster. Having a fast test suite is very important, as it makes it more desirable to run the tests more often.

- We have not written the actual PersistenceManager implementation yet.

To test that the PetStore interacts with the PersistenceManager in the correct way, we can use a mock implementation of PersistenceManager. For now, all we want to test is that `PersistenceManager.add()` is called with the correct Pet passed as an argument.

The mock PersistenceManager class is created using the dynamic Mock class from the MockObjects library (described in Chapter 4). This automatically implements the interface of the PersistenceManager. An expectation is added to the PersistenceManager to assert that the `add()` method is called and that the first parameter passed in is the same Pet we declared in the test. After the code under test has been executed, we verify that the expectations set up in the mock have been met.

```java
[TestPetStore.java]

import com.mockobjects.dynamic.Mock;

...

public void testAddPet() {
  // create a pet
  Pet pet = new Pet();

  // setup expectation of PersistenceManager
  Mock mockPM = new Mock(PersistenceManager.class);
  mockPM.expect("add", pet);

  PetStore petStore = new PetStore();
  // pass mock PersistenceManager implementation to petStore
  petStore.setPersistenceManager((PersistenceManager)mockPM.proxy())

  // add pet to store
  petStore.addPet(pet);

  // verify expectation has been met
  mockPM.verify();
}
```

We have a test! Unfortunately, it doesn't compile, so we need to create the classes required to allow the code to compile. These are the PersistenceManager, Pet, and PetStore classes.

```
[Pet.java]

public class Pet {
}

[PetStore.java]

public class PetStore {
  public void setPersistenceManager(PersistenceManager pm) {
    // todo
  }

  public void addPet(Pet pet) {
    // todo
  }
}

[PersistenceManager.java]

public interface PersistenceManager {
  void add(Object obj);
}
```

Note that the interfaces of these classes were driven by our test — we did not create them until we had a test that did not compile.

Now that the code compiles, we can run the test. Red Bar!

```
add(< = Pet@e86da0>) was expected but not called
```

This error is generated by the MockObjects library. It means it expected the add() method to be called with a single argument that should equal a specific Pet instance — but it never was. That is, of course, what we are trying to test.

To allow the PetStore to persist the Pet using the PersistenceManager, it needs a small modification:

```
[PetStore.java]

public class PetStore {

  private PersistenceManager pm;

  public void setPersistenceManager(PersistenceManager pm) {
    this.pm = pm;
  }

  public void addPet(Pet pet) {
```

```
    pm.add(pet);
  }

}
```

Now we can run the test again. Green Bar!

But we're not done yet, because there's no concrete implementation of PersistenceManager.

Implementing the PersistenceManager Using Hibernate

Recall the interface for PersistenceManager:

```
[PersistenceManager.java]

public interface PersistenceManager {
  void add(Object obj);
}
```

We now need an implementation that delegates to Hibernate so the object can be persisted in a relational database. (Hibernate was discussed in Chapter 5.)

But how do we test it? In general it's desirable to avoid hitting the database wherever possible because it ties things to a particular persistence implementation. It's also very slow, making a quick test-code cycle not so quick! However, seeing as this actually is a persistence implementation we are testing, it makes sense to look at the state of the database for the test. Note that as this is the only class in the system that talks to the database, it will be the only test case that talks to the database. All the other test cases shall use mock objects.

This is where *Hypersonic SQL Database (HSQLDB)* makes life easier. It's an Open Source relational database written in pure Java that is SQL and JDBC compliant. What's great is that it gives you the option of keeping the entire database in memory, meaning no files or servers are involved (fast!) and the database contents are forgotten about whenever the connection is closed. It's also in-process which cuts inter-process calls. That doesn't sound all that great because it defeats the purpose of a database, but for unit tests, it's a perfect fit.

So, as usual, we begin with a test. Our PersistenceManager should be able to persist any type of object; however, we already have a Pet class, so we may as well use that.

```
[TestHibernatePersistenceManager.java]

public class TestHibernatePersistenceManager extends TestCase {
  private HibernatePersistenceManager pm;

  protected void setUp() {
    pm = new HibernatePersistenceManager();
```

```
  }

  public void testAddPet() throws Exception {
    pm.add(new Pet());

    // verify a row exists in the database
    assertEquals(1, countRows("PETS"));
  }
}
```

This test also requires the helper `countRows()` method.

[TestHibernatePersistenceManager.java]

```
/** Count rows in a table */
private int countRows(String tableName) throws SQLException {
  Connection jdbcConnection = pm.getConnection();
  Statement stmt = jdbcConnection.createStatement();
  ResultSet rs = stmt.executeQuery("SELECT COUNT(*) FROM " + tableName);
rs.next();
return rs.getInt(1);}
```

At last, we have a test. Of course, it doesn't compile yet. We need to add the HibernatePersistenceManager class and implement the `add()` and `getConnection()` methods.

[HibernatePersistenceManager.java]

```
package org.petsoar.pets;

import net.sf.hibernate.Session;
import java.sql.Connection;

public class HibernatePersistenceManager implements PersistenceManager {

  /** Implemented from PersistenceManager interface */
  public void add(Object obj) {
    // todo
  }

  public Connection getConnection() {
    return null;
  }
}
```

If we run the test now, we get a NullPointerException in `countRows()`. This is obvious, as the Connection object returned from HibernatePersistence-Manager's `getConnection()` method is null. To tackle this problem, we need to get a Connection object from Hibernate. Hibernate's Session class is responsible for opening a JDBC connection, so we should ask a Session to return us the underlying Connection.

```
public Connection getConnection() {
  return session.connection();
}
```

Of course, it doesn't compile because *session* is not yet defined. The HibernatePersistenceManager needs a chance to initialize itself (so it can connect to the database and start a Hibernate Session) and a chance to clean itself up properly (so it can commit any transactions and disconnect from the database).

To initialize the Hibernate Session instance, a Configuration object is required (a Hibernate-specific class that contains information on how to connect to the database and definitions of how objects map to a relational model), as is a SessionFactory (that actually creates the Sessions).

```
[HibernatePersistenceManager.java]

import net.sf.hibernate.SessionFactory;
import net.sf.hibernate.HibernateException;
import net.sf.hibernate.cfg.Configuration;
import java.sql.Connection;

public class HibernatePersistenceManager implements PersistenceManager {

  private Session session;

  public void init() {
    try {
      // Load Hibernate configuration
      Configuration config = new Configuration();
      config.configure();

      SessionFactory sessionFactory = config.buildSessionFactory();
      session = sessionFactory.openSession();
    } catch (HibernateException e) {
      throw new RuntimeException(e.getMessage(), e);
    }
  }
  ...
}
```

Now we need only to call the `init()` method before any persistence code is run. We call it from the `setUp()` method of the test case:

```
[TestHibernatePersistenceManager.java]

public class TestHibernatePersistenceManager extends TestCase {
```

```
private HibernatePersistenceManager pm;

protected void setUp() {
  pm = new HibernatePersistenceManager();
  pm.init();
}
...
}
```

To see how we're progressing, we can run the test. Red Bar!

```
net.sf.hibernate.HibernateException: /hibernate.cfg.xml not found
at net.sf.hibernate.cfg.Configuration.configure(Configuration.java:673)
```

Hibernate expects a file named `hibernate.cfg.xml` in the classpath. This file contains all the information Hibernate needs for connecting to the database. So, we create the file:

```
[hibernate.cfg.xml]

<hibernate-configuration>
  <session-factory name="/jndi/PetSoarSessionFactory">
    <!-- properties -->
    <property name="hibernate.connection.driver_class">
      org.hsqldb.jdbcDriver
    </property>
    <property name="hibernate.connection.url">jdbc:hsqldb:.</property>
    <property name="hibernate.connection.username">sa</property>
    <property name="hibernate.connection.password"></property>
    <property name="hibernate.connection.pool_size">4</property>
    <property name="hibernate.dialect">
      net.sf.hibernate.dialect.HSQLDialect
    </property>
  </session-factory>
</hibernate-configuration>
```

Note that this configuration is useful only for running the tests using HSQL. For production, we will define another `hibernate.cfg.xml` file, but this one contains the information for connecting to a real database such as Oracle or MySQL or any other relational database. To successfully run the test cases with the in-memory HSQL database, we make sure this file is placed in the classpath of the test cases.

NOTE HSQLDB returns an in-memory database when specifying the JDBC URL "jdbc:hsqldb:". This memory will be discarded when the connection is closed. No external files or servers are required.

Now we can run the test again. Red Bar!

```
Unknown table name PETS
```

We forgot to create the PETS table and its columns. But we don't need to issue any SQL CREATE TABLE statement for creating the table. We can use Hibernate's SchemaUpdate class. Hibernate can generate the database schema for us. It does that by looking at the xml mapping files. So we refactor init() and invoke SchemaUpdate from there.

```
[TestHibernatePersistenceManager.java]

import net.sf.hibernate.tool.hbm2ddl.SchemaUpdate;

public class HibernatePersistenceManager implements PersistenceManager {
...

  public void init() {
    try {
      // Load Hibernate configuration
      Configuration config = new Configuration();
      config.configure();

      // update database schema if required
      try {
        new SchemaUpdate(config).execute(false);
      } catch (SQLException e) {
        log.fatal("Cannot update schema",e);
        throw new RuntimeException("Cannot update schema",e);
      }

      SessionFactory sessionFactory = config.buildSessionFactory();
      session = sessionFactory.openSession();
    } catch (HibernateException e) {
      throw new RuntimeException(e.getMessage(), e);
    }
  }
}
```

SchemaUpdate can also be invoked off-line via the command line, and there's even an Ant task for incorporating it with your build. Because our test database is an in-memory database, we don't need to use the off-line mode. Instead, we call it during initialization of HibernatePersistenceManager before any other persistence code is executed. We also need to modify hibernate.cfg.xml like this:

```
[hibernate.cfg.xml]

<hibernate-configuration>
  <session-factory name="/jndi/PetSoarSessionFactory">
```

```
          . . .
      <mapping resource="org/petsoar/pets/Pet.hbm.xml"/>
    </session-factory>
  </hibernate-configuration>
```

A `<mapping/>` element must be added to the `hibernate.cfg.xml` file. This element tells Hibernate which mapping files to use. Hibernate can create the PETS table and its columns by looking at this mapping file. A mapping file for a class is a file placed in the classpath that follows the `package-name/classname.hbm.xml` naming convention.

Now that we've invoked SchemaUpdate, we can expect to have a table in place when the test starts running. We're ready to run the test again. Red Bar!

This is because Hibernate can't find the `Pet.hbm.xml` mapping file. To do this, we can either manually create this XML file or mark the class with additional JavaDoc tags and let XDoclet do the hard work instead (see Chapter 9).

A primary key also needs to be added to the Pet class so it can be uniquely identified.

```
[Pet.java]

package org.petsoar.pets;

/**
 * @hibernate.class table="PETS"
 */
public class Pet {

  private long id;

  /**
   * @hibernate.id column="PETID" generator-class="vm.long"
   */
  public long getId() {
    return id;
  }

  public void setId(long id) {
    this.id = id;
  }
}
```

After adding the JavaDoc tags to the Pet class, the hibernatedoclet target of the build must be run — this generates the appropriate `Pet.hbm.xml` mapping file. Running the test now yields another Red Bar:

```
expected:<1> but was:<0>
```

The countRows() method returned zero; that means no row was found in the PETS table while we were expecting that a row should be due to the call to the add() method. We're making progress, and the Red Bar has reassured us that our test is actually testing properly.

We need to now implement the add() method properly. We implemented it before in the easiest possible way, by just putting a to-do comment in it! In Chapter 5, we see that to access the Hibernate object store, we use the Session interface. To add something to the object store, we need only to call session.saveOrUpdate().

```
[HibernatePersistenceManager.java]

package org.petsoar.pets;

import net.sf.hibernate.Session;
import net.sf.hibernate.HibernateException;

public class HibernatePersistenceManager implements PersistenceManager {
...
  private Session session;

  public void add(Object obj) {
    try {
      session.saveOrUpdate(obj);
    } catch (HibernateException e) {
      throw new RuntimeException("Could not persist object :"
                                 + e.getMessage(), e);
    }
  }
}
```

The add() method simply calls saveOrUpdate() and inserts a new record to the database if the record is new or updates the database if the record already exists.

TIP The Session.saveOrUpdate() **method throws a checked exception: HibernateException. However, this is implementation specific, and adding this to the method signature of** PersistenceManager.add() **would mix implementation specifics into the interface. For this reason, the exception is caught and rethrown as an unchecked RuntimeException.**

You may choose another approach for handling exceptions, such as rethrowing a custom exception, logging, invoking a callback for a recovery procedure, or using checked exceptions throughout your implementation. For every opinion on "proper" exception handling, you'll find a counterargument. We've just gone for the simplest thing.

We need also to ensure that the Hibernate session is cleaned up properly. This involves flushing all unwritten data, committing the transaction, and closing the session. We add a new method to HibernatePersistenceManager and consequently to the PersistenceManager interface.

```
[HibernatePersistenceManager.java]

public void dispose() {
  try {
    try {
      session.flush();
      session.connection().commit();
    } finally {
      session.close();
    }
  } catch(Exception e) {
      throw new PersistenceException("Couldn't close the session", e);
  }
}
```

The test can be modified to accommodate this extra method by adding a call to the `dispose()` method in the `tearDown()` method. So, whenever we're finished executing a test case, the session is politely freed. By using the `tearDown()` method of JUnit (which is always run before and after each test — regardless of the result), an in-memory database can be created and destroyed. By closing the database connection in the `tearDown()` method, we make sure the database resources are freed and the next test executed acquires a fresh database connection.

```
[TestHibernatePersistenceManager.java]

protected void tearDown() throws Exception {
  // end transaction and free up persistence manager.
  pm.dispose();
}
```

Our test is passing. That means that a row is being added to the table when we call `PersistenceManager.add()`. That's good, but we need a bit more reassurance that it is actually persisting the object state correctly.

We extend our unit test to verify that the correct row, not just any row, has been added to the table after the `HibernatePersistenceManager.add()` method has been called. Here's the original test to refresh your memory:

```
[TestHibernatePersistenceManager.java]

public void testAddPet() throws Exception {
  // add an object to the database
```

```
    pm.add(new Pet());

    // verify a row exists in the database
    assertEquals(1, countRows("PETS"));
}
```

To improve this, we extend the test so that it creates a table with more than one column and verifies that each column contains the correct data, as specified by fields of the object to be persisted.

```
[TestHibernatePersistenceManager.java]

public void testAddPet() throws Exception {
    // sanity check
    assertEquals(0, countRows("PETS"));

    // set some fields
    Pet pet = new Pet();
    pet.setName("Garfield");

    // add an object to the database
    pm.add(pet);

    // verify a row exists in the database
    assertEquals(1, countRows("PETS"));

    // verify row contains correct values
    Connection jdbcConnection = pm.getConnection();
    Statement stmt = jdbcConnection.createStatement();
    ResultSet rs = stmt.executeQuery("SELECT * FROM PETS WHERE PETID = "
                                     + pet.getId());
    rs.next();
    assertEquals("Garfield", rs.getString("NAME"));
}
```

Once again, the test won't compile because extra fields need to be added to the Pet class. Let's do that now:

```
[Pet.java]

package org.petsoar.pet;

/**
 * @hibernate.class table="PETS"
 */
public class Pet {

    private long id;
    private String name;
```

```
/**
 * @hibernate.id column="PETID" generator-class="increment"
 */
public long getId() {
  return id;
}

public void setId(long id) {
  this.id = id;
}

/**
 * @hibernate.property column="NAME"
 */
public String getName() {
  return name;
}

public void setName(String name) {
  this.name = name;
}
}
```

Now we can run the test again. Green Bar!

Hibernate has kicked into action and has automatically mapped the fields of the Pet class to the columns in the database. It just works!

We now have a PersistenceManager implementation capable of adding plain Java objects to a table in the database.

Where We Are

The components are now in place for adding a Pet to the store. Looking back, we have a Pet class containing the details of a Pet and a PetStore component that allows the store's contents to be modified. The actual code for persistence has been abstracted away from the PetStore and placed into a generic PersistenceManager component.

Once we have a PetStore instance, adding a new Pet is as simple as:

```
Pet pet = new Pet();
pet.setName("Garfield");
petStore.add(pet);
```

Now is a good time to go back and look at the classes and tests we have just created. Notice how all the Hibernate-related code is placed in one class. Notice the simplicity of the other classes.

Retrieving Pets

Of course, it's pointless adding pets to the store unless they can later be retrieved.

To get the ball rolling, a test can be added to TestHibernatePersistenceManager that adds some pets and tests that they can be retrieved properly:

```
[TestHibernatePersistenceManager.java]

public void testRetrievePets() throws Exception {
  // add some pets
  Pet pet1 = new Pet();
  pet1.setName("Garfield");
  pm.add(pet1);
  Pet pet2 = new Pet();
  pet2.setName("Odie");
  pm.add(pet2);

  // verify pets are in database
  List pets = pm.findAll();
  assertEquals(2, pets.size());
  assertEquals("Garfield", ((Pet)pets.get(0)).getName());
  assertEquals("Odie", ((Pet)pets.get(1)).getName());
}
```

This skeleton for the test is in place. A couple of Pets are added. We then call the `findAll()` method to retrieve a List of these creatures and assure that the List contains what we expect it to.

As usual, the test doesn't compile yet — there's no `findAll()` method. This can quickly be added to the HibernatePersistenceManager class and PersistenceManager interface.

```
[PersistenceManager.java]

public interface PersistenceManager {

  void add(Object obj);

  List findAll();
}


[HibernatePersistenceManager.java]

public class HibernatePersistenceManager implements PersistenceManager {

  ...
```

```
public List findAll() {
  return null;
}
}
```

The test compiles but now results in a NullPointerException because findAll() returns null. In order to implement this method, we need to provide Hibernate with a query string using the Hibernate Query Language.

[HibernatePersistenceManager.java]

```
public List findAll() {
  try {
    return session.find("FROM pet IN CLASS org.petsoar.pets.Pet");
  } catch (HibernateException e) {
    throw new RuntimeException(e.getMessage(), e);
  }
}
```

This simple query says, "return all objects of class org.petsoar.pets.Pet." Now the test passes with a Green Bar!

Now that the generic PersistenceManager is capable of retrieving objects that have been added, the PetStore needs to provide the domain specific getPets() method.

Thanks to our previous test, we are confident that the PersistenceManager implementation is capable of retrieving all Pets using the findAll() method. As our tests are to be rerun often, it will be immediately apparent if this is no longer the case.

With this assurance, to test the PetStore we can avoid hitting the database altogether and use a mock object instead. This dramatically reduces the time to run the unit tests as the application gets larger.

The following test is added:

[TestPetStore.java]

```
public void testRetrievePets() {
  // setup expectation of PersistenceManager
  Mock mockPM = new Mock(PersistenceManager.class);
  mockPM.expectAndReturn("findAll", Collections.EMPTY_LIST);

  PetStore petStore = new PetStore();
  // pass mock PersistenceManager implementation to petStore
  petStore.setPersistenceManager((PersistenceManager)mockPM.proxy());
  List result = petStore.getPets();

  assertTrue(result.isEmpty());
```

```
    // verify expectation has been met
    mockPM.verify();
}
```

This creates a mock PersistenceManager implementation and sets an expectation stating that findAll() should be called on it. Note that the method expectAndReturn() is used for this, as the findAll() method is not void — it needs to know what it should return when it is called. The second parameter to expectAndReturn() is the return value. In our test, we are simply providing an empty list.

Next, the PetStore instance is created and passed the mock PersistenceManager before we call the method we want to test — getPets(). Finally, we check that the call returned the empty list is set up on the mock and that the mock's expectations have been met.

To get the test to compile, a method needs to be added to PetStore:

```
[PetStore.java]

package org.petsoar.pets;

import java.util.List;

public class PetStore {

  private PersistenceManager pm;

  public void setPersistenceManager(PersistenceManager pm) {
    this.pm = pm;
  }

  public void addPet(Pet pet) {
    pm.add(pet);
  }

  public List getPets() {
    return null;
  }
}
```

Before the test can pass, we need to implement this new method:

```
[PetStore.java]

  public List getPets() {
    return pm.findAll();
  }
```

Green Bar!

TIP In many cases, it's tempting to skip the failing test by writing the test and implementation in one step. Although this may save a small amount of time (typically only a few seconds — not much longer than it takes to run the test), it should be avoided because a failing test acts as an additional test — it tests the test. Without a failing test, there is no assurance that the test is testing what it should be.

Retrieving a Single Pet

As well as retrieving all the Pets in the PetStore, it is essential to retrieve a single Pet based on its unique identifier.

As usual, we shall implement this by starting out with a test. A simple way to test it is to add two Pets, obtain their IDs, and test that the same Pets can be retrieved using the IDs.

```
[TestPersistenceManager.java]

public void testGetById() throws Exception {
    // add two pets
    Pet pet1 = new Pet();
    pet1.setName("Garfield");
    pm.add(pet1);
    Pet pet2 = new Pet();
    pet2.setName("Odie");
    pm.add(pet2);

    // get the unique ids for the added pets
    long id1 = pet1.getId();
    long id2 = pet2.getId();

    // verify names match ids
    assertEquals("Garfield", ((Pet)pm.getById(id1)).getName());
    assertEquals("Odie", ((Pet)pm.getById(id2)).getName());
}
```

To get the test to compile, a method needs be added to the PersistenceManager interface and HibernatePersistenceManager class.

```
[PersistenceManager.java]

public interface PersistenceManager {

    void add(Object obj);

    List findAll();

    Object getById(long id);
```

```
}

[HibernatePersistenceManager.java]

public class HibernatePersistenceManager implements PersistenceManager {
  ...

  public Object getById(long id) {
    return null;
  }
}
```

Running the test yields the Red Bar. A NullPointerException is thrown.

Hibernate provides the simple `load()` method for retrieving a single object. It is passed a java.lang.Class to identify which type of object is to be loaded and the unique identifier:

```
[HibernatePersistenceManager.java]

  public Object getById(long id) {
    try {
      return session.load(Pet.class, new Long(id));
    } catch (HibernateException e) {
      throw new RuntimeException(e.getMessage(), e);
    }
  }
```

Running the test again gives the Green Bar!

The PetStore class needs the ability to allow its clients to look up a Pet by a unique ID. To test this, we can simply provide a mock PersistenceManager to the PetStore and verify that it is called properly from the PetStore.

```
[TestHibernatePersisenceManager.java]

public void testGetPetById() {
  Mock mockPM = new Mock(PersistenceManager.class);
  mockPM.expectAndReturn("getById", new Long(99L), new Pet());

  PetStore petStore = new PetStore();
  // pass mock PersistenceManager implementation to petStore
  petStore.setPersistenceManager((PersistenceManager)mockPM.proxy());

  Pet pet = petStore.getPetById(99L);

  assertNotNull(pet);
  mockPM.verify();
}
```

The expectAndReturn() method takes three parameters. The first is the name of the method that is expected to be called. The second is what it expects to receive as a parameter when called. The third is the value it should return. Again, the test fails, so we'll need to implement the new method:

```
[PetStore.java]

public class PetStore {


  ...

  public Pet getPetById(long id) {
    return (Pet)pm.getById(id);
  }
}
```

Green Bar! It's now easy to retrieve all Pets from the PetStore or just a specific Pet by its ID. One last thing before we're finished here. The test can be refactored to remove duplication between the test methods by initializing the PetStore and mock object in the setUp() method.

```
[TestPetStore.java]

public class TestPetStore extends TestCase {

  private Mock mockPM;
  private PetStore petStore;

  protected void setUp() {
    mockPM = new Mock(PersistenceManager.class);
    petStore = new PetStore();
    petStore.setPersistenceManager((PersistenceManager)mockPM.proxy());
  }

  public void testAddPet() {
    // create a pet
    Pet pet = new Pet();

    // setup expectation of PersistenceManager
    mockPM.expect("add", pet);

    // add pet to store
    petStore.addPet(pet);

    // verify expectation has been met
    mockPM.verify();
  }

  public void testGetPets() {
    // setup expectation of PersistenceManager
```

```
        mockPM.expectAndReturn("findAll", Collections.EMPTY_LIST);

        List result = petStore.getPets();

        assertTrue(result.isEmpty());

        // verify expectation has been met
        mockPM.verify();

    }

    public void testGetPetById() {
        mockPM.expectAndReturn("getById", new Long(99L), new Pet());

        Pet pet = petStore.getPetById(99L);

        assertNotNull(pet);
        mockPM.verify();
    }
}
```

Where We Are

We now have a very clean API to the PetStore. Look at the interface of the members of the PetStore class:

```
[PetStore.java]

public class PetStore {
  public void addPet(Pet pet) { ... }
  public List getPets() { ... }
  public Pet getPetById(long id) { ... }
}
```

Pet itself is just a plain old Java object with getters and setters. The PetStore is a simple class. Backing the PetStore is a PersistenceManager that can be used by other components for persisting other types of objects. The resulting code is very clean.

It's time to look back at the code and remove any duplication and improve it. One improvement we can make is to remove the countRows() method from the TestHibernatePersistenceManager and replace it with a call to the findAll() method of PersistenceManager. So, we refactor the following code:

```
[TestHibernatePersistenceManager.java]

public void testAddPet() throws Exception {
  // sanity check
```

```
        assertEquals(0, countRows("PETS"));

        // set some fields
        Pet pet = new Pet();
        pet.setName("Garfield");

        // add an object to the database
        pm.add(pet);

        // verify a row exists in the database
        assertEquals(1, countRows("PETS"));

        // verify row contains correct values
        Connection jdbcConnection = pm.getConnection();
        Statement stmt = jdbcConnection.createStatement();
        ResultSet rs = stmt.executeQuery("SELECT * FROM PETS WHERE PETID = "
                                         + pet.getId());
        rs.next();
        assertEquals("Garfield", rs.getString("NAME"));
    }
```

We replace the countRows() call with a call to findAll() or getById().
Needless to say, we can also remove countRows() altogether, since it's no
longer used.

```
[TestHibernatePersistenceManager.java]

public void testAddPet() throws Exception {
    // sanity check
    assertEquals(0, countRows("PETS"));

    // set some fields
    Pet pet = new Pet();
    pet.setName("Garfield");

    // add an object to the database
    pm.add(pet);

    // verify a row exists in the database
    pet = pm.getById(pet.getId());
    assertNotNull(pet);

    // verify row contains correct values
    assertEquals("Garfield",pet.getName());
}
```

Persisting the Categories

When we started this chapter, we mentioned that the store needs the capability to categorize Pets. A *category* class can be introduced for this.

Before we begin modifying the PetStore, we must ensure that the Hibernate-PersistenceManager is capable of persisting classes other than Pet.

```
[TestHibernatePersistenceManager.java]

public void testAddAndRetrieveCategories() throws Exception {
    Category category = new Category();
    category.setName("Dogs");
    pm.add(category);

    // verify objects are in database

    List categories = pm.findAll();
    assertEquals(1, categories.size());
    assertEquals("Dogs", ((Category)categories.get(0)).getName());
}
```

In writing the test, it becomes apparent that the findAll() method is not sufficient because it must be able to distinguish whether you want to find all the Pets or Categories. We need to change that — but not just yet, because the code is not compiling (it is very hard to refactor code when it doesn't compile).

To get the test compiling, we need to add a Category class with a name property. We will speed up slightly now and add the unique identifier and Hibernate mapping data at the same time.

```
[Category.java]

package org.petsoar.categories;

/**
 * @hibernate.class table="CATEGORIES"
 */
public class Category {

    private long id;
    private String name;

    /**
     * @hibernate.id column="CATEGORYID" generator-class="increment"
     */
    public long getId() {
```

```
    return id;
  }

  public void setId(long id) {
    this.id = id;
  }

  /**
   * @hibernate.property column="NAME"
   */
  public String getName() {
    return name;
  }

  public void setName(String name) {
    this.name = name;
  }


}
```

Now that the test compiles, we can look at how we can modify the `findAll()` method so we can narrow the list down to that of a particular type.

The simplest thing would be to pass an argument stating which class to return. This could be a java.lang.String or java.lang.Class. We will go with the latter because it's less prone to error (the compiler will catch typos).

```
[TestHibernatePersistenceManager.java]

public void testAddAndRetrieveCategories() throws Exception {
  Category category = new Category();
  category.setName("Dogs");
  pm.add(category);

  // verify objects are in database

  List categories = pm.findAll(Category.class);
  assertEquals(1, categories.size());
  assertEquals("Dogs", ((Category)categories.get(0)).getName());
}
```

To get the test to compile, the signature of `findAll()` must be changed throughout the code to take another argument of type java.lang.Class.

```
[PersistenceManager.java]

public interface PersistenceManager {

  ...
```

```
    List findAll(Class cls);

    ...

}


[HibernatePersistenceManager.java]

public class HibernatePersistenceManager implements PersistenceManager {

    ...

    public List findAll(Class cls) {
      try {
        return session.find("FROM pet IN CLASS " + cls.getName());
      } catch (HibernateException e) {
        throw new RuntimeException(e.getMessage(), e);
      }
    }

    ...

}
```

There is also a call to this method in the PetStore class. This can have the appropriate parameter passed.

```
[PetStore.java]

public class PetStore {

  // ...

  public List getPets() {
    return pm.findAll(Pet.class);
  }

  // ...
}
```

TIP Many modern IDEs provide a feature for performing refactorings like this. Investigate your environment — it can save you a lot of time.

The test now compiles. We run it and get a Red Bar!

Unexpectedly, there are now two failing tests. Obviously, we have not implemented the code to allow the test we just wrote to pass. However, in introducing the new parameter, we've broken one of the existing tests.

```
TestPetStore.testRetrievePets():
wrong number of arguments expected:<0> but was:<1>
```

This is because we also need to modify the mock object to expect a parameter when called:

```
[TestPetStore.java]

public void testRetrievePets() {
    // setup expectation of PersistenceManager
    mockPM.expectAndReturn("findAll", Pet.class, Collections.EMPTY_LIST);

    List result = petStore.getPets();

    assertTrue(result.isEmpty());

    // verify expectation has been met
    mockPM.verify();
}
```

We can run the tests again — another Red Bar, but this time with only one failing test.

```
Unmapped class: org.petsoar.pets.Category
```

Unfortunately, even though we've marked the Category class with Hibernate doclet tags, the Configuration does not know about the class. This is resolved by modifying the `hibernate.cfg.xml` file:

```
[hibernate.cfg.xml]

<hibernate-configuration>
  <session-factory name="/jndi/PetSoarSessionFactory">
    ...
    <mapping resource="org/petsoar/pets/Pet.hbm.xml"/>
    <mapping resource="org/petsoar/categories/Category.hbm.xml"/>
  </session-factory>
</hibernate-configuration>
```

Now we can run the test again. Green Bar! Our PersistenceManager is now capable of storing and retrieving different types of classes.

This generality should also be applied to the `PersistenceManager` `.getById()` method, and the Category-specific classes can be added to PetStore. We will skip the details of implementing this because the same techniques apply that have been previously illustrated.

Where We Are

The PetStore now supports storage of Pets and Categories:

```
[PetStore.java]

public class PetStore {
  public void addPet(Pet pet) { ... }
  public List getPets() { ... }
  public Pet getPetById(long id) { ... }

  public void addCategory(Category category) { ... }
  public List getCategories() { ... }
  public Category getCategoryById(long id) { ... }
}
```

Still, the implementation of PetStore is remarkably simple, and the Pet and Category classes are plain old Java objects.

The next step is allowing Category to contain Pets and a Pet to be assigned to a Category.

Implementing the Category-Pet Relation

We should be able to group Pets in a parent Category. As usual, we start by writing the test for this scenario:

```
[TestHibernatePersistenceManager.java]

public void testAddPetsToCategory() throws Exception {
  Category category = new Category();
  category.setName("yy");

  pm.save(category);

  Pet pet = new Pet();
  pet.setName("xx");

  category.addPet(pet);

  // verify category contains the pet
  assertEquals(1, category.getPets().size());
  assertTrue(category.getPets().contains(pet));

  // verify pet has a reference to the parent category
  assertEquals(category, pet.getCategory());
}
```

Here, we first create a new Category and save it; then a Pet is created and added to the Category and saved. We verify that the Pet was successfully added.

But this code does not update the database at all, so we enhance the test to do that, too.

```
[TestHibernatePersistenceManager.java]

public void testAddPetsToCategory() throws Exception {
    Category category = new Category();
    category.setName("yy");

    pm.save(category);

    Pet pet = new Pet();
    pet.setName("xx");

    category.addPet(pet);

    // verify category contains the pet
    assertEquals(1, category.getPets().size());
    assertTrue(category.getPets().contains(pet));

    // verify pet has a reference to the parent category
    assertEquals(category, pet.getCategory());

    // now save it
    pm.save(pet);

    // retrieve them from the database
    category= (Category)pm.getById(Category.class, category.getId());
    pet= (Pet)pm.getById(Pet.class, pet.getId());

    // verify category contains the pet
    assertEquals(1, category.getPets().size());
    assertTrue(category.getPets().contains(pet));

    // verify pet has a reference to the parent category
    assertEquals(category, pet.getCategory());
}
```

Just to make sure the database content is also correct, we load the two objects by calling getById() and verify it again. But there's still a problem. It doesn't yet compile, since there's no addPet in Category and no getCategory in Pet either.

```
[Category.java]

public class Category {

    public void addPet(Pet pet) {
        //todo
```

```
    }
    public List getPets() {
        return null;
    }
    ...
}
```

Pet.java

```
public class Pet {

    public Category getCategory() {
        return null;
    }
    ...
}
```

Now it compiles. We can run the test. Red Bar! That's because getPets returns null, so we correct it.

```
[Category.java]

public class Category {

    private List pets = new ArrayList();

    public void addPet(Pet pet) {
        //todo
    }
    public List getPets() {
        return pets;
    }
    ...
}
```

We can run the test again. Red Bar!

```
junit.framework.AssertionFailedError: expected:<1> but was:<0>
```

That's what we expected because addPet was not implemented correctly. So we change addPet.

```
[Category.java]

    public void addPet(Pet pet) {
        getPets().add(pet);
    }
```

We run the test again and Red Bar!

```
junit.framework.AssertionFailedError:
    expected:<org.petsoar.categories.Category@a23610> but was:<null>
```

So, the second assertion fails. Although Category does contain the new Pet, the reference from Pet to its parent Category is null. We modify addPet() and set the reference.

```
[Category.java]

    public void addPet(Pet pet) {
        getPets().add(pet);
        pet.setCategory(this);
    }
```

But it doesn't compile yet because there's no setCategory() method in class Pet.

```
[Pet.java]

    public void setCategory(Category category) {
    }
```

Still the same Red Bar! That's because setCategory is not implemented. We add a property and implement the setter method correctly.

```
[Pet.java]

public class Pet {

    private Category category;

    public void setCategory(Category category) {
        this.category=category;
    }

    . . .
}
```

Now the first two assertions should pass and they do, but we get a Red Bar! The third assertion failed. There's a problem in the mapping part. We now need to define a mapping between Category and Pet for Hibernate. We can do this using the XDoclet tags in the Category and Pet classes:

```
[Category.java]

public class Category {

    /**
```

```
 * @hibernate.list table="PETS" lazy="true" cascade="all"
 * @hibernate.collection-one-to-many class="org.petsoar.pets.Pet"
 * @hibernate.collection-key column="CATEGORY"
 */
public List getPets() {
    return pets;
}


...
}


[Pet.java]

public class Pet {

    /**
     * @hibernate.many-to-one cascade="none" column="CATEGORY"
     */
    public Category getCategory() {
        return null;
    }


    ...
}
```

The specified @hibernate.list tag tells Hibernate that it's a 1-n relation and that the other end of the relation is stored in the PETS table. Note the lazy parameter of this tag. Setting its value to true means the Pets of a Category are not loaded when the Category is loaded from the database; rather, Hibernate waits until getPets() is called and then loads the associated Pets. The @hibernate.collection-one-to-many tag is there to tell Hibernate about the type of the contents of the List. Without this tag, Hibernate doesn't know objects of which type should be created when the List is loaded into memory from the database. The column parameter of the @hibernate.collection-key tag specifies the name of the foreign key column in the PETS table that references the parent Category in the CATEGORIES table.

The getCategory() method of class Pet is also tagged, but with the many-to-one Hibernate tag. The relation is modeled in the database with a foreign key in the PETS table holding the primary key of the parent category in it from the CATEGORIES table. The cascade parameter is important here. The value of none here means upon inserting, saving, or deleting a Pet, the associated Category is left untouched. A value of delete would mean "delete the associated Category when the Pet is deleted," which is obviously not something we want to happen. A value of save would mean save the associated Category, too, but that's not what we need either, because we want the parent Category to not change when the Pet gets edited.

We are now ready to run the test again. Red Bar!

```
net.sf.hibernate.PropertyNotFoundException: Could not find a setter for
property pets in class org.petsoar.categories.Category
```

For any persistable property, there should also be a setter method specified. We add the method.

```
[Category.java]

    public void setPets(List pets) {
        this.pets = pets;
    }
```

We also add the setter method for Pet's category property. We give the test another run and finally, Green Bar!

So now we're sure that the two ends of the association between Pet and Category are correct, and they are correctly saved and loaded from the database. We follow this procedure for other methods such as `removePet()`. They are not shown here because the procedure looks quite similar to this one.

We should also support grouping of Categories under another Category. This is easily accomplished by adding a `categories` property of type java.util.List and the familiar `add()` and `remove()` methods, plus another property to represent the parent Category.

Where We Are

We can group Pets in Categories now. We changed both classes to contain information about this association between the two, and the association persists in the database successfully, along with the rest of the fields. We can also group Categories under a parent Category and persist it.

Performance and Maintainability Considerations

We have a clean domain model that can load and save itself from and to a database successfully. By using Hibernate and domain objects, the client code is cleaner than a solution that loads raw data from the database. The domain objects can encapsulate business rules as well as data. Also, they give us the benefit of other OO features such as polymorphism. Instead of working with raw data, we're working with clean and high-level objects representing data.

But couldn't we do the persistence of the domain objects with a lesser amount of code in straight JDBC instead of using Hibernate? Does it perform well? Couldn't we get a better performance by issuing SQL statements directly?

We could write the persistence logic with the same amount of code or perhaps even less code by just using JDBC and executing SQL statements directly. The performance factor is debatable, though, because both solutions have room for lots of optimizations.

The reason we chose to use an object-relational framework like Hibernate is that besides writing the same amount of code for the basic persistence logic, it offers a lot of useful possibilities, too. Let's list them here:

- We don't have to create the database schema by hand. We let Hibernate's SchemaUpdater do that for us. This is a nice added benefit for a TDD scenario. We have less hesitation when refactoring the domain model if we don't have to keep the schema up to date manually.

- By using the XDoclet tags, we have a very nice way of documenting the mapping from classes to database tables. It's more readable this way. A programmer can easily find the mapping for a class or property.

- Because Hibernate takes care of the schema update and mapping from the model to the database, we can easily change the underlying database. If you haven't noticed, we actually used this feature! We used the in-memory HSQL database for the tests, but we certainly can use a real database such as Oracle or MySQL for running the PetSoar site.

- We wrote a single HibernatePersistenceManager class, and it performs persistence for any kind of object, be it Pet, Category, or whatever. We don't have to write specific DAO classes for each type. Now that HibernatePersistenceManager, is written we can focus solely on the business logic of the application.

- By pushing a switch, we can ask Hibernate to load multiple dependent objects with a single SQL SELECT statement. All we have to do is add an outer-join= "true" to the @hibernate.list tag. It tells Hibernate to mix multiple SQL queries into a single query that uses SQL's OUTER JOIN.

- We can easily cache the objects loaded from the database in the memory. By caching all Pets and Categories, we can significantly reduce the need for any database access and improve the performance. We just add a @hibernate.jcs-cache tag to the classes that should be cached, and Hibernate, under the covers, handles caching instances of the class by using Apache's JCS package. JCS is a flexible framework for caching objects. By setting up its configuration file, we can control the exact caching behavior, for example how long the objects should be cached in memory and so on.

- Lazy loading is another out-of-the-box benefit of Hibernate. We can configure Hibernate to lazily load objects. By defining a proxy, we can tell Hibernate to load the contents of an object from the database only when one of its accessor methods is called. Defining a proxy is as simple as adding a proxy parameter to the @hibernate.class tag. For example, to lazy-load Pet, we just add a @hibernate.class proxy="org.petsoar.pets.Pet" and Hibernate takes care of lazy loading it!

- Another important and useful lazy-loading strategy could be lazily loading dependent objects of an object. For example, we could improve performance by not loading Pets of a Category when the Category is loaded from the database. Only when the `getPets()` method of Category is called, Pets of that Category are loaded. This is also easy to implement with Hibernate. We just add a `@hibernate.list lazy="true"` to the `getPets()` method. Under the covers, Hibernate intercepts the `getPets()` call and loads the associated Pets. Note that it's all done transparently by Hibernate. We don't have to change any code to take advantage of this performance optimization; no specific DAO code is written.

We can effectively do TDD and we can easily optimize our database performance by using the right Hibernate configuration elements.

Summary

In this chapter, we created the domain model for the application. The domain model consists of a PetStore class that has several methods for saving and retrieving Pet and Category classes. PetStore does its job by delegating the hard persistence job to a separate PersistenceManager interface. We implemented a default implementation of PersistenceManager by creating a HibernatePersistenceManager, which persists objects by using the Hibernate OR mapping framework.

We learned how to configure HibernatePersistenceManager to work with the relational database by using Hibernate's Configuration class and the hibernate.cfg.xml file. We configured it to use the in-memory HSQL database for the test. Using HSQL made it possible for us to run all the tests dealing with database access in a fraction of a second. We also learned how and where to open and close Hibernate Session objects.

We then expanded Pet and Category classes and implemented the code for grouping some Pets under a Category and also grouping some Categories under a parent Category.

For implementing these classes, we used TDD techniques. Using TDD led to a very clean and tested API for the domain model and the persistence framework.

CHAPTER 16

Creating a Web-Based Interface

In this chapter, we will explore the process of connecting the domain model presented in Chapter 15 to the user interface. We will do this, as we did with the domain model, using a TDD process. In PetSoar, the MVC framework we have chosen to use is OpenSymphony WebWork version 2.0. We chose this framework because of its rich features as well as its ability to make testing of actions very easy. However, the concepts presented here can most likely be applied toward any MVC framework or even toward your own home-brewed design.

While we cannot go over every Web interface in PetSoar, we will discuss a common situation most developers are familiar with: the need to create, read, update, and delete domain objects (CRUD). Given that we're writing a Pet-Store, there is no better domain object to choose for this task than the Pet model. We will start by adding pets; then we'll move on to viewing those newly created pets, building a way to update the Pets, and, finally, building a way to delete the Pets. When all is said and done, you should have a strong grasp of using TDD in a Web environment using WebWork or any other technology of your choosing.

Adding a Pet

Using the persistence model and domain object developed in the Chapter 15, we will now build a way for pets to be added to the PetStore by building a WebWork *action* that will house the business logic needed to implement this requirement. One of the nice things about WebWork is that it is very easy to use in TDD development. We will first look at the business logic and then the HTML for the Web interfaces. Without further ado, we will write the first tests.

Creating the AddPet Action

Before a unit test can actually be coded, we need to sort out what we want to achieve and, as such, what we need to test. *Specifically, we need to retrieve a name from a field on the Web page and create a Pet using that value.* Let's just write down our expectations and work from there. Remember that we don't need to test that the Pet is actually added to the database. We can just test that the `PetStore.addPet()` method is called, via a mock. The real PetStore is already tested elsewhere and assumed to work perfectly! Here's a test that shows what we're expecting to do:

```
public void testAddPet() throws Exception {
    // create the mock PetStore
    Mock mockPetStore = new Mock(PetStore.class);
    PetStore petStore = (PetStore) mockPetStore.proxy();

    // create pet that should be added to the pet store
    Pet expectedPet = new Pet();
    expectedPet.setName("bob");
    mockPetStore.expect("savePet", expectedPet);

    // create an action and give it the required parameters & resources
    AddPet action = new AddPet();
    action.setPetStore(petStore);
    action.setName("bob");

    // execute the action and verify results
    String result = action.execute();
    assertEquals(Action.SUCCESS, result);
    assertEquals(expectedPet, action.getPet());
    mockPetStore.verify();
}
```

So what did we do here? Let's take a look. First, we set up a mock PetStore instance (mockPetStore); then we created a Pet that we expect to be added to the PetStore. Finally, we created an instance of some sort of AddPet action (we don't know how this works yet). After creating the AddPet action, you can see that we "gave" it a few values: the name of the pet to be created, "bob," and the PetStore that this new pet will be added to.

Last, we execute the WebWork action (AddPet) and verify that it did indeed return a code equal to SUCCESS as well as ensure that the action does indeed return the expected pet. Furthermore, using the MockObjects API, we can verify that the pet was indeed added to the PetStore.

Of course, this test won't really run if AddPet doesn't yet exist, which means we need to write stubs now. So, we do that and then run the tests — Red Bar. Great, that's exactly what we expected!

Before we go ahead and implement AddPet such that we get a Green Bar, let's see if there are any other tests we might want to write. Note that this test only tests the situation when a valid name is given to the action, resulting in a SUCCESS return code. But what if no name is given to AddPet? We would assume that AddPet returns an ERROR code instead, as well as an error message explaining what went wrong. Let's make a test:

```java
public void testAddPetNoName() throws Exception {
    Mock mockPetStore = new Mock(PetStore.class);
    PetStore petStore =  (PetStore) mockPetStore.proxy();
    // mockPetStore has no expectations set, meaning the test
    // will fail if any method is called on it.

    AddPet action = new AddPet();
    action.setPetStore(petStore);
    String result = action.execute();

    assertEquals(Action.ERROR, result);
    assertEquals("Please enter a valid pet name.",
                (String) action.getFieldErrors().get("name"));
    assertNull(action.getPet());
    mockPetStore.verify();
}
```

Do you notice that this test and the last test both have some duplicate code? That is a sure sign that it's time to do some refactoring — which is just another step in TDD. We can see that the creation of the mock PetStore, as well as the action, is the same in both tests. Let's move these duplicate code chunks over to the setUp() method of our unit test, with the final unit test class looking like this:

```java
public class TestAddPet extends TestCase {
    private Mock mockPetStore;
    private AddPet action;

    protected void setUp() throws Exception {
```

```
        mockPetStore = new Mock(PetStore.class);
        PetStore petStore =  (PetStore) mockPetStore.proxy();

        action = new AddPet();
        action.setPetStore(petStore);
    }

    public void testAddPet() throws Exception {
        Pet expectedPet = new Pet();
        expectedPet.setName("bob");
        mockPetStore.expect("savePet", expectedPet);

        action.setName("bob");
        String result = action.execute();

        assertEquals(Action.SUCCESS, result);
        assertEquals(expectedPet, action.getPet());
        mockPetStore.verify();
    }

    public void testAddPetNoName() throws Exception {
      // mockPetStore has no expectations set, meaning the test
      // will fail if any method is called on it.

        String result = action.execute();

        assertEquals(Action.ERROR, result);
        assertEquals("Please enter a valid pet name.",
                    (String) action.getFieldErrors().get("name"));
        assertNull(action.getPet());
        mockPetStore.verify();
    }
}
```

Up to this point, this exercise has been fairly academic. We've been doing the same TDD process that we've been showcasing for the last two chapters. Now we get into the guts, where the actual business logic will go: the Web-Work action. After ensuring that the AddPet stub does exist and that these tests compile, run, and fail (Red Bar), we can finally begin to write Java code inside of those stubs and continue to run the test until we pass with a Green Bar. The final AddPet class looks like this:

```
public class AddPet extends ActionSupport implements PetStoreAware {
    private PetStore petStore;
    private String name;
    private Pet pet;

    public String execute() throws Exception {
        if (name == null || name.equals("")) {
```

```
            addFieldError("name", "Please enter a valid pet name.");
            return ERROR;
        }

        pet = new Pet();
        pet.setName(name);
        petStore.savePet(pet);

        return SUCCESS;
    }

    public void setPetStore(PetStore petStore) {
        this.petStore = petStore;
    }

    public Pet getPet() {
        return pet;
    }

    public void setName(String name) {
        this.name = name;
    }
}
```

There you have it, a complete and working WebWork action that adds a new pet to the database (via the PetStore service). Everything should look very simple and straightforward, except for the part where AddPet implements PetStoreAware. What is that all about?

Recall that in Chapter 14 we discussed *Inversion of Control (IoC)*. This interface tells XWork's IoC container that, in order for the action to run, it must be given an instance of a PetStore resource. This is done by calling the setPetStore() method before the execute() method is called.

The interface to enable XWork to automatically pass the PetStore into the action using IoC looks like this:

```
public interface PetStoreAware {
    void setPetStore(PetStore petStore);
}
```

Creating Views for AddPet

It's great that we have a working action, but that doesn't get us much if there isn't a user interface that works in tandem with it. Logically, we need to represent three views: an area where the user can input the pet's name, a place where error messages can be displayed, and a screen to signal to the user that the pet was successfully added. We can combine the input and error views into a single view, because it turns out to be very useful in terms of functionality for the user. This enables you to display error messages alongside the form field that was entered incorrectly, so the user can easily correct inputs and resubmit.

Therefore, we will use a very simple HTML view. Let's look at the addpet.jsp page first. This page will be used as the initial INPUT view:

```
[addpet.jsp]

<%@ taglib uri="webwork" prefix="webwork" %>
<html>
<head>
    <title>Add A Pet</title>
</head>

<body>
    <table>
        <form action="AddPet.action">
            <webwork:textfield label="Name" name="name" />

            <tr><td colspan="2">
                <input type="submit" value="Add">
            </td></tr>
        </form>
    </table>
</body>
</html>
```

This HTML is bare-bones and would not be acceptable as a final user interface. However, it does the job it needs to do with a minimum level of fluff. As you can see, the form consists of two elements: a textfield and a submit button. We use WebWork's JSP taglibs to make presenting the textfield extremely simple. The webwork:textfield tag is very nice because it will automatically search for field-error messages and, if they exist, display them above the HTML INPUT control. Furthermore, it provides a standard look and feel for each input element, which will be discussed in more detail in Chapter 17.

Now that we've created the INPUT view, we must create a SUCCESS view. This is needed so that the user can have some sort of validation that the data just entered was indeed processed by the application correctly. This SUCCESS view will act as that confirmation and reassure the user. Therefore, your SUCCESS views should always try to include some reference to the action before. In our case, it would be nice to show the user which Pet was just added to the PetStore. Luckily, we have a getPet() method in the action, which returns the created Pet, so this is relatively trivial.

Here is the success view — addpet-success.jsp: (from now on, we will include only the relevant HTML contents to help focus on the important parts of the page, assuming all pages have the proper enclosing HTML elements, such as BODY and HEAD).

```
[addpet-success.jsp]

<html>
<head>
  <title>Pet added</title>
</head>
<body>

Success - your pet called <b><webwork:property value="pet.name" /></b>
was successfully added!

</body>
</html>
```

Here we have a nice use of WebWork's property tag. This tag evaluates the expression given and prints the value of that expression. The expression pet.name is valid because our action, AddPet, has a getPet() method, and the Pet in turn has a getName() method. Therefore, pet.name is essentially calling action.getPet().getName(). Using this tag, we can correctly display the name of the Pet that was just added to the database, thereby confirming the operation with the user.

Finally, we need to create an ERROR view to be displayed if the user enters anything that is invalid. When an error occurs, the user should be able to amend the data entered in the form. So instead of creating a new view, we can reuse the existing addpet.jsp view.

Tying It All Together

Now that we've successfully created the action as well as the views, the only thing left to do is provide the glue that binds them all together. This is done by modifying xwork.xml and adding an entry for the AddPet action:

```
<action name="AddPet" class="org.petsoar.actions.inventory.AddPet">
    <interceptor-ref name="defaultStack"/>
    <result name="error">
        <param name="location">addpet.jsp</param>
    </result>
    <result name="success">
        <param name="location">addpet-success.jsp</param>
    </result>
</action>
```

Notice that the input view is not actually specified here. That matches with what we wrote in the AddPet action: we were returning only SUCCESS or ERROR, not INPUT. The reason for this is that input is really just the first page during the control flow (`addpet.jsp`), so just pointing the browser there takes care of the need for an input view. As long as `addpet.jsp` submits to AddPet.action, as we already saw, the flow will continue as desired by either following the SUCCESS view or the ERROR view.

The only thing left to do is launch the application server and ensure that all this stuff works correctly. If you are deploying this on your desktop, the URL will be `http://localhost:8080/inventory/addpet.jsp` and should look exactly like Figure 16.1.

Even though we've unit tested the AddPet action, nothing replaces a true integration or user-acceptance test. Go ahead and try various inputs to the name field, including no name. You should either be presented with an ERROR message, or the SUCCESS message if all went well. The point is that while there shouldn't be any surprises because of the development approach we took, it's always good to do a sanity check at the end. Figure 16.2 shows the flow in which the actions, views, and results interact with each other.

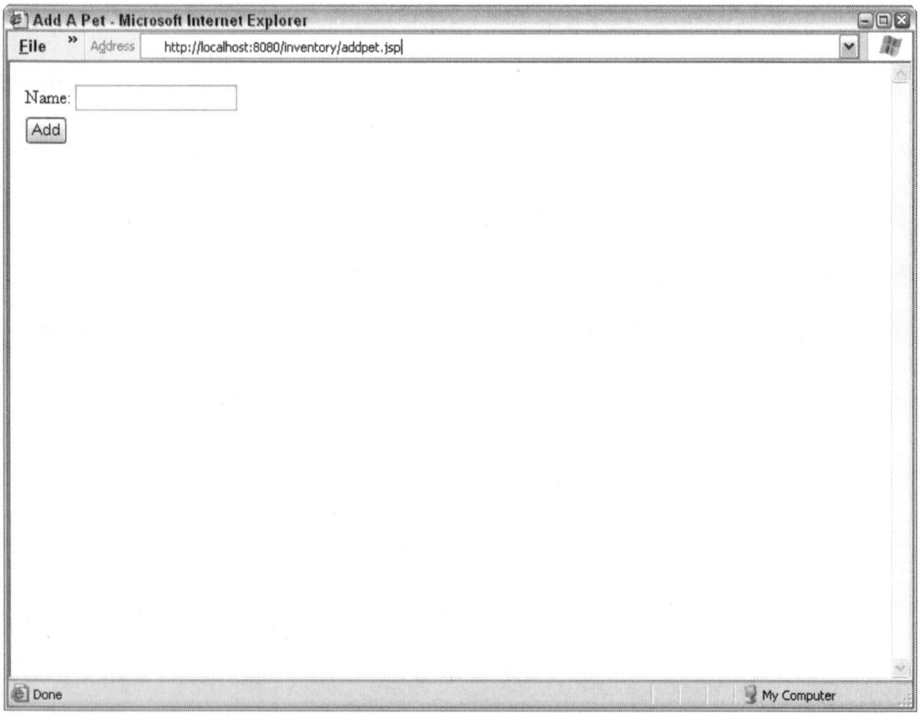

Figure 16.1 Screenshot of the above URL

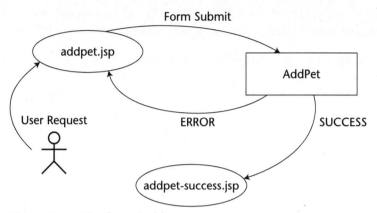

Figure 16.2 The flow of adding a pet

Congratulations! Take a breath. We've now created our first fully TDD Web-Work action, complete with user interfaces, to create a domain model object (a Pet!). As always, the thing to notice here is the sheer simplicity of it all. It's not over yet, though. We've done only the C (Create) part of CRUD. Before we can move onto U (Update), we should write an action to view a Pet. This is generally a good practice, because this action is a useful SUCCESS view for other actions (like Create and Update). Let's look at ViewPet next.

Displaying a Pet

At this point, we're going to speed things up a bit, as you've probably gotten the hang of TDD by now and displaying a Pet isn't *that* different from adding a Pet. So we're going to be cutting steps out of what we show you. But that doesn't mean they didn't happen, so you shouldn't skip them when you develop in a similar situation. We just didn't want to bore you, that's all!

Creating the ViewPet Action

The first thing we need to do is identify the inputs and outputs of this action. The required input to view a Pet would be the Pet's unique ID. The output of this action, of course, would be the Pet itself. Simple enough. So let's now take these inputs and outputs and come up with a few situations that we might want to test:

1. *Retrieve a Pet with a valid ID (for example, 123)* — This is the normal, expected behavior of the ViewPet action.

2. *Act accordingly if the ID given is invalid* — This is when the ID is either totally invalid (such as negative) or there is no Pet in the database with the given ID.

3. *Act accordingly if the ID is not given at all* — We should also be able to handle situations where the ID is never given to the action.

The complete test case for these situations is as follows:

```
public class TestViewPet extends TestCase {
    private Mock mockPetStore;
    private ViewPet action;

    protected void setUp() throws Exception {
        mockPetStore = new Mock(PetStore.class);
        PetStore petStore = (PetStore) mockPetStore.proxy();

        action = new ViewPet();
        action.setPetStore(petStore);
    }

    public void testViewPet() throws Exception {
        Pet existingPet = new Pet();
        existingPet.setName("harry");
        existingPet.setId(1);

        Pet expectedPet = new Pet();
        expectedPet.setName("harry");
        expectedPet.setId(1);

        mockPetStore.expectAndReturn("getPet", new Long(1),existingPet);
        action.setId(1);

        String result = action.execute();

        assertEquals(Action.SUCCESS, result);
        assertEquals(expectedPet, action.getPet());
        mockPetStore.verify();
    }

    public void testViewPetInvalidId() throws Exception {
        action.setId(-1);
        testViewPetNoId();
    }

    public void testViewPetNoId() throws Exception {
        mockPetStore.expectAndReturn("getPet", P.ANY_ARGS, null);

        String result = action.execute();

        assertEquals(Action.ERROR, result);
        assertEquals(1, action.getActionErrors().size());
        assertEquals("Invalid pet selected.",
            action.getActionErrors().iterator().next());
```

```
        assertNull(action.getPet());
        mockPetStore.verify();
    }
}
```

Notice that the last two tests, `testViewPetNoId` and `testViewPet` `InvalidId`, were very similar. The only difference was that one set an invalid Pet ID, while one didn't set an ID at all. Because they otherwise shared the exact same tests and assertions, we've refactored `testViewPetInvalidId` to just build upon `testViewPetNoId`. When writing tests, you can often break out assertion code so that it can be used by many similar tests, as we did in this case.

Next we must implement ViewPet until we end up with a Green Bar. The end result is as follows:

```
public class ViewPet extends ActionSupport implements PetStoreAware {
    private PetStore petStore;
    private long id;
    private Pet pet;

    public String execute() throws Exception {
        this.pet = petStore.getPet(id);

        if (pet == null) {
            addActionError("Invalid pet selected.");
            return ERROR;
        }

        return SUCCESS;
    }

    public void setPetStore(PetStore petStore) {
        this.petStore = petStore;
    }

    public Pet getPet() {
        return pet;
    }

    public void setId(long id) {
        this.id = id;
    }
}
```

That's it! Now we need to create views for this action. As we can see in the code, there is a SUCCESS view as well as an ERROR view that we need to build. We won't be creating any INPUT views as we did for AddPet because we're planning to pass in the ID of the Pet through a URL parameter, not using an HTML form.

The SUCCESS view looks like this:

```
[viewpet.jsp]
<html>
<head>
  <title>View Pet</title>
</head>
<body>
  <b>ID:</b> <webwork:property value="pet.id" /><br>
  <b>Name:</b> <webwork:property value="pet.name" /><br>
</body>
</html>
```

And the ERROR view looks like this:

```
[error.jsp]

<%@ taglib uri="webwork" prefix="webwork" %>
<html>
<head>
    <title>Error</title>
</head>
<body>

    Errors occurred:
    <ul>
        <webwork:iterator value="actionErrors">
            <li><webwork:property/></li>
        </webwork:iterator>
    </ul>

</body>
</html>
```

The ERROR view iterates over the list of actionErrors, a feature provided by ActionSupport, the base class for ViewPet. And now, just as with AddPet, all that is left is to update xwork.xml to tie it all together:

```
<action name="viewpet" class="org.petsoar.actions.inventory.ViewPet">
    <interceptor-ref name="defaultStack"/>

    <result name="error">
        <param name="location">error.jsp</param>
    </result>
    <result name="success">
        <param name="location">viewpet.jsp</param>
    </result>
</action>
```

That's it. You can now fire up PetSoar, create a pet, and view it using this newly created action. Point your browser to a URL such as `http://localhost:8080/inventory/viewpet.action?id=123`, where 123 is a valid Pet ID. A nice side effect of this design is that as new properties are added to the Pet object, our ViewPet code doesn't need to change at all. If you look at the code again, you'll see that there is no mention of the Pet's name, even though we refer to it in `viewpet.jsp`.

That's because we're retrieving the entire Pet object graph from the PetStore, and then WebWork's expression language is navigating that graph from the webwork:property tag we used in `viewpet.jsp`. For example, if a new property "gender" were added to the Pet object, we could just modify `viewpet.jsp` to display the property value of "pet.gender."

Refactoring the Actions

Let's stop for a moment now and look back at the AddPet action, views, and configuration. Recall that the SUCCESS view for AddPet pointed to `addpet-success.jsp`, which printed the Pet's name. A more robust way of doing this would be to have the SUCCESS view of AddPet actually invoke the ViewPet action for the new pet ID. There are two reasons why:

1. By redirecting to the ViewPet action, we no longer need to maintain both `addpet-success.jsp` and `viewpet.jsp`, as `addpet-success.jsp` is now obsolete. More important, doing this streamlines the user interface flow and presents the user with a minimal set of views to work with, thereby simplifying the user experience on the site.

2. By returning a redirect, we remove the potential problem of people creating *two* Pets! Currently, after posting to the AddPet action, your browser location bar will read `http://localhost:8080/inventory/AddPet.action`. If you reload the page, another Pet with the same name will be created, even though you most likely didn't mean to do that. The solution to this problem is to return an HTTP redirect to the ViewPet action. This means your browser will be now be pointing to `http://localhost:8080/inventory/ViewPet.action?id=4` after creating a new Pet (where 4 is the ID of the new pet). Any reloading of the page will simply result in viewing the ViewPet page again, no extra data!

HANDLING MULTIPLE SUBMIT REQUESTS

By redirecting to the ViewPet action, we effectively solved the problem of users clicking the Refresh button on their browser and causing multiple submits. But what about if the user clicks the Submit button in rapid succession, causing multiple submit requests? Ensuring that this behavior doesn't break your application is one of the hardest tasks when developing a Web-based application because of the stateless nature of HTTP and the fairly limited feature set in browsers.

The most common way employed is to use JavaScript to ensure that the button may only be clicked one time. When logging in to NetFlix.com, for example, the login button changes to a "Please wait" image after the first click. While this solution generally works and is very user-friendly, it fails for browsers with JavaScript disabled. It merely masks the bug without actually solving the problem.

Another more powerful technique that can be employed is to associate a unique ID with every form input. This ID, or token, would then be used as a handshaking identifier that is only allowed to be used once in the lifetime of the application. If a form is submitted a second time with that same token, the server-side processing is halted and an error is returned. This is a much safer approach, but is generally not acceptable. Users might double-click the Submit button and be presented with an error message even though their request went through perfectly fine the first time.

What we really want is to combine the best of both worlds: safe server-side support combined with a pleasant user interface. We can do this by using WebWork's built-in token interceptor and generator support. You can associate each form with a unique token via the webwork:token JSP tag, and then, by using the TokenSessionStoreInterceptor, all secondary requests with the same token will be redirected to what the original output would have looked like. The end result is that impatient users that double- or triple-click will still be presented with the same results that a normal, single click would.

Using this feature is extremely simple: add a webwork:token tag in your JSP form:

```
<form action="AddPet.action">
    <webwork:token/>
    <webwork:textfield label="Name" name="name" />
    <tr><td colspan="2">
        <input type="submit" value="Add">
    </td></tr>
</form>
```

In your `xwork.xml` **configuration file, just add the token interceptor to the action's stack, as shown here:**

```
<action name="addpet"
        class="org.petsoar.actions.inventory.AddPet">
    <interceptor-ref name="defaultStack"/>
    <interceptor-ref name="token-session"/>

    <result name="error">
        <param name="location">addpet.jsp</param>
    </result>
    <result name="success" type="dispatcher">
        <param name="location">
               viewpet.action?id=${pet.id}
        </param>
    </result>
</action>
```

Where the interceptor reference named token-session is associated with the class com.opensymphony.webwork.interceptor.TokenSessionStoreInterceptor.

Refactoring doesn't always come in the form of code changes. In this case, we can refactor `addpet-success.jsp` out of existence by merely modifying `xwork.xml` again:

```
<action name="addpet" class="org.petsoar.actions.inventory.AddPet">
    <interceptor-ref name="defaultStack"/>

    <result name="error">
        <param name="location">addpet.jsp</param>
    </result>
    <result name="success" type="redirect">
        <param name="location">viewpet.action?id=${pet.id}</param>
    </result>
</action>
```

As you can see, we've changed the SUCCESS result to be of type redirect. We now pass the given Pet ID to the ViewPet action and everything automatically works. This very simple change is why MVC frameworks are so useful and powerful. All we needed to do was change one small configuration element, and we successfully got rid of a somewhat nasty integration bug. Finally, we can delete `addpet-success.jsp`.

In Figure 16.2, we show you the original flow for adding a Pet. Now that we've made this change, the flow has changed just a little bit, as seen in Figure 16.3.

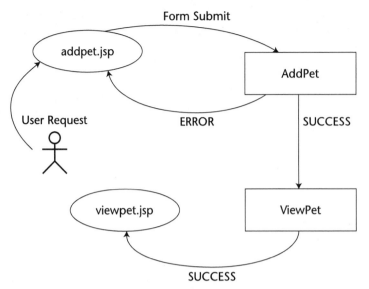

Figure 16.3   The new flow for adding a Pet, using the ViewPet action

As mentioned in Chapter 6, WebWork supports many kinds of result types besides the default dispatcher type and the redirect type used here. These various results can greatly change the behavior of your application, and you should plan out carefully how you intend to use them.

In this section, we sped up the TDD cycles used to create ViewPet, but also focused on more advanced refactoring that may not necessarily come from code changes. We will continue to refactor both code and noncode throughout the remainder of the chapter in this same manner.

Editing a Pet

So far, we've done only the "CR" and have the "UD" left to do. So, let's start attacking the U of CRUD and make an EditPet action. Just as we did before, let's figure out what the edit pet scenario is supposed to do and then decide on what we should test. The process flow is:

1. We retrieve the Pet information and return the user to an input page that contains all the existing data prefilled out for the user, thereby making incremental changes very easy.

2. The user modifies the data in the form elements and submits it.

3. The pet is retrieved from the database, the new fields are updated, and the changes are then stored in the database.

Looking at this process flow, we can identify what tests we might want to do, which are shown as follows:

1. *Normal behavior* — Expected and valid inputs are given and the update to the database is therefore completed successfully.

2. *Invalid data elements* — The Pet ID is correctly given, but the name of the Pet is invalid (missing or blank), causing an error-return code.

3. *Incorrect identifier* — The Pet ID given to the action is totally incorrect, causing an error-return code.

Here is the test case that we came up with to satisfy these three conditions:

```
public class TestEditPet extends TestCase {
    private Mock mockPetStore;
    private EditPet action;
    private Pet existingPet;

    protected void setUp() throws Exception {
        mockPetStore = new Mock(PetStore.class);
        PetStore petStore = (PetStore) mockPetStore.proxy();

        action = new EditPet();
        action.setPetStore(petStore);

        existingPet = new Pet();
        existingPet.setName("bob");
        existingPet.setId(1);
    }

    public void testEditPet() throws Exception {
        mockPetStore.expectAndReturn("getPet", new Long(1),existingPet);

        Pet expectedPet = new Pet();
        expectedPet.setName("bill");
        expectedPet.setId(1);

        mockPetStore.expect("savePet", expectedPet);

        action.getPet().setId(1);
        action.getPet().setName("bill");

        String result = action.execute();

        assertEquals(Action.SUCCESS, result);
        mockPetStore.verify();
    }

    public void testEditPetNoName() throws Exception {
        mockPetStore.expectAndReturn("getPet", new Long(1),existingPet);

        action.getPet().setId(1);
```

```
        String result = action.execute();

        assertEquals(Action.ERROR, result);
        assertEquals(1, action.getFieldErrors().size());
        assertEquals("Please enter a valid pet name.",
            action.getFieldErrors().get("pet.name"));
        mockPetStore.verify();
    }

    public void testEditPetInvalidId() throws Exception {
        String result = action.execute();

        assertEquals(Action.ERROR, result);
        assertEquals(1, action.getActionErrors().size());
        assertEquals("Please enter a valid pet ID.",
            action.getActionErrors().iterator().next());
        assertEquals(new Pet(), action.getPet());
        mockPetStore.verify();
    }
}
```

Starting with a Red Bar and developing EditPet until a Green Bar is found, the result is:

```
public class EditPet extends ActionSupport implements PetStoreAware {
    private PetStore petStore;
    private Pet pet = new Pet();

    public String execute() throws Exception {
        if (pet.getId() < 1 || petStore.getPet(pet.getId()) == null) {
            addActionError("Please enter a valid pet ID.");
            return ERROR;
        } else if (pet.getName() == null || pet.getName().equals("")) {
            addFieldError("pet.name", "Please enter a valid pet name.");
            return ERROR;
        }

        petStore.savePet(pet);

        return SUCCESS;
    }

    public void setPetStore(PetStore petStore) {
        this.petStore = petStore;
    }

    public Pet getPet() {
        return pet;
    }
}
```

Checking Validity

Why `pet.getId()  <  1`? By looking at the Pet class, we can see that by default the ID value is 0, so this test will check for invalid IDs. We must also check that the ID we are given by the user's browser is a valid one. Hence, we try to retrieve the existing Pet with that ID and check that it exists. The second if statement checks that the name of the Pet is valid, as we indicated we wanted to look for in test #2.

Quickly jumping into the views, we know that we need a few views: one for data entry (INPUT), one for confirmation (SUCCESS), and one for error messages (ERROR). Following the procedure we did with ViewPet and AddPet, we will do the following:

1. *SUCCESS* — This will be a redirect to ViewPet, just like AddPet does.

2. *INPUT* — We will need to create a simple data-entry page for updating Pets.

3. *ERROR* — Error messages can be displayed inline in the INPUT view.

And now we create `editpet.jsp`:

```
[editpet.jsp]

<html>
<head>
    <title>Edit Pet</title>
</head>
<body>
    <table>
        <form action="editpet.action">
            <webwork:textfield label="Name" name="pet.name" />
            <webwork:hidden name="pet.id" />

            <tr><td colspan="2">
                <input type="submit" value="Update">
            </td></tr>
        </form>
    </table>
</body>
</html>
```

The interesting thing to note here is the use of the webwork:hidden tag. This essentially ensures that the Pet we are trying to edit is correctly remembered during an otherwise stateless protocol session (HTTP).

Tying It All Together — Take II

Now it is time to tie everything together again. But this time, it's a little different than it was for AddPet and ViewPet. That is because, unlike with AddPet, we can't just send the user off to the INPUT view directly. That is because we must prefetch the existing Pet information so that the input fields aren't empty. What we need to do is retrieve the Pet information, then display editpet.jsp.

Lucky for us, we already wrote this code. Can you guess which action does this? ViewPet, of course! The only difference with ViewPet is that its SUCCESS view sends off to viewpet.jsp, not to editpet.jsp. Not a problem. We can create an alias of ViewPet that can be used for our purposes. Following is the new xwork.xml configuration. See how ViewPet is used for two different actions but has slightly different uses:

```xml
<action name="viewpet" class="org.petsoar.actions.inventory.ViewPet">
    <interceptor-ref name="defaultStack"/>

    <result name="error">
        <param name="location">error.jsp</param>
    </result>
    <result name="success">
        <param name="location">viewpet.jsp</param>
    </result>
</action>

<action name="editpetload"
        class="org.petsoar.actions.inventory.ViewPet">
    <interceptor-ref name="defaultStack"/>

    <result name="error">
        <param name="location">error.jsp</param>
    </result>
    <result name="success">
        <param name="location">editpet.jsp</param>
    </result>
</action>

<action name="editpet" class="org.petsoar.actions.inventory.EditPet">
    <interceptor-ref name="defaultStack"/>

    <result name="error">
        <param name="location">editpet.jsp</param>
    </result>
    <result name="success" type="redirect">
        <param name="location">viewpet.action?id=${pet.id}</param>
    </result>
</action>
```

Once again, fire up PetSoar and point your browser to `http://local host:8080/invetory/editpetload.action?id=123` and see it all in action. We're now "CRU," with only a "D" left to implement. So let's do it!

Get that Pet Out of Here!

It's a great day for Bob the pet, as he's been sold and is well on his way to a life-time of love and happiness. But Bob's leaving does mean one thing for us: we need to get him out of the database so no one else thinks he's still available for purchase. As usual, let's get started with what this action will do and what we need to test.

NOTE Deleting data from the database is the most sensitive operation out of the CRUD process. Therefore, we must be very careful to properly warn the user, as well as to ensure that the user has clearly confirmed his or her intentions to us. A simple way to do this is to require that a confirm input be be given to our action and that its value be non-null.

Other times, delete is nothing more than turning on a "delete flag," and you may or may not require this extra step of confirmation. Many systems don't actually delete data, as it could break referential integrity if, for example, PetSoar is tracking Pet history or sales.

Because we'll be asking for some sort of confirmation of this process, we'll need to test three unique cases:

1. The confirmation element is given to us, and the Pet is successfully removed, resulting in a SUCCESS return code.

2. The Pet ID given is invalid, resulting in an ERROR return code.

3. The user decided against deleting this Pet and has not provided the confirmation we are looking for. This will result in a CANCEL return code.

The test case looks like this:

```
public class TestRemovePet extends TestCase {
    private RemovePet action;
    private Mock mockPetStore;

    protected void setUp() throws Exception {
        mockPetStore = new Mock(PetStore.class);
        PetStore petStore = (PetStore) mockPetStore.proxy();

        action = new RemovePet();
```

```
        action.setPetStore(petStore);
    }

    public void testRemovePet() throws Exception {
        Pet pet = new Pet();
        pet.setName("zizi the zebra");
        mockPetStore.matchAndReturn("getPet", pet);
        mockPetStore.expect("removePet", pet);

        action.setId(1);
        action.setConfirm("foo");

        String result = action.execute();

        assertEquals(Action.SUCCESS, result);
        mockPetStore.verify();
    }

    public void testInvalidIdEntered() throws Exception {
        mockPetStore.matchAndReturn("getPet", null);

        String result = action.execute();

        assertEquals(Action.ERROR, result);
        assertEquals(1, action.getActionErrors().size());
        assertEquals("Invalid pet selected.",
            action.getActionErrors().iterator().next());
        mockPetStore.verify();
    }

    public void testCancel() throws Exception {
        Pet pet = new Pet();
        pet.setName("zizi the zebra");
        mockPetStore.matchAndReturn("getPet", pet);

        action.setId(1);

        String result = action.execute();

        assertEquals("cancel", result);
        mockPetStore.verify();
    }
}
}
```

Note that, in testInvalidIdEntered, we make the mock object return null for any call to getPet. This is a nice little trick for when you are testing for situations like an invalid Pet ID. You might want to remember this one!

NOTE Another way to handle confirmation of important tasks, such as deleting a Pet, is to use JavaScript to ask the user if he or she really wishes to go ahead with this process. This is a very nice user interface mechanism and works well when JavaScript is not disabled on the browser. However, we don't like to depend on it as *the* way to confirm a user's intentions, because it is not guaranteed that JavaScript will indeed be working on the client. The best technique is to use both JavaScript as well as a server-side confirmation technique, as we do here.

So now we create the stubs. Test. Rinse. Repeat. Green Bar. Stop. And what we have is:

```
public class RemovePet extends ActionSupport implements PetStoreAware {
    private PetStore petStore;
    private long id;
    private Pet pet;
    private String confirm;

    public String execute() throws Exception {
        this.pet = petStore.getPet(id);

        if (pet == null) {
            addActionError("Invalid pet selected.");
            return ERROR;
        }

        if (confirm != null) {
            petStore.removePet(pet);
            return SUCCESS;
        } else {
            return "cancel";
        }
    }

    public void setPetStore(PetStore petStore) {
        this.petStore = petStore;
    }

    public Pet getPet() {
        return pet;
    }

    public void setId(long id) {
        this.id = id;
    }

    public void setConfirm(String confirm) {
        this.confirm = confirm;
    }
}
```

Note that the confirm element needs to be non-null. We don't actually check for any value. That is why in our test case we set the value to "foo" and it still worked correctly. The reason for this will become very clear once we create the view for this action, which we will do right now.

```
[removepet.jsp]

<html>
<head>
    <title>Remove Pet</title>
</head>
<body>
    <table>
        <form action="removepet.action">
            <webwork:hidden name="id" />

            <tr><td colspan="2">
                Are you sure you want to delete
                <webwork:property value="pet.name" />?<br>

                <input type="submit" name="confirm" value="Remove">
                <input type="submit" value="Cancel">
            </td></tr>
        </form>
    </table>
</body>
</html>
```

Of special importance is how we handled the confirm input. Notice that the Remove button is named "confirm," but the Cancel button has no name. Both are Submit buttons, so both will cause RemovePet to be executed. The only difference is that if Remove is clicked, RemovePet.setConfirm will be called with the argument of "Remove." This is a simple (but powerful) way for us to handle different behavior based upon the button the user clicks.

Lastly, let's quickly add the required elements to xwork.xml. Just as we did with EditPet, we will be creating an alias for ViewPet that we will use with a different view: removepet.jsp. Here is what the configuration now looks like:

```
<action name="removepetload"
        class="org.petsoar.actions.inventory.ViewPet">
    <interceptor-ref name="defaultStack"/>

    <result name="error">
        <param name="location">error.jsp</param>
    </result>
```

```
        <result name="success">
            <param name="location">removepet.jsp</param>
        </result>
    </action>

    <action name="removepet"
            class="org.petsoar.actions.inventory.RemovePet">
        <interceptor-ref name="defaultStack"/>

        <result name="error">
            <param name="location">error.jsp</param>
        </result>
        <result name="success" type="redirect">
            <param name="location">default.jsp</param>
        </result>
        <result name="cancel" type="redirect">
            <param name="location">viewpet.action?id=${pet.id}</param>
        </result>
    </action>
```

Notice we have a view other than SUCCESS, ERROR, or INPUT: CANCEL. All we do when the CANCEL result is found is redirect the user to viewing the Pet the user just decided not to delete.

Congratulations! We've just completed the CRUD cycle and have working code for all four data actions. But we're not finished just yet. As explained in Chapter 13, TDD says you should always look over your code you just wrote and see if there is anymore refactoring that can be done. As it turns out, there are a few things we can make better through the process of refactoring, so let's get started.

Refactoring the CRUD

While AddPet, ViewPet, EditPet, and RemovePet are all very nice on their own, there appears to be plenty of room for optimizations via refactoring. Be careful not to make any changes that affect the behavior of the code, such as adding new features. Since tests are already written, we can refactor and we should still get a Green Bar.

This is a vital step in the process. Often, when developing Web-tier actions, you'll find that over time you will end up with many actions with duplicate or close-to-duplicate portions of code. In this section, we will look at three refactorings that will make the four actions we've created contain much less duplication of code, thereby making already simple classes that much simpler.

Removing Duplication in ViewPet and RemovePet

Looking back at ViewPet and RemovePet, we see that they are strikingly similar. To refresh your memory, here is ViewPet:

```
public class ViewPet extends ActionSupport implements PetStoreAware {
    private PetStore petStore;
    private long id;
    private Pet pet;

    public String execute() throws Exception {
        this.pet = petStore.getPet(id);

        if (pet == null) {
            addActionError("Invalid pet selected.");
            return ERROR;
        }

        return SUCCESS;
    }

    public void setPetStore(PetStore petStore) {
        this.petStore = petStore;
    }

    public Pet getPet() {
        return pet;
    }

    public long getId() {
        return id;
    }

    public void setId(long id) {
        this.id = id;
    }
}
```

RemovePet looks like this:

```
public class RemovePet extends ActionSupport implements PetStoreAware {
    private PetStore petStore;
    private long id;
    private Pet pet;
    private String confirm;

    public String execute() throws Exception {
        this.pet = petstore.getPet(id);

        if (pet == null) {
            addActionError("Invalid pet selected.");
```

```
            return ERROR;
        }

        if (confirm != null) {
            petstore.removePet(pet);
            return SUCCESS;
        } else {
            return "cancel";
        }
    }

    public void setPetStore(PetStore petStore) {
        this.petStore = petStore;
    }

    public Pet getPet() {
        return pet;
    }

    public void setId(long id) {
        this.id = id;
    }

    public void setConfirm(String confirm) {
        this.confirm = confirm;
    }
}
```

As you can see, both actions have very similar structures. RemovePet has an extra field (confirm) and a slightly more complicated execute method, but otherwise they are carbon copies. Let's fix that, since duplicating of code is always bad. We can do that by simply making RemovePet *extend* ViewPet and change it's execute method to take advantage of this new class hierarchy. RemovePet is now much smaller:

```
public class RemovePet extends ViewPet {
    private String confirm;

    public String execute() throws Exception {
        String result = super.execute();

        if (hasErrors()) {
            return result;
        }

        if (confirm != null) {
            petStore.removePet(pet);
            return SUCCESS;
        } else {
```

```
                return "cancel";
        }
    }

    public void setConfirm(String confirm) {
        this.confirm = confirm;
    }
}
```

What we did is have RemovePet's execute() method first execute its superclass execute() method. Then it checks to see if that execution caused any errors to be reported, and, if so, it terminates processing. The rest of the method is just as it was before the refactoring. Also, note that the only field we specify for RemovePet is confirm, as all the other fields are already part of ViewPet.

We also changed ViewPet slightly. All of its fields were changed from private to protected to allow RemovePet to access them. After doing this, all that is left is to run the unit tests for ViewPet and RemovePet. Green Bar! That means the refactoring was successful and we don't have to worry about the code changes, since our tests just guaranteed the changes didn't break anything.

Odd One Out

If you recall, AddPet behaved a little differently from the other three actions. Instead of setting "pet.name," the input was just the name field of the action. Why not make all the actions standard so we can further remove duplicate code? What this means is, rather than specifying the name directly, the Pet POJO will have its name field set instead. Here's our new AddPet action:

```java
public class AddPet extends ActionSupport implements PetStoreAware {
    private PetStore petStore;
    private Pet pet = new Pet();

    public String execute() throws Exception {
        if (pet.getName() == null || pet.getName().equals("")) {
            addFieldError("pet.name", "Please enter a valid pet name.");
            return ERROR;
        }

        petStore.savePet(pet);

        return SUCCESS;
    }

    public void setPetStore(PetStore petStore) {
        this.petStore = petStore;
```

```
        }

        public Pet getPet() {
            return pet;
        }
    }
```

Not bad. Let's run the tests to confirm our refactoring was successful. Red Bar! Uh oh, what happened? After a bit of investigation, we see that the problem is that the tests are still looking for errors reported on "name" and we've changed it to "pet.name." So let's refactor our test case to accommodate this new change. The relevant parts are highlighted here:

```
public void testAddPet() throws Exception {
    ...
    action.getPet().setName("bob");
    ...
}

public void testAddPetNoName() throws Exception {
    ...
    assertEquals("Please enter a valid pet name.",
        (String) action.getFieldErrors().get("pet.name"));
    ...
}
```

Likewise, we need to update our addpet.jsp view to also accommodate this change. The new webwork:textfield tag will look like this:

```
<webwork:textfield label="Name" name="pet.name" />
```

Having made this change, we can now clearly see the overlap between AddPet and EditPet. Both have the exact same fields, a "blank" Pet POJO, and similar execute methods. The only difference is that EditPet requires that the Pet ID be valid before updating the database. Refactoring more, we get EditPet to look like this:

```
public class EditPet extends AddPet {
    public String execute() throws Exception {
        if (pet.getId() < 1 || petStore.getPet(pet.getId()) == null) {
            addActionError("Please enter a valid pet ID.");
            return ERROR;
        }

        return super.execute();
    }
}
```

It's the incredible shrinking code! It's amazing how simple these actions are getting. All the while, our refactoring is validated through the unit tests reporting Green Bar. The only change needed for AddPet is that its fields are now protected, just as we did with ViewPet.

Note that EditPet uses its superclass execute method *after* it validates the incoming data. This is different from when RemovePet used its superclass *before* any data processing occurred. The order of when to use the superclass execute method is entirely determined by the object hierarchy and the requirements as to what should be executed first.

Performing One Last Refactor

We've successfully turned EditPet and RemovePet into very simple actions, but there is still quite a bit of code duplication between ViewPet and AddPet. Both have a PetStore field, as well as a Pet, including their associated getter and setter methods. What we can do is move these common elements into an abstract class that doesn't actually process anything, but provides a base for ViewPet and AddPet to extend from. What we end up with is this:

```java
public abstract class AbstractPetAction extends ActionSupport
        implements PetStoreAware {
    protected PetStore petStore;
    protected Pet pet = new Pet();

    public void setPetStore(PetStore petstore) {
        this.petstore = petstore;
    }

    public Pet getPet() {
        return pet;
    }
}

public class ViewPet extends AbstractPetAction {
    private long id;

    public String execute() throws Exception {
        this.pet = petStore.getPet(id);

        if (pet == null) {
            addActionError("Invalid pet selected.");
            return ERROR;
        }

        return SUCCESS;
```

```
        }

        public long getId() {
            return id;
        }

        public void setId(long id) {
            this.id = id;
        }
    }

    public class AddPet extends AbstractPetAction {
        public String execute() throws Exception {
            if (pet.getName() == null || pet.getName().equals("")) {
                addFieldError("pet.name", "Please enter a valid pet name.");
                return ERROR;
            }

            petStore.savePet(pet);

            return SUCCESS;
        }
    }
```

Once again, run the unit tests to ensure that this refactor didn't break any-thing. Green Bar, Good. We've successfully turned four simple actions into four incredibly simple actions, all in a very short time thanks to our unit tests. Comparing the old object hierarchy (shown in Figure 16.4) with our new, very nice Object-Oriented design (shown in Figure 16.5), we can see that object reuse is much more prominent in this new design.

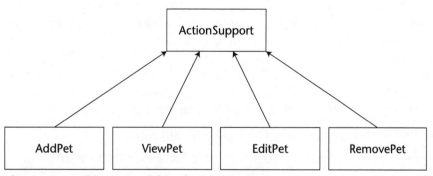

Figure 16.4   Old UML model for the CRUD actions

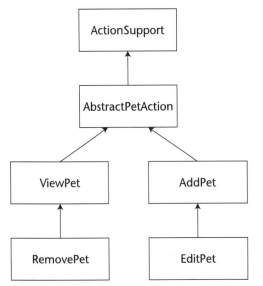

Figure 16.5 New UML model for the CRUD actions

Decoupling the Validation

Even after the refactoring and a more organized object model, there is still one thing that reeks of "code smell": the data validation logic is tied to the actions themselves. It would be nice if we could extract this so that the actions focus only on their sole task, not worrying about valid input parameters. Fortunately, XWork comes with a very nice validation framework we can use to do this.

The validation framework provides a clean separation of concerns. To use the validation portion of WebWork, we must first provide a list of possible validator classes that will do the validation against user input. WebWork comes with a nice set of classes already built for us that we can use, so we'll just stick with the default `validators.xml` file shipped with WebWork. This file will be placed in the classpath (WEB-INF/classes) alongside `xwork.xml`.

The default set of validator classes that we can use are as follows:

- *required* — Reports an error if a field has a null value.
- *requiredstring* — Reports an error if a field has a null value or an empty string value.
- *int* — Reports an error if an integer is not within a specified range.
- *date* — Reports an error if a date is not within a specified range.
- *expression* — Reports an error if the given expression does not evaluate to true. This is the most powerful validator.

USING XWORK COMMANDS

As you've seen, we've been using the ViewPet action as an alias for editpetload and removepetload. We've also now refactored the four CRUD action classes to eliminate duplication of code, as shown in comparison between the new and old UML diagrams. While using ViewPet as an alias is one way to achieve this goal, there is another way to do this: using XWork commands.

As explained in Chapter 6, XWork executes an action's execute method by default. However, you can specify other methods in the configuration that you wish to be executed when an action alias is invoked. So, rather than making editpetload alias to ViewPet directly, it would have been possible for us to make editpetload alias to a method in EditPet action called `doLoad()`. The end result is pretty much the same, so the choice is entirely stylistic and up to you. For your convenience, we've provided what the action aliases might look like for editing a Pet if you were to choose this approach:

```
<action name="editpetload"
        class="org.petsoar.actions.inventory.EditPet"
        method="doLoad">
    <interceptor-ref name="defaultStack"/>

    <result name="error">
        <param name="location">viewpet.jsp</param>
    </result>
    <result name="success">
        <param name="location">editpet.jsp</param>
    </result>
</action>

<action name="editpet"
        class="org.petsoar.actions.inventory.EditPet">
    <interceptor-ref name="defaultStack"/>

    <result name="error">
        <param name="location">editpet.jsp</param>
    </result>
    <result name="success" type="redirect">
        <param name="location">
            viewpet.action?id=${pet.id}
        </param>
    </result>
</action>
```

As indicated by the bold area, the only difference is that editpetload is now calling `doLoad()` in the EditPet action, rather than calling ViewPet's `execute()` method. The advantage of this is that each action class is in complete control of its behavior. The disadvantage is that now each action class needs an extra method that will most likely end up calling a superclass method, as we did in our refactored design. The choice is yours as to which style you prefer.

Now let's take a look at the AddPet action. Currently, its execute() method looks like the following:

```
public String execute() throws Exception {
    if (pet.getName() == null || pet.getName().equals("")) {
        addFieldError("pet.name", "Please enter a valid pet name.");
        return ERROR;
    }

    petstore.savePet(pet);

    return SUCCESS;
}
```

Notice that the check on pet.getName() is exactly what the required string validator does! So let's use this validator for AddPet. We can do this by creating a validation XML file using either the class name of the action or the alias name of the action as given in xwork.xml. We will place AddPet-validation.xml in the same package of AddPet, and it will be picked up automatically. Here's what it looks like:

```
<validators>
    <field name="pet.name">
        <field-validator type="requiredstring">
            <message>Please enter a valid pet name.</message>
        </field-validator>
    </field>
</validators>
```

One nice thing about the validation framework is that error messages can be customized by referring to expressions using the notation ${ . . . }, just as we did for the redirects to the ViewPet action. That means you could customize error messages to print values that the user enters, making the error message carry more clarity.

We could have had the error message say, "Please enter a valid Pet name. You entered ${pet.name}." But we didn't do that because we know that if an error message is printed, it will have an empty value anyway, so there was no point in attempting to print it. However, often you do want to specify values in your error messages, so this is a very powerful feature. For example, an error message might say, "Please enter an int between 1 and 10; you entered 11."

> **NOTE** WebWork, and it's underlying core, XWork, are very capable of supporting internationalization. While the error message presented here does not support i18n, XWork does provide support for loading error messages from resource bundles, giving full compatability for i18n by using the optional "key" attribute to the message element and providing resource bundles for the Action.

Now that we've moved the validation logic to a configuration file, let's remove it from AddPet's execute method. The new method will look like this:

```
public String execute() throws Exception {
    if (hasErrors()) {
        return ERROR;
    }

    petstore.savePet(pet);

    return SUCCESS;
}
```

Not too shabby! More validation rules can be added at any time without changing the action code at all. We have achieved a complete decoupling of validation and action. Even better, because EditPet extends AddPet, the same validation rules will also be applied toward the EditPet action. We're now finished with refactoring our CRUD actions and have achieved a very simple set of actions that are fully unit tested, nicely organized, and have no duplication of code. Not bad at all.

But one question remains: How easy are these actions to add functionality to? All we've been talking about is Pets having either an ID or a name. Very often with Web applications, new data fields are added to domain objects. The actions that suffer the most from this kind of change are the CRUD classes. What if new fields are added to the Pet class, such as gender or description? Can our design easily accommodate for that? Let's find out.

Changing the Pet

Suppose our boss has given us the task of adding various fields to the Pet domain object because currently we have only a name and ID field, which really isn't enough to be useful for a fully functional PetStore. Our boss wants to double that number of fields by adding gender and description to the Pets. Normally, we might be a bit unhappy, especially after all this work we've just gone though. While this might seem to be a fairly large undertaking, it turns out that this is the simplest process of this whole chapter!

It's trivial for us to add new fields to the pet. Why? Because we have a complete unit test suite, a nicely structured object hierarchy thanks to our refactoring, and views and validations that are completely decoupled from the Java code. Without further delay, let's get started by looking at all four of our CRUD actions, starting with AddPet.

Recall that we had refactored AddPet to use the Pet POJO rather than have individual fields in the action class itself. Because we did that, the action code doesn't need to be updated at all. Assuming that gender and description are both optional fields, all that needs to be updated is the view, addpet.jsp:

```
<form action="addpet.action">
    <webwork:textfield label="Name" name="pet.name" />
    <webwork:select label="Gender" name="pet.gender"
                    list="{'Unknown', 'Male', 'Female'}" />
    <webwork:textarea label="Description" name="pet.description" />

    <tr><td colspan="2">
        <input type="submit" value="Add">
    </td></tr>
</form>
```

The only change here is that the two new fields were added to the view using WebWork's select and text-area controls. The gender field was given a choice of three options (Unknown, Male, and Female). Is that really are there is to it? Maybe our boss isn't such a bad guy after all!

So now we load up our application server and verify that this new functionality works — or at least we think it works. It's pretty hard to tell when the ViewPet page isn't showing these fields. So, let's fix that by updating viewpet.jsp to display these new values:

```
<b>ID:</b> <webwork:property value="pet.id" /><br>
<b>Name:</b> <webwork:property value="pet.name" /><br>
<b>Gender:</b> <webwork:property value="pet.gender" /><br>
<b>Description:</b> <webwork:property value="pet.description" /><br>
```

Again, amazingly simple. Our boss is going to love us! Quickly moving on to update, we see that the same exact changes made to viewpet.jsp are needed for editpet.jsp:

```
<webwork:textfield label="Name" name="pet.name" />
<webwork:select label="Gender" name="pet.gender"
                list="{'Unknown', 'Male', 'Female'}" />
<webwork:textarea label="Description" name="pet.description" />
```

Finally, does RemovePet need to change? Since its views don't need to display these other fields, we don't need to do anything at all. Just for the sake of safety, we can run our unit tests one more time. Green Bar. But of course they would pass; we never changed the actions!

And that is the amazing part. We've actually modified our domain object and its corresponding CRUD actions with only six lines of HTML and JSP (excluding the changes to the Pet class itself, of course). We'll be getting to go home early today.

Summary

There you have it, the beginning of the Web interface for PetSoar. Of course, we're not finished yet. We still have a *lot* of cleanup to do with the views, as they are currently way too simple and ugly. Chapter 17 discusses tips and techniques how we can make this user interface much better looking.

So, what did we learn today? Creating actions for the Web interface is not nearly as hard as it sounds. Refactoring those actions should be done at all times, because the refactorings will save you time down the road, as we just showed when we added two new fields to the Pet. We demonstrated simple usage of the validation framework and how it cleanly decouples the view, action, and validation logic into three distinct parts. Overall, we showed you how we can extend from the domain objects developed in Chapter 15 and easily create a Web interface in almost no time.

chapter 17

Defining Navigation, Layout, Look, and Feel

In Chapter 16, we explored how to use WebWork to tie in domain objects to interact with a Web interface. We focused mainly on the actions that bind HTML to the domain objects, leaving the HTML in a bare-bones state. In this chapter, we will discuss various techniques and technologies that can make the *Web* in your Web application much better in both design and look. Starting from the lowest level, we will discuss how HTML can be componentized and folded into common reusable libraries. We will then take this same logic and apply it toward high-level elements common in your pages. Finally, we will look at various options for beatifying your pages with the help of a graphic designer. The technologies discussed include WebWork, SiteMesh, and Cascading Style Sheets.

Componentizing Form Widgets

In Chapter 16, we show how simple it is to add new fields to your domain object. We add *description* and *gender* to the Pet object and essentially get the new features for free because our action code doesn't have to be modified at all. The only change needed is to update our JSPs to include calls to Web-Work's rich set of UI tags. These tags automatically create the required HTML to input the new data such as gender and description.

But what if you want something other than a simple select box or text field? Let's suppose that you're now tasked to add another new field to the Pet class: birthdate. Just as we do in the last chapter, the only Java code that needs to change is Pet.java itself — the actions will automatically work. But what about the input fields in the JSPs? Are they also just as simple?

The short answer is "yes." Assuming that you want users to enter date information using a simple text field, all that is needed is making yet another webwork:textfield tag call from your JSP file. But often people don't want to enter dates by hand. They'd rather have a popup calendar or three drop-down select boxes representing month, day, and year. These are more complex than the previous WebWork tags we use in the previous chapter.

Luckily, WebWork caters to users like us who require more advanced usage from the user interface form widgets. Through the use of the generic webwork:component tag, we can create custom, reusable user-interface elements that have the same look and feel that the existing form elements do.

Suppose that it is decided that a popup calendar is the best option for our user interface. We've already found a nice Open Source JavaScript calendar program, so most of the hard work is already taken care of. Without worrying about components just yet, let's see how we might use this calendar without any fancy tag libraries:

```
<tr>
    <td>Birthdate:</td>
    <td>
    <script language="JavaScript"
           src="/decorators/datepicker.js"></script>
    <input type="text" name="pet.birthdate">
    <a href="javascript:show_calendar('/', 'editform',
           document.editform, 'pet.birthdate');">
        <img src="/images/icons/cal.gif" width="16" height="16"
           border="0" alt="Pick a date"></a>
    </td>
</tr>
```

NOTE Note that, in the previous example, we assumed that PetSoar has been deployed to the root context of your application server. This was done for the sake of brevity only. A more robust solution would be to replace instances of / with <% request.getContextPath() %>, which we have done in the actual application. In general, you should always prepend any absolute URL with a call to getContextPath. It's the only way to ensure your application is totally portable.

The show_calendar() JavaScript function requires that the form be given a name. We've chosen to call the form editform, which means that the form tag must also contain this name. Otherwise, the JavaScript would not be able to find the input element and set it with the selected date.

```
<form action="editpet.action" name="editform">
    <webwork:textfield ... />
    <webwork:select ... />
    <tr>
        <td>Birthday</td>
        ...
    </tr>
</form>
```

That's it! Now we've got a working popup calendar that can be used to select birthdates. But there are a couple problems:

1. It looks odd to see the `<tr>` and `<td>` tags beside the much slicker-looking WebWork tags that take care of the table formatting for you.

2. If we want to use this same type of input in another form (such as when adding a Pet rather than editing), we can't just copy the preceding text directly. The form name must be changed from `editform` to `addform`.

The first problem can be addressed with a simple JSP include tag or directive, but the second problem is a bit more complex. Somehow, values in `editpet.jsp` or `addpet.jsp` need to be passed in to the widget so that the form name can be given to the calendar function. JSP has support for this using jsp:include and jsp:param, but WebWork offers a more powerful and graceful alternative: *component tags*. The WebWork component tags are a set of predefined JSP tags that allow you to turn form controls, their error messages, and surrounding basic HTML into reusable components.

WebWork's component tags are nicer than the jsp:include (used beside jsp:param) for several reasons:

1. Parameters passed using jsp:param can only be string values. Parameters passed to WebWork tags, using webwork:param, can be any object that can be retrieved through XWork's powerful expression language.

2. Using jsp:include means that you are tying your included component (a date picker in this case) to your view code. If you ever want to change the file that is being included, you have to modify all pages that include the original date picker to include a new date picker.

3. WebWork's UI tags come with support for "themes." These themes allow you to change the look and behavior of all the components by simply changing a single configuration element. By default, the theme is "xhtml," which are simple XHTML-compliant UI tags. These could be changed to interactive Java Applets or any other style for data entry very easily, with no need to change the JSPs *using* the components.

Using the new webwork:component tag, what does the HTML in `editpet`
`.jsp` look like now? Following are all of the input components for editing
Pets, including the new support for the generic date picker:

```
<webwork:textfield label="Name" name="pet.name" />
<webwork:select label="Gender" name="pet.gender"
                list="{'Unknown', 'Male', 'Female'}" />
<webwork:textarea label="Description" name="pet.description" />
<webwork:component label="Birthdate" template="datepicker.vm"
                name="pet.birthdate">
   <webwork:param name="formname" value="'editform'" />
</webwork:component>
```

The HTML we previously had has been abstracted to a component that we
have yet to write: `datepicker.vm`. Components in WebWork are written in
the Velocity templating language because it offers unparalleled speed in all
Servlet containers. Before we look at the contents of `datepicker.vm`, let's
carefully look at what this component tag is actually doing.

There are three attributes in the webwork:component tag that we are using:
label, name, and template. These attributes are discussed in more detail in
Chapter 6, but let's briefly highlight the ones used in this particular example:

- *Label* — The text value that will be displayed on the Web.

- *Name* — The field name that will be set by WebWork. In this case, it is a
  representation of a path in the object graph, resulting in an equivalent
  call to `action.getPet().setBirthdate()`.

- *Template* — The `Velocity` file that does the rendering and display
  logic for a particular component.

All that is left to write is the actual contents for `datepicker.vm`:

```
#parse( "/decorators/xhtml/controlheader.vm" )
<script language="JavaScript" src="/decorators/datepicker.js"></script>
<input type="text" name="${tag.Name}" value="$!{tag.ActualValue}"/>
<a href="javascript:show_calendar('/', '${tag.Params.get("formname")}',
        document.${tag.Params.get("formname")}, '${tag.Name}');">
   <img src="/images/icons/cal.gif" width="16" height="16"
        border="0" alt="Pick a date">
</a>
#parse( "/decorators/xhtml/controlfooter.vm" )
```

Though it might look a little scary at first, this is really nothing new. The only
difference is the syntax that you might be used to, such as JSP. Rather than `<%=
foo %>` or `<webwork:property value="foo"/>`, we use `$foo`. Everything
else is pretty much the same. As you can see here, the logic in this small file is
exactly what we need based upon the original static HTML previously written.

Note that the content here is slightly simplified, again for the sake of brevity.
A complete date-picker component might want other properties to be

specified, such as the size of the input box, date format, a marker indicating the field is required, and so on. Also, at the moment, we can only include one of these date-picker components in the page at once, because the JavaScript include will be duplicated, causing an error on most browsers. However, this suits our needs for now and is acceptable. In the future, we could modify the tag to use a Boolean parameter to indicate that the JS had already been included and whether to include it again.

Now that we've looked at the smallest-level component in our forms, a form widget, let's move up one level and see if there are ways we can componentize other parts of our pages.

Forming a Better Look and Feel

Moving on, let's see if we can improve the look and feel of the form in editpet.jsp, while still maintaining a nicely componentized architecture. But before we try to make a nice architecture, let's just try to make the user interface look nice. Just as premature optimization can hurt a project, so can premature architecture design — especially when doing TDD.

Most forms should have some sort of title as well as a detailed description of what the form is all about. Without this kind of information, it is much harder for the user to quickly discern the purpose of the form. We place this information in to our editpet.jsp and now the form is much more usable than it was previously:

```
<table>
    <tr><td colspan="2">
        <h2>Edit a Pet</h2>
        This form will edit an existing pet. If you want to add a pet,
        use a different form!
    </td></tr>
    <form action="editpet.action">
        <webwork:hidden name="pet.id" />
        <webwork:textfield label="Name" name="pet.name" />
        <webwork:select label="Gender" name="pet.gender"
                        list="{'Unknown', 'Male', 'Female'}" />
        <webwork:textarea label="Description" name="pet.description"
                          rows="6" cols="40"/>
        <webwork:component label="Birthdate" template="datepicker.vm"
                           name="pet.birthdate">
            <webwork:param name="formname" value="'editform'" />
        </webwork:component>

        <tr><td colspan="2">
            <input type="submit" value="Add">
        </td></tr>
    </form>
</table>
```

This does the job (albeit the HTML is getting crowded), but we'll soon find ourselves creating this same HTML for other forms, such as adding pets or removing pets. Clearly, we don't want to duplicate this style each time. We could use a jsp:include directive, but again there is a better alternative: SiteMesh's inline decorator support.

As discussed in Chapter 7, SiteMesh has support for inline decoration of content. It just so happens that this example is a perfect fit for using SiteMesh. Why is that? Neither JSP includes nor WebWork's component tag supports processing the body of a tag as content to be decorated. This is where SiteMesh really shines. Using the body of the tag as the content to be decorated is important, as the body can be generated dynamically using other JSP tags.

Changing the previous example to use the SiteMesh decorator application tag, the new editpet.jsp is now:

```
<page:applyDecorator name="/decorators/petform.jsp">
      <page:param name="title">Edit a Pet</page:param>
      <page:param name="description">
         This form will edit a pet. If you want to add a pet,
         use a different form!
      </page:param>

      <webwork:hidden name="pet.id" />
      <webwork:textfield label="Name" name="pet.name" />
      <webwork:select label="Gender" name="pet.gender"
                   list="{'Unknown', 'Male', 'Female'}" />
      <webwork:textarea label="Description" name="pet.description"
                      rows="6" cols="40"/>
      <webwork:component label="Birthdate" template="datepicker.vm"
                      name="pet.birthdate">
         <webwork:param name="formname" value="'editform'" />
      </webwork:component>
</page:applyDecorator>
```

The content of petform.jsp is now as follows:

```
<%@ taglib uri="sitemesh-decorator" prefix="decorator" %>
<table>
    <tr><td colspan="2">
        <h2><decorator:getProperty property="title" /></h2>
        <decorator:getProperty property="description" />
    </td></tr>
    <form action="editpet.action">
        <decorator:body />

        <tr><td colspan="2">
```

```
            <input type="submit" value="Edit">
        </td></tr>
    </form>
</table>
```

Okay, what's happening here? There are two magical things that SiteMesh is letting us do. One we've already seen with WebWork: the ability to pass parameters to our component. The second magical thing occurring is that SiteMesh decorators, such as `petform.jsp`, can pull the content inside of the page:applyDecorator tag and insert it into the text of the decorator using the decorator:body tag. This means that all the webwork tags have been evaluated to HTML and are then included inside of the form we define in `petform.jsp`.

As you can see, `editpet.jsp` is passing two parameters to our decorator (`petform.jsp`): *title* and *description*. These values are then used to create the form UI elements that we desire. But we need to actually specify a couple more parameters besides the obvious ones that affect the UI. For example, `petform.jsp` cannot yet be used in other pages that require forms because it still submits to editpet.action and its button is still displaying "Add." This can be easily fixed by introducing more parameters: *action* and *button*. The changes in `petform.jsp` are now:

```
<form action="<decorator:getProperty property="action" />">
    <decorator:body />

    <tr><td colspan="2">
        <input type="submit"
                value="<decorator:getProperty property="button" />">
    </td></tr>
</form>
```

So, `editpet.jsp` now looks like this:

```
<%@ taglib uri="webwork" prefix="webwork" %>
<%@ taglib uri="sitemesh-page" prefix="page" %>
<html>
<head>
    <title>Edit A Pet</title>
</head>

<body>
    <page:applyDecorator name="/decorators/petform.jsp">
        <page:param name="action">editpet.action</page:param>
        <page:param name="button">Edit</page:param>
        <page:param name="title">Edit a Pet</page:param>
```

```
        <page:param name="description">
            This form will edit a pet. If you want to add a pet,
            use a different form!
        </page:param>

        <webwork:textfield label="Name" name="pet.name" />
        <webwork:select label="Gender" name="pet.gender"
                    list="{'Unknown', 'Male', 'Female'}" />
        <webwork:textarea label="Description" name="pet.description"
                    rows="6" cols="40"/>
        <webwork:component label="Birthdate" template="datepicker.vm"
                    name="pet.birthdate">
            <webwork:param name="formname" value="'editform'" />
        </webwork:component>
    </page:applyDecorator>
</body>
</html>
```

Now editpet.jsp has moved from being HTML content to being a collection of components, making maintenance much easier. Notice that the only HTML in the page is the enclosing HTML elements, which are extremely basic. Anytime we need to display a form, we can use this decorator and give our entire site a standardized look and feel. Any changes to petform.jsp will be reflected throughout the site. Besides the obvious benefit of being able to put content into our inline decorators (something jsp:includes doesn't have an easy time dealing with), there is another gain of not having to refer to petform.jsp directly. A simple change in the page:applyDecorator tag to the following lets us refer to the decorator by an alias:

```
<page:applyDecorator name="petform">
...
</page:applyDecorator>
```

All that we need to do is modify SiteMesh's decorators.xml configuration to indicate what this alias maps to:

```
<decorators defaultdir="/decorators">
    <decorator name="petform" page="petform.jsp" />
</decorators>
```

We've now componentized both individual form widgets as well as the form itself. Now let's look at ways to customize the look and feel of the entire page, leaving a very nice, professional style throughout the application.

Using a Touch of Style

Components are very powerful for Web design, but without a nice look and feel, the application will never be fully accepted by users. Good site design is a goal that is incredibly hard to reach and takes years of know-how in the usability and design fields to truly understand. It's not expected that developers such as us have this kind of experience. However, it doesn't hurt to know a bit about the technologies that enable good user-interface design.

A good design makes use of compatible color tones, attractive, readable fonts, clean table layouts, and sensible image and text placement. The best way to control these various elements is through the use of *Cascading Style Sheets (CSS)*. A CSS is a great way to separate the look and feel of your application from the implementation. In an ideal world, we'd like to be able to have graphic designers work directly on files such as `editpet.jsp`. But even as simple as that file is, it's not suitable for HTML-heads to modify directly, because the tags can be confusing and most WYSIWYG tools don't understand JSP taglibs.

The solution is to write the JSPs yourself, make the HTML refer to CSS styles, and then let graphics designers modify the style sheets to their heart's content. As you can see in Figures 17.1 and 17.2, applying well thought-out style sheets to your HTML pages can make a world of a difference.

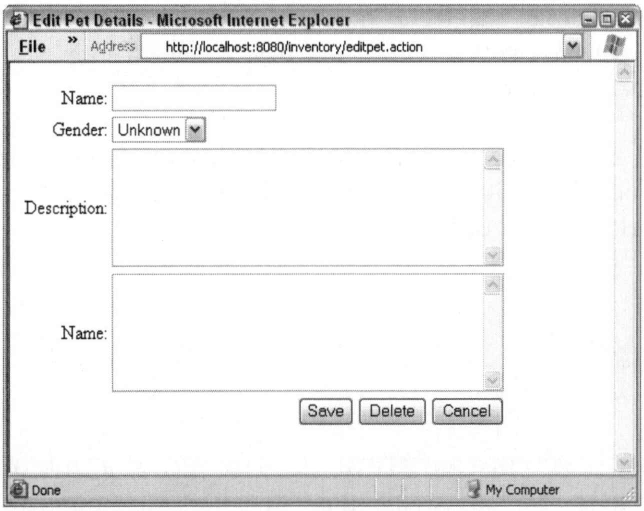

Figure 17.1   Editing a pet without CSS

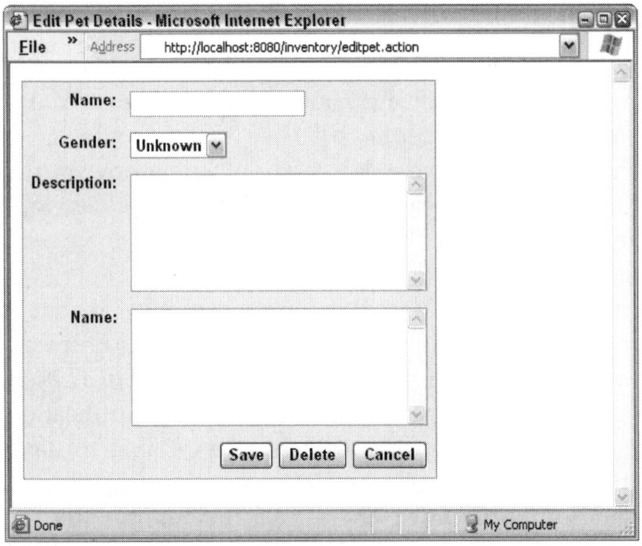

Figure 17.2 Editing a pet with CSS

NOTE As good as CSS makes our pages look, it isn't perfect. After all, what technology is? Different browsers use CSS in different ways, and it is sometimes impossible to get a page to look the same on all platforms. For example, Netscape 4.0 has terrible support for style sheets. Likewise, small inconsistencies can be found in different versions of Internet Explorer, as well as in Mozilla, Opera, and Netscape. Nevertheless, style sheets are your best bet for a (mostly) standard user interface that looks good.

Clearly, using CSS can make a big impact on your application. How does this CSS get applied to our HTML? It's as simple as adding a reference to our style sheet in the HEAD element of our HTML.

```
<head>
    <title>Edit A Pet</title>
    <link rel="stylesheet" type="text/css" href="/decorators/style.css">
</head>
...
```

All that needs to happen now is that any HTML element (such as a table or group of text) that needs to be specially styled must have its "class" defined. Classes are detailed in the style sheets (`style.css`) and then referenced in the HTML file itself (`editpet.jsp`). For example, if we want to style a table element for when it's supposed to look like a form, we do the following:

```
<table class="form">
...
</table>
```

Remember that because we're now using SiteMesh to do form componentization, this change only happens in one place: `petform.jsp`. Likewise, the default WebWork UI templates (such as textfield, select, and so on) all have predefined CSS classes that you can override in your style sheets. Suddenly, graphic designers have much more control over the style of your application than it previously appeared.

Defining classes for each HTML element may seem like a lot of work — and it can be. But it's important that you don't rely on only the style sheet to dictate the user interface's look and feel. While it is possible to use CSS to control the look of *all* tables, doing that is probably undesirable if you are only trying to make the look of a form. Investing some upfront time in the types of items in your pages you'd like to style will allow designers to have more control over the user interface than just the HTML element types such as *table, font, h1, p,* and others.

You can probably consult with your graphic designer to determine when unique classes should be defined and when styles can be applied to all element types. For example, using classes for tables is generally a good idea because tables are used in numerous places in your pages, and stylizing all of them would probably not turn out as expected. On the other hand, styling all paragraph tags (<p>) might not have an adverse effect on the user interface.

A sample of the style sheet used for PetSoar is shown here:

```
/* Standard HTML elements */
h1 {
    font-size: 19pt;
    font-weight: normal;
    color: #1f4ca5;
    font-family: arial;
}
h2 {
    font-size: 13pt;
    color: #663366;
    font-family: arial;
}

/* Form style table */
.form {
    border: 1px solid;
    border-color: buttonshadow;
    background-color: #eeeeee;
}
.form td, .form th {
    vertical-align: top;
    font: menu;
    padding: 5;
}
.form th {
        text-align: left;
```

```
            font-weight: bold;
            background-color: #dddddd;
    }
    .form .errorRow input {
        background-color: #ffcccc;
    }
    .form .label {
            font-weight: bold;
    }
    .form .error {
        color: red;
    }
    .form input, .form select, .form textarea {
        font: menu;
    }
```

The form-related styles are specifically for the `petform.jsp` decorator as well as the styles that WebWork supports by default. Now, error messages will show up as dark-red text on a light-red background, and labels will show up as bold. Pretty neat!

Fully understanding and taking advantage of CSS is well beyond the scope of this book. There are many great HTML design books that can teach you the ins and outs of advanced Web-page design, but this should give you a general overview and show you why knowledge of this technology is important to developers such as yourself.

The one thing that is perplexing with CSS is that the style sheet must be referenced in every single HEAD tag. This leaves open the possibility of forgetting to make the link or a typo in the link, resulting in a non-stylized page. We will now discuss ways to avoid this problem as well as discuss advanced ways to provide for a consistent layout and navigation.

Navigating to a Better User Interface

While we find that CSS is a great technology for making clean, beautiful Web pages, we've also seen that it can sometimes be tricky to set up, especially in large applications where there are hundreds of HTML and JSP pages. We need to find a way to link the style sheet to each and every page in a consistent manner. Not only that, but, in general, we probably want to have the same headers and footers on every page so that there is a consistent navigation throughout.

The knee-jerk reaction to this problem is again to use jsp:include. But once again, while jsp:include does help alleviate this problem, there are better solutions! Before jumping into the alternatives, let's look at how we can tackle this problem using includes. Here is what a sample HTML file might look like.

```
<html>
    <jsp:include page="/includes/header.jsp">
        <jsp:param name="title" value="PetSoar - Edit a Pet"/>
    </jsp:include>

    normal HTML and JSP tags go here.

    <jsp:include page="/includes/footer.jsp"/>
</html>
```

Now let's look at how this would be done using SiteMesh, as discussed in Chapter 7:

```
<html>
    <head>
        <title>Edit a Pet</title>
    </head>

    normal HTML and JSP tags go here.
</html>
```

The second example is so much simpler and cleaner because we no longer have to make explicit calls to include content. Instead, SiteMesh passively is parsing the HTML your page evaluates to and modifying it to display a standard look and feel (such as navigation bars, headers, footers, titles, and, of course, correct links to style sheets).

Some other advantages of decorators over includes are:

- Includes must be tightly bound to every single JSP.

- Includes don't work for non-JSP content, such as HTML or XML converted to HTML, or even non-Java technologies such as Perl or PHP.

- Includes are very static. Changing their behavior at runtime is not the most straightforward task.

Because SiteMesh parses existing HTML and integrates it into decorators, which are also complete HTML files, the job for site designers is much easier now. Rather than have to deal with includes that hide away basics such as TITLE and HEAD tags, designers can work with more complete HTML files. However, depending on your ratio of normal HTML to JSP tags, this may or may not be a major benefit for you.

Here is an extremely trimmed-down version of the actual PetSoar decorator, just to give you a taste of how decorators can be used:

```
<%@ taglib uri="sitemesh-decorator" prefix="decorator" %>
<html>
 <head>
  <title>PetSoar - <decorator:title default="Your Pet Store" /></title>
  <link rel="stylesheet" type="text/css" href="/decorators/style.css">
  <decorator:head />
 </head>
 <body>
  <table>
   <tr>

    <!-- Start Menu Items -->
    <td>
     <li><a href="/inventory/listpets.action">Inventory</a></li>
     <li><a href="/storefront/listpets.action">Pets</a></li>
    </td>
    <!-- End Menu Items -->

    <td>
     <decorator:body />
    </td>

   </tr>
  </table>
 </body>
</html>
```

Let's examine what this decorator is doing:

- *Style sheet linking* — Now any page that uses this decorator will automatically link to the correct style sheet, without even knowing it.

- *Consistent titles* — Every page will have a title of "PetSoar - " followed by the actual page title or, if it wasn't specified, PetSoar's extremely catchy tagline: "Your Pet Store."

- *Uses HEAD elements* — Any additional HEAD element other than the title, such as links to special JavaScript files, will automatically be added. This allows each page to retain its individuality while also maintaining a standard look.

- *Provides a common navigation* — The menu items will be displayed on every page, providing for a very easy-to-understand and consistent navigation scheme.

All that is left to do is to configure which pages get this decoration. For Pet-Soar, we'd like all pages to look the same way, so it's a very trivial URL pattern that we will map against:

```
<decorators defaultdir="/decorators">
    <decorator name="main" page="main.jsp">
        <pattern>*</pattern>
    </decorator>
</decorators>
```

In your applications, you might require different decorators for different parts of your application. For example, the administrative interface might look different from the rest of the Web pages. All you need to do this is to map "/admin/*" to your admin.jsp decorator page. Because of this, structuring your JSPs and HTML files in a manner that allows for simple URL patterns can prove to be very valuable. As discussed in Chapter 7, there are other kinds of "decorator mappers" that provide much more functionality than demonstrated here.

Summary

In this chapter, we took the very simple HTML examples from Chapter 16 and began to explore various ways we can make them more maintainable, but also good-looking at the same time. By using tag libraries supplied by WebWork and SiteMesh, as well as some simple design practices such as abstraction, we were able to make all the PetSoar JSPs much more maintainable by removing all levels of duplication.

We then looked at Cascading Style Sheets and showed how we could take advantage of their power and leverage their decoupled nature to provide externalized look-and-feel control. Then, using SiteMesh, we showed how some of the limitations of style sheets (such as the requirement to be linked in every page) can be overcome. Finally, we looked at ways to provide standard headers, footers, and navigation bars in PetSoar using standard jsp:include tags as well as more advanced techniques involving SiteMesh.

CHAPTER 18

Implementing Browse and Search Capabilities

In the previous chapters, we focused on the domain model of the PetSoar application and the view and user interface layout portions of it. In this chapter, we implement two of the most important parts of a pet-store site: browsing and searching.

Defining the Application Requirements

It must be possible to view all available Pets and categories and easily navigate through the list. Because there may be a large number of Pets in the store, it should also be possible to view the lists in a paginated way, like most Web-based user interfaces do. So, by using the pagination mechanism, the user would be able to view the list in smaller chunks (ten items per page, for example) and easily navigate among these pages.

A searching system is also essential to our application. Without an effective searching mechanism, users can't find their favorite Pet in our rich list of offered Pets. It should be possible to search the list of Pets and categories with friendly English queries. In other words, we need a smart, full-text searching mechanism for the site.

Browsing the List of Categories

To get started, we will create a ListCategories action class. It's a WebWork command object and encapsulates the category retrieval logic. As usual, we start with the test:

```
[TestListCategories.java]

public class TestListCategories extends TestCase {
    public void testListCategories() throws Exception {
        // setup

        ListCategories action = new ListCategoriesAction();

        // execute
        String result = action.execute();

        // verify
        assertEquals(Action.SUCCESS, result);
    }
}
```

Okay, so we have a test, but it doesn't compile yet. To get it to compile, we create ListCategories:

```
[ListCategories.java]

public class ListCategories implements Action {
    public String execute() {
        // todo
        return SUCCESS;
    }
}
```

The test hasn't actually tested all the categories that have been retrieved. We should first add some categories to the store and then test that the action retrieves them all. We don't need to test whether PetStore performs Category retrieval correctly; we have already created tests for that code in Chapter 15. The only thing we need to test is that ListCategories interacts with PetStore correctly. We can create a mock PetStore object, pass it to the ListCategories object, and verify that ListCategories works with PetStore correctly.

```
[TestListCategories.java]

public class TestListCategories extends TestCase {

    public void testListCategories() throws Exception {
        // setup
        List categories = createSomeCategories();
```

```
            Mock mockPetStore = new Mock(PetStore.class);
            mockPetStore.matchAndReturn("getCategories", categories);

            ListCategories action = new ListCategories();
            action.setPetStore((PetStore)mockPetStore.proxy());

            // execute
            String result = action.execute();

            // verify
            assertEquals(Action.SUCCESS, result);
            assertEquals(categories, action.getCategories());
        }

        private List createSomeCategories() {
            Category category = new Category();
            category.setId(123);
            category.setName("Dogs");
            List result = new ArrayList();
            result.add(category);
            return result;
        }
    }
```

The test `testListCategories` first creates a Category object and configures the `getCategories()` method of the mock PetStore to return a List containing that single Category instance. Finally, we verify that the same List is returned from the `getCategories()` method after executing the action object.

Of course, the tests won't pass at this point because we haven't implemented anything useful yet. Following a few TDD cycles, we get a Green Bar with the following implementation:

```
public class ListCategories implements Action, PetStoreAware {
    private List categories;
    private PetStore petStore;

    public List getCategories() {
        return categories;
    }

    public void setPetStore(PetStore petStore) {
        this.petStore = petStore;
    }

    public String execute() {
        categories = petStore.getCategories();

        return SUCCESS;
    }
}
```

We're now finished implementing the retrieval of the categories of the store. The next thing to do is implement retrieval of all Pets of a specific Category.

Browsing the List of Pets

Users should be able to browse the list of Pets we offer at our store. It should be possible to browse all Pets at once or only Pets of the category the user has selected.

We will first implement the feature that lets the user browse all Pets offered in our site. Then we will implement the feature that makes it possible to browse all Pets of the currently selected category.

We will now introduce a new test class named TestSListPets and a testListAllPets() method in it that tests the correctness of the ListPets class. ListPets is a WebWork action class responsible for performing retrieval of Pets. We introduced the PetStore class in Chapter 15. ListPets uses PetStore for retrieving all the Pets available in the store. We use a mock object for the PetStore instead of using a concrete implementation of it (such as DefaultPetStore, which in turn uses HibernatePersistenceManager to load the Pets from a relational database). By using a mock object, we can test the interaction between ListPets and PetStore in isolation from the rest of the system.

```
[TestListPets.java]

public class TestListPets extends TestCase {

    public void testListAllPets() throws Exception {
        // setup
        List pets = createSomePets();

        Mock mockPetStore = new Mock(PetStore.class);
        mockPetStore.matchAndReturn("getPets", pets);

        ListPets action = new ListPets();
        action.setPetStore((PetStore)mockPetStore.proxy());


        // execute
        String result = action.execute();

        // verify
        assertEquals(Action.SUCCESS, result);
        assertEquals(pets, action.getPets());
    }

    private List createSomePets() {
        Pet pet = new Pet();
```

```
        pet.setId(123);
        pet.setName("Dog");
        List result = new ArrayList();
        result.add(pet);
        return result;
    }
}
```

Since this test is similar to the previous one, we can switch gears and move faster. We add the remaining missing bits and run the test. Here is what the final implementation of ListPets looks like:

```
[ListPets.java]

public class ListPets implements Action, PetStoreAware {
    private PetStore petStore;
    private List pets;

    public void setPetStore(PetStore petStore) {
        this.petStore = petStore;
    }

    public String execute() throws Exception {
        pets = petStore.getPets();
        return SUCCESS;
    }

    public List getPets() {
        return pets;
    }
}
```

We run the test and Green Bar!

We can now move to the second scenario: browsing Pets of a specific Category. We expect ListPets to return only Pets of a specific Category if the ID of a specific Category is given and to return ERROR if the Category cannot be found. We create two new test methods:

```
[TestListPets.java]

public void testListPetsOfCategory() throws Exception {
    // setup
    Pet pet = new Pet();
    pet.setId(456);
    pet.setName("Dog");
    Category category = new Category();
    category.setId(123);
    category.addPet(pet);

    Mock mockPetStore = new Mock(PetStore.class);
```

```
        mockPetStore.expectAndReturn("getCategory", new Long(123), category);

        ListPets action = new ListPets();

        // execute
        action.setCategoryId(123);
        String result = action.execute();

        // verify
        assertEquals(Action.SUCCESS, result);

        mockPetStore.verify();
        assertEquals(category.getPets(), action.getPets());
    }

    public void testListPetsOfAnUnknownCategory() throws Exception {
        Mock mockPetStore = new Mock(PetStore.class);
        mockPetStore.expectAndReturn("getCategory", new Long(666), null);

        ListPets action = new ListPets();

        // execute
        action.setCategoryId(666);
        String result = action.execute();

        // verify
        assertEquals(Action.ERROR, result);

        mockPetStore.verify();
        assertNull(action.getPets());
    }
```

The new `testListPetsOfCategory()` method first creates a Pet object
and adds it to new Category instance, which has an ID of 123. We then configure the mock PetStore instance to return this new Category object when its
`getCategory()` method is called with an argument of 123. In addition to
configuring the Mock object to return the newly created Category object,
`expectAndReturn()` also verifies that `getCategory()` was actually called
with the arguments declared as its second argument. We also need to tell the
ListPets action we're looking for Pets of a Category that has an ID of 123
by calling its `setCategoryId()` method. To complete our test, we now
just need to assert that `getPets()` returns the Pets we expect to be in the 123
Category.

On the other hand, for our second test, `testListPetsOfAnUnknown`
`Category()`, all we need do is set a fictitious Category ID (666), then assert
that there are no Pets retrieved and the action returns an ERROR.

Following the standard TDD process, we implement until we have a Green Bar and the final result ends up as:

```
[ListsPets.java]

public class ListPets implements Action, PetStoreAware {
    private PetStore petStore;
    private List pets;
    private long categoryId;

    public void setCategoryId( long categoryId ) {
        this.categoryId = categoryId;
    }

    public void setPetStore( PetStore petStore ) {
        this.petStore = petStore;
    }

    public String execute() throws Exception {
        if (categoryId != 0) {
            Category parentCategory = petStore.getCategory(0);
            pets = parentCategory.getPets();
        }
        else {
            pets = petStore.getPets();
        }

        return SUCCESS;
    }


    public List getPets() {
        return pets;
    }
}
```

We have an action class for retrieving all Pets or only Pets of a specific Category, as well as tests to cover all possible cases. We can now concentrate on the next requirement: searching Pets.

Searching the Store for Pets

To get started, we will create a Search action class. It's a WebWork command object and encapsulates the searching logic. It must accept a query String and return a list of search hits.

As usual, we start with a test. We want to search for a Pet and retrieve a list of matched Pets:

```
[TestSearch.java]

public class TestSearch extends TestCase {

    public void testSearch() throws Exception {
        Search action = new Search();
        action.setQuery("dog");

        String result = action.execute();
        assertEquals(Action.SUCCESS, result);
    }
}
```

But this test is not sufficient. It hasn't actually tested that the query was executed correctly and that the expected search result was returned. There are two ways we can ensure the search operation was performed correctly.

- Allow the Search class to conduct the Lucene API and actually run the query.
- Don't test the Lucene searching logic itself. Rather, test that the Search class made the correct method calls to the underlying searching mechanism and returned the expected results according to the contract.

We settle on the second approach because it provides a good way to layer the responsibilities of our code and allows us to take baby steps when writing tests and corresponding implementations.

To separate the underlying searching mechanism from our high-level Search action class, we define a Searcher interface. The Search class delegates the actual searching operation to the specified Searcher instance, as the following code shows:

```
[Searcher.java]

public interface Searcher {
    /**
     * Performs the search operation and returns a List of found items.
     */
    List search(String query);
}


[StoreFrontSearch.java]

public class StoreFrontSearch extends ActionSupport {
```

```
        private Searcher searcher;

        public Searcher getSearcher() {
            return searcher;
        }
        public void setSearcher(Searcher searcher) {
            this.searcher = searcher;
        }

        public String execute(String query) throws Exception {
            // todo

            return SUCCESS;
        }
    }
```

We enhance our previous test by introducing Searcher. We haven't written any concrete Searcher implementation yet, and we're not concerned about its implementation details in this stage. As such, we create a mock Searcher for our tests:

```
[TestSearch.java]

public class TestSearch extends TestCase {

    public void testSearch() throws Exception {
        // setup
        List pets = createSomePets();

        Mock mockSearcher = new Mock(Searcher.class);
        mockSearcher.expectAndReturn("search","dog",pets);

        Search action = new Search();
        action.setSearcher((Searcher)mockSearcher.proxy());

        // execute
        action.setQuery("dog");
        String result = action.execute();

        // verify expectation has been met
        mockSearcher.verify();

        assertEquals("success", result);
        assertNotNull(action.getPets());
        assertEquals(1,action.getPets().size());
        assertEquals(pet,action.getPets().get(0));
    }

    private List createSomePets() {
        Pet pet = new Pet();
```

```
        pet.setId(123);
        pet.setName("Billy");
        List result = new ArrayList();
        result.add(pet);
        return result;
    }

}
```

We create a mock Searcher instance in `setUp()` and then expect to see Searcher's `search()` method called with an argument of "dog" by Search. When that call is made by Search, the mock object returns the Pets List that we created and contains a single Pet object that has an ID of 123. Finally, we assert that Search executes successfully, returns SUCCESS, and that its search result is the Pets List that we configured Searcher to return.

Now the code compiles, and we can run the test. Red Bar!

```
search() was expected but not called
```

It means it expected the `search()` method to be called, but it never was. This is the expected behavior and validates that our test is indeed testing a new feature. The next step is, of course, to write code until this test passes. We can do this by allowing Search to correctly delegate the searching operation to Searcher:

```
public String execute() throws Exception {
    setPets(searcher.search(query));

    return SUCCESS;
}
```

Now the code compiles; we can run the test. Green Bar! So far, we've defined the contract of Search. We've also separated the high-level WebWork action from the actual implementation of the searching logic by defining a separate Searcher interface. It's time to move on to creating a concrete implementation for Searcher that uses Lucene.

Implementing LuceneSearcher

We start by defining the test case as well as a LuceneSearcher class that will pass the tests. We need to let LuceneSearcher know where to expect to find the index files. We do that by specifying its `indexDir` property.

NOTE Unlike in the previous tests, we don't use mock objects here because we want to actually test the Lucene searching logic. Because we aren't using in-memory mock objects, these unit tests will run a bit slower than the average test. As explained in Chapter 12, this is a perfect candidate to belong to the SlowUnitTestSuite rather than the normal test suite that runs much faster.

```
[TestLuceneSearcher.java]

public class TestLuceneSearcher extends TestCase {
    private LuceneSearcher luceneSearcher;
    private File indexDir;

    protected void setUp() throws Exception {
        luceneSearcher = new LuceneSearcher();

        // assume index files are stored under the system temp directory
        File tmpDir = new File(System.getProperty("java.io.tmpdir"));
        indexDir = new File(tmpDir, "test-index");
        indexDir.mkdir();

        luceneSearcher.setIndexDir(indexDir.getAbsolutePath());
    }

    public void testSimpleSearch() throws Exception {
        List searchHits = luceneSearcher.search("\"dog\"");

        assertNotNull(searchHits);
        assertEquals(1, searchHits.size());
    }
}
```

Stubbing LuceneSearch, we end up with:

```
[LuceneSearcher.java]

public class LuceneSearcher implements Searcher {
    private String indexDir;
    private String query;

    public void setIndexDir(String indexDir) {
        this.indexDir = indexDir;
    }
    private String getIndexDir() {
        return indexDir;
    }

    // implemented from Searcher interface
    public String getQuery() {
```

```
        return query;
    }

    public void setQuery(String query) {
        this.query = query;
    }

    public List search() {
        // todo: use Lucene's API to perform searching

        return null;
    }
}
```

As expected, the test fails with a Red Bar. To get the tests to pass, the minimum amount of code we can write involves calling Lucene's IndexSearcher class for querying the index. Here is the code:

```
public List search() {
    QueryParser qp = null;
    Query myquery = null;

    try {
        qp = new QueryParser("description",createAnalyzer());
        myquery = qp.parse(query);
    } catch (Exception e) {
        throw new LuceneException("Couldn't parse the query:"+
            e.getMessage());
    }

    IndexSearcher searcher = null;

    try {
        searcher = createSearcher();

        Hits hits = searcher.search(myquery);
        List result = new ArrayList(hits.length());
        for (int i = 0; i < hits.length(); i++) {
            Document doc = hits.doc(i);
            result.add(Long.valueOf(doc.get("handle")));
        }

        return result;
    } catch (Exception e) {
        throw new LuceneException("Couldn't complete search",e);
    } finally {
        try {
            if (searcher != null) {
```

```
                searcher.close();
            }
        } catch( IOException e ) {
            throw new LuceneException("Couldn't complete search",e);
        }
    }
}

public IndexSearcher createSearcher() throws IOException {
    return new IndexSearcher(getDirectory(false));
}

protected Directory getDirectory(boolean create) throws IOException {
    return FSDirectory.getDirectory(indexDir, create);
}

private Analyzer createAnalyzer() {
    return new StandardAnalyzer();
}
```

This is typical Lucene querying code similar to the code we've seen before in Chapter 8. A QueryParser is first created, and then the query is parsed. Next, an IndexSearcher is created and initialized with the parsed query. Finally, a search is performed. Note that we're using the simplest Analyzer type, StandardAnalyzer, which is enough for our purpose of getting the test pass.

Note that the `LuceneSearcher.search()` method actually returns a List containing objects of type Long. Earlier in this chapter, we tested the interaction between StoreFrontSearch and Searcher by assuming that Searcher returns a List of Pets. But as you can see here, we create a List of Longs rather than Pets. TestStoreFrontSearch is not broken, because it uses a mock Searcher object instead of a LuceneSearcher instance, and that mock is correctly set up to return a List of Pets.

Another design possibility here would be returning a value object containing all indexed fields. For example a SearchHitValueObject could be returned in the List, containing the values of indexed fields such as name and description. The advantage of using this value object is that the indexed fields are retrieved from Lucene very fast, and this saves us the performance hit of going to the PersistenceManager to load a Pet object for each search result.

The disadvantage of using a SearchHitValueObject is that there are now two domain objects representing a Pet. This means we need different view components for general browsing and showing search results (one using Pet, the other using SearchHitValueObject), causing duplication in our view layer.

In our case, we have chosen to design both the search and browse capabilities to use the same Pet domain object because it leads to cleaner code. We don't need to be overly concerned with the performance of accessing PersistenceManager repeatedly to retrieve domain objects here because most of these accesses should be cached.

The only tricky design issue is exactly *where* to ask the PersistenceManager for the relevant Pet object from the search results. LuceneSearcher is not the right place, because the search facility should not have dependency on the PersistenceManager. They are both low-level components of the system and should be kept independent of each other. So, we return a List of Longs, and the client is responsible for asking the PersistenceManager for the corresponding Pet object. Later in this chapter, we'll show a neat way to handle this issue without burdening the WebWork action with this task.

Everything looks correct, so let's run the test again. Red Bar!

```
java.io.IOException: C:\temp\test-index not a directory
     at org.apache.lucene.store.FSDirectory.<init>(Unknown Source)
     at org.apache.lucene.store.FSDirectory.getDirectory(Unknown Source)
     at org.apache.lucene.store.FSDirectory.getDirectory(Unknown Source)
     at org.apache.lucene.index.IndexReader.open(Unknown Source)
     at org.apache.lucene.search.IndexSearcher.<init>(Unknown Source)
     at org.petsoar.search.lucene.LuceneSearcher.search(LuceneSearcher
.java:108)
     at org.petsoar.search.lucene.TestLuceneSearcher.TestStoreFrontSearch
(TestLuceneSearcher.java:74)
```

This is happening because there is no *test-index* directory. Recall that we specified this directory as the directory where IndexSearcher should expect to find the indexed files. Of course, there is no directory because we never created it, nor did we index any documents. To do this, we will now focus on writing a LuceneIndexer class.

Note here that we're doing things a little backward to what you might expect. Normally, indexing comes before searching; after all, you can't search without having indexed first. However, in our case, TDD dictates the flow of design, and because we started with StoreFrontSearch, we are writing the Searcher before the Indexer. Let's look at the Indexer now.

Implementing LuceneIndexer

A user must be able to search any information item in the pet store. Since we have a nice domain model behind the application, we naturally want to index those domain objects for faster and more robust searching. LuceneIndexer should be able to accept Pet, Category, or any other object and create Lucene index files for them.

Another important thing we should consider is updating the index whenever the domain objects change. Deleting a domain object should delete the indexed document from the index files as well.

We start with a test, implementing the easiest scenario: indexing newly created Pet objects. We should let LuceneIndexer know where to create the index files. We do that by specifying the indexDir property.

```
[TestLuceneIndexer.java]

public class TestLuceneIndexer extends TestCase {
    private LuceneIndexer luceneIndexer;
    private File indexDir;

    protected void setUp() throws Exception {
        luceneIndexer = new LuceneIndexer();

        // assume index files are stored under the system temp directory
        File tmpDir = new File(System.getProperty("java.io.tmpdir"));
        indexDir = new File(tmpDir, "test-index");
        indexDir.mkdir();

        luceneIndexer.setIndexDir(indexDir.getAbsolutePath());
    }

    public void testIndexNewObject() throws Exception {
        Pet pet = createDog();
        luceneIndexer.index(pet);
    }

    private Pet createDog() {
        Pet pet = new Pet();

        pet.setId(123);
        pet.setName("dog");
        pet.setPersonality("dog");
        pet.setDescription("dog");

        return pet;
    }
}
```

We first create a LuceneIndexer object and set the indexDir property. The testIndexNewObject() method creates a new Pet instance and then tells the LuceneIndexer instance to index it. We can't yet run the test, because we haven't written LuceneIndexer yet. So, we create it.

```
[LuceneIndexer.java]

public class LuceneIndexer {
    private String indexDir;
    private IndexWriter indexWriter;

    public void setIndexDir(String indexDir) {
        this.indexDir = indexDir;
    }
    private String getIndexDir() {
        return indexDir;
    }

    public synchronized void index(Object obj) {
        Analyzer analyzer = createAnalyzer();
        IndexWriter writer = createWriter(analyzer);

        try {
            Document doc = createDocument(obj);
            writer.addDocument(doc);
            writer.optimize();
        } finally {
            writer.close();
        }
    }

    private IndexWriter createWriter(Analyzer analyzer)
        throws IOException {
        return new IndexWriter(getDirectory(false),analyzer,false);
    }

    protected Directory getDirectory(boolean create)
        throws IOException {
        return FSDirectory.getDirectory(indexDir,create);
    }

    private Analyzer createAnalyzer() {
        return new StandardAnalyzer();
    }

    public Document createDocument(Object obj) {
        Document doc = new Document();
        return doc;
    }
}
```

The index() method accepts an Object and, you guessed it, indexes it. To do so, first a Lucene IndexWriter should be created, so the createWriter() method is called. This method creates an IndexWriter that puts the indexed files in the directory that the indexDir property points to. An Analyzer object should be specified for the IndexWriter, so the createAnalyzer() method is called that creates the simplest kind of analyzer we can use, the StandardAnalyzer. Now we create a Lucene Document for the object we are trying to index, add it to the index by invoking addDocument() on the IndexWriter, and finally close the writer by calling its close() method (which frees all allocated resources).

It seems like everything is ready, and we can run the test finally. Green Bar! However, we're not really sure that the index files are actually updated. We can enhance the test and verify that a document was added to the index:

```
public void testIndexNewObject() throws Exception {
    Pet pet = createDog();
    luceneIndexer.index(pet);

    IndexReader indexReader = createReader();
    assertEquals(1,indexReader.numDocs());
    indexReader.close();
}

private IndexReader createReader() throws IOException {
    // assume index files are stored under the system temp directory
    File tmpDir = new File(System.getProperty("java.io.tmpdir"));
    indexDir = new File(tmpDir, "test-index");
    indexDir.mkdir();

    return IndexReader.open(indexDir.getAbsolutePath());
}
```

An IndexReader is opened on the specified index directory. Then we verify that a single document exists in the index directory by asserting that indexReader.numDocs does indeed return 1.

We run the test again, and Green Bar! This means that the Pet we created is actually added to the index. It seems like we're done with the LuceneInexer. The index files are created. We can go back to our LuceneSearcher test and run it again. Recall TestLuceneSearcher:

```
[TestLuceneSearcher.java]

public class TestLuceneSearcher extends TestCase {
...
    public void testSimpleSearch() throws Exception {
        List searchHits = luceneSearcher.search("\"dog\"");

        assertNotNull(searchHits);
        assertEquals(1,searchHits.size());
    }
}
```

We run it again. Red Bar!

```
expected: 1 but was: 0
```

So, although the index files are there and they contain a Document, the search fails to find anything for the query we gave it.

The reason for this failing test is that the query returns no result because the indexed document contains incorrect data. Let's go back and review the piece of code in LuceneIndexer that created the Document object:

```
public Document createDocument(Object obj) {
    Document doc = new Document();
    return doc;
}
```

The document is effectively empty. It contains no fields, no data! We should fill it with correct data by adding some Lucene Fields to it. Let's take the shortest path:

```
public Document createDocument(Object obj) {
    Document doc = new Document();
    Pet pet = (Pet) obj;

    doc.addField(Field.Keyword("handle", pet.getId()));
    doc.addField(Field.Text("name", pet.getName()));
    doc.addField(Field.Text("description", pet.getDescription()));

    return doc;
}
```

We have hard-coded the Pet type here. Obviously, with this strategy, we can't index Category or any other arbitrary object. We note this limitation and just hard-code the Pet type for now. We want to write the least code to make the test pass. Later, we can extend functionality for any type of object.

To make sure the document contains the correct field values, we enhance the test in TestLuceneIndexer:

```
public void testIndexNewObject() throws Exception {
    Pet pet = createDog();
    luceneIndexer.index(pet);

    IndexReader indexReader = luceneIndexer.openIndexReader();
    assertEquals(1, indexReader.numDocs());

    Document doc = indexReader.document(0);
    assertEquals("123", doc.get("handle"));
    assertEquals("dog", doc.get("name"));
    assertEquals("dog", doc.get("description"));

    indexReader.close();
}
```

Green Bar!

We go back to TestLuceneSearcher and run it again. Green Bar as well!

Notice that the behavior of TestLuceneSearcher is dependent on the output of TestLuceneIndexer. In other words, if we don't run TestLuceneIndexer *before* running TestLuceneSearcher, TestLuceneSearcher fails. It clearly violates one of the most important rules of unit testing:

Unit tests should be independent of each other.

That's not the only place we made mistakes. We didn't clean the created index files. If we run the test again, the new documents would be added to the existing index files and the tests would fail. We violated another golden rule:

Successive runs of a unit test shouldn't depend on the output from previous runs of the test.

With some small changes to TestLuceneSearcher, we can make sure that it is not dependent on the output of TestLuceneIndexer. That, of course, doesn't mean we abandon TestLuceneIndexer, as it is a granular test for LuceneIndexer and is still very valuable. Also, we change both tests to make sure the old index files are deleted when we run any of the two tests again. TestLuceneIndexer now has an added `tearDown()` method:

```
public class TestLuceneIndexer extends TestCase {
...
    protected void tearDown() throws Exception {
        indexDir.delete();
    }
...
}
```

After the test is run, `teardown()` is called and we clean up after ourselves by deleting the index directory that was created during the test.

We do the same for TestLuceneSearcher, too, but we also create a fresh index in the `setUp()` method:

```
[TestLuceneSearcher.java]

public class TestLuceneSearcher extends TestCase {
...
    protected void setUp() throws Exception {
        luceneSearcher = new LuceneSearcher();

        // assume index files are stored under the system temp directory
        File tmpDir = new File(System.getProperty("java.io.tmpdir"));
        indexDir = new File(tmpDir, "test-index");
        indexDir.mkdir();

        luceneSearcher.setIndexDir(indexDir.getAbsolutePath());

        luceneIndexer = new LuceneIndexer();
```

```
        luceneIndexer.setIndexDir(indexDir.getAbsolutePath());

        Pet dog = new Pet();
        dog.setId(111);
        dog.setName("dog");
        dog.setImage("dog");
        dog.setDescription("dog");
        luceneIndexer.index(dog);

        Pet cat = new Pet();
        cat.setId(112);
        cat.setName("cat");
        cat.setImage("cat");
        cat.setDescription("cat");
        luceneIndexer.index(cat);

        Pet dogy = new Pet();
        dogy.setId(113);
        dogy.setName("dogy");
        dogy.setImage("dogy");
        dogy.setDescription("dogy");
        luceneIndexer.index(dogy);
    }

    protected void tearDown() throws Exception {
        indexDir.delete();
    }
    ...
}
```

Now TestLuceneSearcher is not dependent on any preexisting index files generated by TestLuceneIndexer, because some test objects are created and indexed in the setUp() method.

There's another bit of refactoring we can do to remove some code duplication. Notice how both LuceneIndexer and LuceneSearcher work with the index directory and duplicate the code responsible for creating IndexWriter objects. So, we extract this code to a separate class called LuceneIndexStore:

```
[LuceneIndexStore.java]

public class LuceneIndexStore {

    private static final String DEFAULT_INDEX_DIR = "index";

    private final String indexDir;
    private IndexWriter indexWriter;

    public LuceneIndexStore() {
        this(DEFAULT_INDEX_DIR);
```

```
        }

        public LuceneIndexStore(String indexDir) {
            this.indexDir = indexDir;
            try {
                new IndexWriter(getDirectory(true), null, true).close();
            } catch (IOException e) {
                throw new LuceneException("Cannot create index directory",
                                          e);
            }
        }

        public IndexReader createReader() throws IOException {
            return IndexReader.open(getDirectory(false));
        }

        public IndexWriter createWriter(Analyzer analyzer)
            throws IOException {
            return new IndexWriter(getDirectory(false), analyzer, false);
        }

        public IndexSearcher createSearcher() throws IOException {
            return new IndexSearcher(getDirectory(false));
        }

        public int getNumDocs() throws IOException {
            IndexReader reader = createReader();
            int result = reader.numDocs();
            reader.close();
            return result;
        }

        protected Directory getDirectory(boolean create)
            throws IOException {
            return FSDirectory.getDirectory(indexDir, create);
        }
    }
```

Now we just need to change LuceneIndexer and LuceneSearcher to use this new class instead of the old duplicated code:

```
public class LuceneIndexer {
    private LuceneIndexStore indexStore;

    public void setIndexStore(LuceneIndexStore indexStore) {
        this.indexStore = indexStore;
    }

    public synchronized void index(Object obj) {
        try {
```

```
                    Analyzer analyzer = createAnalyzer();
                    IndexWriter writer = indexStore.createWriter(analyzer);
                    try {
                        Document doc = createDocument(obj);
                        writer.addDocument(doc);
                        writer.optimize();
                    } finally {
                        writer.close();
                    }
                } catch (IOException e) {
                    throw new LuceneException("Cannot update index", e);
                }
            }
    ...
    }
```

And in LuceneSearcher:

```
public class LuceneSearcher {
    private LuceneIndexStore indexStore;
    private String query;

    public void setIndexStore(LuceneIndexStore indexStore) {
        this.indexStore = indexStore;
    }

    public List search() {
        QueryParser qp = null;
        Query myquery = null;

        try {
            qp = new QueryParser("description",createAnalyzer());
            myquery = qp.parse(query);
        } catch (Throwable e) {
            throw new LuceneException("Couldn't parse the query:"+
                e.getMessage());
        }

        IndexSearcher searcher = null;

        try {
            searcher = indexStore.createSearcher();

            Hits hits = searcher.search(myquery);
            List result = new ArrayList(hits.length());
            for (int i = 0; i < hits.length(); i++) {
                Document doc = hits.doc(i);
                result.add(Long.valueOf(doc.get("handle")));
            }
```

```
            return result;
        } catch (Throwable e) {
            throw new LuceneException("Couldn't complete search",e);
        } finally {
            try {
                if (searcher!=null) {
                    searcher.close();
                }
            } catch( IOException e ) {
                throw new LuceneException("Couldn't complete search",e);
            }
        }
    }
    ...
}
```

The test cases also duplicate some code related to creating the LuceneIndexer object and the `indexDir` attribute. So, we remove the duplication by introducing a base class for both test cases:

```
[LuceneTestCase.java]

public abstract class LuceneTestCase extends TestCase {
    protected LuceneIndexer luceneIndexer;
    protected LuceneSearcher luceneSearcher;
    protected LuceneIndexStore indexStore;

    private File indexDir;

    protected void setUp() throws Exception {
        File tmpDir = new File(System.getProperty("java.io.tmpdir"));
        indexDir = new File(tmpDir, "test-index");
        indexDir.mkdir();

        indexStore = new LuceneIndexStore(indexDir.getAbsolutePath());

        luceneIndexer = new LuceneIndexer();
        luceneIndexer.setIndexStore(indexStore);

        luceneSearcher = new LuceneSearcher();
        luceneSearcher.setIndexStore(indexStore);
    }

    protected void tearDown() throws Exception {
        indexDir.delete();
    }
}
```

We can safely remove `setUp()` and `tearDown()` from TestLuceneIndexer and TestLuceneSearcher and extend them from LuceneTestCase.

Where We Are

We can index Pets and query them. Both LuceneIndexer and LuceneSearcher perform their jobs perfectly, and all tests are well written and independent of each other, and successive runs produce the same result. We now have clean code and an effective model for indexing objects and querying them.

So, are we done? No, not yet. Recall that our application requirement states that it should be possible to search for both Pets and Categories. We tested it for Pets only. It also states that we support full text searches, yet we support only simple searches because we used the simplest kind of analyzer possible. We also need to support *pagination* of search hits, but currently we return all the search hits at once. We will address these requirements one by one.

Implementing Searching of Any Type of Data

Besides indexing Pets, we want to be able to index and search Category objects. So, we add a test method to TestLuceneIndexer and run it:

```java
public void testIndexNewCategoryObject() throws Exception {
    Category category = createCategory();
    luceneIndexer.index(category);

    IndexReader indexReader = luceneIndexer.openIndexReader();
    assertEquals(1,indexReader.numDocs());

    Document doc = indexReader.document(0);
    assertEquals("456",doc.get("handle"));
    assertEquals("dogs",doc.get("name"));
    assertEquals("",doc.get("image"));

    indexReader.close();
}

private Category createCategory() {
    Category category = new Category();

    category.setId(456);
    category.setName("dogs");

    return category;
}
```

Unfortunately, Red Bar!

```
java.lang.ClassCastException: org.petsoar.categories.Category
    at org.petsoar.search.lucene.LuceneIndexer.createDocument
(LuceneIndexer.java:108)
```

Because we hard-coded the Pet type in `createDocument()`, it fails. To solve this problem, we can either add an if/else and support Category class, too, or refactor it to work with any class. We choose to take the second approach because we are sure that the popularity of the site will soon force us to offer other types of searchable information. Also, it gives us more interesting topics to discuss!

It's a good idea to extract the Document creation logic to a separate class, because LuceneIndexer is a generic utility class and shouldn't bother about domain-model-specific classes. This is clearly the task of a separate entity that knows about the specifics of each domain class and knows how to satisfy LuceneIndexer by returning the correct Document for each type.

A possible design is defining an interface named DocumentFactory and letting Pet and Category implement it by creating Document objects out of their own information. But that's not a good idea, because with that design our domain classes are polluted by indexing-related code. In other words, we cross the boundaries of different layers with that design. A third-party class should handle it.

As usual, we start with a test case. We will create a LuceneDocumentFactory interface and a default implementation derived from it: DefaultLuceneDocumentFactory. A `createDocument()` method is all we need in the LuceneDocumentFactory interface. We also create a test data class called DefaultLuceneDocumentTestData. A Lucene Document object will be created by DefaultLuceneDocumentFactory for this class. Here is the test case:

```
[DefaultLuceneDocumentTestData.java]

public class DefaultLuceneDocumentTestData {
}

[TestDefaultLuceneDocumentFactory.java]

public class TestDefaultLuceneDocumentFactory extends TestCase {
    private DefaultLuceneDocumentFactory defaultLuceneDocumentFactory;

    protected void setUp() throws Exception {
        defaultLuceneDocumentFactory =
            new DefaultLuceneDocumentFactory();
    }

    public void testCreateDocument() throws Exception {
        DefaultLuceneDocumentTestData obj =
```

```
        createDefaultLuceneDocumentTestData();
    Document doc = defaultLuceneDocumentFactory.createDocument(obj);
    assertNotNull(doc);
}

private DefaultLuceneDocumentTestData
    createDefaultLuceneDocumentTestData() {
    return new DefaultLuceneDocumentTestData();
}
}
```

We create a DefaultLuceneDocumentFactory object in the `setUp()` method of the unit test. The test `testCreateDocument()` tests that DefaultLucene-DocumentFactory creates a Document object for the DefaultLuceneDocumentTestData class. We can't yet run the test, since we haven't yet created the DefaultLuceneDocumentFactory class.

```
[LuceneDocumentFactory.java]

public interface LuceneDocumentFactory {
    Document createDocument(Object obj);
}


[DefaultLuceneDocumentFactory.java]

public class DefaultLuceneDocumentFactory
    implements LuceneDocumentFactory {
    public Document createDocument(Object obj) {
        return new Document();
    }
}
```

LuceneDocumentFactory has a single method, `createDocument()`. This method accepts an Object and returns a new Document object. Default-LuceneDocumentFactory is our default implementation for this interface. For the time being, we simply create an empty Document object.

We run the test. Green Bar! Moving on to the next step, we must verify that the created Document object holds correct Fields. To do so, we enhance the test-data class by introducing some properties. Each property is meant to be mapped to a separate Field type:

```
public class DefaultLuceneDocumentTestData {
    private long handleAttr;
    private int textAttr;
    private String keywordAttr;
    private double unIndexedAttr;
    private float unStoredAttr;
    // getter and setter for the above properties goes here
...
}
```

Here, we have introduced five properties. `textAttr`, for example, would be mapped to a Lucene Field.Text object, while `keywordAttr` would be mapped to a Field.Keyword, and so forth for the other properties. Each of these properties is of a different Java type. One is of long type; the other is String, and so on. This is also to make sure that we test different mappings. Now we add to the test case and verify that these properties are correctly mapped to their Lucene counterparts:

```
public void testCreateDocument() throws Exception {
    DefaultLuceneDocumentTestData obj =
        createDefaultLuceneDocumentTestData();
    Document doc = defaultLuceneDocumentFactory.createDocument(obj);

    assertEquals(String.valueOf(obj.getHandleAttr()),
                doc.get("handleField"));
    assertEquals(obj.getKeywordAttr(),
                doc.get("keywordField"));
    assertEquals(String.valueOf(obj.getTextAttr()),
                doc.get("textField"));
    assertEquals(String.valueOf(obj.getUnIndexedAttr()),
                doc.get("unIndexedField"));
    assertEquals(String.valueOf(obj.getUnStoredAttr()),
                doc.get("unStoredField"));
}

private DefaultLuceneDocumentTestData
    createDefaultLuceneDocumentTestData() {
    DefaultLuceneDocumentTestData obj =
        new DefaultLuceneDocumentTestData();

    obj.setHandleAttr(111);
    obj.setKeywordAttr("112");
    obj.setTextAttr(113);
    obj.setUnIndexedAttr(114);
    obj.setUnStoredAttr(115);
    return obj;
}
```

We run the test. Red Bar!

```
expected:<111> but was:<null>
```

That's because the Document object does not hold any fields (we are currently returning an empty Document). We should now write the Document-creation logic in the `createDocument()` method of DefaultLuceneDocumentFactory. But should it know about each and every domain class and create Document objects for each type by evaluating a long list of if/else blocks for each type? No, that's not an attractive solution, because we don't want to code tricky if/else blocks for each new type introduced in the future.

One possible way around this is if we define a way to map the domain object (Pet or Category) to a Document via XML configuration. For Pet, we would have a separate `Pet.lucene.xml` file, and for Category it will be `Category.lucene.xml`. No class would hard-code anything to the domain objects. There should be only a driver that reads the XML file for the domain type at hand and maps it to a Document. For example, the mapping for the test data class would look like this:

```
<configuration>
    <field type="Handle"
        fieldName="handleField" attributeName="handleAttr"/>
    <field type="Keyword"
        fieldName="keywordField" attributeName="keywordAttr"/>
    <field type="Text"
        fieldName="textField" attributeName="textAttr"/>
    <field type="UnIndexed"
        fieldName="unIndexedField" attributeName="unIndexedAttr"/>
    <field type="UnStored"
        fieldName="unStoredField" attributeName="unStoredAttr"/>
</configuration>
```

We define an XML file named `DefaultLuceneDocumentTestData` `.lucene.xml` with the preceding structure. For each property of the class that a Lucene Field should be created, we define a `<field/>` element. The `<field/>` element specifies the type of the Field, the name of the Lucene Field, and the name of the attribute that the value is extracted from.

We refactor the `createDocument` method to the following code. We create an in-memory representation of the contents of the XML file. ClassConfiguration is holding that information.

```
public Document createDocument(Object obj) {
    ClassConfiguration class_config = getClassConfiguration(obj);
    return createDocumentForObjectFromClassConfiguration(
            obj, class_config);
}

private Document createDocumentForObjectFromClassConfiguration(
                Object obj, ClassConfiguration class_config) {
    return new Document();
}
```

We call the `getClassConfiguration()` method to retrieve a ClassConfiguration instance for the object we are going to create a Document for. Then we pass that ClassConfiguration object to a utility method called `create DocumentForObjectFromClassConfiguration()`, which is responsible for using the ClassConfiguration and creating the Document object for the object at hand. ClassConfiguration looks like this:

```
public static final class ClassConfiguration {
    private List fieldConfigurations = new ArrayList();

    public void addFieldConfiguration(
                    FieldConfiguration fieldConfiguration) {
        fieldConfigurations.add(fieldConfiguration);
    }
    public List getFieldConfigurations() {
        return fieldConfigurations;
    }
}

public static final class FieldConfiguration {
    public static final String TYPE_TEXT = "Text";
    public static final String TYPE_KEYWORD = "Keyword";
    public static final String TYPE_UNINDEXED = "UnIndexed";
    public static final String TYPE_UNSTORED = "UnStored";
    public static final String TYPE_HANDLE = "Handle";

    private String type;
    private String fieldName;
    private String attributeName;
    // getter and setter methods for the above properties
...
}
```

ClassConfiguration contains a list of FieldConfiguration objects.

The createDocumentForObjectFromClassConfiguration() method uses the Digester framework from Jakarta to create a ClassConfiguration object with the data retrieved from the XML file.

```
private ClassConfiguration getClassConfiguration(Object obj) {
    String className = obj.getClass().getName();
    String configFileName = className.replace('.','/')+".lucene.xml";
    ClassConfiguration newClassConfig = new ClassConfiguration();

    // create the Digester object and add the necessary rules to it
    Digester digester = new Digester();
    digester.push(newClassConfig);
    digester.addObjectCreate("configuration/field",
        FieldConfiguration.class.getName());
    digester.addSetProperties("configuration/field");
    digester.addSetNext("configuration/field", "addFieldConfiguration",
        FieldConfiguration.class.getName());

    // load the xml file
    InputStream configXml =
        Thread.currentThread().getContextClassLoader()
```

```
                          .getResourceAsStream(configFileName);

        try {
            // parse the xml file and fill the new_class_config object
            digester.parse(new InputStreamReader(configXml));
            return newClassConfig;
        } catch (Exception e) {
            throw new LuceneException(
                "Couldn't load lucene config file successfully, file="+
                config_file_name,e);
        }
    }
```

What is happening here? First, we create an empty ClassConfiguration object and fill it with the XML file contents. Digester is responsible for this task. Chapter 11 covers Digester in great detail.

We can later refactor the getClassConfiguration() method and cache the ClassConfiguration objects.

Now that we have the XML file data loaded into the ClassConfiguration object, we can use that information to create a complete Document object. So, we enhance the createDocumentForObjectFromClassConfiguration() method:

```
private Document createDocumentForObjectFromClassConfiguration(
                Object obj, ClassConfiguration classConfig) {
    Iterator iter = classConfig.getFieldConfigurations().iterator();
    Document doc = new Document();

    // for each FieldConfiguration
    while (iter.hasNext()) {
        FieldConfiguration fieldConfiguration =
            (FieldConfiguration)iter.next();
        String strContent = getStringContentOfAttribute(obj,
                        fieldConfiguration.getAttributeName());
        Field field = null;

        if (fieldConfiguration.getType().equals(
                FieldConfiguration.TYPE_TEXT)) {
            field = Field.Text(
                    fieldConfiguration.getFieldName(), strContent);
        } else if (fieldConfiguration.getType().equals(
                FieldConfiguration.TYPE_KEYWORD)) {
            field = Field.Keyword(
                    fieldConfiguration.getFieldName(), strContent);
        } else if (fieldConfiguration.getType().equals(
                FieldConfiguration.TYPE_UNINDEXED)) {
            field = Field.UnIndexed(
```

```
                                fieldConfiguration.getFieldName(), strContent);
                } else if (fieldConfiguration.getType().equals(
                        FieldConfiguration.TYPE_UNSTORED)) {
                    field = Field.UnStored(
                            fieldConfiguration.getFieldName(), strContent);
                } else if (fieldConfiguration.getType().equals(
                        FieldConfiguration.TYPE_HANDLE)) {
                    field = Field.Keyword(
                            fieldConfiguration.getFieldName(), strContent);
                } else {
                    throw new LuceneException(
                        "Unknown type for a field, fieldName="+
                        fieldConfiguration.getFieldName());
                }

                doc.add(field);
            }

        return doc;
    }
```

What we are doing is looping over every FieldConfiguration object based on the type creating the correct Field object. For example, we create a Field.Text object for a FieldConfiguration with the type of TYPE_TEXT. The String content of the field is extracted from the object by calling a little utility method called `getStringContentOfAttribute()`. This method is implemented like this:

```
String getStringContentOfAttribute(Object obj,String attributeName) {
    try {
        String str = BeanUtils.getProperty(obj,attributeName);

        return (str==null) ? "" : str;
    } catch (Exception e) {
        throw new LuceneException(
            "Couldn't get string content of attribute, attributeName="+
            attributeName);
    }
}
```

Using Jakarta Commons BeanUtils, we can retrieve the String representation of the attribute. Without BeanUtils, we would have to write lots of ugly if/else blocks to deal with different Java types, as well as complicated Java reflection code.

It's now time to go back to our good-old test case and run it again with the new logic. Recall the test case:

```
public void testCreateDocument() throws Exception {
    DefaultLuceneDocumentTestData obj =
        createDefaultLuceneDocumentTestData();
    Document doc = defaultLuceneDocumentFactory.createDocument(obj);

    assertEquals(String.valueOf(obj.getHandleAttr()),
                 doc.get("handleField"));
    assertEquals(obj.getKeywordAttr(),
                 doc.get("keywordField"));
    assertEquals(String.valueOf(obj.getTextAttr()),
                 doc.get("textField"));
    assertEquals(String.value(obj.getUnIndexedAttr()),
                 doc.get("unIndexedField"));
    assertEquals(String.valueOf(obj.getUnStoredAttr()),
                 doc.get("unStoredField"));
}
```

Previously, it failed because the Document was empty, but now we have filled the Document object using an XML-based mapping file. Running the test now results in a Green Bar. The only thing left undone is refactoring LuceneIndexer to work with the LuceneDocumentFactory:

```
[LuceneIndexer.java]

public class LuceneIndexer {
    ...
    private LuceneDocumentFactory luceneDocumentFactory;

    public synchronized void index(Object obj) {
        unIndex(obj);
        try {
            Analyzer analyzer = createAnalyzer();
            IndexWriter writer = indexStore.createWriter(analyzer);
            try {
                Document doc =
                    luceneDocumentFactory.createDocument(obj);
                writer.addDocument(doc);
                writer.optimize();
            } finally {
                writer.close();
            }
        } catch (IOException e) {
            throw new LuceneException("Cannot update index", e);
        }
    }
    ...
}
```

To make sure we didn't break LuceneIndexer, we run the TestLuceneIndexer test case. Red Bar! A NullPointerException shows up because `lucene DocumentFactory` is null. The caller of LuceneIndexer should specify which LuceneDocumentFactory class should be used. We now refactor the `setUp()` method of the test case.

```
protected void setUp() throws Exception {
    File tmpDir = new File(System.getProperty("java.io.tmpdir"));
    indexDir = new File(tmpDir, "test-index");
    indexDir.mkdir();

    luceneDocumentFactory = new DefaultLuceneDocumentFactory();

    indexStore = new LuceneIndexStore(indexDir.getAbsolutePath());

    luceneIndexer = new LuceneIndexer();
    luceneIndexer.setIndexStore(indexStore);
    luceneIndexer.setLuceneDocumentFactory(luceneDocumentFactory);

    luceneSearcher = new LuceneSearcher();
    luceneSearcher.setIndexStore(indexStore);
    luceneSearcher.setLuceneDocumentFactory(luceneDocumentFactory);
}
```

We run the test again and Green Bar!

Where We Are

We've refactored LuceneIndexer to delegate the Document-creation logic to an external LuceneDocumentFactory. We created a default implementation for it. The DefaultLuceneDocumentFactory reads an XML file to learn about the object-to-Lucene-Document mapping and creates a new Document object using this mapping.

We have now solved the problem of indexing different domain objects. We can make Pet be indexed by creating the `Pet.lucene.xml` file. We can make Category be indexed by creating the `Category.lucene.xml` file. Likewise, we can index any other data type in the future using the same technique.

Implementing Full-Text Searches

The most important component in implementing a smart and user-friendly full-text search capability is the analyzer. Using an inappropriate analyzer might make searches awkward and disappoint users by returning unexpected or even empty search results. Previously, we used the most bare-bones Analyzer class only for the sake of simplicity. It is time to review the analyzer we chose and replace it with an appropriate analyzer based on the searching requirements of our application.

Recall that LuceneIndexer and LuceneSearcher both had a create Analyzer() method defined:

```
private Analyzer createAnalyzer() {
    return new StandardAnalyzer();
}
```

We should remove the duplication and make them both use a single implementation. We can move this method to the LuceneDocumentFactory interface and provide a default implementation in DefaultLuceneDocumentFactory. Refactoring LuceneIndexer and LucenceSearcher:

```
private Analyzer createAnalyzer() {
    return luceneDocumentFactory.createAnalyzer();
}
```

Now we define the createAnalyzer() method in LuceneDocument-Factory and implement it in DefaultLuceneDocumentFactory by creating an Analyzer class more in line with our application requirements.

```
[LuceneDocumentFactory.java]

public interface LuceneDocumentFactory {
    Document createDocument(Object obj);
    Analyzer createAnalyzer();
}

[DefaultLuceneDocumentFactory.java]

public class DefaultLuceneDocumentFactory
    implements LuceneDocumentFactory {
...
    public Analyzer createAnalyzer() {
        return new DefaultAnalyzer();
    }

    public static class DefaultAnalyzer extends Analyzer {
        public TokenStream tokenStream(String fieldName,
                                       Reader reader) {
          LetterTokenizer tokenizer = new LetterTokenizer(reader);
          TokenStream result = null;
          result = new LowerCaseFilter(tokenizer);
          result = new StopFilter(result,
                              StopAnalyzer.ENGLISH_STOP_WORDS);
          result = new PorterStemFilter(result);

          return result;
        }
    }
}
```

We've defined a new class, DefaultAnalyzer, that extends Lucene's Analyzer abstract base class and implements its `tokenStream()` method by creating a TokenStream class composed of a few TokenFilters. TokenStream is responsible for tokenizing a String, such as a query or field of a Document. TokenStream is internally used by Lucene's engine to enumerate over every token in a String; so whenever we index something, the fields of the document are tokenized. Later when we query the documents, the query is also tokenized, and both tokenized forms are compared to each other. In essence, the outcome of the query is determined by the TokenStream used.

A TokenFilter is a TokenStream whose input is another TokenStream. First, we divide the String into letters by using LetterTokenizer; then each letter (which is now a token) is converted to lowercase form by the nested Lower-CaseFilter; then common English stop words are removed from the list of tokens, and finally the Porter algorithm is applied over the tokens.

By using this sequence of TokenFilters, we make sure all common queries we expect are answered correctly. We make sure the query is not case-sensitive and that searching for "puppy" and "puppies" returns the same results (this is the Porter algorithm at work). We would create a different analyzer if we were to support different languages. Different languages have different stop words and different rules for recognizing separate letters. Fortunately, our site is not yet internationalized, so what we've done so far satisfies our current needs.

Implementing Pagination

Pagination makes it possible for users to view lists because search results are displayed in smaller chunks (ten items per each page, for example). This makes navigating between these pages easy. Both StoreFrontListPets and StoreFrontSearch should support pagination. We chose to work with domain objects in both of these actions, meaning they both return a List of Pet objects. A common code can be written to page through the List of Pets originated from both browse and search operations. So, if 200 Pets are to be displayed for browsing and we show 20 Pets per page, accessing items 0 to 19 of this List gives us all the Pets that we display in page 1.

You might realize that, with this strategy, we first load 200 Pets from the database and then just iterate over the first 20 of them. There is a huge overhead here because, although we show only 20 Pets to the user, we load 200! To overcome this overhead we should simply load only the Pets that we want to show now and postpone loading the rest of the Pets to when the user navigates to the pages containing those Pets.

Look at the StoreFrontListPets action. It works with PetStore, which in turn delegates the actual database access operation to a PersistenceManager instance. HibernatePersistenceManager is the implementation we're using.

Thanks to Hibernate's proxy facility, we can easily tell Hibernate to load only the Pets that are actually needed for display. All we have to do is to add a proxy parameter to Pet's @hibernate.class XDoclet tag:

```
/**
 * A creature.
 * @hibernate.class table="PETS" proxy="org.petsoar.pets.Pet"
 */
public class Pet {
...
}
```

What this parameter does is to tell Hibernate to lazy-load Pet objects. Whenever we do a call to `Session.load()` or `Session.find()`, Hibernate just creates an empty proxy object instead of a fully loaded Pet. As soon as one of the property methods (such as `Pet.getName()`) is accessed, it goes to the database and loads that Pet. The proxy parameter of the @hibernate.class tag has the name of the proxy class in it; in this case, we used the same Pet class, which means an empty Pet object is created and treated as a proxy for a real Pet object.

By adding this single doclet parameter to Pet, we instruct Hibernate to lazily load all Pets. It solves our problem of loading 200 Pets at once when we only need to show 20 per page.

But what about the StoreFrontSearch action? A query can return a large number of Pets as well. Recall that earlier in this chapter we coded LuceneSearcher to return only the IDs (Long) of found Pets, not the Pet objects themselves. To get the Pet objects from those IDs, we need to ask a PersistenceManager instance for help. A PersistenceManager implementation, such as Hibernate-PersistenceManager, can turn those IDs into Pet objects by communicating with the database. However, it should only access the database or, more specifically, the PersistenceManager, for those Pets that need to be displayed.

We solve this problem by introducing a LazyLoaderList class. A LazyLoaderList derives from java.util.List and contains the IDs of Pets. It loads the actual Pet object by asking a PersistenceManager object whenever the `get(int index)` method is called for an index of the List.

Let's write some test code to demonstrate this behavior:

```
[TestLazyLoaderList.java]

public class TestLazyLoaderList extends TestCase {
    private Mock mockPersistenceManager;
    private List lazyList;

    protected void setUp() throws Exception {
```

```
        mockPersistenceManager = new Mock(PersistenceManager.class);
        // add 123 and 456 ids to the List
        List idsList = new ArrayList();
        idsList.add(new Long(123));
        idsList.add(new Long(456));

        // create a LazyLoaderList wrapper around idsList
        lazyList = new LazyLoaderList(idsList,
            (PersistenceManager) mockPersistenceManager.proxy(),
            String.class);
    }

    public void testListContainsCorrectNumberOfElements()
                                            throws Exception {
        // assert LazyLoaderList contains two elements
        assertEquals(2, lazyList.size());
    }

    public void testOnlyLoadsItemsWhenNeeded() throws Exception {
        // access the first element, it should call
        // PersistenceManager's getById method
        mockPersistenceManager.expectAndReturn("getById",
            C.eq(String.class, new Long(123)), "123");
        assertEquals("123", lazyList.get(0));
        mockPersistenceManager.verify();

        // now access the second element, it should call
        // PersistenceManager's getById method
        mockPersistenceManager.reset();
        mockPersistenceManager.expectAndReturn("getById",
            C.eq(String.class, new Long(123)), "123");
        assertEquals("456", lazyList.get(1));
        mockPersistenceManager.verify();

        // now access the first element again, this time it should
        // not call PersistenceManager's getById method, because it has
        // already loaded it once by calling getById before
        mockPersistenceManager.reset();
        mockPersistenceManager.expectAndReturn("getById",
            C.eq(String.class, new Long(123)), "123");
        assertEquals("123", lazyList.get(0));
        mockPersistenceManager.verify();

    }
}
```

In this test, we create a LazyLoaderList based upon an ArrayList. That ArrayList contains two Long objects. Upon calling the get(index) method on this List, LazyLoaderList asks the PersistenceManager to retrieve an object from the database based upon the data type (the class) and the ID of the domain object.

The implementation of LazyLoaderList is as follows:

```java
public class LazyLoaderList extends ArrayList {
    private List decoratedList;
    private BitSet loadedListBitSet;
    private PersistenceManager persistenceManager;
    private Class type;

    public LazyLoaderList(List decoratedList,
                          PersistenceManager persistenceManager,
                          Class type) {
        this.decoratedList = decoratedList;
        loadedListBitSet = new BitSet(decoratedList.size());
        this.persistenceManager = persistenceManager;
        this.type = type;
    }

    public int size() {
        return decoratedList.size();
    }

    public boolean isEmpty() {
        return decoratedList.isEmpty();
    }

    public Object get(int index) {
        if( loadedListBitSet.get(index) == false ) {
            Long id = (Long) decoratedList.get(index);
            Object lazyLoadedObj = persistenceManager.getById(type,
                                              id.longValue());

            loadedListBitSet.set(index);
            decoratedList.set(index, lazyLoadedObj);
        }

        return decoratedList.get(index);
    }
}
```

LazyLoaderList is backed by a java.util.BitSet, which is simply a long list of bits. So, whenever `get(index)` is called, we check whether the bit in the specified index is set or not. If it's not set, PersistenceManager is asked to load the domain object for us. Otherwise, it's already loaded, and we just return the object in that index.

With this simple class, we can very cleanly handle pagination and lazy loading of Pets in the Search action. We just decorate the List of IDs that Searcher returned us with a LazyLoaderList and presto, the search result is lazy loaded! Here is how Search uses this new class:

```
[Search.java]

private PersistenceManager persistenceManager;
public void setPersistenceManager(PersistenceManager pm) {
    this.persistenceManager = pm;
}

public String execute() throws Exception {
    searcher.setQuery(query);
    setPets(searcher.search());

    return SUCCESS;
}

public void setPets( List items ) {
    decorateWithLazyLoaderList(items);
}

protected void decorateWithLazyLoaderList(List items) {
    this.items = Collections.unmodifiableList(
        new LazyLoaderList(items, persistenceManager, Pet.class));
}
```

The `Search.execute()` method calls setpets(), and it decorates the List of IDs that Searcher returned with a LazyLoaderList. The PersistenceManager is also passed to it. With this mechanism, we get pagination for free. Neither PersistenceManager nor Searcher has to deal with pagination code directly. And both browse-and-search features use high-level domain objects while still being efficient.

Tying It All Together

Let's wrap up this chapter by creating a GUI for browsing Pets and searching them. We create a `listpets.jsp` file. This view shows either all Pets in stock or the result of a search operation. As we've seen before, because both browse and search produce a list of Pets as their output, we can just write a single JSP file and use it for both of them. Here is how `listpets.jsp` is defined:

```
[listpets.jsp]

<%@ taglib uri="webwork" prefix="ww" %>
<%@ taglib uri="webwork" prefix="ui" %>
<html>
    <body>
        <form action="search.action" method="get">
            <table class="form">
                <ui:textfield label="Search" name="query"/>
            </table>
        </form>

        <ww:iterator value="pets">
            <table class="form" width="100%">
                <tr>
                    <th>
                        <ww:property value="name"/>
                    </th>
                </tr>
                <tr>
                    <td>
                        <b>Gender: </b><ww:property value="gender"/><br>
                        <ww:property value="description"/>
                    </td>
                </tr>
            </table>
            <br>
        </ww:iterator>

    </body>
</html>
```

It's a very simple WebWork JSP view: an HTML form at the top of the page for performing a search, then a ww:iterator tag to iterate over all Pets produced by the action object redirecting to this page. The action class is either StoreFrontListPets or Search, as defined in the xwork.xml configuration file:

```
[xwork.xml]

<xwork>
...
    <package name="storefront" extends="default"
            namespace="storefront/">
        <action name="listpets"
            class="org.petsoar.actions.storefront.ListPets">
            <interceptor-ref name="defaultStack"/>

            <result name="success">
                <param name="location">listpets.jsp</param>
```

```
            </result>
        </action>

        <action name="search"
              class="org.petsoar.actions.storefront.Search">
            <interceptor-ref name="defaultStack"/>

            <result name="success">
                <param name="location">listpets.jsp</param>
            </result>
        </action>
    </package>
</xwork>
```

Note that both search and listpets are configured to redirect to `listpets` `.jsp` after successfully doing their job of producing a list of Pets.

Supporting pagination is as easy as changing the iterator tag to this:

```
[listpets.jsp]

<ww:iterator value="pets.subList(@startIndex,@endIndex)">
...
</ww:iterator>
```

Because the Pets object is a java.util.List, we can easily call its subList() method and a get a List containing only the elements of the original Pets List that is in indices `startIndex` and `endIndex`. So, if `startIndex` is 0 and `endIndex` is 19, we iterate over the first 20 Pets of the original List. Both `startIndex` and `endIndex` are request parameters passed as part of the URL for this action.

Summary

In this chapter, we first implemented a ListCategories WebWork action class that deals with browsing the list of categories of Pets offered in the site. As usual, a test case was written for it.

Then we implemented a ListPets action class to deal with browsing the list of all the offered Pets. A change to this class made it possible to retrieve and browse only Pets of a specific Category.

After implementing browsing of categories and Pets, we moved to implementing the search facility. A Search WebWork action was written. But, instead of putting the searching logic in this UI-level class, we delegated the responsibility to a specialized Searcher interface. We created a concrete implementation for it called LuceneSearcher that uses Lucene API to perform the actual full-text search operation. To do searches, information should be available in indexed format in some index files. So, we introduced a LuceneIndexer class. LuceneIndexer creates a Lucene Document object for each searchable domain object. To support creating Document objects for different types of domain classes (such as Pet and Category) and to make the Document creation code cleaner, we introduced a separate interface for this task called LuceneDocumentFactory and a default implementation for it called Default-LuceneDocumentFactory that stores information needed for mapping domain objects to Document objects in XML files.

By this stage, we had a working indexing and searching system. To support more sophisticated and smarter full-text searching, we replaced the simple Lucene analyzer type we used before with a new one capable of handling case-sensitive and other language-specific issues.

Both browse and search need pagination support. We introduced pagination to ListPets by using Hibernate's proxy feature. Search, on the other hand, used a decorator List to lazily load found Pets. From a client's perspective, both search and browse work with a List of domain objects and a single code can be written to page through them.

Finally, we created some JSP files that hook to the WebWork actions we developed before and displayed the result to end users.

CHAPTER 19

Adding a Shopping Cart

In this chapter, we will implement the business logic and user interface for creating a shopping cart. A user should be able to add Pets to the shopping cart, view the contents of the shopping cart, and finally perform a checkout. Upon checking out, an Order should be created from the shopping cart containing the list of purchased Pets.

Creating a Shopping Cart

A shopping cart is nothing but a list of products to be purchased. The user should be able to add Pets to the shopping cart, remove any of the Pets from it, and view its contents.

We start implementing the shopping cart at the domain-model level. We first create the domain object representing the shopping cart in our application and provide the methods for adding Pets to it, removing Pets from it, and getting the list of the Pets already added to the cart.

We create a TestShoppingCart class and write some code for the three operations that the ShoppingCart should support:

```
package org.petsoar.cart;

import org.petsoar.pets.Pet;
import junit.framework.TestCase;
```

```
public class TestShoppingCart extends TestCase {
    public void testAddAndRemovePet() {
        Pet pet = new Pet();
        pet.setId(1);
        pet.setName("Bill");
        pet.setDescription("Bill is a cat");
        pet.setGender(Pet.MALE);
        pet.setPersonality("timid");

        ShoppingCart cart = new ShoppingCart();
        assertTrue(cart.isEmpty());
        assertEquals(0,cart.getPets().size());

        cart.addPet(pet);
        assertFalse(cart.isEmpty());
        assertEquals(1,cart.size());
        assertEquals(1,cart.getPets().size());
        assertEquals(pet,cart.getPets().get(0));

        cart.removePet(pet);
        assertTrue(cart.isEmpty());
        assertEquals(0,cart.size());
        assertEquals(0,cart.getPets().size());
    }
}
```

The test method is self-explanatory and very simple. Initially, it checks to see if the cart is empty; then a Pet is added and verified that it has been added successfully. Finally, the Pet is removed and verified that it's been removed successfully.

Next, we should define the ShoppingCart class to satisfy the assertions of the test method. ShoppingCart can simply have a List of Pets, or we can use more sophisticated approaches such as saving ShoppingCart in a database or just putting the ShoppingCart of a user to the HTTP session of that user. To keep the options open and to separate the interface from the implementation, we make ShoppingCart an interface and create concrete implementations for it based on the current requirements of the site. Another good side effect of making ShoppingCart an interface is that we can use mock objects in our tests.

We use a simple strategy for now: no long-term persistence in a database. We simply add Pets to a List and attach the ShoppingCart object to the HTTP session of the user. We create a class named SimpleShoppingCart and modify the test method to create an instance of this type.

```
public void testAddAndRemovePet() {
    Pet pet = new Pet();
    pet.setId(1);
    pet.setName("Bill");
```

```
        pet.setDescription("Bill is a cat");
        pet.setGender(Pet.MALE);
        pet.setPersonality("timid");

        ShoppingCart cart = new SimpleShoppingCart();
        ...
    }
```

The ShoppingCart interface is defined as follows:

```
package org.petsoar.cart;

import org.petsoar.pets.Pet;
import java.util.List;

public interface ShoppingCart {
    public boolean addPet(Pet pet);
    public boolean removePet(Pet pet);

    public boolean isEmpty();
    public int size();

    public List getPets();
}
```

All the common operations we'd expect from a typical ShoppingCart are defined here.

The SimpleShoppingCart concrete class provides a very simple implementation of this interface. It keeps track of the Pets added to the cart by a java.util.List property. It's not persistable. It doesn't have any @hibernate tags.

```
package org.petsoar.cart;

import org.petsoar.pets.Pet;
import java.util.ArrayList;
import java.util.List;

public class SimpleShoppingCart implements ShoppingCart {
    private List pets = new ArrayList();

    public boolean addPet(Pet pet) {
        return pets.add(pet);
    }
    public boolean removePet(Pet pet) {
        return pets.remove(pet);
    }

    public boolean isEmpty() {
        return pets.isEmpty();
```

```
        }
        public int size() {
            return pets.size();
        }
        public List getPets() {
            return Collections.unmodifiableList(pets);
        }
    }
```

It is necessary to alter the test to instantiate the SimpleShoppingCart implementation.

We fast forwarded here a little bit and skipped the TDD cycle we learned in previous chapters to talk about the more interesting techniques used in the remainder of this chapter.

Creating the WebWork Actions

Now that the ShoppingCart interface is defined and a concrete implementation of it is also created, we can move on to defining the WebWork action classes for adding and removing Pets to and from a ShoppingCart.

We start by creating the AddPetToShoppingCart action class, as usual by defining the test case first. AddPetToShoppingCart accepts a `petId`, which it then uses to retrieve the Pet object with that ID from PetStore; then it adds that Pet to the ShoppingCart.

```
package org.petsoar.actions.cart;

import com.opensymphony.xwork.Action;
import com.mockobjects.dynamic.Mock;
import org.petsoar.cart.ShoppingCart;
import org.petsoar.pets.PetStore;
import org.petsoar.pets.Pet;

public class TestAddPetToShoppingCart extends TestCase
{
    private AddPetToShoppingCart action;
    private Mock mockPetStore;
    private Mock mockShoppingCart;
    private Pet pet;

    protected void setUp() throws Exception {
        mockShoppingCart = new Mock(ShoppingCart.class);
        mockPetStore = new Mock(PetStore.class);

        action = new AddPetToShoppingCart();
```

```
            action.setPetStore((PetStore)mockPetStore.proxy());

            pet = new Pet();
            pet.setId(123);
        }

        public void testAddPet() throws Exception {
            action.setShoppingCart((ShoppingCart) mockShoppingCart.proxy());
            mockPetStore.matchAndReturn("getPet", new Long(123), pet);
            mockShoppingCart.expect("addPet", pet);

            action.setPetId(123);
            String result = action.execute();

            assertEquals(Action.SUCCESS, result);
            mockPetStore.verify();
            mockShoppingCart.verify();
        }
    }
```

We use mock objects instead of concrete implementations of PetStore and
ShoppingCart. After all, we want to verify that the correct methods of those
interfaces are called for in all the cases that AddPetToShoppingCart should be
able to respond to.

The implementation for the AddPetToShoppingCart action is as follows:

```
package org.petsoar.actions.cart;

import org.petsoar.pets.Pet;
import org.petsoar.pets.PetStore;
import org.petsoar.pets.PetStoreAware;
import org.petsoar.cart.ShoppingCart;

import junit.framework.TestCase;
import com.mockobjects.dynamic.Mock;

public class AddPetToShoppingCart implements Action,
    ShoppingCartAware, PetStoreAware {
    private long petId;
    private PetStore petStore;
    protected ShoppingCart shoppingCart;

    public void setShoppingCart(ShoppingCart shoppingCart) {
        this.shoppingCart = shoppingCart;
    }
    public void setPetStore(PetStore petStore) {
        this.petStore = petStore;
    }
    public void setPetId(long petId) {
```

```
        this.petId = petId;
    }

    public String execute() throws Exception {
        if (shoppingCart == null || petId == 0) {
            return ERROR;
        }

        Pet pet = petStore.getPet(petId);
        if (pet == null)
            return ERROR;

        shoppingCart.addPet(pet);
        return SUCCESS;
    }
}
```

By implementing the ShoppingCartAware and PetStoreAware interfaces, we use the IoC framework of WebWork to pass ShoppingCart and PetStore objects to the action. The concrete type of these interfaces and the scope of them are defined in the components.xml file, as shown here:

```
<component>
    <scope>request</scope>
    <class>org.petsoar.pets.DefaultPetStore</class>
    <enabler>org.petsoar.pets.PetStoreAware</enabler>
</component>
<component>
    <scope>session</scope>
    <class>org.petsoar.cart.SimpleShoppingCart</class>
    <enabler>org.petsoar.cart.SimpleShoppingAware</enabler>
</component>
```

By using the IoC support of WebWork, we can easily request WebWork to create a SimpleShoppingCart object when the HTTP session for a user is created. In other words, an empty SimpleShoppingCart is created and attached to the session object when the user starts browsing the site. When the user clicks a link to add a Pet to the shopping cart, the selected Pet is retrieved from PetStore and added to the ShoppingCart instance.

As you can see, thanks to the IoC capabilities of WebWork, we don't have to pollute the execute() method of the action with logic for creating a specific ShoppingCart and adding it to the underlying HTTP session. WebWork under the covers does that. AddPetToShoppingCart contains only high-level business logic for dealing with the job it's supposed to do: adding a pet to the shopping cart of the user.

Checking Out the Shopping Cart

The process of checking out is quite straightforward. When the Check Out button is clicked, the contents of the shopping cart are listed for the user, as well as billing and shipping information that should be filled out by the user. Then, when all the information is entered, the order is submitted when the user clicks the Save Order button.

To fulfill this scenario, we need two actions: an action that performs the checkout and shows the order information page as the result and another action that saves the order.

We call the first action CheckOut. It simply creates an Order object containing the ShoppingCart of the user and fills some other information from the User object. The Order object is then used in the `vieworder.jsp` page to show the contents of the order to the user.

So we start by defining TestCheckOut.

```
package org.petsoar.order;

import com.opensymphony.xwork.Action;
import org.petsoar.actions.cart.AbstractShoppingCartTest;
import org.petsoar.actions.order.CheckOut;
import org.petsoar.cart.ShoppingCart;

public class TestCheckOut extends AbstractShoppingCartTest {
    private CheckOut action;

    protected void setUp() throws Exception {
        super.setUp();

        action = new CheckOut();
    }

    public void testCheckOut() throws Exception {
        action.setShoppingCart((ShoppingCart)mockShoppingCart.proxy());
        String result = action.execute();

        assertEquals(Action.SUCCESS, result);
        assertEquals(mockShoppingCart,
            action.getOrder().getShoppingCart());
    }

    public void testCheckOutNoShoppingCart() throws Exception {
        action.setShoppingCart(null);
        String result = action.execute();

        assertEquals(Action.ERROR, result);
    }
}
```

The `testCheckOut()` method creates a mock ShoppingCart object. After executing the CheckOut action, the mock ShoppingCart instance should be set in the Order object created as a result of running CheckOut. As you can see, TestCheckOut derives from AbstractShoppingCartTest. AbstractShopping-CartTest is introduced to remove the duplicated code from TestCheckOut and TestAddPetToShoppingCart classes because both need to deal with a ShoppingCart. AbstractShoppingCartTest is defined like this:

```
package org.petsoar.actions.cart;

import junit.framework.TestCase;
import com.mockobjects.dynamic.Mock;
import org.petsoar.cart.ShoppingCart;

public abstract class AbstractShoppingCartTest extends TestCase {
    protected Mock mockShoppingCart;

    protected void setUp() throws Exception {
        mockShoppingCart = new Mock(ShoppingCart.class);
    }
}
```

Finally, let's see what the CheckOut class looks like.

```
package org.petsoar.actions.order;

import org.petsoar.cart.ShoppingCart;
import org.petsoar.actions.cart.AbstractShoppingCartAction;
import org.petsoar.order.Order;

public class CheckOut extends AbstractShoppingCartAction {
    private Order order = new Order();

    public ShoppingCart getShoppingCart() {
        return shoppingCart;
    }
    public Order getOrder() {
        return order;
    }

    public String execute() throws Exception {
        if( shoppingCart == null ) {
            return ERROR;
        }
        else {
```

```
            order.setShoppingCart(shoppingCart);

            //todo: fill some of the order info from the User object

            return SUCCESS;
        }
    }
}
```

It simply creates an Order object and fills it with the ShoppingCart and User information. Again, we removed some code duplication from AddPetTo-ShoppingCart and CheckOut classes and introduced an abstract class for action classes dealing with ShoppingCart:

```
package org.petsoar.actions.cart;

import com.opensymphony.xwork.Action;
import org.petsoar.cart.ShoppingCartAware;
import org.petsoar.cart.ShoppingCart;

public abstract class AbstractShoppingCartAction
                        implements Action, ShoppingCartAware {
    protected ShoppingCart shoppingCart;

    public void setShoppingCart(ShoppingCart shoppingCart) {
        this.shoppingCart = shoppingCart;
    }
}
```

Now the only incomplete part of this story is the Order object itself. Order has a ShoppingCart property, as well as shipping, billing, and credit-card information that are later entered by user when the order is saved. Order can become quite a heavy and polluted class because of these various types of information. It's a good idea to hold shipping, billing, and credit-card information in separate classes for more clarity. Thus, Order has references to the ShipmentInfo, BillingInfo, and CreditCardInfo classes. These classes contain only relevant information to their scope.

Order also needs a status field. Valid statuses are Pending and Shipped. Total price is another field of Order. It's the sum of all the prices of Pets added to the order.

Order needs long-term persistence. It should be stored in the database for later reference and order tracking. So, the Order class and the dependent ShipmentInfo, BillingInfo, and CreditCardInfo classes should be annotated with XDoclet tags to make Order persistable.

Order is defined like this:

```
package org.petsoar.order;

import org.petsoar.cart.ShoppingCart;
import java.math.BigDecimal;

public class Order {
    public static final String ORDER_STATUS_PENDING = "Pending";
    public static final String ORDER_STATUS_SHIPPED = "Shipped";

    private long id;
    private ShipmentInfo shipmentInfo = new ShipmentInfo();
    private BillingInfo billingInfo = new BillingInfo();
    private CreditCardInfo creditCardInfo = new CreditCardInfo();
    private ShoppingCart shoppingCart;
    private BigDecimal totalPrice;
    private String status = ORDER_STATUS_PENDING;

    /**
     * @hibernate.id column="ORDERID" generator-class="increment"
     */
    public long getId() {
        return id;
    }
    public void setId(long id) {
        this.id=id;
    }

    /**
     * @hibernate.component
     */
    public ShipmentInfo getShipmentInfo() {
        return shipmentInfo;
    }
    public void setShipmentInfo(ShipmentInfo shipmentInfo) {
        this.shipmentInfo = shipmentInfo;
    }

    /**
     * @hibernate.component
     */
    public BillingInfo getBillingInfo() {
        return billingInfo;
    }
    public void setBillingInfo(BillingInfo billingInfo) {
        this.billingInfo = billingInfo;
    }

    /**
```

```
 * @hibernate.component
 */
public CreditCardInfo getCreditCardInfo() {
    return creditCardInfo;
}
public void setCreditCardInfo(CreditCardInfo creditCardInfo) {
    this.creditCardInfo = creditCardInfo;
}


/**
 * @hibernate.component
 */
public ShoppingCart getShoppingCart() {
    return shoppingCart;
}
public void setShoppingCart(ShoppingCart shoppingCart) {
    this.shoppingCart = shoppingCart;
}


/**
 * The total price.
 * @hibernate.property column="PRICE"
 */
public BigDecimal getTotalPrice() {
    return totalPrice;
}
public void setTotalPrice(BigDecimal totalPrice) {
    this.totalPrice = totalPrice;
}


/**
 * The status of the Order.
 * @hibernate.property column="STATUS"
 */
public String getStatus() {
    return status;
}
public void setStatus(String status) {
    if (status.equals(ORDER_STATUS_PENDING) ||
        status.equals(ORDER_STATUS_SHIPPED)) {
        this.status = status;
    } else {
        throw new IllegalArgumentException("Invalid orderStatus");
    }
}
}
```

The implementation is incredibly simple and self-explanatory. The only part worthy of explanation is the use of the @hibernate.component XDoclet tag that is defined for the getter methods of the dependent objects (for example, the getter for CreditCardInfo):

```
/**
 * @hibernate.component
 */
public CreditCardInfo getCreditCardInfo() {
    return creditCardInfo;
}
```

According to Hibernate's vocabulary, a *component* is an object dependent on its parent object and cannot live without its parent, nor does it have a primary key. CreditCardInfo is such a class. It cannot live without the surrounding Order object. It does not need a primary key because, after all, no one would need to look it up independently of its Order using a primary key. We apply the @hibernate.component tag to tell Hibernate that CreditCardInfo is a component of Order and should be persisted in the same table in which Order is persisted. CreditCardInfo is a separate class and has properties of its own, but those properties are stored in the Orders table. Therefore, CreditCardInfo is coded like this:

```
package org.petsoar.order;

import java.util.Date;

public class CreditCardInfo {
    public static final String VISA = "Visa";
    public static final String MASTER_CARD = "Master Card";
    public static final String AMEX = "American Express";
    public static final String UNKNOWN = "Unknown";

    private String creditCardNumber;
    private Date expirationDate;
    private String cardType;

    /**
     * @hibernate.property column="CCNUM" length="20"
     */
    public String getCreditCardNumber() {
        return creditCardNumber;
    }

    public void setCreditCardNumber( String creditCardNumber ) {
        this.creditCardNumber = creditCardNumber;
    }

    /**
     * @hibernate.property column="CCEXPIREDATE"
     */
    public Date getExpirationDate() {
```

```
        return expirationDate;
    }

    public void setExpirationDate( Date expirationDate ) {
        this.expirationDate = expirationDate;
    }

    /**
     * @hibernate.property column="CCTYPE"
     */
    public String getCardType() {
        return cardType;
    }

    public void setCardType(String cardType) {
        if (cardType == null) {
            cardType = UNKNOWN;
        }

        if (cardType.equals(VISA) ||
            cardType.equals(MASTER_CARD) ||
            cardType.equals(AMEX) ||
            cardType.equals(UNKNOWN)) {
            this.cardType = cardType;
        } else {
            throw new IllegalArgumentException("Invalid cardType");
        }
    }
}
```

Note that CreditCardInfo doesn't have a @hibernate.class tag, but the properties are marked with a @hibernate.property tag like the properties of the Order class. Because these properties are all part of a single Orders table in the database, they are all loaded by a single SELECT statement and inserted into the database by a single INSERT statement. The same persistence strategy is used for the ShippingInfo and BillingInfo classes.

Now we just need to add CheckOut to the xwork.xml file:

```
<package name="order" extends="default" namespace="order/">
    <action name="checkout" class="org.petsoar.actions.order.CheckOut">
        <interceptor-ref name="defaultStack"/>

        <result name="success">
            <param name="location">vieworder.jsp</param>
        </result>
        <result name="error">
            <param name="location">/errors/notfound.jsp</param>
        </result>
    </action>
</package>
```

When an Order object is successfully created by the CheckOut action, the vieworder.jsp page is shown to the user. The vieworder.jsp view is a typical order-entry page. All the Pets added to the ShoppingCart are shown, and a big form is displayed where billing, shipping, and credit-card information is entered by the user. Here is the JSP code for this page:

```
<%@ taglib uri="webwork" prefix="webwork" %>
<html>
    <head>
        <title>Details for Order</title>
    </head>
    <body>

    <webwork:property value="order">
    <table cellspacing="0" class="grid">
        <tr>
            <th width="200">Type</th>
            <th width="200">Name</th>
            <th>Price</th>
        </tr>
        <webwork:iterator value="shippingInfo/pets">
            <tr>
                <td>
                    <a href="viewpet.action?id=<ww:property value="id"/>">
                        <webwork:property value="type"/>
                    </a>
                </td>
                <td><webwork:property value="name"/></td>
                <td><webwork:property value="price"/></td>
            </tr>
        </webwork:iterator>
    </table>

    <p>Total price: <webwork:property value="totalPrice"/></p>
    <p>Status: <webwork:property value="status"/></p>

    <form action="saveorder.action" method="post">

      <p>Shipping Information</p>
      <table cellspacing="0" class="grid">
        <webwork:property value="order">
          <webwork:textfield label="First Name" name="shipToFirstName"/>
          <webwork:textfield label="Last Name" name="shipToLastName"/>
          <webwork:textfield label="Address 1" name="address1"/>
          <webwork:textfield label="Address 1" name="address2"/>
          <webwork:textfield label="City" name="city"/>
          <webwork:textfield label="State" name="state"/>
          <webwork:textfield label="Zip Code" name="zipCode"/>
          <webwork:textfield label="Country" name="country"/>
        </ww:property>
      </table>
```

```
    <webwork:hidden value="id"/>">
    <input type="submit" value="Save"/>

</form>
</webwork:property>

</body>
</html>
```

Here, we show you only some parts of the JSP file, notably the part showing the list of the Pets and the part mapping the HTML fields to the ShippingInfo object. As you can see, by using the `<webwork:property value="order">`, we refer to the properties of the Order object without prefixing each with the `order/`. This tag puts the order on the top of the value stack, and any nested property is by default accessible from this new top of value-stack value.

The Save Order button triggers the `saveorder.action`, which is mapped to the SaveOrder action class:

```
<action name="saveorder" class="org.petsoar.actions.order.SaveOrder">
    <interceptor-ref name="defaultStack"/>

    <result name="success">
        <param name="location">ordersaved.jsp</param>
    </result>
    <result name="error">
        <param name="location">saveorder.jsp</param>
    </result>
</action>
```

SaveOrder should validate the information entered by the user and save the Order object in the database. We define a class similar to PetStore for handling everything related to Orders. Let's call this class OrderProcessing. Order-Processing has methods such as `getOrder(long id)`, `saveOrder(Order order)`, and `cancelOrder(Order order)`. As with PetStore, we can actually turn OrderProcessing into an interface instead of a concrete class and separate the interface of the OrderProcessing module from the concrete implementation. So, we define it like this:

```
package org.petsoar.order;

import java.util.List;

public interface OrderProcessing {
    void addOrder(Order order);
    void cancelOrder(Order order);

    List getOrders();
    Order getOrder(long id);
}
```

Having OrderProcessing defined, we can go back and implement the Save-Order action class. A simple test case for SaveOrder checks the correct invocation of the addOrder() method of OrderProcessing from the SaveOrder class, like this:

```
package org.petsoar.order;

import junit.framework.TestCase;
import com.mockobjects.dynamic.Mock;
import com.mockobjects.dynamic.P;
import org.petsoar.actions.order.SaveOrder;
import com.opensymphony.xwork.Action;

public class TestSaveOrder extends TestCase {
    private SaveOrder action;
    private Mock mockOrderProcessing;

    protected void setUp() throws Exception {
        super.setUp();
        mockOrderProcessing = new Mock(OrderProcessing.class);

        action = new SaveOrder();
        action.setOrderProcessing(
                (OrderProcessing)mockOrderProcessing.proxy());
    }

    public void testSaveOrder() throws Exception {
        mockOrderProcessing.expect ("addOrder", P.ANY_ARGS);

        String result = action.execute();

        assertEquals(Action.SUCCESS, result);
        assertNotNull(action.getOrder());
        mockOrderProcessing.verify();
    }
}
```

As you can see, we haven't yet defined any concrete implementation of OrderProcessing, but thanks to mock objects, we can test the functionality without it.

Finally, SaveOrder is implemented with the following code:

```
package org.petsoar.actions.order;

import org.petsoar.order.Order;
import org.petsoar.order.OrderProcessing;
import org.petsoar.order.OrderProcessingAware;
import com.opensymphony.xwork.ActionSupport;

public class SaveOrder extends ActionSupport
```

```
                             implements OrderProcessingAware {
    private Order order = new Order();
    private OrderProcessing orderProcessing;
    private boolean delete, cancel;
    private long id;

    public long getId() {
        return id;
    }
    public void setId(long id) {
        this.id = id;
    }

    public void setOrderProcessing(OrderProcessing orderProcessing) {
        this.orderProcessing = orderProcessing;
    }

    public Order getOrder() {
        return order;
    }

    public void setDelete(String delete) {
        // delete button pressed
        this.delete = true;
    }

    public void setCancel(String cancel) {
        // cancel button pressed
        this.cancel = true;
    }

    public String execute() throws Exception {
        if (!cancel) {
            if (order.getId() == 0) {
                orderProcessing.addOrder(order);
            }
            else {
                Order existingOrder =
                    orderProcessing.getOrder(order.getId());
                if (delete) {
                    orderProcessing.cancelOrder(existingOrder);
                }

                // we can do more fancy stuff here, for example
                // filling the Order object with information from the
                // user's account.
            }
        }
        return SUCCESS;
    }
}
```

SaveOrder implements the OrderProcessingAware enabler interface. Here again, we use the IoC framework included with WebWork. A concrete implementation class defined in the `components.xml` file is passed to the SaveOrder object by WebWork's IoC framework.

The `execute()` method covers adding, canceling, and modifying orders. If the ID parameter is not zero, the user has edited an already existing order; otherwise, it's a new order. The `cancel` property is true when the Cancel button of the form is pressed. It takes the user back to the `vieworder.jsp` page. When the `delete` property is true, the order is canceled by calling the `cancelOrder()` method of OrderProcessing.

```
package org.petsoar.order;

import org.petsoar.persistence.PersistenceAware;
import org.petsoar.persistence.PersistenceManager;

import java.util.List;

public class DefaultOrderProcessing
implements OrderProcessing, PersistenceAware {
    private PersistenceManager persistenceManager;

    public void setPersistenceManager(PersistenceManager pm) {
        this.persistenceManager = pm;
    }

    public void addOrder(Order order) {
        persistenceManager.save(order);
    }

    public void cancelOrder(Order order) {
        persistenceManager.remove(order);
    }

    public List getOrders() {
        return persistenceManager.findAll(Order.class);
    }

    public Order getOrder(long id) {
        return (Order)persistenceManager.getById(Order.class, id);
    }
}
```

All the pieces of the puzzles are in place. The whole checkout and save-order scenario is complete.

Summary

In this chapter, we first implemented a ShoppingCart interface for the shopping cart information. Pets are added and removed to and from this ShoppingCart interface. A simple implementation was provided for this interface called SimpleShoppingCart that holds the information in memory.

Then we implemented the TestAddPetToShoppingCart and AddPetTo-ShoppingCart classes. The AddPetToShoppingCart action class adds a Pet to the shopping cart.

We then implemented the checkout and save-order functionality. Checkout brings up a form where the user enters the shipping, billing, and credit-card information and shows all the Pets in the [CE13]ShoppingCart to the user for verification. This functionality was coded in an action class named CheckOut.

SaveOrder was then created to handle creating or canceling an order. A separate OrderProcessing interface was defined to handle the actual task of adding and canceling an order.

All these classes dealt with an Order object. Order is a concrete Hibernate persistable class. We used Hibernate's component facility to create small dependent classes for the BillingInfo, ShippingInfo, and CreditCardInfo classes. We mapped the properties of these component classes to the same Orders table that the Order itself is saved to.

CHAPTER 20

Securing the Application

No matter what the size or scope of an application (whether it be a small internal project or a gigantic public online book store) security is one of the few areas of application development that must be addressed. Most software developers often overlook protecting the integrity of their information and access to that information until near the end of a project, dismissing security as a small feature that can be tossed in toward the home stretch. While security may not be the most fun item on one's development roadmap, it should not be dismissed either. By not implementing security into an application until right before a product release, it's quite feasible that some security aspects could be overlooked or improperly implemented.

In this chapter, we'll look at the J2EE security model and some of the problems it has for application developers in the real world. Security is a complicated issue, and there are many possible problems and solutions. We will build only a very simple security system that complements the simplicity ethos of the book so far. To complement our simple system, we'll elaborate on a few possible extensions to refactor it into a much more advanced security system. We'll also look briefly at OSUser as a way to provide a pluggable user-management solution.

Understanding J2EE Security

People who are new to J2EE often find that one of the most frustrating areas of the specification (as of J2EE 1.4) is that the security model is very ill-defined. In fact, two areas are mentioned in the "Future Directions" (J2EE.3.7) of the J2EE 1.4 specification:

- *Instance-based access control* — Controlling access to the data based on the content of the data, not just the type of the data.
- *User registration* — A standard way to create new users.

Both of these features are going to be added sometime after J2EE 1.4, and being that J2EE 1.3 servers are just appearing on the market, there is a clear need for something that solves these goals using today's standards. For example, the Servlet specification claims that to secure the /secure directory such that only authorized users in the secure-user role can have access, you would add the following to web.xml:

```
<security-constraint>
 <web-resource-collection>
  <web-resource-name>secure</web-resource-name>
  <description>Secure pages</description>
  <url-pattern>/secure/*</url-pattern>
 </web-resource-collection>
 <auth-constraint>
  <description>Normal PAWS Users</description>
  <role-name>secure-user</role-name>
 </auth-constraint>
</security-constraint>

<login-config>
 <auth-method>BASIC</auth-method>
 <realm-name>PetSoar</realm-name>
</login-config>

<security-role>
 <description>An authorized user</description>
 <role-name>secure-user</role-name>
</security-role>
```

So, what does all this mean? Well, there are a few things going on here. The security-constraint element contains two subelements: web-resource-collection and auth-constraint. The first element defines the URL pattern that is to be secured, and the second element defines the role that has access to the defined resource. The fact that resources can only be protected by a URL pattern is very important, because it makes two issues very clear:

- Securing applications by URL pattern does not allow for fine-grained security, such as securing data based upon its content, as mentioned in the J2EE 1.4 specification.

- Because securing by URL pattern is the only option, organizing your JSP and Web pages in a good hierarchy becomes even more important, as your organization choices will determine how you can secure your application.

The next element is `login-config`, which contains two parts: `auth-method` and `realm-name`. The `auth-method`, according to the Servlet 2.3 specification, can either be BASIC or FORM. The `realm-name` can be any value and is only used for the purposes of identifying the security realm for the entire Web application. FORM and BASIC are different methods used to present a login dialog box, such as a username and password input box, using either an HTML form or the standard HTTP security that summons the familiar popup window shown in Figure 20.1.

NOTE Only one `logic-config` element can be specified. This means that your application can either present login via FORM or BASIC, but it must use the same method for every security-constraint in your application.

The last element is `security-role` and this is nothing more than where you define the roles that were mentioned in the `security-constraint` element previously. In this particular example, the authentication constraint was such that the requesting user must be in the secure-user role. So, in order to use that role, it must be defined, including an optional description element.

Figure 20.1 A typical login dialog box using BASIC authentication

That's it! Using the previous example, any Web resource in the /secure directory will require authentication from all users, with access granted only to those who provide the correct password and also have the secure-user role associated with them. But how are users actually authenticated, and how are they associated with roles? The specification states that it is up to the J2EE vendor (such as JBoss, Resin, or WebLogic) to do this work. How each vendor attacks this problem is very different, so writing portable applications becomes quite a challenge. Some vendors have very simple APIs that you can integrate within just a couple hours of time, while other vendors have incredibly complex APIs that could take weeks to even begin to understand. The internal workings of the vendor match a secure request attempt, such as a request to /secure, to these APIs so that developers can integrate custom security implementations for their applications.

After a user has been authenticated and authorized to access a resource, the username can be accessed via various J2EE APIs. In the case of Servlets, the HttpServletRequest object has a method called `getRemoteUser()` that returns the name of the authenticated user. Likewise, you can test if an authenticated user is in a role with the `isUserInRole()` method. These two methods (and their respective cousins in the EJB APIs) are the only methods that deal with security in J2EE.

To write portable and robust applications, the current J2EE APIs just don't offer enough power and flexibility. It is clear that something else is needed to address these holes in J2EE. One solution is to not use J2EE security at all and instead use your own custom security, including checking for the correct password and role on each request. While this method is very portable and very flexible, it has two major drawbacks:

- You must be very careful to check security constraints in all of your code.

- Integration from the Web-tier to the EJB-tier will not propagate security information correctly.

- The J2EE APIs will no longer work, such that `getRemoteUser()` will only return null and `isUserInRole()` will only return false.

What can be done to address the holes in the J2EE specification without cutting loose any of its features? There are several possible solutions to this problem, and we will examine the simplest one first.

Simplifying Security

Following the spirit of this book, for PetSoar we decided to opt for simplicity above all else (while still meeting all application requirements, of course). Our security implementation will have three main components:

- A request wrapper to wrap all requests
- A security filter to wrap the requests with this wrapper
- A login filter to be applied to any paths that require login and to redirect unauthenticated users to a login action

Let's examine the request wrapper and see what it does and how it helps us bypass existing J2EE security problems while still achieving simplicity.

Using the HTTP Request Wrapper

As stated before, J2EE's security hooks are far too simple for most needs. But just because they are simple does not mean we should abandon them entirely. It is especially important to keep these methods working if there is a need to integrate into some other third-party component that relies on them. By wrapping incoming HttpServletRequest objects with an HttpServletRequestWrapper, we can override the default security methods and link to our custom security, while still providing access through the traditional APIs defined in the Servlet specification. Let's take a look at the wrapper class:

```
public class SecurityHttpRequestWrapper
    extends HttpServletRequestWrapper {
    private HttpServletRequest request;

    public SecurityHttpRequestWrapper(HttpServletRequest request) {
        super(request);
        this.request = request;
    }

    public String getRemoteUser() {
        String user = (String) request.getSession()
                            .getAttribute(LoginFilter.LOGIN_KEY);
        return user;
    }

    public Principal getUserPrincipal() {
        final String name = getRemoteUser();

        return new Principal() {
            public String getName() {
                return name;
            }
        };
    }
}
```

As you can see, the request wrapper is very simple. It overrides only the two methods related to security and lets all other method calls fall through to the original HttpServletRequest object. Because the user's username is stored in a session attribute, we can look it up on demand and use it to provide a trivial implementation for these security methods. Later, if there is a need to store more information than just the username (for example, a complete User object), modifying this code is as simple as changing `getRemoteUser()` to get the username from that information object.

Now let's see where this request wrapper comes into play, through the use of a Servlet filter.

Using the Security Filter

The next step in this process is wrapping all requests with the request wrapper we just examined. We used a *very* simple filter that does this. Note that we have provided only the `doFilter()` method of SecurityFilter for the sake of brevity:

```
public void doFilter(ServletRequest request,
                     ServletResponse response,
                     FilterChain chain)
        throws IOException, ServletException {
    HttpServletRequest req = (HttpServletRequest) request;

    if (!(req instanceof SecurityHttpRequestWrapper)) {
        req = new SecurityHttpRequestWrapper(req);
    }

    chain.doFilter(req, response);
}
```

If the request has already been wrapped, we do nothing. Otherwise, we wrap the request and then let the filter chain carry on as normal, but giving the newly wrapped request to the chain instead. This filter does a great job of wrapping requests, but it does nothing for us in terms of actually securing content. Let's now look at another filter we use to actually do this work.

Using the Login Filter

We now need a filter that listens to all requests and decides whether to allow the request to continue or deny access and direct the user to a login page. This is done with a LoginFilter.

The LoginFilter will allow requests to continue that already have a LOGIN_KEY (the username) set in the session, as we showed in the request wrapper. It will also allow requests to continue that are either to the login JSP or the login action. The login JSP is the page that prompts for the username and password, whereas the login action is the WebWork action that authenticates the input and associates the username in the session with a LOGIN_KEY.

Lastly, any request not to the login JSP or action, nor associated with the correct LOGIN_KEY, will be denied access and directed to the login JSP. The reason that the login JSP and login action must be treated in a special manner is because if they weren't, there would be no way to let an initial request to authenticate come through — a chicken-and-egg problem indeed. Let's look at the code:

```
public class LoginFilter implements Filter {
    public static String LOGIN_KEY = "loggedIn";

    Set extensions;
    String loginAction;
    String loginPage;

    public void init(FilterConfig filterConfig)
            throws ServletException {
        loginPage = filterConfig.getInitParameter("loginPage");
        loginAction = filterConfig.getInitParameter("loginAction");

        extensions = new HashSet();

        String ignoreExtensions =
            filterConfig.getInitParameter("ignoreExtensions");
        StringTokenizer st = new StringTokenizer(ignoreExtensions,
                                                 ", ");

        while (st.hasMoreTokens()) {
            extensions.add(st.nextToken().toLowerCase());
        }
    }

    public void doFilter(ServletRequest request,
                         ServletResponse response,
                         FilterChain chain)
            throws IOException, ServletException {
        HttpServletRequest req = (HttpServletRequest) request;
        HttpServletResponse res = (HttpServletResponse) response;

        String servletPath = req.getServletPath();
        String extension =
            servletPath.substring(servletPath.lastIndexOf('.')
```

```
                                    + 1).toLowerCase();

        if (servletPath.equals(loginAction)
            || servletPath.equals(loginPage)
            || extensions.contains(extension)) {
            // we don't need to secure this path
            chain.doFilter(req, res);
        } else
          if (req.getSession(true).getAttribute(LOGIN_KEY) != null) {
            // we have an authenticated user, keep going
            chain.doFilter(req, res);
        } else {
            // no authenticated user, send them to the login page
            res.sendRedirect(loginPage);
            return;
        }
    }

    public void destroy() { }
}
```

As already explained, the implementation is pretty straightforward to follow. One thing to note is that there is support for ignoring certain extensions. This is useful because besides not wanting to secure the login page and action, you usually do not need to secure images, JavaScript files, and style sheets. The LoginFilter allows you to easily do this.

Making It All Work in Harmony

Tying everything together is now nothing more than a simple exercise of modifying web.xml. But rather than modify the security parts of this XML file, we will instead just apply these two filters on the URL patterns we want to secure. This has the same effect as the Servlet spec's support for security, but automatically works on all application servers. Following are the two filter declarations in web.xml:

```
    ...
    <filter>
        <filter-name>security</filter-name>
        <filter-class>org.petsoar.security.SecurityFilter</filter-class>
    </filter>

    <filter>
        <filter-name>login</filter-name>
```

```
        <filter-class>org.petsoar.security.LoginFilter</filter-class>

        <init-param>
            <param-name>loginPage</param-name>
            <param-value>/login.jsp</param-value>
        </init-param>
        <init-param>
            <param-name>loginAction</param-name>
            <param-value>/login.action</param-value>
        </init-param>
        <init-param>
            <param-name>ignoreExtensions</param-name>
            <param-value>jpeg, gif, css</param-value>
        </init-param>
    </filter>
...
```

Now all that is needed is to map these filters to one or more URL patterns so that they actually secure some content:

```
...
    <filter-mapping>
        <filter-name>security</filter-name>
        <url-pattern>/*</url-pattern>
    </filter-mapping>

    <filter-mapping>
        <filter-name>login</filter-name>
        <url-pattern>/inventory/*</url-pattern>
    </filter-mapping>
...
```

What is happening here might not be entirely clear at first. Most important, the security filter must be applied first, because the request wrapper is central to the entire operation. It must also be applied to all URL paths so that even nonsecure content can still get security information from the HttpServletRequest if needed.

The login filter, on the other hand, is only applied to URL patterns we want to secure by username and password. Securing other URL patterns is as simple as adding a new filter-mapping entry. One such example might be securing /checkout/* so that all orders being checked out require that the user be logged in first.

OSUSER

The simple security framework just outlined is fairly trivial and does about as good of a job as the J2EE security model while providing a vendor-neutral solution. However, writing your own security framework, especially if your requirements are more in-depth, can be a serious undertaking. Thankfully, there is help: OpenSymphony group's creatively named OSUser module (`http://www.opensymphony.com/osuser`).

OSUser has two main parts:

1. *Application support* — A set of generic user-management APIs that your code talks to manage users.

2. *Integration support* — A set of APIs (called Adapters) to integrate into your application server as well as any existing security infrastructure you have in place.

OSUser also provides storage for your users, groups, and user profiles via a set of storage Providers. There is currently a list of prewritten providers that store this data in EJBs, LDAP, JDBC, Hibernate, OFBiz, Memory, Castor, XML files, and other locations. Writing your own providers is a relatively trivial exercise.

The real advantage to OSUser is its centralized API for doing user management, authentication, and authorization. Combined with its broad application support (most major server vendors are supported), you can choose to use your own security framework, J2EE's built-in security, or a mix of both with relative ease.

Using a More Graceful Approach

While the simple solution that we outlined works well and takes advantage of some nice technologies in the Servlet specification (filters and request wrappers), it might be too simple for most real-world needs. Did you catch any of the potential problems that could crop up if you employed this solution?

1. There are currently no "roles" so that there is only one level of security. This is usually not scalable enough for real-world applications.

2. Assigning the filter to more and more URL patterns will quickly bloat web.xml.

3. The URL patterns you can use in the Servlet specification are limited (no regular expressions).

4. Sometimes it might be useful to protect individual WebWork actions rather than URL patterns so we can reuse the action multiple times without worrying if we have protected all the possible URLs.

With these potential holes in mind (as well as any others you might see), what are some possible solutions? Let's look at some extensions that could be made to our security framework. We won't actually implement these extensions, but rather present their possible positive outcomes and how they might be used to address some of the original pitfalls we've identified.

The most obvious addition is to be able to associate roles to different definitions of LoginFilter in web.xml by providing a required role in the init-param of the filter. While this does work, web.xml will quickly become messy, and much of the security logic will soon be stored in a deployment descriptor — not something totally desirable if you have complicated security requirements.

Naturally, the next step is to have a configuration file to manage security concerns. One possible way the configuration file might look is as follows:

```
<security-config>
    <service class="org.petsoar.security.service.WebworkService" />

    <service class="org.petsoar.security.service.PathService">
        <init-param>
            <param-name>config.file</param-name>
            <param-value>/security-paths.xml</param-value>
        </init-param>
    </service>
</security-config>
```

This make-believe configuration file is defining two possible services to manage security. The WebWorkService might act as a guard against unauthorized WebWork action execution requests, regardless of the URL pattern. The PathService, on the other hand, provides protection for URL paths as defined in security-paths.xml, as shown here:

```
<path name="admin">
    <url-pattern>**/admin/*</url-pattern>
    <role-name>admin</role-name>
</path>

<path name="loginrequired">
    <url-pattern>/inventory/*</url-pattern>
    <url-pattern>/checkout/*</url-pattern>
    <role-name>users</role-name>
</path>
```

What is interesting here is that unlike the URL patterns given in web.xml previously, these patterns are more powerful. This is possible because, rather than depending on the weak URL pattern support offered by the Servlet specification, you can now write your own pattern-matching routines in your custom security framework. We hope that these mock configuration files give you an idea of what is possible in the realm of security and provide some food for thought when you begin securing your application.

Summary

In this chapter, we looked at the potential limitations of the current and future J2EE security support. We then looked at a very simple implementation that addresses some of those limitations and is used in PetSoar. Finally, we acknowledged that such a simple approach isn't necessarily feasible for all applications and explored a few simple (but powerful) ideas for providing more robust configuring in your security framework.

The most important thing we hope you take from this chapter is that security is an important feature in your application and that you should address the needs of your application above all else. If the J2EE security support does not let you reach these goals, there are alternatives as we have shown you. And even if you do use J2EE's security, there are Open Source libraries that can make implementing this task even easier.

Index